SLANDERING THE SACRED

CLASS 200 NEW STUDIES IN RELIGION

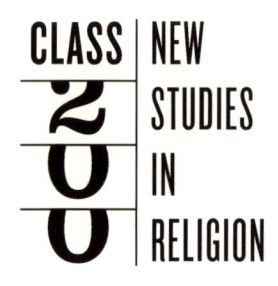

Edited by Kathryn Lofton and John Lardas Modern

Awkward Rituals: Sensations of Governance in Protestant America
Dana Logan

Sincerely Held: American Secularism and Its Believers
Charles McCrary

Unbridled: Studying Religion in Performance
William Robert

Profaning Paul
Cavan W. Concannon

Making a Mantra: Tantric Ritual and Renunciation on the Jain Path to Liberation
Ellen Gough

Neuromatic: or, A Particular History of Religion and the Brain
John Lardas Modern

Kindred Spirits: Friendship and Resistance at the Edges of Modern Catholicism
Brenna Moore

The Privilege of Being Banal: Art, Secularism, and Catholicism in Paris
Elayne Oliphant

Ripples of the Universe: Spirituality in Sedona, Arizona
Susannah Crockford

SLANDERING THE SACRED

Blasphemy Law and
Religious Affect in Colonial India

J. BARTON SCOTT

The University of Chicago Press
Chicago and London

The University of Chicago Press, Chicago 60637
The University of Chicago Press, Ltd., London
© 2023 by The University of Chicago
All rights reserved. No part of this book may be used or reproduced in any manner whatsoever without written permission, except in the case of brief quotations in critical articles and reviews. For more information, contact the University of Chicago Press, 1427 E. 60th St., Chicago, IL 60637.
Published 2023
Printed in the United States of America

32 31 30 29 28 27 26 25 24 23   1 2 3 4 5

ISBN-13: 978-0-226-82488-8 (cloth)
ISBN-13: 978-0-226-82490-1 (paper)
ISBN-13: 978-0-226-82489-5 (e-book)
DOI: https://doi.org/10.7208/chicago/9780226824895.001.0001

Library of Congress Cataloging-in-Publication Data

Names: Scott, J. Barton, author.
Title: Slandering the sacred : blasphemy law and religious affect in colonial India / J. Barton Scott.
Other titles: Class 200, new studies in religion.
Description: Chicago : The University of Chicago Press, 2023. | Series: Class 200: new studies in religion | Includes bibliographical references and index.
Identifiers: LCCN 2022032907 | ISBN 9780226824888 (cloth) | ISBN 9780226824901 (paperback) | ISBN 9780226824895 (e-book)
Subjects: LCSH: India. Indian Penal Code. | Blasphemy—Law and legislation—India—History—19th century. | Blasphemy—Law and legislation—Great Britain—History—19th century. | Libel and slander—India—Religious aspects—History—19th century. | Libel and slander—Great Britain—Religious aspects—History—19th century. | Freedom of expression—India—History—19th century.
Classification: LCC KNS4172.S36 2023 | DDC 345.54/0288—dc23/eng/20220830
LC record available at https://lccn.loc.gov/2022032907e

♾ This paper meets the requirements of ANSI/NISO Z39.48-1992 (Permanence of Paper).

CONTENTS

1 Introduction: Secularizing Blasphemy   1

PART ONE: THE MERRY PROPHET   31

2 A Crisis of the Public: The Rajpal Affair and Its Bodies   33
3 Secularism, High and Low: Making the Blasphemy Bill   54

PART TWO: BLASPHEMY'S EMPIRE   77

4 Codifying Blasphemy: "Religious Feelings" between Colony and Metropole   79
5 Macaulay Unmanned, or, Tom Governs His Feelings   105
6 Libeling Religion: Secularism and the Intimacy of Insult   123

PART THREE: POLEMICS AS ETHICS   137

7 Printing Pain, Ruling Sentiment: A Brief History of Arya Insult   141
8 The Arya Penal Code: Law and the Practice of Documentary Religion   166
9 The Swami and the Prophet: Slandering Lives, Conducting Character   185

10 Conclusion: A Feeling for "Religion"   216

Acknowledgments 231   *Notes* 235   *Index* 287

1

INTRODUCTION

Secularizing Blasphemy

IN TWENTY-FIRST-CENTURY INDIA, "religious sentiments" are often in the news. Bollywood films are said to wound them. So are tweets, political cartoons, television advertisements, Netflix shows, stand-up comedy routines, and scholarly books. In 2014, the pulping of Wendy Doniger's *Hinduism: An Alternative History* even made international headlines. Most of these controversies hinge on the interpretation of a single law: Section 295A of the Indian Penal Code, concerning insults intended to outrage "religious feelings." In this book, I tell the story of how this law came to be, using its unexpected history to anchor a much larger inquiry into secularism and empire, insult and affect.

Enacted in 1927, after a Hindu group published a pamphlet mocking the sex life of the Prophet Muhammad, Section 295A capped a century of efforts to secularize British-imperial blasphemy law. In the century since, it has dogged books and images from *The Satanic Verses* to *The Da Vinci Code*, from the films of Aamir Khan to the paintings of M. F. Hussain.[1] It places a chill on free speech about religion. It extends the power of the state over civil society. It probably even exacerbates the culture of religious controversy that it was designed to fix. Many people, understandably, would like to abolish it.

Yet 295A demarcates a set of problems with no easy solution. The legislators who enacted it foresaw the damage it could do and passed it anyway, a half-despairing measure to curb injurious speech. Their problems are still our problems. Trigger warnings, cancel culture, trolling, fake news—the twenty-first century has, if anything, compounded modernity's free-speech headache.

Section 295A opens a useful window onto these problems precisely because it is a problem too. But what kind of problem? What sort of law is this? One argument for repealing 295A holds that it is a blasphemy law and thus impermissible under postcolonial India's constitutional secularism.[2] That is not quite correct, as this book will show. Section 295A is neither a blasphemy law nor is it antisecular. Rather, it is precisely a secularization of the British common law of blasphemy. Its story is the story of secularism itself, showing how secular law came to govern religion by managing religious affect.

BLASPHEMY NOW

Etymologically, blasphemy is euphemism's cruder cousin, its Greek roots indicating rough speech—insults to the gods. Borrowing a phrase from literary historian Joss Marsh, we could define blasphemy as a "word crime" and thus heuristically distinguish it from heresy (a crime of opinion, which need not be verbalized), iconoclasm (an image crime), or sacrilege (an object or body crime, like submerging a crucifix in human urine).[3] Such distinctions, alas, collapse in practice. Historically, the word *blasphemy* has been used to indicate any and all of the above.

Ever since there have been deities, presumably, humans have been hurling imprecations at them. In recent years, however, this venerable practice has commenced a new chapter. Danish cartoons, Satanic temples, Sweet Jesus Ice Cream—in the twenty-first century, slanders of the sacred are seemingly everywhere, with religion sometimes appearing as little more than a membrane for giving and receiving offense.

Why blasphemy? Why now? One factor is clearly the intense interconnectedness of our hypermediated world, wherein a thumb swipe across a smartphone can hurl insult around the globe in an instant.[4] Religions are not, as once alleged, primarily systems of symbols.[5] Still, in an era defined by the rapid circulation of signs, symbols can seem like religion's most prominent feature—digitalized, decontextualized, and bound for trouble. By this account, our wounded present could be said to have begun sometime around the late 1980s, alongside so-called globalization. To represent it, we could flank Salman Rushdie's *Satanic Verses* (1988) with Andres Serrano's *Piss Christ* (1987) and Madonna's "Like a Prayer" (1989) to form a sort of blasphemous triptych, a rent in the fabric of the sacred that tore across the 1990s and into the twenty-first century.

I think our offended present is older than this. To see why, we need to dial the clock back another half century to the era of high imperialism, globalization's oft-disavowed parent. Rushdie himself, that archangel of blasphemy, points the way. The trouble with the British, says one of the characters in *The Satanic Verses*, is that their history happened overseas, so they do not understand it.[6] Much the same could be said for modern blasphemy.

Too often, histories of blasphemy limit themselves to the geography of "the West" or, as I prefer, the North Atlantic region.[7] In doing so, they get stuck in what I call the Whig-liberal narrative of blasphemous modernity, reciting a litany of martyrs to freethought who, by dying at the hands of inquisitorial religion, gave birth to our secular age—an enlightened epoch of audacious irreverence and salubrious profanation. This narrative coalesced in the eighteenth and nineteenth centuries and tended (not coincidentally, in the age of empire) to focus on the triumphs of white men. Many of this narrative's heroes (James Nayler, Voltaire) should indeed be remembered and even celebrated. Still, the performative effect of its amassment of white male flesh is all too clear. It secures a demographically and geographically circumscribed account of secular modernity that is as intellectually unsatisfying as it is politically objectionable.

To narrate the history of the modern West as though that history can be abstracted from empire is to misrecognize what "the West" was in the first place: a North Atlantic regional identity of presumptively universal significance, crafted from the remains of Latin Christendom through the medium of empire. Empire is the West's ontological prior, the thing through which it came into being. The Whig-liberal narrative of blasphemous modernity cannot, however, make sense of secularism's colonial entanglements because it is itself a product of these entanglements—a historical artifact that needs explaining, not an explanatory apparatus.

To think past the Whig-liberal narrative, then, we also need to think past the entrenched forms of contemporary thought that go by the name secularism, not least the modern concept that Talal Asad has dubbed secularism's "Siamese twin": religion.[8] "The category of religion often works to obfuscate relations of power," writes Lucia Hulsether in a succinct distillation of recent scholarship.[9] That is, the concept of religion that emerged between the seventeenth and nineteenth centuries as secularism's enabling condition worked to create the impression that its referent was a discrete phenomenon, different in kind from other such phenomena ("politics," "economics," etc.) and thus theoretically capable of being sequestered in a discrete social sphere. This sequestration seemed possible partly because the religion concept implied that its object was constitutively otherworldly and therefore disconnected from temporal power relations. Thus did the term *religion* come to demarcate a zone of ongoing political obfuscation—never more so perhaps than in the hands of its secularist critics, who, in presenting their critiques of religion as rooted in transcendent values rather than historically contingent circumstance, often seem to have absorbed religion's own depoliticizing logic.

Consider French prime minister Emmanuel Macron's 2020 public comment on the *Charlie Hebdo* trial. The French, he insisted, have a "freedom to blaspheme" integral to their still more fundamental "freedom of conscience," making the satirical newspaper in question justified in lampooning the Prophet Muhammad.[10] Speaking in the idiom of transcendent French-republican values, Macron deflected the political specificities of the controversy at hand—the racialization and economic marginalization of French Muslims, the unresolved legacies of French colonialism in North Africa—as though questions of "conscience" (i.e., religion) were independent of the political histories of race and empire.[11]

Something similar might be said for another defender of blasphemy, the poet T. S. Eliot. In 1933, Eliot gave a lecture in Virginia where he suggested that blasphemous modernity had run out of steam: modern profanations, leached of real belief, were increasingly empty. In their place, Eliot urged a return to traditionalism, pointing to a contemporary cohort of white "agrarian" poets from the US South as exemplary.[12] What an odd moment in the global culture wars. A Bostonian cosmopolite who, in 1927, became a British-imperial citizen was countering the Whig-liberal narrative of blasphemous modernity by endorsing a settler-colonial agrarian "tradition" that had emerged as plantation capitalism updated itself into a new racialized regime in the half century after the US Civil War. If modern blasphemy appeared hollow to Eliot, this was because he refused to see it in full. Its history had happened partly overseas, circulating on the crosscurrents of empire. The very year Eliot became a British-imperial subject, after all, British India was having its own blasphemy crisis—culminating in Section 295A.

As Rajeev Bhargava has suggested, scholars of North Atlantic secularisms "may need to look sideways" toward India to discover "not only a compressed version of their own history but also a vision of its future."[13] To look sideways is to trace the horizontal latticework of empire and the entangled histories that unfold within it. It is both to connect and to provincialize. French republicanism is not the same as anglophone Whig liberalism, and to pry them apart is to see "the West" dissolving into a richly variegated transcolonial landscape that runs from settler-colonial Virginia to metropolitan Paris to postcolonial Delhi and Bombay. There too, the Whig-liberal narrative of blasphemous modernity has been remarkably tenacious—shaping, among other things, how the Indian left frames its critiques of Hindu nationalism.[14] To think past it, we might begin by reconsidering the problem of how to "secularize" blasphemy.

SECULARIZING BLASPHEMY

It might seem perverse to study blasphemy via what amounts to an absence—Section 295A, which is precisely not a blasphemy law. But, as I hope to show, the conceptually unstable text of 295A can help bring the history of this common-law offense into clearer view.

During the 1927 Legislative Assembly debates over the new 295A, assembly member M. R. Jayakar offered an especially succinct definition of blasphemy. Troubled that his colleagues kept referring to the "Religious Insults Bill" by its popular moniker, the "Blasphemy Bill," Jayakar took the floor to explain why this was a serious mistake. Blasphemy, he said, is an "entirely different offence" from the one proposed: it is an "offense per se against religion." Although a crime in England, where the state was the "upholder of the Church," blasphemy could not be criminalized in India. Central Provinces representative and prominent legal scholar Hari Singh Gour concurred. Where the English monarch was the "defender of the faith," the Government of India was merely the "defender of the peace." Any laws restricting the criticism of religion must be limited to the basis of preventing potential violence.[15]

Section 295A keeps to these limits. It criminalizes "acts intended to outrage the religious feelings of any class, by insulting its religion or religious beliefs." Relegating the noun *religion* to a subordinate clause, it grants religion per se only indirect protection, reserving direct protection to something else—"religious feelings" (of which more anon).

Defining blasphemy as an offense against religion per se might seem intuitive; Jayakar's definition is not wrong. It is, however, misleading—effecting a kind of conceptual sleight of hand. Throughout the nineteenth and early twentieth centuries, British reformers had been trying to secularize blasphemy law. That is, they participated in a cultural logic of secularization that emplotted its actors within we might now call a subtraction story, a drama wherein "religion" would be removed from "law" to purify both.[16] Blasphemy's would-be reformers sought to eliminate what had come to appear as a Christian-theological crime and possibly replace it with some kind of secular equivalent; Jayakar and Gour were heir to this ongoing history when they insisted that the new 295A could not concern itself with offenses against religion per se. They were, in a historically specific sense, secularizers. They were also, however, reterritorializing this secularizing impulse with a subtle semantic shift. The English common law of blasphemy did not protect "religion." It protected Christianity (when the term *religion* was used, it was typically as a functional synonym for Christianity). By trading terms, Jayakar was engaging in an act of secular translation, reinterpreting common law's pasts via his late colonial present in a productive anachronism.[17]

To study the history of English blasphemy law is to discover not a continuous process of secularization, but rather a sequence of historically distinct formations of both the secular (a cultural or epistemic category) and secularism (a political doctrine).[18] The illusion of continuity was created by anachronistically rereading the past in presentist terms, as Jayakar did. The shift from one formation to the next was partly driven by secularism's own questioning power, its impulse to query the line around the religious.[19] Even the most ardently separationist of secular states cannot fully disentangle itself from religion, because to grant freedom to something called "religion" the state first has to demarcate that concept's boundaries, officially recognizing certain practices as religious while withholding recognition from others.[20] The resulting paradox—to disestablish religion, a state first has to establish it—means that the line separating religion from politics will constantly be transgressed, such that the secular state continually needs to police it. This ongoing boundary-work thus serves a productive function in that it tends to extend the state's authority over increasingly minute aspects of social life—an essential but underrecognized side effect of secularism's constitutive language game.

The British knew how to use this game to their advantage: it helped justify colonial rule. As Henry Maine argued in 1861, India was stuck in a stage of social evolution where "a rule of law is not yet discriminated from a rule of religion."[21] It thus needed Britain to educate it, civilizing by secularizing. If we understand colonial secularism as itself constitutively unable to discriminate neatly between "law" and "religion," then its real function would seem to be training the colonized to inhabit its questioning power, learning to query the boundaries of religion to various political ends. This querying happened in multiple languages, with the vernacular press using translation to negotiate the hegemony of the colonial state by exploiting non-equivalence between *religion* and words like *din* and *dharma*.[22] It also happened in English, in official spaces like the Legislative Assembly. As Burmese representative Hla Tun Pru laconically observed in 1927, there remained "certain difficulties with regard to what a religion is."[23] Would the proposed 295A protect atheist or rationalist beliefs? In light of these problems, he asked that the new law not apply to his homeland. (His request was ignored.)

Jayakar too was playing this secularist language game and, in the process, reinterpreting the legal past. For an early modern authority like William Blackstone, blasphemy indicated "contumelious reproaches," "profane scoffing," or "contempt and ridicule" directed at God, Jesus, or the Bible.[24] Blackstone did not mention "religion," the general category—not yet as widely available in 1769 as it would become over the next century or so, as, starting around 1880, talk of "world religions" erupted into self-evident ubiquity.[25] In 1927, then, Jayakar could do things with "religion" that Blackstone could not. He used the concept to rework blasphemy so it could denote insult to *any* world religion, thus making this legal concept serviceable in religiously plural India (he was not, as we shall see, the first to do so). Conceptual instability was perhaps inevitable. Even a not-blasphemy law like 295A remains in an important sense, blasphemy-adjacent. It circulates in a cultural field where the concept of blasphemy is still alive and well, overdetermining 295A's possible meanings—as Jayakar saw, to his frustration, prompting him to engage in more conceptual boundary-work.

As an aside, it bears noting that when scholars consider how best to translate *blasphemy* out of Christianized English, they are engaged in the same historical processes as Jayakar. What does blasphemy look like in Buddhism? Hinduism? Islam? Those questions are ultimately beyond the scope of this book. I would simply caution anyone approaching them to exercise hermeneutic care. Although Islamic legal traditions do detail crimes that overlap with blasphemy, for instance, their typologies of offense—organized around such concepts as *takdhib*, or willful rejection of religious truths, and *sabb al-rasul*, vilification of the Prophet—are not identical to Christianity's.[26] Hinduism offers an even more complicated case. Would one translate blasphemy as *nindastuti*, praising the divine by intimately berating it?[27] Or would one study satire, heterodoxy, and polemic?[28] What about word crimes like a brahman mispronouncing a syllable while reciting the Vedas? Or a woman or subordinated-caste person uttering Vedic words? Such word crimes are also body crimes, of course, linked to the ritual politics of caste and gender.

FORMATIONS OF THE SECULAR: BLASPHEMY AS COMMON LAW OFFENSE

Jayakar's definition of blasphemy would seem to beg a fundamental conceptual question. What is it for religion to suffer offense? To begin exploring this question, one might construct a (surely incomplete) list of the various harms that have been attributed to blasphemous speech over the centuries:[29]

1. Metaphysical harm, as to God or the cosmos.
2. Political harm, as to the state.
3. Harm to the public peace.
4. Spiritual harm to the population, as by corrupting Christian souls.
5. Ethical harm to the population, as by corrupting morals.
6. Harm to the feelings of individuals.
7. Harm to group feelings.
8. Harm to human dignity.

Which of the above counts as harm to religion, per se? Any of them? This question, I think, needs to be answered historically.

Thinking from the above list, a commonsense account of the history of blasphemy law might run as follows: between the seventeenth and twenty-first centuries, an ecclesiastical crime became a political crime, which was then tempered by Victorian reformers before finally—and belatedly—being abolished in 2008 and replaced by a new "racial and religious hatred" law. This is a classic subtraction story of secularization, set in "Little England," that self-contained isle.

Further study reveals a more complex tale. The colonies play a prominent role in articulating Britain's understanding of itself as a secular nation; British secularism was arguably invented in the colonies, especially India. Even the narrowly English story is marked by substantial discontinuity. It is a history of sequential formations of the secular, wherein the very notion of the secular shifts along the way. Case in point: the English word *secularism* is a product of this history. It was coined in 1851 by George Jacob Holyoake, who had been prosecuted for blasphemy a decade earlier.[30] For Holyoake, *secularism* indicated an ethics of being-in-the-world, continuous with the freethinking milieu that drove Victorian blasphemy trials.[31] It was not until later that *secularism* came to denote a political doctrine.

I adumbrate this history here, in schematic form, with particular attention to the nineteenth century.

Formation 1: The Crown's Christianity. In late medieval England, blasphemy was an ecclesiastical crime. It harmed the soul of the speaker. It also potentially caused metaphysical harm. A village church mural from around 1400 depicts a *pietà* surrounded by men cursing, swearing, and otherwise taking the Lord's name in vain. Their injurious words literally dismember the body of Christ in heaven. One swearer holds Jesus's heart, another a chunk of bone, a third his severed foot—freshly yanked from a gorily rendered leg that protrudes from the Virgin's lap.[32]

A new dispensation coalesced in 1676 after a poor farmer named John Taylor exclaimed, repeatedly, that "Christ is a whore-master, and religion is a cheat." Taylor (a member of an antinomian prophetic movement called the Sweet Singers of Israel) was first sent to the madhouse at Bedlam for "bodily correction."[33] Found sane, he was then sent to court, where Justice Matthew Hale, who in the 1660s had presided over witch trials, found him guilty of blasphemy. Hale's decisive words in *Rex v. Taylor* resounded for the next two hundred years: "Christianity is parcel of the laws of England; and therefore to reproach the Christian religion is to speak in subversion of the law."[34]

It is easy to see why Enlightenment thinkers like Thomas Jefferson derided Hale as a theocratic Puritan, invoking a version of the Whig-liberal narrative. We should not, however, follow Jefferson's lead. Hale was a secularizer. In saying that Christianity was "parcel" of English law, he was claiming that parcel for the king—insisting that Crown courts could try a crime previously belonging to ecclesiastical courts.[35] This is secularization in the most literal sense. The verb *secularize* was first used in English to describe Henry VIII's seizure of monasteries and other church property for the Crown, converting these sacred or eternal things into worldly or temporal ones. In this early modern formation of the secular, then, Christianity was being appropriated as a political symbol open to worldly administration—a move with precedent in the late medieval period now harnessed to the needs of the early modern state.[36]

Formation 2: Victorian Decency. English and (after the 1707 Act of Union with Scotland) British blasphemers went quiet for most of a century before piping up again in the 1790s to distribute cheap reprints of Thomas Paine's *Age of Reason* (1794) and other Enlightenment tracts. Decades of trials followed, sweeping up alleged blasphemers both famous and obscure before culminating in the case that decisively revised the common law of blasphemy.

In *Regina v. Ramsay and Foote* (1883), Lord Chief Justice John Coleridge (a relative of the poet) held that in an age when Jews, Catholics, and Nonconforming Protestants had been granted civil rights, Christianity was no longer part of the law in any simple way. He thus redefined blasphemy as a stylistic offense, a crime of manner not matter.[37] "If the decencies of controversy are observed," he wrote, "even the fundamentals of religion may be attacked without the writer being guilty of blasphemous libel."[38] Doubt God all you like, that is, but do not (like the accused publishers of the *Freethinker*, George Foote and William Ramsay) print a picture of him showing his buttocks to Moses on Mt. Sinai (a riff on Exodus 33:23: "Thou shalt see my back parts: but my face shall not be seen") (see figure 1). One might be inclined to view Coleridge as a secularizer, muting Hale's theocratic impulse. This reading, however, simply reinscribes the nineteenth century's own Whig-liberal paradigm. It is more productive to take Coleridge as articulating a specifically Victorian formation of secularism as biopolitical project—one that shifted the paradigmatic locus of the theologico-political from the sovereign to the social body as a site for the regulation of manners, morals, and public decency.

"Decency," that most primly Victorian of terms, implied a constellation of raced, classed, and gendered values. Its class valence was especially glaring. The nineteenth century's most heavily prosecuted rationalist tracts were addressed to working-class readers and often linked to radical political movements. Upmarket "literary" texts (with the adjective conferring cultural status) were prosecuted less frequently because they seemed less threatening to class hierarchies.[39] As *Freethinker* editor George Foote noted, his journal was on trial not just for its "coarse" language (to use Coleridge's classed adjective), but also because it was cheap. Notably, it featured pictures, that most demotic of media.

Empire and its racialized tropes were never far away. Foote called the Bible a Victorian "fetish," invoking the ethnological term associated with "primitive" religions.[40] Another Victorian blasphemer said the Bible was so barbaric as to constitute a "disgrace to orang-outangs, much less to men."[41] Yet another described the biblical God as vicious, like a "painted savage," and "more bloodthirsty than a Bengal tiger."[42] When blasphemers accused Christianity of savagery, law accused them of a parallel incivility. Everyone seemed to agree on the value accorded "civilization" itself, that racializing, imperial term.[43] Victorian debates about blasphemy, one might say, were debates about how best to produce a certain kind of religio-racial subject, trained in proper decorum by both law and social mores.[44]

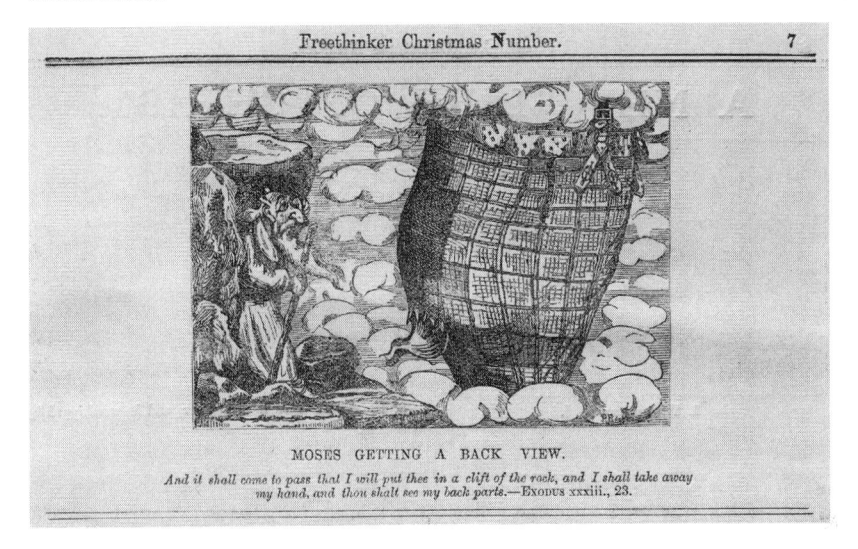

FIGURE 1. "Moses Getting a Back View." *Freethinker*. Christmas 1882. Courtesy of Thomas Fisher Rare Book Library, University of Toronto.

Perhaps the decisive move of Enlightenment blasphemers had been to reimagine blasphemy as a tool for social reform, a means of advancing the cause of civilization. Where once blasphemy had been a discrete act (whether sin or recreation), now it would be both an identity and a mission.[45] Blasphemy was a moral act, with the blasphemer dedicated in service to reason—an inversion or antithesis of Christian missionaries. These dueling missions then smashed together in a religio-racial civilizational assemblage that sprawled out onto the world stage.

This assemblage's religio-racial subjects were also gendered subjects. *Regina v. Ramsay and Foote* belonged to a cluster of intertwined trials that included the 1877 prosecution of Annie Besant and Charles Bradlaugh for obscenity after they distributed copies of a banned birth control tract, *The Fruits of Philosophy* (1832).[46] If Besant, Foote, and company saw freethought and birth control as conjoined causes, their opponents (organizations such as the Society for the Prevention of Vice) saw them as conjoined problems. An image, such as the *Freethinker*'s divine bottom, could then scandalously concretize this struggle over Victorian bodies.

For Coleridge, it was these bodies' emotional capacities that mattered most. By redefining blasphemy as a stylistic crime, he also redefined it as an affective crime. Only "indecent and offensive attacks" on religion "calculated to outrage the feelings of the general body of the community" would, by his standard, be punished.[47] (That verb, *outrage*, would also appear in 295A.) Decent criticisms too were defined by their affect, but Coleridge struggled to find the words to describe it. Legally permissible criticism of religion would need to have "a grave, an earnest, a reverent, I am almost tempted to say a religious tone." Coleridge proposed John Stuart Mill, the noted agnostic, as a paradigm for his reverent critic—underscoring the irony of describing good criticism as quasi-religious criticism. In Coleridge's hands, "religion" metamorphosed from message to medium. It became a tone or style, manifested in a decorum or habitus that even an agnostic could achieve. Thus transformed, the religious became the precondition of shared civic life.

Formation 3: Racial and Religious Hatred. In 1921, John Gott became the last man in Britain jailed for blasphemy (or, precisely, for outraging "religious feelings") after comparing Jesus to a circus clown and distributing birth control tracts in East London.[48] In 1977, Denis Lemon became the last man in Britain convicted and fined for blasphemy for publishing a homoerotic poem about the crucifixion in his small-circulation paper, the *Gay News* (judge and jury agreed that saying, of Jesus, that "the shaft still throbbed, anointed with death's final ejaculation" was in breach of good taste).[49] By this time, however, the Victorian formation of the secular was in the process of collapsing, a vestige of an earlier era. After *Ramsay*, legal reformers complained that courts should have abolished, not updated, blasphemy law. After *Lemon*, this complaint grew louder. In 1981, a commission was created to assess whether blasphemy law should be reformed or abolished; it recommended outright abolition.[50] In 1990, during the Rushdie debacle, the UK Action Committee on Islamic Affairs joined with the Archbishop of Canterbury and Chief Rabbi to ask that blasphemy law be broadened to protect all religions, with the Church of England serving as a sort of interfaith anchor, *primer inter pares* much like England herself in the Commonwealth.[51] The Law Lords rejected the proposal.

A solution to the problem of blasphemy did not emerge for another fifteen years. In 2006, Parliament passed the Racial and Religious Hatred Act, which outlawed religious hate speech. Incitement of "racial hatred" had been legally prohibited since the 1960s, and there had been occasional proposals to broaden these laws to include religion. The impetus for finally doing so came from the post-9/11 moment, with its alarming increase in anti-Muslim hate crimes and attendant racialization of Muslimness. The concept of "hate speech," dating to the 1980s, offered a new basis for restricting religious insult (a development I consider further in chapter 10). With the new law in place, Parliament was finally, in 2008, able to abolish blasphemy as common-law offense.[52] Hate speech made blasphemy redundant.

SECULARISM IN THE COLONIES

The Indian lawmakers who enacted Section 295A were thinking via this English legal history. They referenced blasphemy cases from the previous half century, wondered whether English law applied in the colony, and rattled off names of British skeptics who had kept their comments within the bounds of decency.[53] Jayakar, a trained lawyer, would certainly have known this material. When he defined blasphemy as an offense per se against religion, perhaps he was thinking of Justice Hale's ruling in *Rex v. Taylor*.

Section 295A, however, pointed to a notably different set of harms—and a substantially confused one at that. This confusion grew out of the court case that prompted the colonial government to add a new religion section to the Indian Penal Code: *Rajpal v. Emperor*.[54] The trial concerned an anonymously authored tract, the *Rangila Rasul* (The merry Prophet), published by a man named Mahashe Rajpal. Charged under Section 153A of the Code with having created "enmity or hatred" between religious classes, Rajpal was taken to court for what proved a prolonged (nearly three-year) trial. In May 1927, the Lahore High Court finally acquitted Rajpal on appeal. Its decision, written by Justice Kanwar Dalip Singh, conceded that the *Rangila Rasul* was indeed a "scurrilous satire on the founder of the Muslim religion," but insisted that it was not therefore also a slander on "the Muhammadan religion as such," nor did it necessarily render Muslims "objects worthy of enmity or hatred." Singh thus demarcated three distinct offenses: libel of the dead, defamation of religion (i.e., blasphemy), and group defamation. The court could not, Singh argued, consider the empirical "reaction of a particular class" in assessing whether a given text was offensive, but must base its rulings on textual evidence alone. By this standard, the *Rangila Rasul* is slippery: the text clearly states that its criticisms of Muhammad do not imply a criticism of Islam. Thus, although "decent persons of whatever community" should feel "contempt" for the tract, it could not be proscribed under 153A. Singh closed his judgment by suggesting that government create a new section that would directly prohibit insults to religion without making that offense dependent on the production of class enmity.

Singh's decision seemed downright bizarre to many of his contemporaries. One bureaucrat scrawled a handwritten note on the official government file describing the decision as "rather metaphysical"—so convoluted, that is, as to be worthy of a philosopher.[55] Perhaps this is why, when government bureaucrats proposed a new law two months later, they did the precise thing Singh's decision would seem to disallow: they made insult to religion criminal only insofar as it produces "outrage" in religious "classes," thus framing an offense substantially redundant with Section 153A and its class "enmity." Sensing this redundancy, Hari Singh Gour (the legal scholar and Legislative Assembly member) proposed that the Assembly scrap 295A entirely and instead add a new religion-specific section alongside 153A in the Code's chapter on "offenses against the public tranquility" (where, in 1898, 153A had been appended to a section about riots).[56]

To see why colonial bureaucrats were unable to disentangle religious insult (and thus blasphemy) from religious classes or populations, let us visit the history of English blasphemy law once again, resituating it within a transcolonial framework. By the time that John Taylor was dragged to court in 1676, England was already an empire. The British secularism that emerged thereafter emerged contrapuntally, through the interplay of colony and metropole.[57] India sounded an especially clear note in this counterpoint, because of both its political and economic importance and its religious diversity.[58] It was, and remains, a major laboratory of secular modernity.

For heuristic purposes, one might divide the history of Indian secularism into three principal periods: Company secularism (1600–1858), late colonial secularism (1858–1947), and postcolonial secularism (1947–). This schema is potentially useful for seeing how postcolonial secularism emerged from the secularisms that preceded it.

Postcolonial Indian secularism is often celebrated as nationally distinctive because it is defined around ideals of religious neutrality (*dharma nirpekshata*) and respect for all religions (*sarva dharma samabhava*) rather than the punctilious church-state separation that animates, in different ways, French and US secularisms.[59] Simultaneously a political ideal and a cultural imaginary, Indian secularism's ethos of pluralist inclusion assumed iconic form on postcolonial cinema screens with their melodramas of Mother India receiving blood transfusions from her Hindu, Muslim, and Christian sons.[60]

Without denying Indian secularism's distinctive emphasis, it bears stressing that, just as British secularism cannot be extricated from India, Indian secularism cannot be extricated from Britain. Each, as Gauri Viswanathan notes, is at once "the condition and the effect of the other."[61] Or, put slightly differently, empire is the ontological prior of both. In other words, as Saba Mahmood has argued, the "national-political structuration" of secularism happens from within secularism as global political project, one predicated on transnational institutions and their universalizing impulses.[62] By putting India back into this transcolonial framework, we can better see the South Asian circulation of multiple varietals of secularism—not just the 1920s tolerance secularism that would later be enshrined as postcolonial ideal (see chapter 3) but also the separation secularism that underlaid Jayakar's and Gour's insistence on the impossibility of a secular blasphemy law.

This transcolonial history could be said to have begun in 1600 with the creation of the East India Company. The Company subsequently developed alongside political modernity, experimenting with religious "toleration" at the same moment that John Locke was writing on that theme, and talking about religious "free exercise" in 1776, during the moment of the Atlantic-world revolutions.[63] Especially from the late eighteenth century forward, Company secularism did not stipulate separation between religion and state. Instead, the Company set out to rule its Hindu and Muslim subjects according to their own laws and customs, thus incorporating religious law (or a version of it) into the secular-state apparatus.

This basic orientation continued when Queen Victoria assumed direct rule of her colony in 1858 through a proclamation that affirmed her own Christian "convictions" while renouncing the "right" to impose those convictions on her Indian subjects. Her government, she promised, would "abstain from all interference" in "religious belief or worship."[64] Victoria's very title was shaped by secularist imperatives. When, in 1877, she was proclaimed "Empress of India," her advisers translated this phrase into Hindustani, slightly awkwardly, as *Kaisar-i-Hind*, thus avoiding the potential religious association of words like *chakravartin* or *shahanshah*.[65] She would be a latter-day "Caesar," the culmination of a grand—and grandly secular—imperial lineage. As Viceroy Robert Bulwer-Lytton opined at an official Delhi dinner celebrating the new empress, India's diversity of "race" and "creed" posed "administrative problems unsolved by Caesar, unsolved by Charlemagne, unsolved by Akbar."[66] He thus put Britain at the technical-administrative frontier of secular empire as political form, defined by the twinned management of race and religion.

In the late nineteenth century, the colonial state increasingly turned to the new academic discipline of anthropology for authoritative knowledge about South Asian races, castes, and creeds. The result was what has been called the ethnographic state, a political formation that saw religion primarily as an object of empirical study.[67] Religion also cued a security question, a problem of endemic populational violence requiring skilled technical management. Bureaucrats were especially concerned about preventing a recurrence of the 1857 uprisings (a.k.a. the "Sepoy Mutiny"), allegedly sparked by wounded religious sentiments.

It is no mistake that Indian secularism emerged first as a managerial question and only later as a question of rights. As Partha Chatterjee has argued, the liberal-constitutional state came late to colonies like India, where other political rationalities—especially governmentality—predominated throughout the nineteenth and early twentieth centuries. The North Atlantic world had citizens; the colonies had subjects. Indeed, according to Chatterjee, even the postcolonial Indian state more often operates within a logic of governmentality than of rights, giving rise to the distinctive form of counter-politics that Chatterjee calls the politics of the governed.[68]

When we talk about secularism, we typically think via the citizen (as by discussing Article 25 of the postcolonial Indian constitution, with its guarantee of freedoms of religion and conscience). It is consistently harder to imagine secularism from within the terms of governmentality, which is why both popular and legal discourse have remained consistently unable to see secularism clearly. Secularism has a "dual character," as Mahmood suggests; it is split between a "promise of freedom" and a "regulatory impulse."[69] Refracting Mahmood through Chatterjee's account of the differential emergence of the modern state form in colony and metropole, I argue that colonial secularism operated via two distinct political rationalities or logics: a liberal-constitutional secularism, addressed to the rights of the citizen, and a governmental secularism, addressed to the administrative management of empirical populations. The former promised freedom; the latter delivered regulation. In colonial India, the contradiction between these two political rationalities was often resolved through a pedagogic narrative, rendering a conceptual hiatus as a temporal hiatus. One day, religiously excitable subjects would mature into citizens. Until then, they required the paternalism of colonial law, a tool for educating subjects toward a perpetually deferred future freedom.

If the structural tension between juridico-legal and governmental rationalities is intrinsic to the modern state form, it is nonetheless articulated in historically specific ways. Here, I give this tension a period-specific gloss by talking about the liberal-constitutional and ethnographic (i.e., governmental) states. I further suggest that, in late colonial India, one important modality of governmental secularism was penal secularism—that is, a secularism that takes religion as a potentially violent criminal object in need of reform or reeducation.

VIOLENCE AND THE EDUCATION OF RELIGIOUS SENTIMENT

The Indian Penal Code was originally written by Thomas Babington Macaulay, the colonial ideologue now better known for his 1835 "Minute on Education," which proposed teaching Shakespeare and Milton in India to create a class of ersatz Englishman—a charter text for colonial mimicry.[70] Written immediately after the "Minute," the Code expressed a parallel pedagogic project. It would turn Indians into "manly" British subjects (Macaulay's adjective), including by training them to moderate their excitable feelings.[71] Here, law serves more than a strictly juridico-legal function. It does pedagogic work, becoming part of the apparatus of colonial governmentality. It operates via the education of affect.

Macaulay's 1837 draft Code responded directly to early nineteenth-century British blasphemy trials. In 1833, Macaulay proposed to Parliament a means of reconceptualizing blasphemy as an affective crime. In India, he implemented that proposal. His Code did not include a blasphemy law. Instead, it criminalized "wounding the religious feelings of any person."[72] That language became law in 1860 as Section 298. In 1927, it was supplemented by 295A. These colonial statutes were part of the same entangled history as the 1883 *Ramsay* ruling, which similarly redefined blasphemy as an affective crime.

In both Britain and India, "religious feelings" were a proxy for violence. "Blasphemy," as a Victorian guide to libel law put it, is "an outrage on men's religious feelings, tending to a breach of the peace."[73] Forty years later, 295A would use nearly identical language. In this phraseology, the meaning of "religious feelings" is overdetermined. To speak of "outraging religious feelings" is to indicate one feeling in particular: outrage. In the lead-up to the passage of 295A, a colonial bureaucrat offhandedly remarked that the "unfortunate state of feeling" between Hindus and Muslim regularly results in "deplorable outbreaks of passion."[74] This was not just euphemism. It was catachrestic displacement. When it came to religion, passion meant violence and violence, passion.

Laws like 295A were designed to prevent such passions from forming. The dark irony is that they probably just intensified them, with law's repressive or censorial function perversely inciting a profusion of forbidden speech.[75] Polemicists learned to speak law's language, alleging that their "religious feelings" had been outraged, and thus performatively constituting those feelings in the very act of transmitting them to others. "Religious feelings," then, were not something external to law that the colonial state could step in to manage. They grew along the trellis of law, taking shape around the bureaucratic state apparatus. This was education of a kind—just not the kind lawmakers said they intended. Law contained the script for communal violence. It educated its subjects in outrage.

If such dynamics are hard to see, it is perhaps because liberalism—as a theory of speech acts, not just a political theory—has a hard time accounting for the force of political speech. As eminent Victorian Walter Bagehot succinctly glossed the matter in 1867, liberalism indicates "government by discussion."[76] It places ultimate authority in the deliberations of parliamentary bodies and thus, by extension, in the critical deliberations of the civic public. Liberalism's ideal of deliberative reason, as is now well-known, works to occlude the body and its affects as political sites. It has thus also, historically, worked to exclude categories of person understood via the body (i.e., women and racialized people), whether by insisting that their bodies are too particular (thus having insufficient vantage on the general good) or too emotional (and thus insufficiently rational-deliberative).

Victorian liberals, meanwhile, also did a spectacularly bad job of accounting for the performative conditions of their own speech. All law carries the implicit threat of physical violence, it being the modern state's monopoly on legitimate violence—its ability to arrest, imprison, or kill—that lends its words the "force of law." In colonial situations, law's implicit force tends to be strongly racialized. In British India, for instance, the force of law undergirded the mundane acts of white violence that were a commonplace feature of social life. "Disorderly" whites, in their very bodies, quoted the racialized state, thus arrogating its implicit power—and undermining its ability to symbolize the rule of law.[77] Colonial officials found various ways to disavow such violence. One important tactic was displacing "state" violence onto Indian "society" as religious conflict, thus refusing to see the state's role in constituting Hindu-Muslim communalism (a disavowal enabled by the very distinction between "state" and "society," those grand abstractions)

Metropolitan writers like Bagehot (who inherited his position as editor of *The Economist* from his father-in-law, who died in India) engaged in similar acts of disavowal. When Bagehot turned discussion into a political symbol, he invested it with a perlocutionary force that extended beyond Parliament, that temple of deliberation, to facilitate imperial rule. It was discussion, he argued, that had catapulted Britain to the forefront of world civilizations and allowed it to colonize places like India—unskilled at critical chatter, and thus stuck in an arrested state of civilizational development. This racist cant imbues Bagehot's "government by discussion" with a secondary sense. If discussion is what justified the British government in India, then discussion became a byword for empire, an ideological cultural norm around which Britain constructed a narrative of global hegemony. Discussion exerted force to order colonized bodies.

Nor was Bagehot alone in treating discussion in this way. James Fitzjames Stephen—the writer, judge, and former Indian colonial official (and, later, uncle to novelist Virginia Woolf)—thought extensively about the distinction between force and persuasion in his 1873 response to John Stuart Mill's *On Liberty*. Where Mill had suggested that despotic force was appropriate for "children" and "barbarians" (i.e., India), reserving "liberty" and "free discussion" for mature nations (like Britain), Stephen insisted that the difference between a "rough and a civilized society" is not that the former uses "force" where the latter uses "persuasion," but that the latter uses force with more care.[78] He then set about undermining the distinction between the two.

This distinction had a venerable lineage. In his *Letter Concerning Toleration* (1689), for instance, John Locke also differentiated between the "outward force" of the magistrate and the "inward persuasion of the mind." Because outward force cannot change inward belief, he argued, the state must tolerate religious difference. This argument seems to construe religion as a purely mental affair, disjoined from the body. And yet Locke knew (or at least elsewhere seemed worried that) religion refuses such distinctions. It is a habitus that burrows deep into bodies before those bodies have full access to language and thus to deliberative persuasion.[79]

For Stephen too, religion seemed a site where force and persuasion verge together. (Like Macaulay, he sprang from the clans of Clapham Common, that Anglican-evangelical stronghold, with a certain kind of religious discipline written into his family being.) "Religion and morality are and always must be essentially coercive systems," he fumed. Though they might start with the "persuasion" of a small group, they inevitably culminate in "command," the forceful conversion of many.[80] Indeed, he explained, although the relation between "force" and "persuasion" is sometimes conflated with the relation between "temporal" and "spiritual" power (i.e., politics and religion), religion's force is quasi-physical. Religion thus helps show how persuasion and force "are neither opposed to nor really altogether distinct from each other. They are alternative means of influencing mankind. . . . Persuasion, indeed, is a kind of force . . . applied through the mind," just as force, in turn, is "a kind of persuasion."[81] The secular-liberal Mill is thus more akin to a religious figure like John Calvin than he might care to admit: both men apply force to reform society.[82] They install—to use one of Stephen's recurrent metaphors—canals, grooves, and other waterworks to get stagnant ponds moving, creating systems that direct behavior by harnessing external forces (friction, gravity, etc.).[83] Liberty, refracted through a theorization of religion, dissipates into a structure of well-calibrated constraints.

This is precisely why religion provides a useful metaphor for colonial law. As Stephen opined in 1876 (with acute sardonicism), in India, law is the "gospel of the English." This phrase would seem an ironic (and likely unconscious) reworking of Justice Hale's dictum that Christianity is parcel of the laws of England. In India, of course, English law was emphatically not Christian, but rather religiously neutral. For it to function as a gospel, then, the gospel would need to be stripped of theological contents—becoming a metaphor for a manner or modality of secular rule. As a "new religion," wrote Stephen, law would produce a "moral conquest more striking, more durable, and far more solid than the physical conquest which rendered it possible."[84] Here, Stephen is trying to find language to describe the pedagogic force of law, a force that shapes subjects while remaining distinct from overtly physical conquest. He lands on the word *moral*, which underscores this force's proximity to religion (probably echoing the eighteenth-century sense of *moral* as including both the sentimental and the ethical).

Stephen's question here is, I think, still a live one. How does law's pedagogic, governmental, or persuasive force differ from and relate to its juridico-legal force? Both act on bodies, but in different ways. To develop an answer to this question, we need not follow Stephen in his antique terminology. What the nineteenth century called moral force, more recent scholarship has called affect.

RELIGIOUS AFFECT AS PUBLIC FEELING

The interdisciplinary field of affect theory, which emerged in the 1990s at the intersection of queer theory and poststructuralism and later absorbed various strands of British cultural studies and psychoanalysis, has, more recently, entered conversations in religious studies, critically reframing an older set of scholarly themes.[85] "Religion always begins with an emotion," declared Cornelis Tiele in 1899, writing toward the end of a period in which theorists of religion—from Friedrich Schleiermacher in the 1790s to Rudolph Otto in the 1910s—had increasingly come to see their object of study as primarily a species of feeling.[86]

While affect theory lurks behind much of the analysis in *Slandering the Sacred*, it only occasionally steps into the limelight. To me, it has seemed relatively more productive to think with (and also against) the period-specific concepts circulating in my historical archive, with the term *affect* a tool for getting critical traction on phrases like "religious feelings." In the eighteenth century, one spoke of passions, sentiments, and affections—philosophical terms that conjoined the mental to the moral, often with theological valence. In the early nineteenth century, this moral lexicon was partly displaced by the word *emotion*, which previously had denoted political or meteorological unrest; now it was redeployed as a scientizing term for describing the human mind. Its popularizers included James and John Stuart Mill, key patrons of the Indian Penal Code.[87] These shifting English-language concepts shaped developments in South Asian vernacular languages. For example, an Urdu-language treatise on modern psychology like Abdul Majid Daryabadi's *Falsafa-e Jazbat* (The philosophy of emotions, 1914) separated the emotional from the moral, a sharp departure from older discourses on civility or the "polishing of ethics" (*tahzib ul-akhlaq*).[88] These concept-histories also inflected colonial jurisprudence. In 1915, a lower court in north India held that because religion is "rooted in the emotions and sentiments," religious arguments are pointless. They never change minds. They only hurt feelings.[89]

This book's dive into historical feeling is not just empirical, however. Throughout, I work to develop modes of theorization immanent to my historical archives. I also consistently make critical moves indebted to contemporary affect theory, especially around the question of what have been described oxymoronically as "public feelings."[90] What better phrase to capture the "feelings" of 295A? Writing sentiment into the very text of law, 295A turns law itself into something like a sentimental literary genre—a mode of writing defined by the transmission of affect.

To understand this sentimental text, we need to dispense with the notion that emotions somehow exist interior to the individual human psyche. Even inward feelings, after all, are more outward than we like to think. They creep along the skin, linger in rooms, connect us to embodied others.[91] The word *affect* brings this connectivity into clearer view: it denotes a body's ability to be affected by forces external to it (so too, etymologically, do *emotion* and *passion*, respectively indicating "moved" and "passive" bodies).

By focusing on public feelings—or, rather, on affect as a mobile force that is neither public nor private/personal—we can also productively reframe the history of secularism. As Joan Wallach Scott has argued, what we understand as secularism emerged in tandem with the modern public/private distinction that coalesced in the late eighteenth century. This distinction was strongly gendered, linked with the newly regnant ideal of the bourgeois home as temple of feminine domesticity. For long-nineteenth-century secularism, then, woman, sentiment, and religion appeared as correlate entities, all constitutively disbarred from public. Secularism was a patriarchal project. (Only later, as Scott argues, did secularism reinvent itself as a feminist project, defined against racialized, and especially Muslim, postcolonial populations.)[92]

We can see these histories converging on a turn-of-the-twentieth-century figure like William James. Famously, his *Varieties of Religious Experience* (1902) defines religion as "the feelings, acts, and experiences of individual men in their solitude, so far as they apprehend themselves to stand in relation to whatever they may consider the divine."[93] This sequestering of religion within the confines of the heart was both a protestantizing and a gendered move. In a telling aside, James quips that to study religion is to be "literally bathed in sentiment" and confesses that he is "almost appalled at the amount of emotionality" in his text.[94] Try to imagine James delivering what was originally a lecture series to a roomful of besuited Scottish gentlemen in Edinburgh, narrating intense emotional experiences (including a few of his own, duly anonymized) in a paradigmatically public venue. Turning solitary feelings into public ones, he staged a kind of performative contradiction—registered in his body as a gendered squirm. James inhabited a gendered structure of secularist feeling.

This structure looked slightly different in turn-of-the-century India. Because colonialism disbarred elite Indian men from full participation in public life, these men turned to the inner sphere of literature, culture, domesticity, and religion as a zone of potential sovereignty, one where they could exercise self-rule without British interference.[95] The result was what some scholars have depicted as a sort of secondary colonization, an invasion of the home by bourgeois men who set about imposing new restrictions on the lives of bourgeois women, including through language education as site for the production of sexual difference.[96] Duly sentimentalized, these women then became the symbolic heart of the religious "communities" that mediated elite-male access to the institutions of the colonial public.

This bourgeois-masculine public was, importantly, a formation of the parlor not the street.[97] Its mores were *savarna* (privileged-caste) mores, with the question of the late colonial public thus inseparable from the late colonial rearticulation of the caste sensorium. If caste, in its various iterations, implies both a spatial-sensory order (a distribution of bodies in urban and village spaces phenomenologically coded around affectively charged practices of touch, smell, sight, etc.) and a sexual order (a violent enforcement of caste endogamy), both orders were undergoing structural transformation in the late nineteenth and early twentieth centuries.[98] This shift in the sensible infrastructures of caste was evident in the new modes of political religion that followed from B. G. Tilak's reinvented Ganesh Chathurti festival, bringing religious images out of the sacred enclosure of brahmanical temples and into the public or *sarvajanik* street.[99] It was likewise evident in the cheaply printed pages of polemical religious tracts, which developed an aesthetics of obscenity that stoked affects integral to the *savarna* sensorium (repulsion, disgust)—often by referencing either saliva (linked to the brahmanical ideology of purity/pollution) or forms of labor traditionally associated with subordinated castes (sex work, human waste removal)—even as the promiscuous circulation of cheap tactile print potentially unsettled caste mores.[100] Caste reterritorialized Victorian "decency" by overlaying a *savarna* habitus onto the bourgeois-Victorian habitus of bodily or spatial enclosure. A similar overlay of caste and class informed the mores of *ashraf* (elite) Muslims.

This was the affective structure into which the *Rangila Rasul* was launched in 1924. The tract satirizes the Prophet Muhammad by depicting him as a libidinous fool unable to restrain his desire for wives. It also explicitly contrasts Muhammad with paragons of male celibacy: the Buddha, Jesus, and Swami Dayananda Saraswati, the founder of the religious society that published the tract, the Arya Samaj. "Even in a very, very old philosopher like me, feelings are stirred up when my women or religion is insulted," remarked a member of the 1927 Legislative Assembly when pondering such polemics. His comment neatly distills the cultural logic of late colonial secularism, wherein a reconstituted patriarchy asserted simultaneous control over "woman" and "religion" as twinned inner objects.[101] This secularism's religious feelings were gendered feelings. They were perhaps specifically the feelings of men, whose excitable bodies became sites for the articulation of various ethico-political discourses on self-control or self-rule. They were also caste-inflected feelings. Not incidentally, Arya Samajists were prominent advocates of caste reform, conducting *shuddhi* or purification ceremonies that ritually transformed Dalits, Muslims, and others (including, at various points, Europeans and East Africans) into *savarna* Hindus—thus simultaneously affirming and unsettling the caste order.

Such rhetoric did not disappear after 1927. Stereotyped depictions of hypersexualized, Muslim masculinity remain alarmingly familiar in twenty-first-century India. Neither did the Indian Penal Code disappear. It remains law across the countries of former British India (India, Pakistan, Bangladesh, and Myanmar). If the Code's religious feelings are simultaneously intimate and official—shaping the affective reactions of particular bodies by placing those bodies in a legal frame—then they are also simultaneously local and geopolitical, linked to empire as an affective architecture designed to organize bodies and their conduct at a global scale.

THE TRANSCOLONIAL "INDIAN" PENAL CODE: A LEGAL INFRASTRUCTURE OF WORLD RELIGIONS?

The Indian Penal Code was never just Indian. It emerged from the interstitial space connecting India to Britain (see chapter 4). And the British soon imposed it, with minimal changes, on a host of other colonies: Sri Lanka, Singapore, Malaysia, Kenya, Malawi, Tanzania, Uganda, Zanzibar, Zambia, Gambia, Yemen, Cyprus, Fiji, Vanuatu, Tuvalu, the Solomon Islands, the Seychelles, and, for a time, part of Nigeria.[102] It also, via a more circuitous path, shaped criminal law in the white-settler colonies of Australia and Canada. In 1877, James Fitzjames Stephen published an English criminal code modeled on the Indian one. (A major Macaulay fan, Stephen wrote in 1872 that comparing the Indian Penal Code to English common law was "like comparing cosmos with chaos.")[103] The Stephen code then became the model for the 1892 Canadian Penal Code (created to extend criminal jurisdiction nationally after the 1885 North-West Rebellion of Métis and First Nations communities; it included a prohibition on blasphemous libels that exceed "decent language") and the 1899 Queensland Criminal Code in Australia.[104] This cluster of anglophone texts subsequently entered the toolkit of legal reformers in places like Thailand (1908) and Egypt (1919), who drafted religion sections strikingly reminiscent of the Indian ones.[105] So, seemingly, did reformers in British Palestine (1936).[106]

This transcolonial tale is hardly unique. A similar story could presumably be constructed for French civil law. The question then arises: To what extent have globally mobile secular-legal texts served as the infrastructure for "world religions" (that post-1880s notion), as both global cultural form and global structure of feeling? Many of these codes use the word *religion*, after all. Many also, in one way or another, mention "religious feelings." (While 295A exists only in South Asia, the British adapted Section 298, with its wounded feelings, to other colonies.) If we want to study the global circulation of religious affect, do we need to start from colonial-secular law as unseen infrastructure of "religious" feeling?

I pose this question rhetorically. Answering it is beyond the scope of this (and probably any single) book. I will bring this introduction to a close by simply sketching one synecdochic piece of this larger history—the Indian Penal Code's influence in Britain—to return us to where we began: the inadequacy of a Whig-liberal narrative of blasphemous modernity that forgets how much of the history of North Atlantic secularism happened overseas in the colonies.

Macaulay dreamed that his Indian Penal Code would one day return to Britain. His contemporaries mistrusted radical legal reform, but perhaps future lawmakers would resolve to "be at least as well off as their Hindoo vassals" by adopting his cutting-edge code.[107] That metropolitan mimicry never quite happened; the Macaulay Code was a colonial boomerang that did not land. Still, it hovered over English legal debates for more than a century, exerting clear force by articulating a sort of conceptual outer limit for British secularism—especially when it came to blasphemy.

The Code's influence began in the 1830s and '40s with a criminal law commission chaired by Henry Brougham.[108] For blasphemy law, however, the real story begins after the 1883 *Ramsay* ruling, which prompted an outcry from legal reformers. By redefining blasphemy, these reformers argued, Coleridge preserved a crime that should have been either abolished or broadened to cover all religions.[109] Some reformers proposed replacing English blasphemy law with a version of India's Section 298.[110] Others sounded notes of caution, including J. F. Stephen, who worried that such a law would place excessive constraint on British speech. He nonetheless ended up endorsing the idea.[111] Six years earlier, Stephen's Macaulayan English criminal code had begrudgingly retained the crime of blasphemous libel, bowing to precedent while also noting (wishfully?) that this crime was "practically obsolete."[112] Now it looked like it would finally become so. In 1887, Cambridge law professor and member of Parliament Courtney Kenny introduced a 298-style bill that would have made wounding religious feelings a misdemeanor; it went nowhere. In 1889, Charles Bradlaugh proposed another bill that would have abolished blasphemy outright. It failed too.[113]

For the next century, British legal reformers kept looking to India. In a 1922 article on blasphemy law, Kenny even quoted Hari Singh Gour.[114] In 1930, Parliament considered an updated version of Kenny's 1887 bill, but was deterred by complaints that it would protect "crank religions" like Spiritualism and Christian Science.[115] Blasphemy then went on hiatus until the *Gay News* case, after which the House of Lords once again looked to the Indian Penal Code as a model of how to govern religion in a "plural society."[116] A 1981 commission concluded that the Code was in fact the only viable model for reforming blasphemy law—but then decided that its liabilities were sufficiently dire that it was better to abolish blasphemy altogether.[117] A 2002 House of Lords committee went so far as to solicit an official statement from Indian attorney-general Soli Sorabjee, who explained that the Indian Penal Code had fostered "intolerance, divisiveness, and unreasonable interference with freedom of expression," amplifying conflict by prompting "fundamentalists" to "invoke the criminal machinery against each other's religions."[118] This was hardly a ringing endorsement. In any case, a different solution to blasphemy law was at hand: the post-1980s notion of hate speech.

It bears stressing that Britain was not somehow uniquely "behind" in the timeline of secular-legal modernity. The United States, for instance, was also still grappling with blasphemy law in the mid-twentieth century (state blasphemy statutes that dated to the colonial period had been prosecuted throughout the nineteenth century and were not deemed unconstitutional until 1952).[119] If one is thinking in these linear terms, however, India was certainly "ahead" of its North Atlantic counterparts in reconceiving blasphemy as a secular crime. It is thus a perhaps uniquely rich site for thinking about the history of blasphemy—and, more broadly, how secular law has come to regulate something called "religion" by regulating feelings.

WHERE THIS BOOK GOES FROM HERE

Slandering the Sacred pursues these themes by digging into a particular set of historical archives. This method implies an argument. To see legal feelings clearly, we need to push past the phenomenologically thin generalities of law itself to think via concrete historical conjunctures that allow us to see religious affect as simultaneously official (structured by bureaucratic, legal, and other institutions) and intimate (lodged in historically situated human bodies). Working toward such an account, this book traces an arc from "public" to "private" and back again, hoping to throw the public/private distinction into productive confusion.

Part I opens with an analysis of "the public" as a category in global crisis. Through a detailed analysis of the 1927 Rajpal affair (the controversy that ended, or at least seemed to end, with the passage of Section 295A), it asks how the 1920s crisis of the public prompted a related crisis for late colonial secularism. The rest of the book circles around the Rajpal affair, with parts II and III respectively pursuing the prehistory of the two texts that collided in this 1927 scandal: the Indian Penal Code, as secular-legal book, and the *Rangila Rasul*, as polemic religious tract. While this organization might seem to reify the distinction between "law" and "religion," the account developed across these six chapters works to confuse that distinction. We find a secular law shaped profoundly by religious histories and religious words exerting a quasi-legal force. Law and religion thus appear not only as complementary technologies for the governance of emotion, but also as profoundly intertwined ones.

Part II, "Blasphemy's Empire," begins in the same vein as part I, exploring a public history of the Indian Penal Code by excavating the intellectual world of the early nineteenth century. It then pivots. Chapter 5, "Macaulay Unmanned," marks a shift in the arc of the book, moving from the public register of law to what will at first glance appear a surprisingly domestic set of concerns: Macaulay's incestuous love for his sisters and readerly rebellion against his evangelical father. In sympathy with recent scholarship on the intimacy of empire, I ask how one lawmaker used the paper object of a penal code as a tool for the governance of his own feelings, with Company paper thus rendered an intimate artifact. Chapter 6 returns to legal history to stay with the category confusion that arises from chapter 5. Tracing a brief history of the concept of libel between the seventeenth and late nineteenth centuries, it asks how the distinction between religion and politics emerged in tandem with the distinction between public and private.

Part III, "Polemics as Ethics," shifts to what might seem the most local or limited of the histories in *Slandering the Sacred*. The reader will discover, however, that by diving deep into the world of the Arya Samaj—the Hindu reform society behind the *Rangila Rasul*—we can come to a more satisfying theoretical account of the secular-legal governance of religion. Only in part III do the major themes broached earlier in the book come to fruition:

forceful words, excitable bodies, slanderous intimacies. As in my discussion of Macaulay's domestic sentiments, I take Arya affect as synecdochic of larger political structures, its microscopic granularity a lens for seeing those structures in altered perspective. Not least, Arya affect foregrounds the embodied realm of gender, race, and caste—which is to say, the realm of religion as a set of technologies for the government of the body and its conduct—as a key site for the cultural production of law.

The Aryas have typically been represented in scholarship as pioneers of communalist hate speech and thus progenitors of the Hindu right. That is not wrong. Still, it is not the whole story. The reader will meet a somewhat different Arya Samaj here. By working to produce a slight shift in how we see the Aryas, I am also, by extension, working to reframe the phenomenon of "fanatic speech" for which the Aryas often serve as exemplars. Not only did Aryas presume the Indian Penal Code (which went into effect thirteen years before the Samaj was founded) as key background condition for their injurious words (chapter 8) but they also used words to achieve some of the same ends as colonial law, including managing religious affect (chapter 7). Sometimes Foucauldian, sometimes Kittlerian, my account of Arya speech is rooted in the materiality of historically specific discourse networks or inscription systems, from print to photography to poster art. It thus hews close to particular scenes and texts: speechifying schoolgirls, purloined letters, middlebrow biographies, and more. Chapter 9 brings *Slandering the Sacred* full circle by constructing a cultural history of the genre of religious biography that the *Rangila Rasul* lampooned, and with it, a cultural history of the prophet as figure of comparative religion.

The framers of Section 295A expressly exempted scholarly writing from the scope of that law. It thus perhaps bears noting that my aims and intentions in writing this book are entirely scholarly. Frustrated with the repetitive, often-hackneyed debates about religion and free speech in the twenty-first century, I have tried to revisit one formative moment in the history of our blasphemous present to ask whether, by seeing it differently, we might also come to see ourselves differently. I return to these contemporary questions in the conclusion.

A note on the text: To write a book about blasphemy without quoting blasphemous material is like writing about art without any pictures. It leaves the reader blind. I thus quote some potentially offensive material here. I trust the reader to approach this material in the scholarly spirit in which the book was written. Even seemingly spontaneous embodied responses participate in, and are shaped by, historically sedimented structures of feeling.

By addressing the reader as a potential scholar, I thus invite them to do the scholarly work of historicizing their own emotions. A given reader's affective response to quoted material is implicated in the very histories this book attempts to explicate—and would thus, ideally, become part of the reader's own archive of cultural analysis.

Speaking of scholarly: Translations are my own unless otherwise indicated. With an eye to a nonspecialist readership, I have restricted diacritics to the endnotes.

I
THE MERRY PROPHET

02

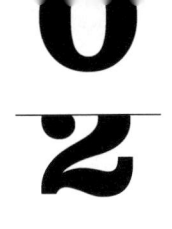

A CRISIS OF THE PUBLIC

The Rajpal Affair and Its Bodies

WHEN MAHASHE RAJPAL PUBLISHED THE *Rangila Rasul* (The merry Prophet) in 1924, he surely realized it would offend readers of Urdu in Lahore, where he ran his bookshop. He presumably did not expect a major national controversy ending in his murder. Charged by the government with fomenting hatred between religious communities, Rajpal spent almost three years on trial before he was finally—and unexpectedly—acquitted by the Lahore High Court in 1927. A public outcry ensued, leading the central government to add a new section, 295A, to the Indian Penal Code to criminalize publications that intentionally outrage religious feelings. That law seemed to resolve the crisis. Then, in 1929, a man upset about the *Rangila Rasul* walked into Rajpal's bookshop and stabbed him to death.

Even a century later, recounting these events risks narrative trouble. The Rajpal affair was shaped in advance by a set of cultural scripts that overdetermined the actions available to any given individual. Many of these scripts remain very much alive in the twenty-first century—not least the Islamophobic scripts that would take Rajpal's murder as proof of their own facticity without seeing how this event unfolded from within a version of those same narratives. The empirical "fact" conceals a set of historical contingencies that its apparent facticity or givenness works to naturalize. The work of critical scholarship is to try to break free from such narratives. Still, one should not naïvely underestimate their power to reassert themselves.

Problems begin with how to name the events at hand. To call them the *Rangila Rasul* affair is arguably to repeat, with every use, the "indecent assault" on Islam implied by that tract's title. Some Muslim-owned newspapers in 1927 urged that the controversy be called the Rajpal affair instead.[1] I mostly follow that recommendation. Why was this title such a problem? Even by itself, the word *rangila* was said to be a "diabolical outrage on decency."[2] Literally meaning "colorful," it implies (in the words of the 1927 government translator) "drink and debauchery," indicating a person "who is sexually low in morals and leads a gay and fast life."[3] Or, as an 1884 dictionary has it, a *rangila* is "a man of pleasure; a rake, a sybarite."[4] To call the Prophet (or *rasul*) a *rangila*, then, is to depict him as a foppish dandy.[5] To soften that charge, I opt for the most neutral period-specific translation: "The Merry Prophet."

My aim here is to denaturalize the Rajpal affair and the communalist scripts instantiated in it. Toward that end, I approach the controversy as a global event—one that expresses not dueling religious "fanaticisms" but rather the constitutive antinomies of secular modernity.[6] The affair was certainly global. Public outcry against the *Rangila Rasul* started in Lahore, then rippled steadily outward—first to other Punjabi cities, then onward to Kanpur and Allahabad, Calcutta and Madras, Burma and Ceylon, Africa and England.[7] The House of Commons briefly discussed it, as did newspapers like the *Manchester Guardian*.[8] Even global celebrities weighed in, as when Arthur Conan Doyle, the detective-fiction author and Spiritualist, became the first signatory to a petition circulated by London's Ahmadiyya Mosque asking the Privy Council to overturn the Lahore court ruling.[9] In 1925, Pandit Chamupati, the tract's anonymous author, quietly left India for a Vedic mission tour of British East Africa.[10] The *Rangila Rasul* traveled too, and along similar diaspora pathways. In 1931, it popped up in Fiji.[11]

Thinking from these global flows, I argue that the Rajpal affair staged a crisis not just for Indian secularism but also for the Indian "public," sharing in a transcolonial moment wherein this key category of modern political thought seemed to be unraveling. This exploration of the category of the public launches a line of inquiry that will run throughout *Slandering the Sacred*: how do religious feelings emerge in and through the material infrastructures of the public, especially print media and the reading body?

PHANTOM PUBLICS, GOVERNED PUBLICS

Colonial administrators had long presented the Indian public as somehow deficient. It was too communal, too cantankerous, too divided by language and region. This alleged deficiency worked to justify colonial rule. "It may be that the public mind of India may expand under our system till it has outgrown that system," opined Thomas Macaulay in 1833, shortly before becoming the architect of the Indian Penal Code. "Perhaps by good government we may educate our subjects into a capacity for better government." Whether that day would ever come, Macaulay confessed, he did not know. Until it did, India would require an "enlightened and paternal despotism," benevolently imposed on a colonial public that this narrative trapped in a state of perpetual political immaturity.[12]

If the Indian public had been in crisis since the nineteenth century, in the 1920s the "Western" public finally caught up to it. A series of books calling the concept of the public into question appeared across the North Atlantic world, especially the United States and Germany: Ferdinand Tönnies's *Critique of Public Opinion* (1922), Carl Schmitt's *The Crisis of Parliamentary Democracy* (1923), Walter Lippmann's *Public Opinion* (1922) and *The Phantom Public* (1925), and John Dewey's *The Public and Its Problems* (1927). Some of these authors argued that the classically liberal ideal of the deliberative public sphere needed to be abandoned. Others rushed to the public's defense. Taken together, however, they articulated a set of problems strikingly resonant with colonial conditions.

Any schematic summary of complex global processes necessarily simplifies those processes. Still, if we want to make sense of the 1920s crisis of the public, we could do worse than to follow Partha Chatterjee in his schematic narrative about the geographic inversions of global modernity. From the eighteenth century forward, Chatterjee tells us, North Atlantic states redefined themselves around the ideals of liberal democracy, including the rights of the citizen and the sovereignty of the public. In the colonies, meanwhile, those same states were pursuing a markedly different form of rule. In technical terms, one could say that, in the metropole, the dominant political rationality was juridico-legal sovereignty, while in the colonies it was governmentality.[13] That is, where imperial Britain had a liberal-constitutional state addressed to the rights of abstracted citizens, colonial India had an ethnographic state addressed to the empirical management of socially heterogeneous populations—an archipelago of communities defined around religion, caste, and tribe.[14]

As the British gradually introduced parliamentary institutions in India in the early twentieth century, this situation began to change. The ethnographic state, which had fully emerged only in the late nineteenth century, was becoming overlaid with something like a liberal-constitutional state, a development that culminated in Indian independence. We can feel the tension between these two political grammars in Herbert Risley's argument for increased censorship during debates preceding the restrictive 1910 Press Act. In India, Risley insisted, "there is very little public opinion and its place must be supplied by the law" as "public educator."[15] Like Macaulay, Risley saw the colonial government as a paternal despot. Unlike Macaulay, this professional ethnologist had spent the previous thirty years making anthropometric measurements of "nasal indexes" and "facial angles" and expressing delight that caste endogamy had made India such a fertile field for race science.[16] His career since the 1860s had coincided with the rise of the ethnographic state, culminating in appointments as Census Commissioner and Director of Ethnography.[17] Risley saw India as populated by racialized bodies that needed mapping and managing. How jarring it must have been for him to see those bodies speaking via the institutional forms of the liberal public—as they would only do more in the decades to come.

We should not, however, take this shift as some kind of Macaulayan maturation. Rather, with Chatterjee, it is more productive to invert the usual temporal order of global modernity by taking the colonial case as paradigmatic. By the end of the twentieth century, governmentality and its populational politics would become the dominant face of politics worldwide, displacing liberal-constitutional logics even in the North Atlantic region. Macaulay was wrong, in other words. The Indian public did not have to catch up to Britain. The British public had to catch up to a modernity that had already emerged in India, realizing that it too was just a managed population—and always had been.

The public sphere theorists of the 1920s were registering this precise insight, their books a hinge or pivot in governmentality's northward swing. Perhaps the clearest text in this regard is Lippmann's *Public Opinion* (1922). Narrating what he calls a "disenchantment" with the foundational myths of modern democracy, Lippman describes the citizen awakening to the realization that "his sovereignty is a fiction. He reigns in theory, but in fact he does not govern." Group psychology and communications science were proving their ability to manipulate the public, turning its opinions into just another factory product—what Lippmann called "manufactured consent." Real power belonged to the manufacturers. The public was a phantom, and always had been. Modern states should face reality and reorganize governance around the rule of experts—refashioning themselves, in other words, to look more like the colonies, where experts had been ruling all along.[18]

Nowadays, Lippmann's sense of agony over the decline of publics can seem almost quaint. In the twenty-first century, we take it for granted that elections revolve around marketing firms managing microdemographics and social psychologists using the latest techniques to "nudge" (in the trade jargon) particular populations to the polls. To the extent that we assume that publics work in this way, we live in the age of governmentality, not the age of the citizen (although the citizen is certainly still with us). We thus, if Chatterjee is correct, live in a modernity that arrived first in colonial contexts like British India.

There are concrete connections between US public sphere theorists of the 1920s and their South Asian contemporaries: Lippmann corresponded with Lajpat Rai; Dewey was B. R. Ambedkar's professor at Columbia.[19] It would be interesting to develop a comparative political theory of the public by thinking from such pairings. Here I pursue a different tactic by asking what formations of the public were visible in late colonial India. My presumption is that the category of the public cannot be applied to South Asian materials from the outside like some kind of theoretical laminate but needs to be critically rethought via its genealogical links to India and empire.[20]

Late colonial India was enacting a reverse movement to the one that Lippmann describes for the United States. If the US liberal public was on the wane in the 1920s, the Indian liberal public was on the rise, institutionalized in representative bodies like the Legislative Assembly, established in 1919. In form, these parliamentary bodies were largely liberal-constitutional. With their members standing for religious communities as well as districts, however, they also relied heavily on the conceptual structures of the ethnographic state, thus expressing the contradiction between these two political rationalities in an especially clear way. In a parallel articulation of the same contradiction, late colonial newspapers were faulted for representing not *the* public but rather particular publics (Hindu, Muslim, etc.)—publics that, because of their particularity, were not really public at all.[21] In eighteenth-century political thought, the generality of the public was contrasted with the parochialism of local interests. These late colonial particularities were something else. Far from local, they indicated a form of generalized collectivity mapped and managed by the apparatus of the ethnographic state: the population.

A phrase like "the Hindu public" thus masks a substantial conceptual tension. In it, *Hindu* denotes a bound seriality or enumerable population; *public* indicates an unbound seriality, its edges extending ambiguously outward to include whoever might happen to pick up a given text. Does a Muslim who reads a Hindu newspaper become part of the Hindu public for the duration of her reading? That such a question is even possible indicates the conceptual hiatus between population and public as modes of collective identity.[22]

A Hindu public is thus neither a public nor a population, but rather sits uneasily at the intersection of the two. I will describe such formations as "populational publics." With this term, I mean to redescribe what is sometimes called a counterpublic—a word that can be used to conflate several distinct entities.[23] A populational public is not a niche consumer public (e.g., the public of a golf magazine), nor is it an oppositional public (e.g., the readership of a feminist or labor-movement journal, defined around political opinion rather than ascribed identity). It would, however, seem to correlate to two paradigm cases of the counterpublic: a gay magazine and a Black church. Like a late colonial Hindu newspaper, these cultural forms are defined by their ambiguity of address. Anyone *could* read a gay magazine or attend a Black church, but only certain kinds of persons are likely to do so.[24] This hiatus between potential and actual audience expresses the related hiatus between the open-edged public and the enumerable population, paralleling the internal structure of late colonial populational publics. (Indeed, it is perhaps because they too had been objects of governmentality—hailed as populations, and thus partly analogous to parallel populations in the colonies—that subaltern social formations in the United States have been productive sites from which to retheorize the North Atlantic public.) This comparison, however, begs a clarification of terms. Describing such populational publics as counterpublics seems to imply that they are also necessarily oppositional publics, with the empirical fact of their subalternity an expression of political dissent. That conceptual conflation might, in some cases, be warranted. It can also, however, elide historical and political complexity. The late colonial Hindu public, for instance, was precisely not subaltern insofar as it reinforced caste and class privilege even as it was simultaneously the contingently subalternized object of colonial forms of knowledge.

Such abstract formations of human collectivity collide in concrete material things—most pertinently for my purposes here, paper artifacts and reading bodies. To bring this materiality into clearer view, let us return to the story of the Rajpal affair.

A RED-EYED READER TAKES THE STAND

The *Rangila Rasul* was, in the first instance, a bundle of paper, the latest volley in a pamphlet war among Lahore's rival religious societies—Hindu and Muslim, Christian and Sikh. Ostensibly a riposte to *Unnisvi Sadi ka*

Maharshi (A nineteenth-century maharishi), a tract published by Ahmadi Muslims criticizing the founder of the Arya Samaj, the *Rangila Rasul* reached a much wider audience. Its first edition of a thousand copies, printed in May 1924, quickly gave way to a second.[25]

If the primal scene of religious offense is a scene of solitary reading, of intimate congress between book and body, then perhaps the signal moment in the early history of the *Rangila Rasul* was when somebody sent a copy to M. K. Gandhi. In June 1924, Gandhi publicly condemned the tract in the pages of *Young India*. Pleading for religious "tolerance" and begging religious leaders to publish "clean literature" instead of filthy polemics, he refused to inflict on his readers the discomfort he himself had undergone, declining to even summarize the *Rangila Rasul*'s contents.[26] A model of ascetic forbearance and self-abnegating tolerance, Gandhi presumably hoped to arrest the flow of injurious affect by focusing readerly pain on his own body.[27] Ironically, his condemnation probably helped launch the *Rangila Rasul* onto its infamous career. Soon a chorus of printed voices was attesting to how the tract had "wounded the hearts of Muslims" with its "uncivil" and "dirty" language.[28]

In July 1924, the Punjab government registered proceedings against Rajpal, the tract's publisher, under Section 153A of the Indian Penal Code, charging him with promoting enmity or hatred between Hindus and Muslims. Hearings began that October but—prolonged by procedural delays and two appeals—did not conclude until May 1927, when the Lahore High Court overturned the lower court rulings to acquit Rajpal. In Justice Kanwar Dalip Singh's idiosyncratic reasoning, slanders of the Prophet are not necessarily also slanders of Islam and thus cannot be presumed to induce enmity in Muslims. The public briefly scratched its head. Then it mobilized. Starting in late May, telegrams and petitions poured into government offices, with protests following in June and July.

Colonial officials waited before acting, hoping that the judicial system would resolve the crisis on its own. They were watching two pending court cases—the first involving a sexual-scatological biography of the Prophet, the *Vichitra Jivan* (A strange life, 1923), the second an article depicting him suffering in hell, published in Amritsar's *Risala-i-Vartman* (Contemporary journal) in May 1927.

Both trials foregrounded the quasi-literary question of reader response. How would a given reader react to one of these controversial texts? The judge in the *Vichitra Jivan* case, Justice Dalal, tried to imagine himself in the position of an ordinary Muslim reader and concluded that he would definitely proceed from hating the tract's author to hating all Hindus.[29] The prosecution in the *Vartman* case saved the court such imaginative acrobatics by calling actual readers to the stand. "On reading this article, I received the most terrible shock," reported one of these witnesses, Maulvi Muhammad Daud Ghaznavi of Amritsar. "Blood came to my eyes when I read it. Intense hatred was created in me against the editor, the author, the publisher and the community, the Arya Samaj and Hindu Sabha by this article."[30] Although the defense countered by insisting that Ghaznavi's "shock" was a different emotion than legally actionable "hatred," the judge ultimately convicted both author and editor.[31] The witness testimony seems to have worked.

Ghaznavi's testimony functioned in court as a performative enactment of the wounded public. Now, of course, we have no unmediated access to his original act of reading. Did he first encounter the article "Sair-i-Dozakh" (A trip to hell) not in the pages of the *Risala-i-Vartman* but on a poster that Ahmadis had plastered around Lahore to protest the offending article?[32] Or was he one of the Muslims who apparently sometimes bought the *Risala-i-Vartman* in the market?[33] That question had possible legal implications if reprinting the article was taken as an independent offense. It matters little, however, to Ghaznavi's performance on the witness stand.

The stand acts as a sort of confessional stall, a space physically constructed to facilitate the elicitation of feeling. One imagines that, as Ghaznavi narrated his initial reading, he relived and thus reperformed his affective response. He feels a shock. His eyes turn red. This physiological reaction would orient Ghaznavi's body to the physical object of the newspaper or poster on which the article was printed. That paper artifact would, in turn, orient him toward an unseen multitude of bodies: Hindus, the class. (It is perhaps ironic that the Arya Samajists, who for decades protested they were not Hindus, became paradigmatic of this class during the Rajpal affair.) In this scenario, the printed page functions as a sort of fetish object. Like the commodity fetish, it stands in for a set of human relations, displacing and absorbing a collective flesh.

According to the prosecution, the author and editor of the offending article had acted "in a representative capacity."[34] They represented all Hindus, which was why readers' enmity toward them necessarily translated into legally actionable class enmity. What kind of representation is this? Perhaps the *Risala-i-Vartman* represented Hindus by giving voice to Hindu public opinion, thus standing in the place of Hindus as would a political representative (i.e., Gayatri Spivak's *Vertretung*). Perhaps it represented Hindus more symbolically, portraying them by metonymic proxy like a sort of ethnographic specimen (i.e., Spivak's *Darstellung*).[35] Probably the *Risala-i-Vartman* did both. That is, it operated simultaneously within the political logics of the liberal-constitutional and the ethnographic state, representing both the public (which speaks) and the population (which is spoken for), with "the Hindu" emerging from the intersection of the two. Nor was the printed page the only physical entity in court representing community in this way. On the witness stand, Ghaznavi's reading body would have functioned in parallel with the printed text. The court took him as a representative type, speaking for and feeling on behalf of a populational class, Muslims. Like the printed page, his body implied multitudes.

If printed texts were able to produce a visceral response in readers, this was partly because late colonial religious polemics had developed a markedly corporeal aesthetic, writing populational bodies into their very prose. Several vivid instances of this aesthetic can be found in the June 1924 issue of another Lahore paper, the *Guru Ghantal* (The knave) (quickly prosecuted by government for promulgating communal enmity), which fuses sexuality, obscenity, and community to a truly remarkable degree.[36] One article describes a sex worker trying to convert a Hindu Jat on behalf of her Sufi pir; while they are having intercourse, she "passes excreta." Another article, in relaying hadith about the Prophet's bodily functions, describes Islam as a "philosophy of urine and nightsoil." Yet another describes God tripping a cleric so that he falls flat on his face before God grabs him by the ears to throw him into hell. A cartoon shows a doctor operating on God's ear so that he might better hear prayers during Ramadan.[37]

These grotesque physicalizations bring the heavens down to inglorious earth, lodging the sacred in the domain of touch, violence, and bodily fluid—a domain marked by caste and gender, among other axes of social and populational identity. These articles' anti-Muslim valence cannot be readily separated from their misogyny, nor from their scatological obsessions. In at least some late colonial writing, there is an explicit link made between human excreta and *savarna* ideas about ritual pollution, predicated on forms of labor traditionally associated with subordinated castes. Some period rhetoric worked to redirect *savarna* disgust (*ghrna*) away from Dalits and toward Muslims.[38]

The Arya Samaj, as we shall see in later chapters, was especially adept at this style of corporeal rhetoric. It also developed new ceremonies for the ritual "purification" of the body (*shuddhi*) with expressly populational intent. Founded four years after the first Indian census of 1871, the Samaj arose in tandem with a new social imaginary of number.[39] By the 1920s, Aryas were among the most prominent exponents of the idea that Hindus were a "dying race," undermined by conversion as well as the natality rates of rival religions, especially Islam. One popular 1924 tract sounded an "alarm bell," predicting that the Muslim population would increase exponentially like compound interest on a bank account.[40] Pandit Chamupati, the anonymous *Rangila Rasul* author, was clearly aware of such rhetoric. In May 1924 (the very month the *Rangila Rasul* was published) his journal, the *Arya*, published an article fretting about Dalit conversion to Islam, Buddhism, and Christianity. In June, it published a series of articles refuting Gandhi's arguments against proselytization. "Can every Muslim be made into an Arya?" it asked. The answer, apparently, was yes.[41]

As a tract obsessed with sexuality, the *Rangila Rasul* played on such biopolitical anxieties. It would have circulated alongside other allegedly obscene texts of the period, from Pandey Bechan Sharma's *Chocolate* (1927) to D. H. Lawrence's *Lady Chatterley's Lover* (1928) to popular sexology manuals.[42] The *Rangila Rasul* weaponized smut for communalist ends, playing on tropes of hypersexual Muslim masculinity to stoke a sexual paranoia that also reinforced gendered power structures—as through abduction narratives that were used to restrict the mobility of bourgeois caste-Hindu women.[43] Thus, in the *Rangila Rasul*, Muslim men appear as a sexual threat to the Hindu joint family. "Every country has its own customs," explains the tract's first-person narrator. In India, it is the custom for a man to treat a woman as his religious sister (*dharm ki bahen*) or mother; Arabia has no such custom, as can allegedly be seen from the life of the Prophet. He should have honored the women whom the tract tendentiously refers to as Mother Khadijah and Daughter Ayesha as fictive kin. Instead, he sexualized and married them. He also allegedly sexualized other female kin, as by marrying Zainab, his adopted son Zayd's ex-wife. "Now the reader can understand why Muhammad hesitated to make any woman his mother or daughter."[44] The tract goes on to suggest that even learned South Asian Muslims remain ignorant of the subcontinent's sexual-familial norms, thus implying that they are both cultural aliens and sexual threats in the Hinduized space of the subcontinent.

One can and should refute this Islamophobic account of the Prophet's life. A tactic pursued by Muslim writers in 1927 was to argue that Muhammad married Zainab in a reformist spirit, curbing social abuses resulting from the pre-Islamic custom of temporary marriage.[45] Later historians have argued that Hindu communalist writers of this period were projecting an incest anxiety endemic to the joint family structure (focused especially, but not exclusively, on brother- and sister-in-law pairings) onto a Muslim religious other.[46]

Here, I pursue a different tactic by focusing on the representative function that the *Rangila Rasul* affords to the Prophet. When the Lahore High Court argued that in satirizing Muhammad, the tract did not therefore also satirize Islam or Muslims, it was either obtuse or disingenuous. The pamphlet's Prophet is a figure for Muslims as biopolitical population. Depicted as comically unable to control his sexual impulses and insistently physicalized, this caricature seems calculated to produce a visceral response in Muslim readers. That response then implicates those offended bodies in a larger forcefield, a structure of feeling immanent to the historically specific institutions of the late colonial populational public.

A SPECIAL KIND OF FEELING

To get a better sense for how such feelings were structured, we need to move beyond the scene of solitary reading to consider the civic meetings that came to define the Rajpal affair by midsummer. Some of these gatherings were organized by religious associations, such as Panipat's Anjuman-i-Islamia; others were sponsored by private individuals, as when Mrs. Khwaja Hasan Nizami hosted a meeting of Delhi's Muslim ladies.[47] Most or all culminated in an official expression of sentiment—a formal resolution stating that the feelings of the assembled persons had been wounded by recent events, including not just the words of the *Rangila Rasul* but also those of the Lahore High Court. Resolutions could then be sent by letter or telegram to a government office or published in a newspaper like Lahore's *Muslim Outlook* ("The Only Muslim Daily Published in English in India"). An archive of public feelings, these resolutions attest to "abhorrence and disgust," "pain and consternation," the "shattering [of] Muslim hearts and wounding [of] their religious sentiments."[48]

While it is impossible to reconstruct a full ethnographic account of these meetings, we do have relatively detailed descriptions of some of them, including a June 1927 assembly at Peshawar's Islamia Club. Its main hall was apparently so packed with Muslims "of all shade of opinion" (Shias, Sunnis,

Ahmadis, Ahl-i-Hadis, etc.) that hundreds of people spilled out into the corridor, unable to find seats. When the speakers took the stage, "a special kind of feeling" descended on the room. Soon everyone was "weeping." After tears came parliamentary resolutions. Four of these were moved, seconded, and then passed unanimously, expressing "sorrow and disappointment" at the actions of the Lahore court and asking government to pass a temporary law preventing attacks on religious founders while a more permanent measure was devised.[49]

Such an event is best understood as performatively constituting the public opinion that it purports to reveal. It structures inchoate affect (a special kind of feeling) into a legible collective emotion (sorrow). There is something deeply oxymoronic about legislating feeling in this way. As a genre of writing, the parliamentary resolution would seem about as sentimental as *Robert's Rules of Order*—which is to say, not sentimental at all. The special kind of feeling that descended on the Peshawar meeting cannot, then, be reduced to the collective sorrow expressed in the concluding resolution. The two necessarily existed in a kind of structural tension.

To parse this tension, we might turn to a book published fifteen years earlier, Émile Durkheim's *Elementary Forms of Religious Life* (1912), identifying the Islamia Club's special kind of feeling as collective effervescence—a quasi-electric affect emerging from and immanent to gatherings of human bodies.[50] Durkheim asked how such effervescence becomes concretized in symbols of the collective, or what he called "totems," mediatory representations that emerge simultaneously with affect in a mutually constitutive dialectic relation.[51] Invoking Durkheim here might seem to foreground religion, thus positioning the Prophet Muhammad as our Peshawar meeting's totemic symbol. But if we take the *Elementary Forms* as not really being about "religion" at all, but rather about "society" as secular-modern social imaginary, then a different picture emerges, one as complex as the *Elementary Forms* itself (a transcolonial text wherein "primitive" Aboriginals in British-colonial Australia are overlaid palimpsestically on "modern" imperial France, and both rerouted through Indigenous North America via the Anishinaabemowin word *doodem*, producing a political semantics of religion wherein the religious is always already collapsing into the secular and both into empire). By this account, the Peshawar meeting's more potent totem was the parliamentary resolution—the secular-liberal medium, not its "religious" message—which represented the Muslim public in two senses at once. It both conveyed public opinion to the state (i.e., *Vertretung*) and reflected the gathered group to itself to bring that group into self-conscious being (i.e., *Darstellung*, recast as Durkheimian process). Attendees presumably did identify with the resolution's expression of sorrow, but their act of identification was, necessarily, just that—an effort, cemented in the ritual assent of a vote, to suture self into a collectivity defined around institutionally mediated affect.

The Rajpal affair was a saga of such secular-liberal institutional forms. Its summer meetings were the very model of deliberative reason. Citizens gather in civic assemblies. The press reports public opinion. Elected or appointed representatives echo these civic voices (as when Muslim members of the Council of State filed petitions to the viceroy attesting to the state of Muslim feelings).[52] Government listens, ultimately creating a new law. And yet, for the most part, these meetings were not read this way, but were taken instead as evidence of hyperemotional religious fanaticism. "The Mussalmans of India have gone mad," wrote Motilal Nehru to his son in July, with evident distaste.[53] Sectors of the Hindi press depicted Muslims' "religious fervor" or *mazhabi josh* (i.e., zeal, passion, boiling, or excitement) as almost inhuman.[54] "A storm has sprung up in the Muslim world," stated one paper.[55] The "Punjabi wind" has spread to Nagpur, reported another.[56] The "fire of communalism" was flaring because of the "*Rangila Rasul* movement [*andolan*]," wrote a third.[57] Who would not be alarmed by such fiery weather?

Contrary to what these meteorological metaphors imply, of course, this was not some atavistic eruption of irrational affect. It was a storm of *sabhas*—of meetings, petitions, procedural demands for a judge's resignation, and threats of boycott. Even hostile writers had a hard time suppressing this fact, with the recurrence of an English bureaucratic lexicon (e.g., *prastav pas karna*, to "pass" a resolution) undercutting efforts to blame the affair on the innate "fanaticism" of the Muslim community (*jati*).[58] Religious affect was located not "in" Muslims, as one headline suggested, but was rather an emergent property of the "public meeting" (*sarvajanik sabha*) as civic-political form.[59]

Such feelings could be described, oxymoronically, as *procedural effervescence*—an affect emerging in and through the routinized, rationalized procedures of parliamentary liberalism, wherein liberal institutions become bureaucratic nodes for the transmission of affect. Presumably all liberal publics produce feelings of this sort, or at least have the potential to.

BEWARE THE "MONSTER MEETING"

These dynamics come into clearer view if we turn to the "monster meetings" of June and July 1927. This phrase, in common use during the Rajpal affair, had circulated in Britain since at least the 1870s and in India since at least 1907, alongside related phrases like "monster petition" and "monster demonstration."[60] With striking rhetorical efficiency, the term yokes the deliberative public (the meeting) to the riotous crowd (the monster), thus succinctly expressing a constitutive anxiety of Victorian and late colonial liberalisms. As political representation was extended to the masses, elites worried that any public might suddenly transform into a monstrously demotic multitude. Liberalism's longstanding fear of large numbers thus entered a phase of acute panic indexed by 1890s crowd theory and stretching into the 1920s, when Lippmann was still assessing the political propensities of what he called the "bewildered herd."[61]

In early May 1927, just prior to the *Rajpal* ruling, Hindu-Muslim riots had convulsed Lahore.[62] That summer, the government fretted that protesting crowds would provoke more riots. (One bureaucrat deemed the likelihood low—unless someone happened to assassinate Justice Dalip Singh.)[63] Worries are understandable. Speakers at monster meetings reportedly used intemperate language, calling Singh "an empty-brained ass" and the other Lahore court justices "bastards and scoundrels." Some even threatened violence against Rajpal.[64] When violence did erupt, however, it seems to have been provoked by the police. In early July, the Punjab government imposed a curfew. Protestors poured into the streets anyway, and police attacked them—with "the swish and the thud of the lathis" resounding in the night.[65]

To see these crowd dynamics in action, let us consider the "very large public meeting" held in Delhi on July 1 at 8:00 p.m. on a parade ground across from the fish market, with organizers including members of the Khilafat Committee. Five speaker platforms were erected, decorated with flags, and equipped with gas lanterns. Volunteers dispersed to manage the gathering crowd, while police watched from a slight distance on horse and foot. An opening prayer was followed by several speeches, culminating with Maulana Muhammad Ali reading a resolution attesting to the "extreme sorrow and anger" of Delhi Muslims at the *Rajpal* decision and asking for the crowd's verbal assent to this representation of its feelings.[66]

As at the indoor Peshawar meeting described above, this resolution would have both structured feelings at the event itself and then gone on to circulate in press and government offices. Or, at least, the potential for such circulation was presumed, a performative condition implied by the very act of passing a resolution, with future circulation retroactively validating a given assembly's claim to speak for the Muslim public. Monster meetings were thus inseparable from newspaper headlines like the one that appeared in the *Muslim Outlook* in late June: "Ultimatum of Lahore Musalmans: Fifty Thousand Speak as One Man: Mr. Justice Dalip Singh Must Go."[67] If it is hyperbolic to suppose that fifty thousand people could speak with a single voice, it is just as misleading to suggest that any of those thousands actually speaks. Their unified voice is the aftereffect of an interlinked chain of mediated acts of representation, a leviathan monster that literalizes the metaphoric operation whereby the *Muslim Outlook* claims to speak on behalf of a populational public.

This, importantly, is a physical operation. A paper like the *Muslim Outlook* metonymically concretizes its public, a teeming mass implicit in every page. In June, the *Outlook*'s editor and publisher, Syed Dilawar Shah Bukhari and Noor ul-Haq, were jailed for contempt of the Lahore High Court, prompting a vocal outcry against this clear abridgment of press freedoms. One concerned citizen wrote that the court might as well "commit the whole Musalman Community to jail," as Bukhari and ul-Haq were "only guilty of expressing public opinion" by putting "in black and white what every Musalman is saying."[68] This comment neatly distills the representative logic of the populational public. Bukhari and ul-Haq did not just represent readers of their newspaper (i.e., their public). They represented all Indian Muslims (i.e., a census-certified population), a political body that seemed to hover over them in their jail cells as ghostly extension of their editorial flesh.

Rather than being effaced by this chain of representations, then, it is perhaps more correct to say that the physicality of the crowd was sublated—ferried secretly into the very heart of the print public. Publics were ghosts or phantoms, purposefully forgetting the bodies that were their ground and condition of being. "The public," as Gabriel Tarde (Durkheim's sometime nemesis) explained in 1901, "could be defined as a potential crowd." Where the latter is monstrously physical, the former is a "purely spiritual collectivity," gathered at a distance through mind alone. Using the term *spiritual* to indicate less a religious quality than a negation of the body, Tarde explained that publics operate through "the transportation of force over distance." He called this force "thought."[69] One might do better to call it "affect," thus resisting Tarde's dephysicalization of reading. Books link bodies, with the physicality of paper convening a fleshy collective, a sort of virtual crowd.

Tarde's use of the word *spiritual* to describe print publics resonates with the reading life of one of late colonial India's most prominent public sphere theorists: M. K. Gandhi. Gandhi's early experiments in print asceticism echoed his distinctive style of crowd politics, wherein the crowd itself was subjected to ascetic discipline and thus partly dephysicalized, its body force (*sharir-bal*) converted into soul force (*atma-bal*). Such spiritualization was necessarily fraught. Crowds are hard to contain, as Gandhi learned the hard way in 1922, when a group of protestors torched a police station, killing those inside.[70] Where crowds go, the potential for body force follows.

Gandhi was an implicit presence at our mass meetings, and not just incidentally via the Khilafatists (his allies in the 1920–22 Non-Cooperation Movement).[71] Some commentators described that summer's mass mobilization as a "Muslim Satyagraha."[72] This moniker raised eyebrows: the *Hindu Sansar* jibed that it would be more accurately described as "*duragraha*" (misguided zeal).[73] Still, it was accurate enough. Orators adjusted Gandhi's religious symbolism, as by taking Hussain ibn Ali (Muhammad's grandson, who died at the battle of Karbala) as their key symbol for taking suffering onto the self in the name of a righteous cause.[74] The core operation, however, is much the same: the suffering religious body transmutes physical pain into moral force. Hussain thus appears, like Gandhi, as an ascetic subject. Or perhaps it is that Gandhi appears like Hussain—a sacrificial subject, his asceticism constructed around the question of violence.[75]

THE MARTYR AND THE MASS BODY

Violence certainly shaped the Rajpal affair, which was bracketed by death. In December 1926, the prominent Arya Samajist Swami Shraddhananda was assassinated by a man named Abdul Rashid, his gun hidden in the folds of a blanket.[76] In late September 1927, a man named Khuda Baksh came into Rajpal's Arya bookshop and attacked him with a knife.[77] Rajpal survived. Then, in 1929, in a second bookshop stabbing, Ilm-ud-din succeeded where Khuda Baksh had failed.[78] Rajpal became a martyr. Hanged for his crime, Ilm-ud-din became one too.[79]

These acts of violence were, as suggested above, enactments of cultural scripts that preceded and overdetermined their possible meanings, inscribing these murders into communalist narratives of Muslim fanaticism. To complicate that picture, we might draw out how the Aryas sanctified their martyrs by appealing to a neo-Vedic symbolism of ascetic and ritual self-sacrifice in which these twinned modes of self-negation became fused with acts of print-reading. Where ordinary people die of winter illnesses, one periodical explained, "blessed men" like Swami Shraddhananda become "sacrifices on the altar of dharma."[80] Where Vedic priests pour ghee into the ritual fire, explained another, the martyr pours himself—the light of his body joining effulgently with the flame. It is this sacrifice, this negation of self, that makes the martyr a true "ascetic" (*sanyasi*) or "world renouncer" (*sarvatyagi*). As was often the case in Arya writing, such Vedic imagery slips easily into polytheistic references of a kind Aryas officially disavowed (the fire god Agni; a garland-bearing "goddess of victory"). More pertinently to my argument here, these metaphors configure spiritualized print as a medium of self-sacrifice, interpellating the reader in this Vedic ritual by addressing him directly: "Who will make the first offering?"[81]

The martyr cults of the 1920s and '30s were simultaneously "political" and "religious," straddling both sides of this historically contingent conceptual distinction. One writer compared Khuda Baksh, unfavorably, to Sacco and Vanzetti (the Italian American anarchists executed in August 1927).[82] In 1928, the Arya Samaj would gain another martyr—Lala Lajpat Rai, whose murder prompted Bhagat Singh and associates to shoot a Lahore policeman, leading in turn to their 1931 hanging and posthumous martyr cult, immortalized in iconic poster art.[83] Even the iconoclastic Aryas used images to mediate martyrdom. Consider the cover of a 1935 volume published by the firm Rajpal and Sons to commemorate the father's death six years earlier (a volume proscribed by the colonial state, see figure 2). A pair of braceleted female hands emerge from a nimbus-ringed and decidedly feminized flame to gesture toward a Vedic fire altar or *havan-kund*. Beams of light radiate upward, simultaneously demarcating the distinct shape of the altar and incorporating it into the semicircular disc of a shining sun. Its art deco vibe fuses timeless tradition with sleek modernity. This image echoes others of its moment, from the elongated fingers of the nationalist Bengal School to the braceleted Lakshmi, ensconced by sunbeams, in a 1920s advertisement for Rising Sun Oil, an imported Russian kerosene.[84] Perhaps that Lakshmi is quoted here, a hidden presence in this aniconic Arya image. Regardless, the picture's rhetorical thrust is clear. It hails the viewer directly, as though cajoling him (or her?) to enter the flame—becoming the *balidan* or sacrifice indicated in writing at the top of the page.

The magazine opens onto a series of articles on religious themes. One explains how, in the Vedas, the "spiritual meaning of sacrifice is self-

FIGURE 2. *Balidan* (Sacrifice) (Lahore) vol. 2, no. 1 (April 1935). Cover. © The British Library Board. Shelfmark PP Hin F 35.

surrender."[85] Another compares the martyr to the "ecstatic [*mast*] fakir." The prison is his hut, the gallows his tongs, the noose his garland, the funeral pyre his incense.[86] "What is life?" muses a third. Its essence is not "in living" or simply counting up years, as is assumed by "worldly people" and the "general public" (*sarvasadharan*). Only the martyr "is alive in the true meaning of the word." The "life that is hidden in death" is written on his body like a *tika* or sanctifying mark, visible on "mahatmas" like Socrates,

Jesus, Giordano Bruno, and Dayananda Saraswati. Mother India needs such men. "We have a need not for the living, but for the dying."[87]

In the middle of the magazine, the reader finds a *balidan-chitravali*, an album of martyrs. Photographs of the Arya dead, starting with Dayananda himself, are reproduced in red ink (indicating auspiciousness? blood?) covering pages and pages, although with resolution too low to warrant reproduction here. Particularly prominent coverage is given to "Dharmvir Rajpal" (i.e., Rajpal, the religious hero). A full-page portrait, taken when he was alive, shows him suited, turbaned, and mustached; a caption describes the circumstances of his death. The next page features three photos of his 1929 funeral procession—in front of the hospital, in Anarkali bazaar, on the way to the cremation ground. According to government files, the processing crowd used Rajpal's bier as a battering ram to push through police lines. Though this action might seem a grotesque literalization of body power or *sharir-bal*, it perhaps more accurately attests to the totemic power of absent bodies. The funeral bier was empty. Authorities had refused to hand over Rajpal's corpse.[88] In the printed image, the red ink is sufficiently muddled to make the crowd indistinct, a blur converging around the inkless white space of Rajpal's unoccupied shroud—a literally empty totemic signifier. Absence draws the eye, orienting the reader's body and leading it along a chain of signification: printed image, photograph, shroud, corpse. "Every Hindu is Rajpal," remarked an Arya writer in 1948, recalling Rajpal's funeral.[89] The sentence asserts equivalence among at least four non-equivalent bodies: the deceased publisher, the processing crowd, the Hindu population, and the reader, whom this passage seems to invite to identify with Rajpal and thus with Hindus. Crowd, population, reader, corpse—it is perhaps precisely because these bodies cannot be reconciled that their equivalence must be asserted.

In these late colonial martyr texts, we see something like a neo-Vedic necropolitics, wherein the ascetic corpse becomes a site for sacralizing the nation.[90] The martyred corpse turns muscular Hinduism on its head—either a grotesque inversion of the Arya cult of bodily improvement or, perhaps, its logical and necessary obverse (see figure 3).[91] Where yoga, athletics, and sexual restraint were, in the words of a June 1927 article, "techniques for increasing bodily strength," the martyr sacrifices these gains in a single instant of ecstatic expenditure.[92] His self-negating, spiritualized flesh becomes a means of bringing the Vedic nation into physical being—or so these articles imply. More immanent to the page is the moral force that the

FIGURE 3. "Arya Vyayamshala Khagaria (Munger) ke Kasrati Purush" (The athletic men of the Arya gymnasium Khagaria). Shitalprasad Vaidya, *Shrimaddayanand Chitravali* (Calcutta: Vedic Pustakalaya, 1925). © The British Library Board. Shelfmark Hin.D.1519.

Vedic print object wields by enjoining its readers toward self-sacrifice. Here, Vedic print asserts a power over life and death that is in some sense parallel to that of law. Vedic necropolitics collides with colonial biopolitics, two interlocking schemas for governing the public and its bodies.

CONCLUSION: "A BRUTAL ORGY OF ABUSE"

This chapter has tried to shift our angle of approach onto the Rajpal affair by framing this crisis of late colonial secularism as a crisis of the public that expressed conceptual antimonies central to modernity at large—publics versus populations, readers versus crowds, procedure versus affect. Since the nineteenth century, colonial ideologues had disparaged the Indian public as constitutively backward. It turns out, the very conditions of its alleged deficiency were what pointed the way toward the global future. Colonial India anticipated the kind of governmentalized public that worried political and media theorists of the 1920s and later (arguably) came to underlay new theorizations of the counterpublic.

Late colonial publics were persistently physicalized—with commentators describing, for example, how "virulent" newspapers packed their pages with "rabid writings" and "venomous propaganda," resulting in a "brutal orgy of abuse" toward religion.[93] Such rhetoric takes sex, disease, and poison as metaphors for the communication of affect, implying that print media infects its readers' bodies with dangerous feelings that pose a threat to the public order. One might respond to such charges by insisting that religious actors in late colonial India were actually secular-rational actors. This move, however, risks reifying the conceptual distinctions on which Islamophobic rhetoric in particular was based—presuming, as it did, that any expression of religious sentiment was evidence of madness. It would seem more productive to clarify how "religious" sentiment was always already implicated in the internal contradictions of secular-liberal procedural and institutional forms, which became media for the cultivation of embodied affect. Because these affects were always physical transmissions (not, *pace* Tarde, spiritual ones), they could draw bodies together, sometimes violently. Law, with its normative claims on bodily behavior, was enmeshed in the circuits of violence it sought to manage.

The bodies of the Rajpal affair were configured in a variety of ways. They were public bodies, populational bodies, crowd bodies, and ascetic or sacrificial bodies, with none of these forms of collectivity fully reconcilable to the others. They were also intimate bodies—in their very affectivity, refusing neat divisions between public and private. This interstitial ground was where religious affect circulated. The question was how best to manage it or arrest its circulation.

3

SECULARISM, HIGH AND LOW

Making the Blasphemy Bill

IN LATE AUGUST 1927, MEMBERS of India's Legislative Assembly headed to Shimla, the colonial summer capital. These 145 men—some appointed, some elected—formed a parliamentary body, the lower house of a bicameral legislature, created in 1919 as an experiment in devolving powers to Indians. This year, they were faced with a "Religious Insults Bill" (or, in popular parlance, a "Blasphemy Bill") adding a new section to the Indian Penal Code to criminalize outraging religious feelings. The legislators did not like the law, sent to them for approval by central government bureaucrats. Overwhelmingly, they saw it as "a very great danger" poised to "muzzle" the press, "hamper" scholarship, and place a general chill on free speech.[1] They passed it anyway. Faced with the ongoing crisis of the Rajpal affair, the legislators decided that a bad solution was better than no solution at all.

Where the previous chapter approached the Rajpal affair from the bottom up, analyzing the popular mobilization against the *Rangila Rasul* as a crisis of the colonial public, this chapter approaches it from the top down, asking how lawmakers sought to manage this crisis through the terms of an emergent Indian secularism. That secularism was shaped by a strong internal tension. If the late colonial civic sphere was organized around two distinct and partly contradictory notions of human collectivity—the public and the population—the late colonial state was structured around a parallel split between what I will call a liberal-constitutional or high secularism and a governmental or low secularism. These distinct political grammars respectively hailed citizens and subjects, publics and populations, seeing religion alternately as a form of privatized belief and a trait of administered communities.[2]

Perched in the hill station of Shimla, the members of the Legislative

Assembly tended to think via the high, articulating a set of secular norms (e.g., freedom of expression) for which the unwashed masses were not yet ready. Replicating a core temporal trope of colonial rule (freedom, but not yet), these elites framed the passage of 295A as a necessary concession to the social fact of religious conflict—a response to a temporary emergency that required an exception to liberal-constitutional norms. That exception became a site for the expression of a distinct political logic. Section 295A articulated what could be called a penal secularism or, more broadly, a governmental secularism—addressed not to rights, but to the technical management of religio-racial bodies organized into endemically violent populations.

I pursue this argument in what may at first seem a counterintuitive manner. Starting with the legislators' own excitable bodies, gathered in Shimla, I ask how parliamentary flesh functioned as a trace of the low within the high, revealing the contradictory role of the body within the liberal-deliberative "public." Opening outward from the scene in Shimla, I analyze the text of 295A, showing how populational "outrage" functions as affective proxy for crowd violence. I then situate this law within a more general history of Indian secularism in the 1920s. By bringing low or governmental secularism into clearer view, I suggest, we can better appreciate how the Indian secularist tolerance ideal worked to conjoin the state to society, with folk practices of communal harmony marshaled as a technology for keeping the peace. This touting of folk tolerance as proxy for state secularism further worked to position Hinduism, or a culturalized version thereof, as the natural substrate of the Indian secular, thus reinforcing caste-Hindu hegemony. The full complexity of tolerance as social/legal norm can be seen in the secularist aesthetics of Sarojini Naidu, whose nationalist poetry provides historical context for a key slogan of the Rajpal affair: "Respect for All Prophets."

BODY COUNT, WORD COUNT:
A DELIBERATIVE EMERGENCY

Every year, the British colonial government in India headed to the hills for six months or more, a seasonal migration said to involve more tea parties than official business.[3] "Come down from your hills and govern," jibed a 1917 newspaper editorial.[4] The Raj ignored this advice. Even as it granted more power to Indians with the 1919 Montagu-Chelmsford reforms, it continued to invest in its summer capital, breaking ground on a new Legislative Assembly building in 1920.[5]

Shimla, as M. K. Gandhi declared after a 1921 visit, was the real "symbol of India's slavery." Its racialized labor made Gandhi queasy: hill station elites hitched subordinated-caste men to rickshaws like animals. So did the implications of its altitude. To rule from Shimla, he said, was like running a shop from a building's "five hundredth storey"—absurd, insulting, and ineffective. He warned of a future in which "discrimination is not between white and coloured, but between high and low," asking that India return government to the demotic ground, lest it end up ejecting the British while retaining their colonial power structures.[6]

High and low—Gandhi's binary distills the deep structure of the late colonial state and, with it, late colonial secularism. Two formations of the secular clashed during the Rajpal affair. One was high: the juridico-legal secularism of liberal constitutionalism, directed to the rights and freedoms of the citizen and aligned with the ideal of the deliberative public. The other was low: the governmental secularism of the ethnographic state, directed to the well-being of populations plagued by what the state saw as endemic religious violence. Each of these political rationalities corresponded to a distinct way of talking about religiously offensive speech. Sometimes, the Shimla legislators spoke of rights—a right to freedom of religion or freedom of speech, even a right not to be offended. At other times, they spoke of populational violence—how to predict it, how to curb it, when to leave it be.

The latent disjuncture between these political grammars flashed into view during moments of crisis, notably around questions of censorship. The British imperial project in India was structured around a fundamental ideological indecision: was it liberal-democratic or authoritarian in nature?[7] Where its liberal impulse was loath to restrain the press, its authoritarian impulse (obsessed, in the 1920s, with "security") was loath not to.[8] The colonial state thus never developed systematic censorship policies, but rather passed censorship laws on an ad hoc basis, in response to periodic crises like the Rajpal affair.[9] In debates around these laws, we can see conceptual conflicts around the nature of colonial rule with particular clarity.

The pivot between political logics relied on precisely the sorts of class distinction that worried Gandhi. "If India were constituted of inhabitants like those who come into this Assembly there would be no trouble," remarked Pandit Thakur Das Bhargava after hearing his colleagues dilate on the virtues of religious tolerance. Alas, he continued, "the man in the street has not got these noble things in his heart."[10] Other legislators agreed.

Insults to religion are downright "ungentlemanly," said one.[11] They were like "hot chestnuts," said another, referencing what he described as an English street food and thus positioning religious insult as a distinctly down-market delectation. "People like to have hot things to warm their cold blood up."[12]

The speech of our urbane parliamentarians might seem different in kind from such hot language. Yet the legislators were less coolly self-controlled than they would have us believe. An "atmosphere of panic" clouded the proceedings of the Legislative Assembly.[13] "Born of a panic," the so-called Blasphemy Bill was also "being hustled in a panic."[14] In just over a month, it was drafted, sent to committee, debated, and enacted, all without "any formal attempt to elicit public opinion."[15] When one member asked to slow the bill down by a few months so that it could be shared with the public, someone reportedly cried out "hysterically," "Who would carry the dead bodies?"[16]

This emotive appeal reveals a constitutive tension of the Rajpal affair. There was, to put the matter crudely, a grotesque disjuncture between body count and word count—between what one assembly member described as the "tragedies" unfolding outside the Chamber's "serene atmosphere" and the lengthy deliberations happening within.[17] Section 295A attempted to rule bodies through words, to fix "religious feelings" into legal language so that those feelings, potentialities in bodies, could be better controlled. But procedural liberalism's ideal of unhurried deliberation, its leisurely semiosis, was badly synchronized to the irruptive temporality of mass violence.

Liberalism as a mode of government by discussion famously tends to occlude the body. At least in its classic form, it prizes argument that pulls away from the interested particularities of the flesh to speak in the disinterested voice of universal reason. This rhetorical disavowal would seem to position violent or excessively affective physicality as exterior to parliamentary spaces. But that, of course, is an illusion. Not only can lawmakers inflict renewed injury by quoting injurious speech; legal speech inflicts a physical force all its own, sublimating state violence into the force of law. The summer protestors understood this: they were protesting the juridical words of the Lahore High Court as much as, or more than, the "religious" words of the *Rangila Rasul*.

Liberalism, let us say, positions the speaking or writing body as a site of performative contradiction, placing a speaker or writer's irreducibly embodied status under an erasure that is necessarily incomplete. This erasure, furthermore, is consolidated by the very media forms that give the historian access to legislative proceedings. Official transcripts of parliamentary debates (most paradigmatically, Hansard's) are paper artifacts that do performative work. They literalize the Victorian-liberal ideal of government by discussion by reducing legislators to their words, transmuting bodies into pure speech—a sort of deliberative-liberal apotheosis, wherein media infrastructure replicates the political-cultural logic that gave rise to it.

To bring these occluded bodies into better view—and thus see how the legislators' bodies functioned as a trace of the excitable crowd within the ethereal halls of deliberative reason, an eruption of the low into the high—let us try to imagine ourselves as physically present in Shimla in August 1927. The members of the Legislative Assembly would, presumably, have peered out onto misty hills while crossing the neoclassical portico of their Council Chamber, completed in 1925, maybe fretting about the protests down in the summer dust of the plains. Inside the chamber doors, they joined a roomful of male bodies—visually marked, including through clothes, as British and Indian, Hindu and Muslim—settling into seats. At one end of the chamber, a raised dais featured a Burmese-made teak throne, with fluted columns culminating in a crown, and an empty box. The former was reserved for the assembly president (in 1927, Vithalbhai Patel); the latter symbolized the absent viceroy (Lord Irwin) and thus also the royal body of the emperor, George V.[18]

This scene articulates a political syntax in which each body serves a representative function—or, rather, two. The legislator is both a political spokesman giving voice to a constituency (i.e., Gayatri Spivak's *Vertretung* or "rhetoric-as-persuasion"), as well as a symbol or synecdochic proxy for that same constituency as enumerable population (i.e., *Darstellung* or "rhetoric-as-trope").[19] If this doubled structure characterizes all political representation (there is no *Vertretung* without *Darstellung*), it is nonetheless articulated in historically specific ways. In early twentieth-century India, I am suggesting (in an argument that loops Spivak through Chatterjee), the first type of representation was aligned with the newly emergent liberal-constitutional state instantiated in institutions like the Legislative Assembly. The second was aligned with the late nineteenth-century ethnographic state that undergirded and entered into assemblage with those same liberal-constitutional institutions—with seats in the Legislative Assembly organized, for instance, by district *and* religious community. The representatives in Shimla were both parliamentary orators, participating in liberalism's aesthetics of persuasion, and ethnographic types, physical specimens of religious and other kinds of population.

They were, importantly, male specimens—their very presence in the public space of the Legislative Assembly evidence of a historically specific formation of gender that bore directly on the problem of religious feelings. If political representation in late colonial India was structured around religious community, religious community was structured around women (specifically bourgeois, *savarna* women) as its idealized inner essence.[20] The symbolic entanglement of "woman" and "religion" was, moreover, crucial to the affective power of both. "Even in a very, very old philosopher like me, feelings are stirred up when my women or religion is insulted," reflected Madras's M. K. Acharya while pondering the *Rangila Rasul*.[21] It is not just that Acharya asserts elite men's control over "their" women as integrally linked to other kinds of public rights, including the right to freedom of religion.[22] It is that his superannuated passions register a historically specific structure of feeling in which woman and religion appear as prior to bourgeois-male subjectivity as such, an intimate inclusion within the public male body. "Feelings are stirred." If affect renders the stoic philosopher passive by compromising his self-control, it can do so because that philosopher's performance of self-control is moored in his gendered being. This gender politics then intersects with the biopolitical regulation of the religious population's implicitly violent affects.

Even in Shimla, on the five-hundredth floor, in other words, there was excitable flesh requiring emotional management—the bodies of the legislators themselves, whose representative flesh was continuous with the mass body of India's administrated populations. In addressing a new law about religious feelings to those down-market multitudes, our legislators were perhaps unwittingly also addressing that law to their own feeling bodies. Where the human body goes, there too goes the ground.

RELIGIONS, FEELINGS, CLASSES: THE TEXT OF 295A

To see how the new law configured its populational feelings, let us turn to the text of Section 295A as originally enacted in 1927: "Whoever, with deliberate and malicious intention of outraging the religious feelings of any class of His Majesty's subjects, by words, either spoken or written, or by visible representations, insults or attempts to insult the religion or the religious beliefs of that class, shall be punished with imprisonment of either description for a term which may extend to two years, or with fine, or with both." A marginal heading distills the core of the offense: "acts intended to outrage religious feelings of any class, by insulting its religion or religious beliefs."[23]

Circuitous syntax abounds here because 295A describes a conceptually circuitous crime. It references but ultimately disavows the crime of blasphemy (i.e., insults to religion per se), affording direct protection not to religion but rather religious feelings. This conceptual hierarchy is clearly indicated in the marginal heading, where insults to religion are sidelined to a subordinate clause. Confoundingly, 295A uses the word *religion* or variations thereupon three different times: *religion, religious beliefs,* and *religious feelings*. It is as though whoever wrote 295A hoped that repetition might stabilize the meaning of this notoriously unstable term. Instead, it creates a sort of a semantic perpetual-motion machine, a tautological loop in which each of the three instances of *religion* keeps defining the others.

This redundancy seems to have been a response to Dalip Singh's decision in *Rajpal v. Emperor*, which differentiated among insults to the Prophet, Islam, and Muslims. The new 295A would prohibit all three. In it, as the special committee assigned to amend the law explained, the noun *religion* indicates entities like Islam, while the phrase "religious beliefs" is meant to ensure that "an attack on a founder is not omitted from the scope of the section."[24] (This reduction of a sacred person to a belief would seem typical of secular law, which tends to understand religion as consisting of lists of propositions that can feel as dry and technical as law itself.) Section 295A still, however, clearly grants primary protection to populational entities like Muslims, indicated here by the phrase "the religious feelings of any class." This is the phrase at the crux of the law, and the reason why 295A ended up being substantially redundant with Section 153A.

Like 153A's "enmity," 295A's "religious feelings" indicate an affect intrinsically linked to the violent crowd (153A was appended to 153, about inciting riots). In context, the meaning of 295A's "religious feelings" is quite restricted. Indeed, in the phrase "outraging religious feelings," the verb overdetermines the noun such that only one feeling would seem plausibly indicated by the law: outrage itself. This irritated the law's critics. As Orissa's Pandit Nilakantha Das complained to his colleagues at the Legislative Assembly, to reduce religious feelings to "ruffled feelings" means "nothing but blasphemy to religion."[25] His feelings apparently outraged by 295A, Das effectively accused the new law of being in violation of itself.

For Das's injury to be actionable under 295A, however, he would have needed to allege that his feelings were "class" feelings. In historical context, this word indicated India's religious, linguistic, caste, and tribal communities, invoking the apparatus of the ethnographic state. Section 153A had used the same word to describe "class" enmity or hatred. Notably, when the Lahore High Court proposed language for a new law bypassing 153A, it avoided the word *class*, speaking instead of "pamphlets published with the intention of wounding the religious feelings of any *person*" (my emphasis). The bureaucrats who adapted this language into 295A made two significant changes, both presumably to limit 295A's scope: they increased the affective threshold of offensive by changing "wounding" to "outraging" and increased its numeric threshold by changing "person" to "class." This change begs what would seem a key question: Can "classes" feel? If so, in what sense? Surely they feel differently than "persons" do.

Finally, it bears noting the obvious: all of these words are in English, the language of colonial law. Translating legal terms into South Asian vernacular languages was, moreover, potentially tricky, in that even a seemingly simple noun like *religion* was not quite equivalent to possible analogues such as *dharm, din, mazzhab, panth*, and *sampradaya*. While I have not seen an official 1927 government translation of 295A, period press gives a sense for how people were rendering its core terms. In Hindi, for instance, M. M. Malaviya's *Abhyudaya* reported how the British government was making it a crime "to intentionally insult the religion [*dharm*] of any class [*jati*] of the emperor's subjects [*samrat ki praja*]" or to "wound religious feelings" (*dharmik bhavas*).[26] To see a different set of translation choices, we might consult an earlier text, the official 1861 Hindi translation of Section 298 (of which, see chapter 4). There, the "intention of wounding religious feelings" is rendered as the intention to give grief or pain to conscience in matters of belief (*antahkarn ko mat ke vishay mein . . . duhkh dene ka prayojan*). Other sections in the Code's religion chapter speak of criticizing the doctrines of a religious lineage (*kisi sampradaya ke mat ko ninda*).[27] In this 1861 text, religion would seem to align more with opinion (*mat*) than with feeling (*bhava*), and *dharm* seems not yet to have settled into its now-standard role as *religion*'s obvious translation.

Section 295A, in short, articulated a specific formation of legal secularism that departed both from nineteenth century and, even more so, early modern precedent. Where a court decision like *Rex v. Taylor* took Christianity as "parcel" of the laws of England, Section 295A took "religion" as an object external to law, a social fact in need of proper management. It is legally relevant only when it threatens to breach the peace. Law thus regulates "religion" only indirectly by regulating "religious feelings" (i.e., "outrage"), an affective proxy for populational violence.

Censorship laws often end up inciting more of whatever variety of speech they seek to suppress, and 295A appears to have abided by this general rule.

It established religion as a site for the cultivation of outrage as public feeling. Any class alleging offense under 295A necessarily presents itself to the state as a religious class situationally defined by its "religious feelings." This is true even for a class that might not, in other circumstances, be understood as primarily religious (as when Rajputs alleged a 295A offense against the 2017 film *Padmaavat*, for suggesting romantic intimacy between a Muslim king and Rajput queen). Penal secularism, it would seem, works to redefine religion around highly transmissible forms of public feeling.

SECULARISM FROM THE FIVE-HUNDREDTH FLOOR

To see how 295A's penal secularism fits into the larger story of Indian secularism is to see how Indian secularism itself was perhaps always already an affective project—constructed around governmental secularism more than liberal-constitutional secularism. What is now commonsensically referred to as "Indian secularism" did not emerge as such until the 1940s, born of the Constituent Assembly debates that decided the shape of the postcolonial Indian constitution.[28] (While the word *secular* did not feature in the original version of that document, it did feature in the debates.)[29] This was the moment when, as Shabnum Tejani has argued, it suddenly became self-evident that there was a distinctively Indian varietal of secularism that could, like anticolonial nationalism before it, unify India's fissiparous parts into a harmoniously pluralist whole.

This project was not exactly new: it built on policies of inclusionary neutrality that dated to the Company period. Nor was it ideologically neutral. This newly emergent Indian secularism worked to reinforce dominant-caste Hindu hegemony. Indeed, it did deft rhetorical work. By identifying religious difference (i.e., communalism) as the postcolonial nation's defining problem, secularism deflected attention away from caste difference, rendered as "intrareligious" dispute.[30] It then displaced the "communal problem" onto the minority group configured from within that problem, with Indian Muslims made to carry the metonymic burden of religious conflict as such.[31] Dalits and Muslims were, once again, rendered marginal to a polity constructed around caste Hindus—with even the rhetorical construction "Dalits and Muslims" recentering *savarna* Hindus by bifurcating caste and religion, thereby repressing the caste question within South Asian Islam.[32]

It bears stating that to narrate the history of Indian secularism in this way is to make no claims about the intentions of particular historical actors. This is a tale of genealogical emergence, a gradual reorganization of the background conditions of political and social thought.

If speaking of Indian secularism prior to the 1940s risks anachronism, it also helps show how the rhetorical moves consolidated in the 1940s had been developing for decades. They were certainly well-developed in the 1920s. Especially notable in this regard is the emergence of what Cassie Adcock has called the "tolerance ideal"—that is, the notion (associated especially with Gandhi) that India's distinctive form of secularism is rooted in culturally distinctive traditions of pluralism and folk tolerance. If "communalism" was Indian secularism's defining problem, "tolerance" was its trademark solution, the means by which it marked itself as nationally "Indian" and thus categorically different from "Western" secularism. As was especially evident in debates about religious conversion, "tolerance" was marked as a distinctively Hindu value (contrasted with the allegedly intolerant practice of proselytization in "Semitic" religions like Christianity and Islam—a move that also delegitimated Dalit conversion). The tolerance ideal thus worked to position a form of culturalized Hinduism as the very substrate of the Indian secular.[33]

We can see these multiple threads converging on the Rajpal affair. The controversy certainly involved plenty of tolerance talk—much of it portraying Islam as a proselytizing and thus inherently intolerant religion, some of it arguing that Islam enshrines tolerance as its highest ideal, some of it arguing against conversion per se.[34] The affair also showcased styles of secularism less frequently associated with India, from the separation secularism of Hari Singh Gour and M. R. Jayakar (see chapter 1) to invocations of the "religious liberties" ostensibly guaranteed by Queen Victoria.[35] Even the word *secular* cropped up at various points. Both the Lahore *Tribune* and *The People* used it as an antonym for "religionism" or religious factionalism.[36] Secularism, the latter suggested, was a means of differentiating between "democracy" and "theocracy," of purifying religion of politics so that it could recenter itself on "godliness."[37]

For my purposes here, however, the affair's two most indicative uses of the word *secular* are found in the Legislative Assembly debates. First, S. Srinivasa Iyengar urged his fellow legislators to approach 295A "not from the point of view of pure religion" but via "secular considerations" about "peace and good will."[38] Second, "home member" James Crerar said that as an instrument of a "secular government," 295A should be understood as "securing the rights and enforcing the obligations of good citizenship and of protecting society from the consequences which might otherwise ensue."[39] Making much the same point as Gour and Jayakar, but actually using the word *secular*, Iyengar and Crerar insisted that secular governments should govern speech about religion only when that speech risks provoking violence.

Crerar's comment further situates this potential violence within a conceptual prevarication. He begins by speaking about the "rights" of citizens, but immediately shifts to talking about "enforcing the obligations of *good* citizenship" (emphasis added). In doing so, he also shifts conceptual territory, moving from citizenship as formal political status to citizenship as social or moral norm. In colonial India, this prevarication was often used to imply that colonized subjects must become good citizens before they could be granted real political rights, with law's moral or pedagogic project thus positioned as the precondition for its juridical project. When discussing the Indian Penal Code, such prevarication was perhaps inevitable. A penal code is not a rights-granting constitution. It can reference the rights of the citizen but, properly speaking, cannot itself hail citizens, at least not in the formal political sense. It can, however, define and demarcate the bad citizen, a potential criminal from whom society must be defended.

It is easy to say, with Punjab governor Malcolm Hailey that in crafting 295A, lawmakers were trying to strike a balance between "freedom of discussion" and preservation of "public tranquility."[40] That ease, however, elides the conceptual chasm between these two phrases, which imply distinct political rationalities. The first gestures to the rights of the citizen, the second to the problem of populational violence. It is not that violence is a minor glitch that can be fully accounted for from within the terms of liberal-constitutional government. Violence indicates a zone of exception, a site where another political rationality becomes visible.

INCULCATING THE PEACE: PRACTICING TOLERANCE, GOVERNING RELIGION

"Secular considerations" of peace and good will (to recall Iyengar)—of promoting religious tolerance as a norm of good citizenship—certainly structured conversation at the Legislative Assembly. Its members enacted 295A hoping the new law would help to disseminate these norms to the man in the street, configured as immature citizen.

In doing so, they intervened in a field of power that was emerging as integral to the anticolonial struggle, at least in its Gandhian iteration. Recall that Gandhi, an early reader of the *Rangila Rasul*, had refused to even summarize the tract's contents in his journal *Young India*, thus arresting (or so he hoped) the transmission of injurious affect. Instead, he absorbed injury into his own readerly body in what could be understood as a practice of *satyagraha* (i.e., passive resistance or "holding the truth"), taking suffering onto the self to convert it into moral force (i.e., *atmabal*). Gandhi, as he wrote elsewhere, hoped that all religious actors would self-censor in this way, with the ascetic refusal to inflict injury on others simultaneously a spiritual practice and a means of claiming power away from the colonial state. Self-censorship precludes state censorship.[41] We might describe Gandhi as engaged in a field of cultural regulation where the repressive function of the state censor becomes redistributed across a range of interconnected institutional sites.[42]

If for Gandhi, in his quasi-anarchist mode, this redistribution of law's repressive function seemed to promise an unraveling of the totalizing power of the modern state form, its actual effects were more ambivalent. Tolerance in late colonial India was a mobile technology for the management of violence, entangling the state in the everyday comportment of its subjects. It was, in other words, a practice of governmentality.[43] It was neither inherently colonial nor inherently anticolonial. Nor was it inherently Gandhian. Many late colonial voices urged civil society to govern itself in this way. "Moral law" alone should govern speech about religion, with society, not the state, fostering a "spirit of tolerance," argued the Calcutta *Forward*.[44] "True liberty" of speech, Muhammad Iqbal urged in an interview, entails not "license" but "moral self-restraint."[45]

To get a further sense for the moral/political structures that emerged from such refusals of state censorship, we might consider Srinivasa Iyengar's remark at the Legislative Assembly: "I myself prefer, like my master and the master of better men—Mahatma Gandhi—that there should be no laws at all punishing anybody and if it were possible by adopting the *satyagrahic* attitude to keep all people in order, that would be an ideal state of things."[46] What appears at first glance as a failure of Gandhian politics is perhaps better read as its ambivalent fulfillment. By underscoring the clear parallelism between *satyagrahic* and legal-secular efforts to maintain public order, Iyengar also indicated the extent to which these were complementary governmental practices, pursuing the same end through different means. By this time, Gandhian practices of massified asceticism had significantly amplified the connective tissue of governmentality, facilitating the transfer of techniques for the conduct of conduct between seemingly discrete registers of rule (e.g., swaraj as both personal and national self-rule). Iyengar, arguably, saw 295A coming to occupy a similar space, annexing the domain of Gandhian countergovernmentality to that of colonial-legal governmentality. Section 295A would do what *satyagraha* could not: keep order.

This attempted annexation of tolerance as socio-moral practice becomes even clearer in a comment from Hari Singh Gour, the legal scholar and assembly member. Suggesting that the Indian state was "pledged to religious neutrality" while its people were "firm believers in religious toleration," he seemed to delineate distinct registers of rule, each implicated in the other and both essential to the preservation of the peace.[47] Toleration as social practice appears here as the obverse face of state secularism, a sort of governmentality-from-below. The two, Gour hoped, would function in tandem. The special committee created to revise 295A were thinking along similar lines when they suggested that "the inculcation of peace is an essential principle of all the great religions practiced in India." Any religion that departs from this principle is, in fact, not "religion" at all but rather criminal "fanaticism."[48] In other words, only peaceful and therefore "great" religions should receive official recognition as "religion," with all the protections pertaining thereto. Here, the tolerance ideal becomes a tool for differentiating between "good" and "bad" religion, thus working to foster the former and incorporate it into a larger set of governmental strategies for securing the peace. Rather than a grassroots practice of folk pluralism, tolerance appears here as a correlate of state secularism, a mode of religion bearing the state's official imprimatur.

Inevitably, of course, the social life of tolerance as moral norm exceeded the colonial state's ability to track or even fully understand it, much less to somehow annex it. This is a complex and often unpredictable field of power relations. To get a better sense for its complexity, let us turn to a previously untold chapter of the Rajpal affair: the story of a lost law that would have prohibited insults not to "religious feelings" but to "prophets," as category of comparative religion.

PROTECTION FOR PROPHETS:
THE STORY OF THE LAW THAT WASN'T

In the rise and fall of the law that wasn't—what I will call (borrowing a phrase from the Lahore *Tribune*)[49] the "Protection for Prophets" law—we can see popular thinkers working through the implications of a still-emergent Indian secularism, a secularism defined not by church-state separation but by an ethos of respect for all religions. This style of secularism opened a new conceptual horizon: a fully secular blasphemy law. For separation secularists like Hari Singh Gour and M. R. Jayakar, a secular blasphemy law is a categorical impossibility; blasphemy, as theological offense, cannot be secularized without ceasing to be blasphemy. For tolerance secularists, however, a blasphemy law can remain secular as long as it protects all religions equally. What is more, tolerance secularism can even be said to require a blasphemy law to enforce the value of religious respect. Had the "Protection for Prophets" law been enacted, it would have made the Indian government not the defender of *the* faith but rather of *all* faiths—a pragmatic impossibility, but not in this instance a conceptual impossibility.

The story of the lost law began in May 1927, when the Lahore High Court ruled that slander of "the founder of the Muslim religion" was not prohibited under existing sections of the Indian Penal Code. It was thus to be expected that, in the ensuing outcry, many voices clamored for a law that would do just that—prohibit "disrespectful criticism of the founders of religious systems."[50] The question was how such a law might work. Terminology was a problem here, cuing a quandary of comparative religion. If the Indian state was to enact a religiously neutral law, that law needed to be framed around a general category, equally applicable to all religions. But what should that category be? Who, after all, is *like* the Prophet Muhammad? To what sacred species does this individual belong? "Founders" (Justice Singh's word) seemed plausible enough but was never entirely satisfactory. Possible synonyms kept cropping up. Where some civic leaders demanded a temporary ordinance protecting "prophets," others spoke about not just "founders" but also "personalities held sacred by the different classes of His Majesty's subjects."[51] Many proponents of such an ordinance were Muslim, but certainly not all. The Bombay Parsi scholar G. K. Nariman, for instance, published an article in the *Muslim Outlook* in mid-July urging that legal limits be placed on criticism of all "lives of founders of religion."[52]

In late July, this popular movement found its motto: "Respect for All Prophets." The poet and nationalist leader Sarojini Naidu announced this slogan at a public meeting, also in Bombay, where she read a poem praising divinity in religiously eclectic terms.[53] Naidu seems to have devised this slogan in conversation with Maulana Muhammad Ali, the Khilafatist editor of the Urdu newspaper *Hamdard*.[54] Shortly before her Bombay event, Ali declared that India needed a law "making the insulting of prophets and saints and such holy men directly and definitely an offence."[55] A few weeks later, he published draft language for such a law, crafted in consultation with Delhi Muslim leaders.[56] Numbered 297A, it would have been appended to the section of the Code concerning desecrations of the dead:

> Whoever with the intention of wounding the feelings of any person or with the knowledge that feelings of any person are likely to be wounded or that the religion of any person is likely to be insulted thereby, by words either spoken or written or by signs or by legible representation or otherwise, insults any prophet or saint or any other person regarded by any class of persons with similar sanctity or makes or publishes any imputation concerning such a person which directly or indirectly lowers his character in the estimation of others, shall be punished with imprisonment of either description which may extend to three years, or with fine, or with both.

While Ali's law certainly foregrounds wounded feelings, its conceptual scope is quite different from 295A. In framing this eclectic law, Ali explained, he drew on sedition, false trademark, and personal defamation laws, as well as the Code's religion sections.

This was not the only "Protection for Prophets" law published that August. Sivasami Iyer, former advocate general of Madras, wrote another. Concerned that it was not currently an offense in India to "calumniate the founders of religions or . . . even the gods," Iyer proposed a law on the following lines:

> Whoever by words, signs, or visible representations intended to be heard, read, or seen, publishes any remarks of a blasphemous character against any religion or any reputed incarnation thereof or any prophets, saints, or spiritual leaders revered by a class of persons, with the intention of wounding the religious feelings of any class of people or with the knowledge that such attack is likely to wound the feelings of any class of per-

sons, shall be punished with imprisonment of either description for a term which may extend to two years or with fine or with both.[57]

Where the Indian Penal Code had tendentiously eliminated the word "blasphemy" (see chapter 4), Iyer's law conspicuously features it. It also features a potentially fraught taxonomic nomenclature. Who would be protected by this law? Prophets? Saints? Spiritual leaders? Whom do these categories include?

The colonial government must have been aware of these proposals. Its official files contain newspaper clippings of both, and Ali sent a copy directly to the viceroy.[58] Yet when the government published its proposal for 295A in August, there was no mention of sacred persons—presumably at least partly because bureaucrats had already drafted the law in July. Tired of waiting for the courts to overturn *Rajpal*, London's India secretary telegrammed to say that, regardless of what happened, the viceroy should add a new section to the penal code making it a crime "with deliberate intention to insult the religion or the religious feelings of any class of persons."[59] This language was clearly modeled on Dalip Singh's and bypassed the "Protection for Prophets" law entirely.

Even as the new 295A headed to Shimla for approval, popular demand for a "Protection for Prophets" law did not die. In late August, the Calcutta Khilafat Conference (presided over by Muhammad Ali) asked for a law prohibiting "slanders against Prophets and Saints."[60] The Anjuman-i-Ahmadiyya proposed amending the official 295A to explicitly protect "sacred personages" and "safeguard the honour of Prophets, Avatars, and Founders of all religions," including "Sikh gurus" and "Divinely inspired religious reformers."[61] Some members of the Legislative Assembly joined this public chorus. One asked that, in 295A, the phrase "religion or religious beliefs" be replaced with "anyone held in religious esteem or reverence," clarifying that "anyone" should be construed as indicating "anyone or anything, including relics, gods, and goddesses."[62] Another asked that "beliefs" be replaced with "the founder, prophet, or avatar of such religion."[63] A third asked that 295A be rewritten to prohibit insult to "a Prophet, to an Avatar, to a Guru or the founder of a religion."[64]

Proliferating nouns were a problem here, with critics pointing to the impracticality of these demands. "How shall law define who is a prophet?" demanded Lajpat Rai's *The People*. Would the government create a "gazette" of their names? Would this list include avatars, gods, goddesses, and saints? "In India, where the number of religions is really beyond calculation, the matter presents a serious difficulty."[65] In Shimla, Jayakar sarcastically asked whether the law would treat all sacred figures equally or whether it would grade punishment based on a figure's degree of sanctity—ten years imprisonment for slandering a founder, seven for a prophet, five for a guru, nine for an avatar, and so on.[66] H. N. Kunzru wondered how it would handle a figure like Shivaji who, although neither saint nor prophet, is looked upon with "feelings bordering on religious reverence."[67] Where, in short, would protection stop? "We have come down from the Prophets to Shivaji and consequently to Aurangzeb, and I do not see any reason why tomorrow we should not come down to the two Honorable Members from the Punjab," joked the United Provinces' T. A. K. Shervani, eliciting a laugh from his audience.[68] If the law were to cover even "modern-day gurus and saints," worried Bhubanananda Das, then "I might offend the Guru of somebody even in this House." As though to prove his point, Das then noted how easy it is "to grow a beard like my friends [i.e., his fellow assembly members] Mr. Acharya or Pandit Nilakantha Das and pose as a Guru." Even convicts earn fortunes this way.[69] All but inviting his esteemed colleagues to take offense, Das comically underlined the problem with a sacred libel law. It risks catching too many human social relations in its net. When Das went on to suggest that extending legal protection even to minor "godlings" would endanger free speech, one of his colleagues did interject that the word *godlings* was offensive to his religious feelings. This parliamentary debate can feel like performance art, demonstrating the hazards of legal speech.

Perhaps precisely because of its obvious impracticality, the "Protection for Prophets" law provides a useful window onto the history of Indian secularism—and indeed secularism as such. Secularism routinely misrecognizes lived religion, thus failing to provide a phenomenologically textured account of religious affect. The "Protection for Prophets" proposals could be read as attempting to resolve this constitutive problem—the generality of law's necessary failure to coincide with the particularity of life—by writing religious particularity into law through proliferating lists of particular nouns. Those nouns, however, failed to resolve the problem. They remained either too particular or not particular enough. Words like *prophet* and *avatar* might be sites of affective attachment, but they fail to meet the neutrality requirements of Indian secularism. An ostensibly neutral phrase like "sacred personalities," meanwhile, is unlikely to move hearts.

To get a better sense for how these taxonomic nouns work, we might sort them into four clusters. There are the comprehensive categories (sacred personalities, holy persons), the generalized types (founders, reformers, saints), the tradition-specific terms (gurus, pirs, avatars), and the named individuals (Krishna, Jesus, Shivaji, Rammohun Roy). Notably, English functions here as the language of the general (and thus the legal secular), with religiously particular terms coming from other South Asian languages. None of these terms, of course, quite coincides with *prophet* (itself an English translation that potentially elides the distinction between *nabi* and *rasul*).

Secularism rests on such acts of translation, which produce an appearance of commensurability between disparate "religious" worlds.[70] Translation is always local, shaped by historical and linguistic circumstance—with late colonial Hindi, for instance, situated differently than English. In the Hindi press we do find routine references to "religious founders" (*sampradaya ke pravartak* or *dharm-pravartak*).[71] We also find figures like Rama and Krishna, who never quite fit under an umbrella term other than avatar.[72] However, with its multiple linguistic registers coded (by the 1920s) around "religion," Hindi could mark difference in ways that English could not. Thus, an *Abhyudaya* article about Naidu's call to respect all prophets opens by reporting her slogan in a Perso-Arabic idiom (*sabhi paigambaron ki izzat karo*) before shifting into Sanskritized Hindi to explain that she means to protect "preceptors of all religions [*sab dharmon ke acharyom*]." It then reinserts the word *paigambar* (prophet/messenger) in brackets, as though to assure the reader that *paigambars* and *acharyas*, prophets and preceptors, are indeed equivalent—even while semantically insisting on their difference.[73] The cultural fabric of late colonial Indian secularism was woven out of such translational minutiae.

THE GOLDEN BRIDGE OF SYMPATHY: SAROJINI NAIDU'S SECULARIST AESTHETICS

To get a slightly different vantage on the work of translation, let us return to Sarojini Naidu, who premiered the "Respect for All Prophets" slogan. Although a well-known poet, orator, and politician, Naidu is seldom studied as theorist of religion or secularism. Yet as Gandhi's right hand (or at least one of them) and, in 1925, president of the Indian National Congress, she was integral to the Congressite milieu that gave rise to Indian secularism. Congressite secularism was tolerance secularism, defined against the "communal problem." It was also Naidu's secularism. As she wrote in a 1928 letter to Gandhi, "You know that the very core and centre of all my public labour has been—the Hindu-Muslim unity."[74]

In the arc of Naidu's career, the "Respect for All Prophets" movement was at most a minor episode. Her principal biographers do not mention it. She was definitely in Bombay in July 1927, sending out correspondence from her reserved room at the Taj Mahal hotel, where she also hosted a Congress Working Committee meeting on Hindu-Muslim unity.[75] The "Respect for All Prophets" event was, presumably, just a blip in her busy schedule.

It certainly, however, exemplified her ethos of cosmopolitan nationalism—her sense that, to achieve unity in diversity, India would have to push past the space of the nation to think at the level of the globe.[76] In a 1903 lecture, Naidu had defined the "national" against the "sectarian" to stress the cosmopolitan basis of a still-emergent India. One should not take pride in being "a Madrassee," "a Brahmin," or "a Hindu," she pleaded, but in being an Indian—a synthetic identity that subsumes these fissiparous parts. She herself had broken free of sectarian attachment through that most cosmopolitan of activities: travel. "Having enlarged my love, having widened my sympathies, having come into contact with different races, different communities, different religions. . . . I have no prejudice of race, creed, caste, or colour."[77] Naidu's cosmopolitan nationalism was an affective or sentimental project. The idea of India, as she said in a 1917 lecture, was a "golden bridge of sympathy" connecting Hindus and Muslims.[78] Defined against several kinds of sectarianism (region, caste, religion, race) but arguably taking religion as the most paradigmatic (whence the word "sectarian"), Naidu's India, one might say, was a kind of interreligious feeling.

Constructing this golden bridge of sympathy required both affective and aesthetic labor. It also presumed the relative autonomy of the inner domain of sentiment, spirituality, and literature—which, as an internationally acclaimed poet, Naidu knew well. Indeed, Naidu was perhaps uniquely adept at traversing the line between inner and outer, feminine and masculine, tradition and modernity, with her "feminine" literary accomplishments the springboard for her political career.[79]

Naidu's secularist aesthetics, developed in her poetry, thus organized her secularist politics, forming a kind of conceptual or sensible infrastructure for her vision of the nation.[80] Tellingly, her proposal for a law mandating "Respect for All Prophets" was accompanied by her reading a poem "of homage to divinity known by different names in principal religions."[81] The "Protection for Prophets" law would translate poem into policy.

There is no record of which exact poem Naidu recited that July. Perhaps it was "The Call to Evening Prayer," which describes Muslims, Christians, Parsis, and Hindus praying in unison. Perhaps it was "Awake!," which describes children from the same four religions kneeling before Mother India to make offerings.[82] Both poems signal the promise and the pitfalls of Indian tolerance secularism. With their list of four religions (Hinduism, Islam, Christianity, Zoroastrianism)—presumably meant to gesture synecdochally to a larger catalogue of faiths—the poems would seem to reify religious difference as the precondition of inclusivist tolerance. The poems also conceal the exclusions that go into the construction of any such religious roster.[83] Here, Hinduism joins hands with its major late colonial rivals, Islam and Christianity, as well as the politically unthreatening minority religion of Zoroastrianism. Absent are other "Indic" religions like Buddhism, Jainism, and Sikhism—implicitly allowing Hinduism to stand in for and subsume its "cousin" religions, defining the space of the Indic against a trio of "imported" theisms.

What is more, Hinduism is not simply one of the religious particularities joined together by India as secular nation. It is the aesthetic idiom of that joining. The Mother India before whom our diverse children kneel certainly seems like a Hindu goddess. The "evening prayer" is, despite its Islamic moniker, ultimately addressed to Narayana. This basic pattern recurs throughout Naidu's poetry and oratory. She imagines India as a "temple," extols the absorptive capacity of "Vedic culture," and (in a letter to Jawaharlal Nehru) uses a Puranic metaphor to describe the search for Hindu-Muslim unity: "Let us go on churning the ocean till we do evolve some supreme gift of Harmony."[84] It does not follow that she was intentionally advancing some kind of Hindu agenda. Indeed, she tried sporadically to break away from Hindu metaphors—most vividly perhaps in a lecture where she described the Indian nation drinking a patriotic elixir from a golden communion chalice emblazoned on four sides by lotus, crescent, fire, and cross.[85] She also often attributed her secularist ethos to her home city of Hyderabad, which had "solved, without any consciousness that it has done so, the greatest problem that all our political reformers are trying to solve, i.e., the question of Hindu-Muslim unity."[86] In one of her poems, she imagined national brotherhood emerging from offerings made not to Mother India, but to the Hyderabadi Nizam.[87] Still, her reliance on Hindu metaphor is recurrent and indicative. Naidu once, in 1911, described Hinduism as "the most exquisitely poetic and artistic religion in the world."[88] To the extent that she conflated the Hindu with the aesthetic and both with the production of "sympathy" as secularist feeling, Naidu was articulating an internally contradictory politics in which the very doubleness of the Hindu (as both religious particularity and generalized cultural substrate) worked to reinscribe Hinduism's hegemonic centrality.

All secularisms, of course, remain imprinted with religion. Just as US and French secularisms remain symbiotic with Christianity, so did 1920s Congressite secularism remain symbiotic with Hinduism, or at least a version thereof. We might further specify Naidu's Hinduism, at least, as the anglophone Hinduism of "guru English."[89] As a girl, Naidu spoke Hindustani with her parents (who spoke Bengali with each other) and Telugu with the servants. When asked to learn English, she at first refused. After her father punished her for this refusal by locking her in her room, she decided to embrace the language. By her late teens, she was studying in London and Cambridge and meeting the literary tastemakers who would launch her into her poetic career—a "Nightingale of India" crowned in England.[90]

Late colonial English was a key medium for translating between South Asian religions, thus producing a particular kind of cosmopolitan ethos. This ethos emerged partly through the experiments in religious eclecticism pioneered by nineteenth-century movements like the Brahmo Samaj and Theosophical Society.[91] Naidu had links to both. Née Chattopadhyay, she was born to a Bengali Brahmo family in Hyderabad; both her parents knew Keshub Chunder Sen, and she married Mr. Naidu in a Brahmo temple alongside a bridesmaid whose name is recorded simply as "Mrs. Ram Mohan Roy."[92] The theosophist Annie Besant, meanwhile, had accompanied the sixteen-year-old Sarojini on her first trip to Britain, with the two women maintaining sporadic correspondence thereafter.[93]

Naidu's pluralist aesthetic surely owed something to these connections, or at least occupied a related cultural space. It certainly relied on English as medium of interreligious commensuration. It was via English translation, after all, that Naidu was able to produce the effect that—as she put it in a 1911 letter comparing the *Bhagavad Gita* to the Sermon on the Mount— "teachers of all religions have taught the same."[94] When, a few years later, she suggested that Islam and Hinduism "worship the same transcendent spirit," calling it "Allah" and "Parameshwar" respectively, she used English to triangulate between Arabic and Sanskrit.[95] In this quintessentially Indian secular translational tactic, secular-cosmopolitan English sutures together classical languages that it thereby positions as sectarian and particularistic, subordinate to the anglophone secular. The "Protection for Prophets" law made much the same move. It just had a harder task. It is relatively easy to assert the equivalence of abstract terms like *Allah* and *Parameshwar*. Things get trickier when it comes to prophets—concrete and indelibly particular beings.

Naidu's poetry and lectures, it bears stressing, were not just an articulation of tolerance secularism. They were a practice of tolerance secularism, taking aesthetics as a means of organizing the body and its perceptions. Exhorting her audiences to set aside sectarian prejudice by conceiving the divine in translated terms, Naidu was exerting a kind of verbal force—directing India's fractious religions toward tolerance and unity, in sympathy with more statist secularist projects. Adding a "Protection for Prophets" section to the Indian Penal Code would have formalized this connection by writing the ethos of interreligious respect into law, converting a cultural norm into a legal one. In this, the lost law perhaps anticipated the formation of Indian secularism that emerged in the 1940s to shape the early postcolonial period.

CONCLUSION: FEELINGS, HIGH AND LOW

We might take Naidu's "golden bridge of sympathy" between Hindus and Muslim as a paradigmatic practice of what I have described as governmentality-from-below (which is to say, practices for the regulation of conduct that happen from within society). The "Protection for Prophets" law would have built a different kind of bridge, one between low and high, society and state. Or, more precisely—and letting the reified abstractions of "state" and "society" dissipate into concrete networks of governance—between the pedagogic secularism of a document like the Indian Penal Code and the various pedagogic practices developed from within the late colonial cultural domain. That bridge crumbled, partly because no one could figure out how stabilize the translational infrastructure beneath it. So instead of writing "sympathy" or "respect" into law, the colonial state opted for "outrage." In doing so, it created a different kind of bridge—one that invited the colonized to inhabit outrage as legally actionable feeling.

II

BLASPHEMY'S EMPIRE

WHAT KIND OF OFFENSE IS DESCRIBED by Section 295A of the Indian Penal Code? What does this late colonial law tell us about the history of secularism? Part I of this book posed these questions from within the 1920s, hovering over the controversy that prompted the creation of 295A. Part II jumps back in time a century to pursue that section's prehistory. Section 295A was a twentieth-century law built of nineteenth-century parts dating to between roughly 1835, when Thomas Macaulay first drafted the Code, and 1898, when Section 153A and its class enmity were added to it.

Where part I noted the oddity of the public feeling described (and thus, in some sense, created) by 295A and observed how certain species of affect resist translation into law's official lexicon, part II develops a fuller theoretical framework for understanding this affective gap. Rather than imposing theory from above, it tries to theorize immanent to its historical archive (in much the same way that part I theorized the 1920s public), sometimes overtly and sometimes more implicitly—with theory on mute, carried and developed by historical narrative.

My history of the Indian Penal Code's regulation of religious sentiment between the 1830s and 1890s runs as follows. Chapter 4 constructs a transcolonial legal and intellectual history for the Code's 1830s reinvention of blasphemy as affective crime. Thinking with and against Benthamite "pain" and Burkean "prejudice," I suggest that secular law purges itself of sentiment in the same movement that it purges itself of local particularity. Or, at least, it tries to. In practice, it ends up creating new species of feeling, abstract and bureaucratic rather than rooted in traditional (in a Burkean sense) lifeworlds. This work of abstraction is, moreover, not just about legal policy; it is also a practice of the self, a work of affective asceticism.

To see this asceticism clearly, we need to flip abstraction on its head, returning legal codes to the feeling bodies that are their ground and condition of being. Toward that end, chapter 5 trades the "public" archive of moral philosophy for a "private" archive of family feeling, exploring the intimate life of "Tom" Macaulay as hyperemotional transcolonial subject. The tonal transition from chapter 4 to chapter 5 might seem abrupt or idiosyncratic. Precisely for that reason, it is a key moment in the conceptual arc traced by *Slandering the Sacred*. If the gendered organization of social life into public and private spheres was the prior condition of political secularism, how might we rewire this long-nineteenth-century conceptual artifact to see secularism more clearly? Chapter 5 ponders that question by asking how Macaulay invested paper (lawbooks, letters, literature) with affective and at times erotic energy, displacing his incestuous love of his sisters onto his library.

Chapter 6 continues this meditation by asking how the legal concept of libel has functioned as a site where the disarticulation of religion and politics (i.e., blasphemous vs. seditious libel) is closely imbricated with the disarticulation of public and private (as through obscenity or personal defamation law). Sketching a rough history of libel law between the seventeenth and nineteenth centuries, the chapter suggests that old conceptual confusions resurfaced as colonial bureaucrats added new word crimes to the Indian Penal Code between 1870 and 1898. These confusions appeared once again during the 1927 Rajpal affair. Part II closes in the thick of that controversy, with the Lahore press recounting how a man on the witness stand experienced "ungovernable" emotion around an insult to the dead—in this case, not the Prophet Muhammad, but rather the man's father, former British prime minister William Gladstone. This closing scene both echoes the wounded readers of part I and anticipates the core thematic of part III: slanderous polemic as a mode of ethics, a tool for governing self and others.

04

CODIFYING BLASPHEMY

"Religious Feelings" between Colony and Metropole

IT CAME WITH THE CALCUTTA MAIL. The penal code on John Stuart Mill's desk had been commissioned by his employer, the East India Company, four years earlier. Now, in 1837, it was his job to approve the final draft. Deeming it "eminently successful," Mill also noted that a single author's literary style was "distinctly visible" throughout.[1] Although the law commission appointed to draft a new criminal law for India had five members, four got sick soon after work began—so sick that, as commission president Thomas Babington Macaulay complained in an 1836 letter, "it seems likely that I may have to do the whole myself."[2] Apparently, he did.

We have already encountered Macaulay advocating an "enlightened and paternal despotism" for India during an 1833 speech before the House of Commons. It is now time to follow him in the rest of that argument, made during debates over the renewal of the East India Company charter. Despotism is desirable, Macaulay argued, because it can confer blessings that a "free government" cannot—chief among them a legal "code."[3]

Macaulay's speech helped persuade Parliament to require the Company to appoint a commission to reform its legal system; James Mill then nominated Macaulay for the handsomely paid post of commission president. He would be a fresh face from Britain—someone "thoroughly versed in the philosophy of man and government" but sufficiently ignorant of India to enact radical reforms despite the inevitable grumbling of Calcutta's old India hands.[4] India, Mill wrote, would become "the first country on earth to boast of a system of law and judicature as near perfection as the circumstances of the people will admit."[5] (Whether it desired such perfection was irrelevant.)

The self-assured Macaulay took the job, leaving London in early 1834 to write his perfect "code."

In the 1830s, that word would have had a specific set of connotations. Since the 1750s, a codification movement had been building in continental Europe, culminating in such documents as the Napoleonic Code (1804) and Edward Livingston's *System of Penal Law for the State of Louisiana* (1826), both of which Macaulay cited as influences.[6] Although these codes circulated widely—Livingston's, for instance, was adopted in Guatemala in 1835— they tended not to circulate in Britain, where lawmakers felt they reeked of French revolution.[7] It took a Francophile philosopher like Jeremy Bentham to promote "codification" on the English side of the Channel. He coined the word in 1817. To Bentham, English common law seemed a tangled cobweb of senseless custom. He wanted to replace it with a rationally coherent and internally consistent body of law—an "all-comprehensive Code" or "pannomium."[8] When the British legal establishment snubbed his proposals, he and his allies—notably James and John Stuart Mill—turned to the colonies. In the late 1820s, Bentham mailed a copy of his Panopticon writings to Rammohun Roy in Calcutta, dreaming of a model prison in Bengal.[9] In the mid-1830s, James Mill sent a human parcel (Macaulay) to the same colonial metropolis. Macaulay continued to correspond with Mill until the latter's 1836 death, after which John Stuart assumed his father's post.

In a late-life letter, Bentham (who died in 1832) imagined himself becoming India's "dead legislative hand." Macaulay seemed poised to make this macabre dream a reality. Indeed, the Macaulay Code boasts several conspicuously Benthamite features: its spare language, its division into numbered chapters and paragraphs, even its status as "the work of a single hand."[10] It is, however, perhaps not quite as Benthamite as its author liked to claim: much of its substance seems have been drawn verbatim from contemporary English criminal law.[11] When Macaulay insisted that his opus was not "a digest of any existing legal system," he was, it seems, self-mythologizing—casting himself in the heroically masculinist role of philosopher-lawgiver.[12]

Still, it is a trademark Benthamite move that concerns me here. Bentham scorned conventional legal terminology (e.g., treason, tort, libel), arguing that law should be based instead on *a priori* categories arrived at through philosophic reason. He thus packed his writing with technical terms that, to his contemporaries, seemed like needless theoretic jargon. Macaulay avoided Bentham's neologisms. Yet he too tried to substitute "natural" concepts for conventional common-law ones.

Thus, for example, where common law spoke of "blasphemy," Macaulay spoke of "offenses relating to religion." Blasphemy, he thus implied, was an antiquated and accidental concept. It needed fixing. He would replace it with a natural, universal, and *a priori* concept: religion. To the twenty-first-century scholar, this will read like the punchline to a joke. The concept of religion, we now know, is very much the historically contingent product of a provincially North Atlantic, and thence imperial, history. It is every bit as accidental as blasphemy.

Working with this concept at a relatively late phase in its consolidation, Macaulay seems to have taken "religion" as self-evident. He was thus able to cast himself as what we would now call a secularizer, subtracting religion from English law—or, at least, subtracting Christianity, still "parcel" of the laws of England (as Justice Hale had proclaimed one hundred fifty years earlier). India presented an opportunity. Macaulay could use the colony to create a properly secular law, a law that stood benevolently above religious difference in a managerial role. That difference would be concretized in the species of affect that Macaulay dubbed "religious feelings."

In this chapter, I situate those feelings in their native historical milieu, the 1830s. Tacking between Calcutta and London (twin cities of empire), I ask how a newly emergent formation of secularism arose through the contrapuntal interplay of colony and metropole. Macaulay first articulated his reconceived blasphemy law in London while debating the place of Jews and other religious minorities within Anglican Britain—a debate that took empire as its constitutive frame. In proposing a means of regulating religious difference via the regulation of affect, Macaulay also channeled a set of philosophic debates that had been raging for decades. What is it for a body to feel pain in relation to tradition? How should the state manage the distribution of pain and pleasure? Can human bodies' propensity for feeling be reconditioned, and if so, at what cost?

COMPANY SECULARISM IN THE AGE OF REFORM

Macaulay arrived in Calcutta at a very particular moment in the history of what could be called Company secularism. Founded in 1600, the East India Company had long cultivated religious neutrality in its territories, implementing policies that echoed the Atlantic-world secularist experiments of the seventeenth and eighteenth centuries.[13] By 1800, this Company secularism had come to be defined by internal tensions, forming a sort of three-legged stool. The first leg was the principle of religious neutrality: the Company was in India to make money, not save souls. The second, paradoxically, was the official patronage of Hindu and Muslim religious institutions that the Company had inherited from monarchs it displaced. The third was the need to placate Britain's Protestant public, which disapproved of patronizing "heathens," demanded funds for the Anglican church, and insisted that Protestant missionaries of all stripes be granted full access to Company territories. Yanked in different directions, the Company stool wobbled, consistently tipping toward whichever leg had just received the firmest tug.[14]

The pull of Protestant Indophobia got stronger in the 1820s and '30s as it joined with a perhaps unexpected ally: godless utilitarians and other reformist liberals. In 1828, the reform-minded William Bentinck became Bengal's new governor-general. That same year, he emblematically banned the Hindu practice of "suttee" or widow-burning (thus positioning Indian women as the "ground" for culture wars waged between British and Indian men, to recall Lata Mani).[15] This reformist moment lasted until roughly 1835, when Bentinck's term ended, and coincided with a related moment in Britain centered on such legislation as the Catholic Emancipation Act (1829), the Reform Act (1832), and the Slavery Abolition Act (1833). This was Macaulay's moment. He joined Bentinck's government in 1834, when reformist sentiment was at its peak, and returned to Britain in 1838 as it waned.

Reform was a highly plastic term, appealing simultaneously to the rationalizing impulses of the radical Enlightenment, the moralizing imperatives of Protestant evangelicalism, and the civilizing mission of empire. It certainly aligned with the dictates of "liberalism," a Spanish-language neologism of the 1810s that emerged from the Iberian-Atlantic colonial revolutions and then migrated into English, via French, in the 1820s (it was later retrojected onto early modern political thinkers, refigured as exponents of "classical liberalism").[16] When scholars accuse liberalism of ideological complicity with empire, 1830s Calcutta is the paradigm case.[17] Its liberal reformers sought to replace venerable Indian tradition with a modernity manufactured in Britain. To reform was to anglicize. It was also, often, to protestantize.

Anglicizing reformers pitted themselves against an earlier generation of Indophilic Orientalists and, with them, an earlier formation of Company secularism. In the 1770s, Governor-General Warren Hastings had hired a team of Orientalist scholars to produce digests of "Gentoo" (i.e., Hindu) and "Muhammadan" (i.e., Islamic) law so that the Company-state could govern its subjects according to their own customs. The resulting tomes cast a long shadow over subsequent history, giving rise to new bodies of "Anglo-

Hindu" and "Anglo-Muhammadan" jurisprudence that were distinct from and less flexible than their precolonial predecessors, shaped from within by the regularizing impulses of the modern state. Some of Hastings's Orientalists dubbed their tomes "codes," thus suggesting a continuity with the eighteenth-century codification movement. These codes were soon fitted, however, to the norms and procedures of English common law—with, for instance, the principle of *stare decisis* (i.e., precedent) establishing itself by the 1810s in ways that seem to have further reduced legal flexibility.[18]

Reformist liberals disdained this Orientalist apparatus. James Mill, in his *History of British India* (1817), derided William Jones's *Institutes of Hindu Law* (1796) as "a disorderly compilation of loose, vague, stupid, or unintelligible quotations and maxims."[19] Macaulay was just as dismissive, disparaging Company patronage of traditional institutions as "not law, but a kind of rude and capricious equity."[20] Such contempt for all things Indian was racist, to be sure. It also distilled a core theoretic puzzle of North Atlantic modernity: the problem of tradition. Mill's Jones, as Javed Majeed has suggestively argued, both was and was not an Indian figure; at times, he seems to function as a proxy for famed conservative Edmund Burke, who eloquently defended tradition in his widely read critique of the French revolution.[21] For these reformers, India and France functioned as conceptually contiguous or even overlapping territories—the transcolonial terrain of Enlightenment modernity.

The puzzle of tradition was particularly acute when it came to common law, which revered its traditional inheritance. Indeed, Mill's mockery of Jones echoes Bentham's earlier dismissal of William Blackstone's authoritative *Commentaries on the Laws of England* (1765–70), which, according to Bentham, was nothing but a "vast bundle of inconsistencies."[22] In the 1760s, the teenaged Bentham had attended the Oxford lectures of "everything-as-it-should-be Blackstone" and came to revile the older man's Panglossian conservatism. His "lawyercraft," quipped Bentham, was like "priestcraft."[23] Lawyers love unwritten law "for the same reason that the Egyptian priest loved hieroglyphics, for the same reason that the priests of all religions have loved their peculiar dogmas and mysteries": it insulates them from criticism and preserves their power, reputation, and fortune.[24] Speaking in the shared anticlerical idiom of Reformation and Enlightenment, Bentham hoped to "pluck the mask of mystery from the face of Jurisprudence."[25]

This was probably a bad reading of Blackstone, who had also been a "scientifical" systematizer, trying to organize English common law in a single text to put it on par with Roman civil law (Bentham was of Blackstone's party without knowing it).[26] Bentham's critique does, however, help highlight the implicit cultural logic of the codification movement: it was simultaneously an Enlightenment project and an extension of Protestantism's "theology of the book."[27] This was hardly a secret. One of Bentham's acquaintances described his codification-mania as a sort of "legal Protestantism," distilling the fundaments of law into one quasi-biblical tome.[28] Bentham also gleefully described himself as a legal "Luther,"[29] a law-giving Moses pointing to a promised land he would never see.[30]

PERSONAL LAW, PUBLIC FEELINGS

The secular/Protestant Macaulay Code did not replace Anglo-Hindu and Anglo-Muhammadan law. It did, however, facilitate a series of structural changes that permanently altered their status. While these changes were linked to Macaulay's use of the category "religion" (of which, more below), they were more obviously linked to shifts in a concept equally integral to nineteenth-century secularisms: "the public." The story of the Indian Penal Code is also the story of how Hindu and Muslim personal law became semi-coextensive with family law, and thus also with a certain formation of the private.

By the mid-twentieth century, personal law had become functionally equivalent to family or private law across much of the world.[31] In the 1830s, that was not yet the case. Personal law hewed closer to its original (and still technically correct) meaning of nonterritorial law attaching to mobile persons—a law of peoples, not places. German legal theorist Friedrich Carl von Savigny (translated into English in the 1820s) proffered "national law" as a plausible synonym.[32] In the early nineteenth century, the competing principle of *lex loci* was on the rise, establishing the territorially bound nation-state as the structuring feature of most jurisprudence worldwide and eroding earlier modes of legal pluralism.[33] It would eventually displace the law of peoples.

The Indian Penal Code contributed to this shift from peoples to territories. It was expressly territorial law, applying to anyone charged with committing a crime "in some part of British India" regardless of "nation, rank, caste, or creed."[34] While that language comes from the 1860 version of the Code, Macaulay too had promoted territoriality as legal principle—to considerable controversy. When, in 1836, he proposed putting Britons and

Indians under the jurisdiction of the same provincial courts, white Calcutta erupted against what they dubbed the "Black Act," arguing that it violated their "constitutional rights." Where white bodies went, English common law followed; Britons in India were not even Company subjects. Macaulay (who, for all his well-attested racism, advocated formal legal equality) sighed that reformers had been branded "enemies of freedom because we would not suffer a small white aristocracy to domineer over millions."[35]

Personal law, one could say, was a religio-racial formation. It inhered in bodies, not territory. It still does. During the middle decades of the nineteenth century, however, its scope was narrowed in such a way that the division between "religious" personal law and "secular" criminal and procedural law gradually came to be coded as a division between "private" and "public." From the moment of their inception, Anglo-Hindu and Anglo-Muhammadan law had been diminishing in scope. In the 1770s and '80s, Orientalists quietly omitted ritual rules (i.e., "religion," or one formation of it) from their legal compendia, seeing them as irrelevant to Company governance.[36] After the 1830s, when the Company stopped using Persian in its courtrooms (under pressure from anglicizing reformers), it also stopped using Islamicate criminal and procedural law, a constriction later consolidated by the enactment of the Indian Penal Code (1860) and Code of Criminal Procedure (1882). Henceforth, Islamic law would be limited to domestic or private matters, as Hindu law had been for some time.[37] Rather than a law of mobile persons, personal law was now a means of regulating religious difference within a given national territory, with the family (i.e., marriage, adoption, and inheritance) the privileged site for the articulation of such difference. Personal law still hailed religio-racial subjects. Those subjects were now rendered, however, via a new, historically specific formation of property, gender, and the biopolitical reproduction of the population.

This gender politics was also a language politics. The late eighteenth-century Company-state had lavished funds on Arabic, Persian, and Sanskrit until, around the 1830s, its Orientalist enthusiasms were curbed by advocates of English as legal and administrative language. The subsequent anglicization of law was perhaps always uneven (Parsi lawyers, for instance, partially deanglicized colonial law by adapting it to their own ends).[38] Still, legal English did work in significant ways to rhetorically demarcate the boundaries of the colonial public.

As though to signal this fact, the Indian Penal Code uses the word *public* frequently, referencing public servants, public justice, public tranquility, public health, and public nuisance, and organizing its chapters on a descending scale of publicity, from offenses against the state to those against private individuals. Offenses against "the public" (including around religion) occupy a "middle place" between these poles.[39] The term is central enough to the Code's conceptual structure that someone felt the need to add it to the glossary of the 1860 version, clarifying that the "word 'public' includes any class of the public or any community" (a definition that unhelpfully defines the word in terms of itself and then equates it to its sometime antonym, the particularity of community).[40] Translators then had to decide how to render this English-specific concept in South Asian vernaculars (which, in the nineteenth century, had yet to settle on a fixed translation: *pablik, zahir, 'awam, sarvasadharan,* and *sarvajanik* were all circulating as possibilities).[41] The 1861 Hindi translation of the Code opted for *sarvasambandhi,* that which is "connected to all."[42] Postcolonial translations have tended to opt for *lok,* "the people."

The bifurcation of public and personal law worked to structure religious affect in historically determinate ways. Personal law became enmeshed with the inner sphere of domesticity, spirituality, and sentiment, perhaps accruing some of that sphere's affective charge. Criminal and procedural law, by contrast, would seem voided of sentiment, taking culture and religion as external objects of technocratic governance. And yet, perhaps inevitably, they too became sites for the articulation of feeling. In a constitutive irony, the Macaulay Code, in its very effort to extricate itself from religion and the private realm of sentiment, ended up enshrining "religious feelings" into public law.

Its use of the word *religion* acquires salience from within this linguistic and affective structure. *Religion*'s function here, moreover, was arguably new. Eighteenth-century Orientalists had used the term. But it was not, for them, an organizing concept in the same way it was for Macaulay. They organized law (to risk stating the obvious) around the terms "Gentoo/Hindu" and "Muhammadan." As Nathaniel Halhed succinctly explained in his *Code of Gentoo Laws* (1776), it was only "by a proper Attention to each Religion, [that] Justice might take place impartially, according to the Tenets of every Sect."[43] In attending to the "each," then, law would allow "Religion" itself to slip into the background, an enabling condition of legal thought but not the direct object of that thought. The Macaulay Code inverted this conceptual order. In it, Hinduism and Islam are mere "illustrations" of a larger genus, with "religion" (or, more precisely, "religious feelings") the object of legal governance. Hinduism and Islam were thus subsumed within a new or at least different kind of legal-administrative logic—a formation of colonial secularism built around religion as generalized category, articulating an equally generalized form of legal affect.

RELIGIOUS FEELINGS IN THE MACAULAY CODE

While some eighteenth-century Orientalist tomes did include rules about "scandalous and bitter expressions," regulation of religious injury was not their primary purpose.[44] For a penal secularism that saw religion primarily as a source of potential violence, by contrast, the regulation of injury was paramount.

Before we get into specifics, a note of clarification is in order. Most readers familiar with the Code will know its revised 1860 version, not the 1837 draft. For the sake of clarity, I therefore refer to sections by the 1860 numbering system, which is simpler than Macaulay's. The basic conceptual map of offenses remains largely the same, at least in the religion chapter: defiling sacred objects or places of worship (Section 295), disturbing religious assemblies (296), trespassing on burial places (297), and uttering offensive words or making offensive gestures (298). Two offenses were cut prior to 1860: coercion through threats of divine displeasure (moved to the chapter on criminal intimidation) and intentionally causing loss of caste, as by secretly mixing beef broth into a brahman's food.[45] The result was a conceptual streamlining, a foregrounding of what had even in 1837 been the Code's primary concern—religious offense.

The Code conceptualized such offense in subjectivist terms. It worried about harms to human feelings—about things "held sacred" by groups of persons, not sacred things as such. Three of the four religion sections explicitly indicate that the harm in a given action consists in wounded feelings. That the fourth (296) does not mention feelings would seem to indicate why feelings matter in the first place. Disrupting a religious assembly is a crime because it risks crowd violence. It might also harm feelings, but such harm is—one infers from the fact that it is not mentioned—redundant. Religious feelings are a proxy for violence. They threaten a breach of the peace.

Macaulay is quite clear on this point. "There is perhaps no country" but India, he explained in an appendix, "in which the Government has so much to apprehend from religious excitement among the people." This would seem a racializing claim, implying that Indians are uniquely emotional. It is also a claim structured around populational anxiety. In India, fretted Macaulay, a minuscule "Christian" minority (i.e., white; he is not thinking about Indian Christians) governs "millions of Mahomedans" and "tens of millions of Hindoos.... Such a state of things is pregnant with dangers."[46] Danger's midwife, apparently, is religious insult, a speech form that risks populational mayhem. There is rhetorical sleight of hand here: white Britons were not just potential victims of violence but regular perpetrators of it, as Macaulay well knew.[47] Precisely because of such occlusions, however, this passage clearly distills a core logic of the British colonial state. The phrase "religious feelings" indicates a sort of numericized affect, gesturing to endemic populational violence with the potential to morph into mass violence against the colonial state.

Macaulay's approach to these numericized feelings is perhaps most evident in Section 298, which stipulates prison for "whoever, with the deliberate intention of wounding the religious feelings of any person, utters any word or makes any sound in the hearing of that person, or makes any gesture in the sight of that person, or places an object in the sight of that person."[48] This is the closest the Macaulay Code comes to a blasphemy law. Notably, for all its semiotic thoroughness, its list of ways to insult religion does not mention writing—likely a classist oversight, as discussed below.

Macaulay explained that he had designed 298 to "allow all fair latitude to religious discussion" while preventing "intentional insults to what is held sacred by others." No one, he said, can be justified in deliberately "wounding . . . the religious feelings of his neighbors." Much the same held true for the chapter as a whole. It was based on the "true principles of toleration" that all governments should follow, "but from which the British Government in India cannot depart from without risking the dissolution of society. It is this, that every man should be suffered to profess his own religion, and that no man should be suffered to insult the religion of another."[49] Crucially, these twinned principles of toleration paraphrase a speech Macaulay had delivered in Parliament a few years earlier, in 1833: "Every man ought to be at liberty to discuss the evidences of religion; but no man ought to be at liberty to force on the unwilling ears and eyes of others sounds and sights which must cause annoyance and irritation." The government should only punish "nuisance" speech acts that cause "pain and disgust" and "outrage our feelings" by "obtruding" one person's views on another.[50]

Rejoining these twinned texts, we might say that Macaulay's first principle of toleration delineates a necessary liberty or right. The latter delineates a crime. The gap between them articulates a version of what I have been describing as the disjuncture between high or liberal-constitutional and low or governmental secularism. Macaulay's "liberty to discuss" invokes the liberal ideal of the deliberative public. His "liberty to force" (duly disallowed) implies a different political grammar, justifying the capillary governance of social life in order to defend society from dissolution.

Straddling these dual principles, Macaulay eased the gap between them by invoking empire's civilizing mission. Empire would educate India away from force and toward discussion, readying it for rights. Shortly before starting work on the Code, Macaulay penned his now-infamous treatise on colonial pedagogy, the "Minute on Education" (1835). There, he proposed that English literature be used to create "a class of persons Indian in blood and colour, but English in taste, in opinions, in morals, and in intellect."[51] His Code, he hoped, would serve a similarly pedagogic function, training passive Indians to be as "bold and high-spirited" as the English.[52] It would do more than just enforce rules, in other words. It would shape subjects—like literature, an instrument of disciplinary or governmental power.

As Asad Ali Ahmed has argued, the "legal subject posited by the Code is an autonomous liberal subject tempered by Indian prejudices, sensitivities, and particularities."[53] That is, the Code hailed colonized Indians into two subject positions at once. They were asked to be autonomous liberal subjects (the aspirational subjects of liberal-constitutional rights), as well as subjects of local custom or prejudice (the present objects of colonial pedagogy). The Code sutured these positions together by invoking the temporal narrative of the civilizing process.

It would be a mistake to take Macaulay at his word when he implied that this English-language penal code was somehow pristinely English, a document imposed on India from a position of pure exteriority. Macaulay's legal reforms were always already implicated in empire as determining structure. To see how, we need to travel from 1830s Calcutta to the London of a decade earlier.

BLASPHEMY ON TRIAL

In the 1820s, everybody was talking about blasphemy, or so John Stuart Mill later recalled.[54] Richard Carlile, a Fleet Street publisher, had in 1819 been convicted of the crime for marketing cheap reprints of Thomas Paine's *Age of Reason* (1794) to working-class radicals. (His distribution of a banned radical journal, *The Black Dwarf*, and close involvement with the political rally ending in the 1819 Peterloo Massacre further antagonized authorities.) While Richard was in prison, his wife Jane took over the press, followed by his sister Mary Ann. They too were jailed for their troubles. The resulting scandal lasted into 1825.[55]

John Stuart, still a teenager during these years, authored a series of newspaper articles about the Carliles, calling for "unlimited toleration" of controversial religious speech.[56] His father had similar views. "Discussion must have its course," he argued in an 1825 essay, especially when it comes to religion, for to "part with the power" of choosing one's "religious opinions" is to "part with every power."[57] Bentham, their close family friend, went so far as to write Richard Carlile in prison, offering legal advice—and a copy of his *Fragment on Government*.[58] He also borrowed Carlile's name, listing the jailed man as the publisher of his pseudonymous *Analysis of the Influence of Natural Religion on the Temporal Happiness of Mankind* (1822).

In the Macaulay household, by contrast, dissension prevailed. Zachary Macaulay, the prominent evangelical and abolitionist, not only blamed Carlile for the Peterloo Massacre, but also belonged to the Society for the Suppression of Vice that had initiated legal proceedings against the jailed publisher.[59] Thomas, a student at Cambridge, felt differently. Although in letters home, he assured his parents that he had not joined any "democratical societies" or been seduced by what his mother Selina called the "Sons of Anarchy," he had in fact fallen in with campus Benthamites, notably Charles Austin.[60] His student fiction, framed around biblical and Greco-Roman themes, meditated on contemporary concerns: massacre, sacrilege, father-son conflict.[61] Macaulay stood with Carlile. Even in the late 1820s, as his support for Benthamism wavered, his views on blasphemy held firm. When he entered politics in the 1830s, he distanced himself publicly from Carlile's "infidel attacks."[62] At dinner parties, however, he still defended the arch-blasphemer of his youth—and with him, the right to free speech about religion.[63]

As a young parliamentarian, Macaulay made his name speaking on what Karl Marx, writing a decade later (and in the shadow of British reforms), would call "the Jewish question," and it was in this context that he made his most explicitly programmatic statement about blasphemy law.[64] It thus bears thinking with him, at some length, about the pressing question of the day. What was the status of religious minorities within a British empire that was beginning to rethink the Protestant identity that had defined it for more than a century?[65] Should Jews, Catholics, and Protestant Dissenters (i.e., non-Anglicans) be permitted to hold public office? To sit on juries? To attend Oxford and Cambridge? Catholics had been "emancipated" in 1829. Almost immediately, there were calls for a similar removal of civil disabilities on Jews. These efforts failed, at least in the short term: Jewish disabilities were not lifted until 1858. Nonetheless, the Jewish question emerged in these years as a theoretically productive site for rethinking the nation under conditions of empire.[66] Suggestively, the 1833 East India Company charter document states that, in the colony, there will be "no disability for office ... in respect of religion, colour, etc."[67] The colony, once again, succeeded where the metropole failed.

Even in Britain, empire was the horizon of thought against which this new formation of secularism was defined. It is remarkable just how often members of Parliament referred to the colonies while pondering British Jews. Sometimes they used colonial analogies to reinforce anti-Semitic tropes, arguing for disabilities: if admitted to Parliament, Jews would buy their seats like eighteenth-century nabobs.[68] At other times, they argued against disabilities by placing the ambivalent trope of Jewish cosmopolitanism in an imperial frame: with their "universal language," emancipated Jews would "spread the story of British liberality in the remotest corners of the globe."[69] The fundamental question facing Parliament was whether, by extending full rights to Jews as an "alien" community, it would then have to extend the same set of rights to "all British subjects," whether born "in Quebec, Jamaica, Calcutta, or Bombay."[70] Would Parliament have to open its doors to "Turks, and to members of every other religion"?[71] To the extent that these comments conflate race and religion as axes of minority identity, they point to the larger entanglement of the two within empire's civilizational assemblage.[72]

Britishness had long been, and in some ways remained, a religio-racial identity. As that identity shifted, so too did ideas about race, religion, and empire, a frame that breached the gendered "domestic" space of the nation. "If the Jews have not felt towards England like children," opined Macaulay, figuring the nation as a family, "it is because she has treated them like a stepmother."[73] He would welcome minorities with warmer arms—but still not, perhaps, make them fully English. There is, as Gauri Viswanathan has argued, a striking parallel between Macaulay's framing of religious minority in Britain and his slightly later writings about India. Indian subjects of English literary education could mimic Englishness (taste, opinions, morals, intellect), but they remained racialized as Indian (blood, color). Like religious minorities in Britain, their difference was both effaced and retained—with these transcolonial minorities becoming, in Viswanathan's formula, "non-Jewish Jews," "non-Catholic Catholics," "non-Hindu Hindus," and "non-Muslim Muslims."[74] Here as elsewhere, secularism emerges as a means of preserving and managing minority difference.[75]

Blasphemy would be a key site for articulating this revised national identity. As Macaulay put the matter in an 1833 House of Commons speech, "It has been said that it would be monstrous to see a Jew judge try a man for blasphemy. In my opinion it is monstrous to see any judge try a man for blasphemy under the present law."[76] Already in an 1831 essay, Macaulay had rejected the notion that English law was "essentially Christian."[77] Now he was working through the implications of that rejection. His rhetorical flourishes do the conceptual work. The "Jew judge" appears monstrous insofar as he is a category error, a religious body out of place in a Christian court. Macaulay inverts this monstrosity. For him, it is the Christian court that is the category error.

This is the speech where Macaulay first expressed the "true principles of toleration" around which he later constructed the Indian Penal Code's religion chapter. In the 1820s and '30s, the very concept of blasphemy had been on trial in Britain. Macaulay found it guilty. It would serve its sentence overseas in the colonies, coming home reformed.

PRINT, BLASPHEMY, AND THE BOURGEOIS BODY

If blasphemy law was a site for negotiating race, religion, and empire, it was also a site for negotiating class. In nineteenth-century Britain, blasphemy was a classed crime, most often invoked against working-class radical tracts.[78] Hardly a subtext, class was very much on the surface of events. As the prosecution argued in the 1822 Carlile trial, Christianity teaches "deference" and acceptance of suffering to the "lower and illiterate classes." Should the court fail to "protect" them from Carlile's radicalism, "the consequences are too frightful to be contemplated." A book like Paine's *Age of Reason* might be appropriate reading for "the rich, the informed, and the powerful" (i.e., the gentlemen of the jury), but imagine the horror of it getting into the hands of "offspring and domestics."[79] (Carlile, for his part, remained defiant: "I tell Jehovah to his face that I will worship no other God but the Printing-press!")[80] This paranoid argument now reads like some kind of Marxist fever-dream about opiate Christianity. It is true that Paine had explicitly linked the religious "revolution" attempted by *The Age of Reason* to the American and French political revolutions.[81] Still, doubling down on paternalistic rhetoric was perhaps not the most strategic move for class elites.

Macaulay absorbed his era's class predilections. As we have seen, Section 298 omits writing from its otherwise lengthy list of ways to insult religion—a serious limitation in an era when print was the paradigmatic medium of offense. Why this omission? Macaulay did not explicitly say. His rhetorical illustrations, however, are telling. A man, he said in 1833, should be allowed to sell Paine's *Age of Reason* "in a back-shop to those who choose to buy," just as he should be allowed to deliver "a Deistical lecture in a private room to those who choose to listen." He should not be permitted to exhibit a "hideous caricature" of a religious figure in a window facing a major thoroughfare like London's Strand, nor should he be permitted to stand in a public place while shouting "opprobrious epithets" about a religious entity.[82] Say what you like in the private spaces of the bourgeois public, that is, but be careful what you do in the demotic street. Commodified print objects are safe. Rough orality and crude visuality are not. These classed distinctions set up a glaring blind spot: penny-press tracts like the Carliles' that were circulated (and probably read) not in shops or private rooms but in teeming thoroughfares.

Channeling this cluster of class anxieties, Macaulay elaborated his distinction between good and bad speech with vividly somatic metaphors. For a man to force words on unwilling listeners and then say he was "exercising his right of discussion" would be like setting up a yard for butchering horses next to a private residence and insisting one has a right to property. Alternately, it would be like running "naked up and down the public streets" and insisting on one's "right to locomotion."[83] A naked body brushes against buttoned-up gentlemen on a crowded sidewalk. Horse blood seeps under a fence. These illustrations suggest a grotesque blurring of bodily boundaries, securing the physical limits of the self-possessed bourgeois subject, whose very flesh is a form of property akin to a private residence. Macaulay mistrusted spaces where such buffers do not prevail. He also mistrusted speech that, disgustingly and dangerously, connects bodies.

The questions of consent that Macaulay raises are important ones, and it is not my intention to intervene in normative debates about the desirability of certain kinds of speech. Rather, I am interested in how any possible framing of such questions necessarily implies some theory of what it means for a subject to give consent, and thus some theory of the subject. Speaking in very broad terms, we might say that Macaulay's subject is the possessive subject of bourgeois liberalism.[84] Liberals have often distinguished between persuasion and coercion, deliberation and demagoguery, indicating speech either conducive to or destructive of democracy. Macaulay's version of this dichotomy (discussion vs. insult) unfolds from a prior set of assumptions about the relationship of speech to bodies. Good speech works on the mind, presenting the evidences of religion. Bad speech works on the flesh, irritating eyes and ears to produce visceral pain and disgust.

This classed theory of speech traveled with Macaulay to India. He seems to have imagined colonized Indians as analogous to the English poor. Both were, in effect, wards of the bourgeois state. He also, however, reserved space for the emergence of a bourgeois Indian public—or at least that is one way to interpret his omission of printed blasphemies from the Indian Penal Code. It made room for the "public mind of India" to "expand" under British influence, as he put it in his 1833 speech on the Company charter.[85]

A MACHINERY OF THE PEACE: SECULARISM AND VIOLENCE

In both India and Britain, the excitability of religious bodies was linked to the question of population, with the very idea of number forcing into view the apparent incompatibility of liberal-constitutional and governmental secularisms. Consider the comment of Macaulay's colleague James Mackintosh, who in 1830 counseled Parliament to ignore population when deciding whether to grant Jews the same rights it had recently granted Catholics. True, seven million Catholics could disrupt the peace in a way that forty thousand Jews could not. "The House must, however, shut out the consideration of numbers, whether of thousands or millions," as "justice" is no "respecter of multitudes; her rules must be observed towards individuals, and in forming them numbers formed no element."[86] Mackintosh's maxim—that justice is no respecter of multitudes—would seem as succinct a distillation of a liberal-constitutional logic as could be desired. It vests rights in individuals, separating justice from technical decisions about the propensities of populations.

At times, Macaulay thought like Mackintosh. In 1830, for instance, he insisted that British Jews had a "moral right" to full participation in Parliament and, in an 1831 *Edinburgh Review* essay, that the right to access public office was akin to the fundamental rights to property and self-defense.[87] More often, however, he thought by number. This was especially true around blasphemy. In his 1833 Jewish disabilities speech, Macaulay elaborated the hypothetical case of the "Jew judge" by saying that if he himself were a judge in Malta, Britain's majority-Catholic Mediterranean colony, he would punish a Protestant who burned an effigy of the pope; if he were a judge in India, he would punish a Christian who polluted a mosque.[88] These examples are of small religious minorities outraging the sentiments of larger religious groups. Refracting minority through empire, Macaulay suggested that a judge best adjudicates blasphemy by becoming a respecter of multitudes, making an empirical assessment of a population's capacity for serious violence. It is insofar as blasphemy is approached as a technical-administrative problem, inhering in populations, that the minority judge can be a neutral arbiter of it.

This rendering of governance as a set of technical procedures defined by external ends was central to Macaulay's philosophy of secularism. In one essay, he jibed that the idea of "essentially Protestant government" is as nonsensical as that of "essentially Protestant cookery, or essentially Christian horsemanship." These are absurd because cookery and horsemanship are so obviously technical skills, for which religious commitment is irrelevant. Religion has "very much to do with a man's fitness to be a bishop or a rabbi" but "no more to do with his fitness to be a magistrate, a legislator, or a minister of finance, than with his fitness to be a cobbler."[89] Care of souls is just one economically differentiated activity among others. Though its aims might be of highest importance, it does not therefore follow that it should pervade all other activities. Food is more important than art, but this does not mean piano makers should become bakers. The result, as Macaulay put it in another essay, would be "much worse music and much worse bread."[90]

Government, then, is an end-directed technical skill like any other. It exists "for the purpose of keeping the peace, for the purpose of compelling us to settle our disputes by arbitration instead of settling them by blows.... This is the only operation for which the machinery of government is peculiarly adapted."[91] The state is a machinery for keeping the peace. It should govern religion only insofar as religion threatens violence.

THE PAIN IS REAL

To govern properly, therefore, the state must dispense with the problem of religious truth—irrelevant in this technocratic context. For, as Macaulay argued in his Code, "the religion may be false but the pain which such insults give to the professors of that religion is real."[92]

Pain. That most Benthamite of words, the very root of utilitarian governance. "Nature has placed mankind under the governance of two sovereign masters, pain and pleasure," Bentham explained in 1789. To "abjure their empire" is futile. "They govern us in all we do, in all we say, in all we think: every effort we can make to throw off our subjection, will serve but to demonstrate and confirm it."[93] With these words, Bentham announced the dawn of a new political age or, at least, a new political rationality. No longer could monarchs pretend that the state served them. It and they served a higher master. "The end of law is to augment happiness," and it was the state's job to devise new techniques for achieving the greatest happiness of the greatest number.[94]

Utilitarian pain was populational pain, an aggregable affect. It conjoined statistics and psychology, attending to the needs of all and each to articulate what Bentham intended to be a more modern and rational basis for the exercise of power.[95] He had no patience for the juridico-legal conceptual apparatus of liberal constitutionalism; the transcendentalizing notion of human rights seemed, to him, like "nonsense upon stilts."[96] He wanted instead to bring government down to earth, rooting it in the body and its sensations. Such a project of governance would necessarily unfold at several distinct but intersecting sites or registers, from the arteries of state to the capillaries of individual comportment. The ethical utilitarian would read each of his actions through the population, performing a routine "felicific calculus": Will this action produce pleasure or pain? At what intensity, for what duration, in how many persons? "Passion calculates," as Bentham put it, in a droll distillation of utilitarianism's founding paradox.[97]

When Bentham first came up with the idea of utilitarianism—allegedly, in a dream—he described himself, with characteristic irony, as the "founder of a sect."[98] He was proposing a revolution in religious as much as political thought. Religion, in his view, was founded on a "principle of asceticism" that is the precise "inverse" of the "principle of utility."[99] It asks people to "immolate" their happiness on the altar of the transcendent, with God little more than a symbol for maximizing pain in a perverse negation of life itself.[100]

In Bentham's radically materialist ontology, then, pain is "real" in a precise sense. Like pleasure, it is a perceptible entity that can be studied through the philosophical techniques of what Bentham called "somatology." Not so with most human desires and passions, which are, in Bentham's technical sense of the term, "fictitious"—shaped by linguistic convention and ultimately reducible to pleasure and pain.[101] To demonstrate this point, Bentham constructed a complete "table of the springs of action," a taxonomy of affect that sorts the passions according to their motives under subject headings loaded with technical neologisms (e.g., "dyslogistic" feelings).[102]

Bentham wrote about blasphemy at least three times in his sprawling and largely unpublished oeuvre. In the "Essay on the Influence of Time and Place in Matters of Legislation" (1782, first published in French translation in 1802), he reduced blasphemy to a "simple mental injury," potentially severe, that a Hindu, Muslim, Catholic, Jew, or Protestant would experience upon encountering words or images that contemn a sacred object.[103] In an undated fragment about "Offences against Religion," he mocked the idea that Christianity is parcel of English law by quipping that if anyone actually took this dictum seriously, they would demand morally spotless executioners and willingly surrender their belongings to thieves.[104] Finally, in a published 1821 letter to the Spanish Count of Toreno about Iberian-Atlantic penal codes, Bentham proposed punishing "exhibitions" that foist "uneasiness of a religious account" on persons who cannot avoid them (sardonically clarifying that the Almighty requires no such emotional protection). He then said he would apply punishment to no discourses, no matter how revolting, confined to writing, printed books, and private conferences that one enters by "free choice." The problem is sights and sounds inflicted on the "promiscuous multitude," as in a road, market, or church.[105]

That last formulation is virtually identical to Macaulay's 1833 comment on blasphemy. Macaulay would also seem to have been performing a version of the felicific calculus as he weighed different types of speech, permitting only those pains accompanied by some form of "compensating good." Discussion of the "evidences" of religion compensates for pain through its tendency to "elicit truth." Insult has "no such tendency." It just inflames "fanaticism."[106]

I do not want to overstate Bentham's influence on Macaulay, who is probably best understood as a tactical Benthamite. After his university dalliance with philosophic radicals, he broke with utilitarianism by publishing a series of essays against James Mill, to which Mill publicly responded. The two later reconciled, aided by Macaulay's vocal enthusiasm for Mill's notoriously racist *History of British India* ("the greatest historical work which has appeared in our language since that of Gibbon"), leading Mill to nominate Macaulay as law commissioner.[107] In Calcutta, Macaulay told the Mills what they wanted to hear. His reforms, he wrote in 1836, would ingratiate him with the "Benthamites at home" and "make Old Bentham jump in his grave."[108]

Not only was Macaulay at best a tactical Benthamite, but he also almost certainly got Bentham wrong. (So did the Mills.) As Jennifer Pitts has argued, Bentham was a staunch critic of colonialism whose "dead legislative hand" remark was caked with trademark weirdness. In 1836, moreover, the deceased philosopher was not actually in a grave: his mummified corpse or "Auto-Icon" was staying at the home of his friend Thomas Southwood Smith (who later transferred it to University College).[109] Bentham was alluding to the Auto-Icon when he made his crack about becoming British India's "dead legislative hand": "Twenty years after I am dead, I shall be despot, sitting in my chair with Dapple in my hand."[110] Dapple was his walking stick. His corpse still holds it (see figure 4).

It is hard to reconcile the gleeful grotesquerie of the Auto-Icon with the self-serious moralizing of Macaulay and the Mills. This 1832 art object is an imperial text of a kind: Bentham's severed head was mummified according to what was understood to be a Maori process (the result was so disturbing that taxidermists made him a wax head instead). It can also be read as a performative inversion of its textual twin, the dead hand of the Indian Penal Code. Where the Code sought to govern embodied religious feelings, the Auto-Icon parodies religion to void the body of affect. Bentham said that the spectacle of his taxidermized corpse was meant to encourage more people to donate their bodies to science (thus slowing a recent spate of *Frankenstein*-style medical school grave robberies), but that rationale hardly seems to exhaust the Benthamite symbolism of a body that cannot feel pleasure and pain and is open, forever, to the panoptic gaze of unknown others—comically inverting the panopticon's all-seeing but unseen quasi-divine prison guard.[111] The Auto-Icon also upends the sacred gaze elicited by religious icons. Its very name poses a sort of semiotic riddle: how can a body function as a likeness (icon) of itself (auto)? To venture an answer, we might think with Bentham's younger contemporary Ludwig Feuerbach, whose *Essence of Christianity* (1841) described religion as a process of self-alienation, a dialectic projection of human ideals onto an imagined divine Other. The Auto-Icon pulls that divine likeness back into the ipseity of the self-representing body—but not therefore the sensuous plenitude of life. Refusing to be immolated on the altar of the transcendent, this body, in its persistent somaticity, its monstrous rebirth, articulates a Benthamite formation of the secular with perverse clarity. It is philosophic performance art, a body so rationalized that it has entirely lost its ability to feel—thus perhaps confirming the longstanding worries of utilitarianism's critics.

FIGURE 4. The Auto-Icon of Jeremy Bentham, circa 1985. © UCL Educational Media 2021, all rights reserved.

PAIN AND PREJUDICE

Utilitarianism's calculating passions come at a cost, as Bentham knew. The truths of moral science, he wrote, do not flourish "in the same soil with sentiment."[112] One reason for this difficulty is soil itself, or, rather, territory. Although the body's capacity for pleasure and pain is "much the same the world over," its "corporeal sensibility" is shaped by historical and geographic circumstances, including "government, religion, and manners."[113] Bentham's most extensive elaboration of these themes is in the "Essay on the Influence of Time and Place in Matters of Legislation," which considers the concrete case of how English law should be adapted to Bengal. It poses a question about what we might now call culture (a late nineteenth-century concept).[114] Bentham called it "custom," "national character," "national manners," and—to take the concept that will concern me here—"prejudice."

Cautioning the legislator against imposing his own provincial customs on foreign soil, Bentham noted that a people "will sit easy under the yoke of their own prejudices; but they will not sit easy under the prejudices of another people." Government should not "shock" those prejudices with "unnecessary violations." If a high-ranking Hindu refuses to appear in court, just make him cover the expense of being examined at home.[115] A nearly identical formulation appears in Macaulay's 1833 speech on the Company charter. "We propose no rash innovation; we wish to give no shock to the prejudices of any of our subjects." He urged the Company to "assimilate" Indians customs without "wounding those feelings" deriving from religion, nation, and caste.[116] Here, "shocked prejudices" and "wounded feelings" would appear synonymous.

This usage of *prejudice* was common in the early nineteenth century. We now think of prejudice mostly as a feeling harbored toward that which a person is "determined to hate" (to quote Jane Austin's 1813 novel *Pride and Prejudice*, itself an intervention into the theory of sentiments).[117] Historically, it has also indicated various forms of preconceived opinion, sometimes shading into what could be called culture or tradition. In the late eighteenth and early nineteenth centuries, *prejudice* seems to have indicated something like tradition's emotional nimbus. This was true in British India, where Halhed's *Code of Gentoo Laws* noted that one should not pass judgment on Hindu customs, as they align with the "consciences of the people" and are "in conformity to their prejudices."[118] It was also true in blasphemy-obsessed Britain. "No good man will wound the prejudices of his fellow-creatures" needlessly or wantonly, argued a Unitarian minister in 1817, unless "pride and passion" overtake him.[119] In the 1830s, the Jewish question was sometimes framed via this notion of prejudice. Removing Jewish disabilities, argued a Tory member of Parliament, would "run some risk of affronting the religious feelings of the people of this country. These feelings might be called prejudices, but they were honest prejudices," and, as such, should be respected.[120] You can feel the MP talking his way around the negatively charged sense of prejudice here, using the adjective *honest* to justify anti-Semitism.

Probably the most celebrated parliamentarian to use *prejudice* in this broad sense, indicating the precritical habitation of the subject, was Edmund Burke. His *Reflections on the Revolution in France* (1790) rushed to the defense of such "untaught feelings." Rather than "casting away all our old prejudices" like Enlightenment-crazed French revolutionaries, he argued, we should "cherish them because they are prejudices." They emerge organically over untold ages and thus express the "latent wisdom" of the past. Precisely because they are prior to judgment, they orient humans in the present like little else can. "Prejudice renders a man's virtue his habit."[121] Simultaneously the arch-theorist of British conservatism and an important early critic of empire, Burke anchored both his conservatism and his anti-colonialism in veneration of tradition, as Uday Singh Mehta has shown.[122]

With Mehta, let us take "Burke" and "Bentham" not just as individual thinkers but also as ideal types—conceptual poles in an unresolved debate about colonial modernity's relationship to tradition. Bentham aspired "to soar above the mists of prejudice."[123] Burke condemned such reformers as "men of no place," their ideas "stripped of every relation, in all the nakedness and solitude of metaphysical abstraction."[124] Burke liked his ideas clothed in locality. He also liked sentiment, decrying the philosophic radicals for having "banished the affections" and left nothing in their place but "cold hearts" and "mechanic philosophy." While observing the French revolution, he took comfort in the fact that the British had "not yet been completely embowelled of our natural entrails" and "inbred sentiments" like "stuffed birds in a museum." Fortunately for him, he died decades before Bentham's stuffed corpse went on display.[125]

Utilitarianism's mathematicized feelings, a Burkean might say, are phenomenologically thin, at a constitutive remove from lived experience. It is not that utilitarianism has no means of accounting for culture. Bentham's essay on "Place and Time," after all, considered how best to accommodate prejudice. Later, in 1843, John Stuart Mill even proposed a new discipline of "ethology" (a "science of the formation of character") to study how history and geography shape subjectivity.[126] Still, if passion calculates, then calculation risks eroding the passions.

John Stuart learned this the hard way. Subjected to an unusually rigorous educational regimen by his father and Bentham (Greek at three, Latin at eight), his boyhood turned him into a "reasoning machine," or so he later recalled in his *Autobiography*. He was especially skilled at manipulating the "principle of association" behind sentimental attachments, training himself to experience pleasure in activities that promoted general happiness and pain in those that did not. Philosophy, for him, functioned as a "dissolving force" on "prejudice." This proved dangerous. In 1826, Mill sank into a deep depression, realizing that his emotional calculus had been "a perpetual worm at the root both of the passions and of the virtues." It took an emotional encounter with Romantic poetry—with place and literary convention—to restore him to health.[127] Mill's microhistorical melancholy distills a broader cultural conflict. Raised on the Benthamite manipulation of pain, he later came around to a Burkean acceptance of untaught feeling.

Six years older than Mill, Macaulay also veered between Burke and Bentham. He thought that Burke had been "the slave of feelings," letting "reason" cede too much ground to "zeal" in his criticisms of Indian Governor-General Warren Hastings.[128] At the same time, he mistrusted utilitarian abstraction—jibing, of James Mill's essay on government, that "it would not appear that the author was aware that any governments actually existed."[129] Macaulay knew that sentiment and locality were irreducible to human experience. He also knew they were potentially useful. In public, Macaulay remained a respectable Anglican. In private, he was, like the Benthamites, a skeptic or agonistic (a word not coined until 1869; Macaulay invented his own neologism, "acatalepsy" or "incomprehensibility").[130] To explain the discrepancy, he liked to quote Edward Gibbon: "The various modes of worship which prevailed in the Roman world, were all considered by the people as equally true; by the philosopher, as equally false; and by the magistrate, as equally useful." This attitude, said Gibbon, was the key to antiquity's "spirit of toleration."[131] Adapting Gibbon's "spirit of toleration" to a new form of empire, Macaulay was ever the magistrate. He instrumentalized religion for the ends of power.

He also sought pragmatic middle ground between "Bentham" and "Burke," those ideal types, as suggested by his oft-quoted epigrammatic advice for colonial lawmakers (its tripartite structure perhaps echoing Gibbon but more likely Augustine: "In necessary things unity; in doubtful things liberty; in all things charity"): "Uniformity where you can have it, diversity where you must have it; but in all cases certainty."[132] Uniformity: the domain of the legal philosopher. Diversity: the social heterogeneity of tradition and prejudice, which must be accommodated. Certainty: the legal-bureaucratic procedure whereby the relationship between law and society, philosophy and tradition, is fixed and regularized.

CONCLUSION: "RELIGION" AS ABSTRACT FEELING

The "world is governed by associations," wrote Macaulay in an 1837 letter—with an echo (presumably accidental) of Mill's 1826 depression, brought on by overmanipulating the "principle of association" connecting affect to its objects.[133] One could take Macaulay's comment as a maxim on government more generally, applicable to the Indian Penal Code's "religious feelings." This secular-legal document sought to govern religious affect in the colony (and thence eventually the metropole). It was itself governed, however, by a series of interlocking associations—overdetermined by the entangled transcolonial histories of legal codification; Protestant book culture; the regulation of religious and especially Jewish difference; an intermittent disavowal of number as valid rubric for ruling religion; the related figuring of government as a technical machinery for keeping the peace; utilitarian pain management; celebrations of organic tradition; the shifting contours of the public; and transcolonial formations of race, class, gender, and sexuality. The reformulation of blasphemy law unfolded along all these axes at once.

I want to close this chapter's discussion of codified "religious feelings" by using Bentham and Burke (those inadvertent affect theorists) to revisit a question posed above: What kind of structure of legal feeling did the discursive object *religion* imply in the 1830s? If the Code pulled away from Anglo-Hindu and Anglo-Muhammadan personal law, eventually becoming the "public" counterpart to personal law's "private" or intimate sphere, it did this partly via the concept of religion, which subsumed the particularity of Hinduism and Islam into a more abstract category. This conceptual shift would seem to imply a structure of feeling. Personal law was created, precisely, to accommodate prejudice or untaught feeling. It aligned with Burke and the veneration of tradition—changing tradition in the process, to be sure, but still working to provide a viably traditionalist habitation for the subject. The Macaulay Code, by contrast, aligned with Bentham, soaring above time and place in an ethereal zone of pure philosophy. By educating Indians, it would bring social fact (Burkean prejudice) into closer alignment with legal norm (Benthamite abstraction). Where personal law worked to reorganize religious affect from within by administering the particularities of social life, Macaulayan criminal law sought to extricate itself from sentiment, taking religious lifeworlds as an external object of governance. The concept of religion was its lever for doing so.

And yet, despite itself, the Macaulay Code became a site of sentiment.

People now routinely speak its language in expressing their wounded religious feelings. They have, in effect, invested the modern anglophone concept of religion with intense affectivity. Perhaps association got the better of philosophy in the end, infusing even the most abstract of concepts with prejudicial attachment. Nor is this surprising. The philosophic lawmaker tried to soar above time and place. Necessarily, however, his feet remained firmly on the ground.

EPILOGUE: MACAULAY'S LEGAL AFTERLIVES

Macaulay, a subject reshaped in Calcutta, went on to shape Victorian Britain's sense of itself. He wrote his bestselling *History of England*—the Whig history that defined the nation for at least a generation—in the shadow of his Indian experience.[134] His England was, in some sense, born in India. Meanwhile, in India, his penal code stalled. After Macaulay submitted the 1837 draft, his opus was shelved for a quarter century. It was not enacted until 1860, after the 1857 uprisings and the subsequent elimination of the Company, becoming law in 1862.

Why the delay? By 1837, reformist fervor was on the wane. James Mill and Bentham were dead, Bentinck was gone, and even Macaulay was packing his bags. When they saw the new Code, Calcutta's old India hands grumbled as predicted and buried it under judicial comment.[135] By 1841, it seemed like the Macaulay Code might "for any practical purpose" be locked in the Tower of London.[136] Law commissioners came and went. In 1850, John Drinkwater Bethune proposed a more conservative penal code. In 1853, Barnes Peacock started drafting a Code of Criminal Procedure, but soon realized he first needed to resolve the ambiguous state of substantive criminal law. He dusted off Macaulay's draft, revised it lightly, and put it forward for enactment.[137] In 1854, Macaulay wrote his sister Hannah to say that "I cannot but be pleased to find that, at last, the Code on which I bestowed the labor of two of the best years of my life has had justice done to it."[138] He died in 1859, one year too early to see it passed.

05

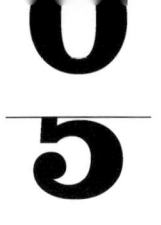

MACAULAY UNMANNED, OR, TOM GOVERNS HIS FEELINGS

PROLOGUE: A LETTER TO A FRIEND

"DEAR ELLIS," IT BEGINS. "THE LAST month has been the most painful that I ever went through. Indeed, I never knew before what it was to be miserable."[1] Thomas Babington Macaulay had been in Calcutta for just over four months when he wrote these words in February 1835. Days earlier, he had penned his "Minute on Education." Soon he would start work on his Indian Penal Code.

The Macaulay who features in histories of modern India is, for the most part, the Macaulay of these public documents. Yet the "Minute" and the Code are, in their way, intimate texts. They are designed to discipline bodies, training "tastes" and "morals" (as in the "Minute") and regulating such private matters as "unnatural" sexuality and visceral responses to religious insult (as in the Code's Sections 377 and 298). Asserting a right to rule India's emotions, these documents also disallow a reciprocal intimacy. As public writing, they imply an author who is himself beyond sentiment, the dispassionate governor of other people's feelings.

It thus becomes tempting to ask a slightly mischievous question: what about the emotional life of Thomas Macaulay? To pose this question is not just to move Macaulay from high to low, asking how his affective body remained an object of governance. It is also to follow the lead of scholarship in critical secular studies that shows how secularism emerged symbiotically with the modern public/private distinction.[2] To get critical distance on the secular, we need to reimagine that distinction, creatively cross-wiring private and public. Toward such a project, one may as well begin with Macaulay's letters—here to his closest friend, Thomas Flower Ellis, residing in Bloomsbury.

This particular letter records a loss. "Early in January, letters from England brought me news of the death of my youngest sister. What she was to me no words can express." A lifelong celibate, Macaulay was strongly attached to his two youngest sisters, Hannah and Margaret. His recent biographers are blunt in their assessment: this was incestuous desire, probably unconsummated.[3] Quasi-romantic bonds between siblings were common in early nineteenth-century Britain. Even in historical context, however, this attachment was extreme. In a December 1834 letter, "Tom" (as his family called him) confessed to Margaret that to love her as he did was "to make war on nature."[4] Weeks later, he discovered she was dead. Words could not express his love or his loss. Was this banal sentimentalism or unspeakable taboo?

Wordlessness undid Macaulay. "Even now, when time has begun to do its healing office, I cannot write about her without being altogether unmanned." In public, Macaulay was a paragon of manly self-rule, an ambassador of imperial masculinity whose Indian Penal Code was meant "to rouse and encourage a manly spirit" of self-assertion in passive colonial subjects.[5] Imperial ideology often invoked gender, with the "natural" hierarchy of masculinity and femininity seeming to justify the racial hierarchies of empire. It is because "the Bengalee is feeble even to effeminacy," wrote Macaulay, that he is "fitted by habit for a foreign yoke."[6] A closely related set of gendered tropes structured political imaginaries within Britain, where liberalism's ideal of the autonomous individual was encapsulated in the figure of the "independent man," a gentleman of means whose property secured both his public position and his intimate authority over household dependents.[7]

The feminized sphere of bourgeois domesticity presented a constitutive risk for the male subjects who traversed its borders. Independent men required intimate bonds, but those bonds threatened their independence. Tom certainly saw domesticity as risky terrain. He once, in a letter to Hannah, wrote dismissively of his East India Company colleague Charles Grant for missing his son. Grant, he said, had "a mind that cannot stand alone. It is—begging your pardon for my want of gallantry—a feminine mind. It turns, like ivy, to some support.... This is a great weakness in a public man."[8] Tom too was like ivy. He clung to his sisters. One winter's evening, while regaling them with tales of his triumphs in Parliament, he described his condition as one of "sweet bondage." "I wish you two ... would hang yourselves," Margaret remembered him saying, "because then I should be the most independent man in the world." His sisters looked at him in shocked silence.[9]

This was the early 1830s, when the struggle to abolish slavery in the British empire was reaching its crescendo—a political context with acute relevance for Macaulay family life, shaped from its inception by the abolitionist fervor of our trio's father, Zachary. In this family, the political resonance of Tom's "sweet bondage" would have been all too clear. His bourgeois white male subjectivity was locked in sentimental chains. The irony is that, without them, he unraveled. This subject's self-possessed masculinity was predicated on a prior dispossession, a production of self via intimate others. As a secondary state, acquired over and against a primary dependence, independence was a project of self-making at perpetual risk of being undone—hence the anxious need to reaffirm it.[10] Sweet bondage was the condition of possibility for "Tom," the intimate man, and thus also for "Macaulay," the public one.

Tom knew only one tool for restoring his manhood: literature. It is a "blessing," he wrote Ellis, to "love books as I love them." A long digression on the Greek classics consumes the rest of the letter, ferrying it toward a socially acceptable closing and cementing Tom's homosocial bond to his classically educated male friend. Macaulay is in good health. His finances are good. He offers Ellis his "kindest remembrances"—and a Latin postscript.

CONCEIT: LEGAL SECULARISM AND THE INTIMACIES OF EMPIRE

This chapter asks what would happen if, as a sort of thought experiment, we took Macaulay's private letters as charter texts of colonial secularism. Taking my cue from Lisa Lowe, I position intimacy as a heuristic, an analytic lens for approaching public events. In the style of her "political economy of intimacy," I try to dislodge the intimate from the domestic sphere, thus courting a sort of category error to get better analytic traction on nineteenth-century separate spheres ideology.[11] It is no secret that empire was an intimate enterprise, lodged in bodily affect and regulating sexual desire so as to maintain racial difference.[12] Empire also regulated sociality, such that even simple expressions of friendship across racial lines could imply a radical reconfiguration of empire's affective architecture.[13] How should such critical insights shape the study of colonial secularism? This chapter explores one possible answer to that question.[14] It takes as its maxim an argument from a recent ethnographic study of postcolonial law: "Kinship is central to the practice of secularism."[15] Something similar held true in the colonial period, I argue. It even held true for Macaulay.

In what follows, I lean heavily on Catherine Hall and on Robert Sullivan, Macaulay's recent biographers—scholarship, like family, being a practice of dependence. To document the emotional lives of prominent public figures is, as Hall argues, to advance a broadly feminist intellectual agenda by insisting on the inextricability of the personal and the political as well as highlighting a cast of supporting characters, often female, typically excluded from historical analysis. It is also to demonstrate the centrality of family to empire itself.[16] "Families like the Macaulays," explains Sullivan, "were economic as well as emotional and cultural units. Their complex interdependence belied the vocabulary of autonomous selfhood that proliferated in much of the nineteenth-century Atlantic world."[17] The Macaulay we meet in Hall's and Sullivan's biographies is indeed an arrogant, racist ideologue, but he is also a chronically depressed, social-isolate reader, debilitated by his incestuous love for his sisters and shaped profoundly by both evangelicalism and empire. This biographical "Tom" has yet to make his way into South Asian studies. This chapter is meant as a step in that direction.

A week before his penal code was published in 1837, Macaulay wrote a letter to Ellis saying that "whether the work proves useful to India or not, it has been of great use, I feel and know, to my own mind."[18] I propose taking this claim seriously. How did the Code shape Macaulay's intimate relation to himself? What "use" did he put it to in his daily practices of self-governance? These are unanswerable questions. Although Macaulay's letters between 1835 and 1837 often mention the Code—noting that work is going slowly, proffering opinions on coauthors—they do not say much about how it felt to write it.[19] Still, as I hope to suggest, it is possible to reconstruct a provisional account of how Macaulay used the Code by taking a broad view of his biography.

Lawmakers make laws, and those laws become part of their makers' daily lives during the time of their making. This near-tautological truth would typically be shuffled aside as being of dubious historical relevance. If, however, one is interested in how multiple registers of governmentality intersect in practice (i.e., techniques for the conduct of conduct including not just law, but also religious norms, manners and mores, ethical precepts, familial networks, etc.), then the necessarily intimate relation between law and lawmaker becomes a potentially promising site of study. For the lawmaker, the intimate is not just the object of law; it is the prior condition of law, the site at which law first emerges. Most scholars have, quite appropriately, posed what could be called—borrowing a term from media studies—a reception question about religion and law. They ask how lawbooks shape the intimate lives of the governed. Here, by contrast, I pose a production question, asking how a lawbook shaped the intimate life of its author.

Alternating between narrative and analysis, I age Macaulay backward from the late 1830s until 1800 (he was born with his century). To understand why Macaulay was unmanned by his passions—etymologically, that which renders the subject passive—we need to understand the historical specificity of his media practices of the book. For him, sisters, semiosis, and secular empire were affectively supercharged precisely because they were so tightly intertwined. To see how, let us give ourselves over to the gossipy pleasures of Tom's story.[20]

TOM LOVES HIS SISTERS

In May 1838, while Thomas Macaulay was on the ship back from India, his father Zachary died. Perhaps at that moment Tom regretted his fantasies of coming home rich—"for the first time in my life, an absolutely free and independent man."[21] He had gone to India partly to extricate himself from his father's financial woes, even to displace his father in the family financial hierarchy. Now, headed home, he was perhaps more independent than he wanted. His three sweetest bonds had been severed while he was away.

Tom (b. 1800) was the oldest of nine children, with Hannah (b. 1810) and Margaret (b. 1812) the two youngest girls. Age difference sparked fondness that intensified as the trio grew into adulthood. In 1830, they even talked about setting up house together. Margaret gushed in her scrapbook that Tom had been the "the object of [her] whole heart" for years, and she had never "felt so worked up about anything" as the idea of moving in with him.[22] Their idyll was short-lived. In 1832, Margaret announced that she was engaged to Edward Cropper, a director at the Liverpool and Manchester Railway. Tom was devastated by the news, greeting it with "a flood of very bitter tears."[23] As he explained in a letter to her a few months later, Margaret had for him taken "the place of a first love. During the years when the imagination is most vivid and the heart most susceptible, my affection for my sisters has prevented me from forming any serious attachment." He now saw his error in having warred "against the nature of things, against the great fundamental law of society." "That women shall leave the home of their birth and contract ties dearer than those of consanguinity is a law as ancient as the first records of the history of our race, and as unchangeable as the constitution of the human body and mind." It was quite a confession. He asked Margaret not to show the letter to Hannah.[24]

Margaret's marriage was like a death to Tom. In early 1833, he sent her a belated wedding gift—a portrait of himself. Enclosed was a letter describing the gift "as a funeral relique—as a memorial of one who, though still living, is separated from you by a gulph like that which parts the living and the dead."[25] The following Christmas, he told Hannah that "instead of wishing to be near [Margaret], I rather shrink from it. She is dead to me; and what I see is only her ghost."[26]

With Margaret gone, Tom transferred all his affections onto Hannah—or as he called her, Nancy. Two weeks after his 1832 confessional letter to Margaret, he was writing Hannah from a party to tell her that "I see some pleasing women here" with "pretty faces" and "orange ribbands," but "none who is worthy to tie the shoe-latchet of my two darling sisters."[27] A few months later, he wrote to say that Margaret "has a husband to look after her; you have only a brother."[28] A week after that, we find him bored in Parliament and looking forward to a little "fondling with my own Nancy."[29]

Such sentiments were, to some extent, typical of a historical period when brother-sister love was celebrated as a desexualized, and thus purified, form of heterosexual romance. Sibling love also served a critical economic function in that it readied bourgeois children to marry their cousins in a world that revolved around endogamous cousin marriage. This was how the era's major British clans (Darwins, Wedgewoods, Wilberforces) retained wealth in family firms.[30] By century's end, the key ethnographers of this intimate sphere (Sigmund Freud, Havelock Ellis) would speculate that the bourgeois family unit was founded on disavowed incestuous desire. One need not be a Freudian, however, to raise an eyebrow at the January 1834 letter in which Tom tells his "pretty" Nancy that "I am your papa now."[31] He was trying (as Hall suggests) to be father, brother, and lover at once.[32] Hannah and Margaret had mothered Tom after their collective mother, Selina Mills Macaulay, died in 1831. Now that a business failure had imperiled Zachary's finances, Tom would reciprocate.[33]

Even by period standards, this kind of language is extreme. When, in the

1870s, Hannah's son George published selections from his famous uncle's letters, he censored overtly romantic language ("pretty," "dearest love") in the letters to his mother.[34] This may partly reflect a shift in social mores at midcentury, after a mid-Victorian panic about sibling incest.[35] Already in the 1830s, however, Tom was clearly self-censoring, asking his sisters to keep his "war on nature" a secret.

Tom wanted Nancy to accompany him to India. Over seventeen months and more than seventy letters—addressed to his "dearest love," "my dear girl," "ever dearest yours"—he pursued a campaign of emotional blackmail. His well-paid position in Calcutta would save their father from debtors' prison, and "whether the period of my exile shall be one of misery or comfort . . . depends on you, my dear, dear Nancy. I can scarcely see the words which I am writing through the tears which force themselves into my eyes. Will you, my own darling . . . go with me?"[36] Hannah went.

They left London in February 1834 on a ship called the *Asia*, arriving in Madras in June. Other than a short trip to Paris, Tom had never been out of Britain—nor apparently did he relish the prospect. A friend who saw him off noted his "foul" and "jaded" complexion and had a distinct sense "he was going to sacrifice his life."[37] Hannah was no better. "If I could have conceived the sufferings of the last twenty-four hours beforehand never would I have placed myself here," she wrote Margaret. "Why did none of my friends intervene."[38] At sea, Tom holed up in his cabin with a stack of books and imagined Hannah enjoying herself on the ship's dance floor. In fact, she was seasick and horribly lonely. "Tom has no conception what I am feeling," she wrote Margaret.[39]

Hannah got to Calcutta before her brother, who had stopped in south India on official business. The separation seems to have been good for her. Before they set sail, an acquaintance had predicted she would "marry some rich Nabob" within six months of arriving in Bengal.[40] The acquaintance was right. Tom arrived in Calcutta in September. Two months later, Hannah was engaged to the well-positioned young East India Company official Charles Trevelyan. They were married at Christmas in the Calcutta cathedral. Tom gave Hannah away. "Everything is dark," he wrote Margaret on Christmas Eve. "I have nothing to love—I have nothing to live for."[41] He did not know that Margaret had died of scarlet fever six months earlier, shortly after her siblings' arrived in India. News of her death was as slow as the imperial mail. For months, Tom had been writing to a ghost.

Our soap opera continues with Hannah somehow persuading Charles to let Tom move in with them so that they could "form one family" in a

Calcutta mansion.[42] It is time, however, to press the pause button and consider what this intimate saga might say about the liberal ideal of the independent man and the early colonial discourse network in which these sibling letters circulated.

COLONIAL GRAPHOMANIA

The intensely sentimentalized nuclear family was, the historians tell us, a "crucible of sexuality" as well as a "training ground for new affective modalities" that went well beyond mere sexual intercourse.[43] Even as adults, Victorian siblings often had surprisingly little heterosexual sex, instead channeling their polymorphous energies into a lush of array of affectively charged practices, from homoerotic friendships to religious piety to relentlessly voluminous production of prose—a sort of "graphomania."[44] The Macaulays were graphomaniacs. They proliferated speeches, journals, scrapbooks, essays, histories, minutes, codes, and, perhaps above all, letters. In this, they were typical of their era's discourse network (to recall the psychoanalytically inflected media archaeology of Friedrich Kittler, for whom gender, language, and material inscription systems develop in tandem to form historically specific structures of semioticized desire).[45]

Tom in particular was a torrent of words. He gave dozens of speeches in and out of Parliament and published thousands of pages of prose. His sisters were integrally involved in these public productions. So as not to compromise his speeches' intrinsic orality, he refused to write them down, instead rehearsing them out loud to Hannah and Margaret who, Hall suggests, were "always the primary audience both for his speeches and his writing."[46] In 1831, relishing his newfound political fame, Tom wrote Hannah to say that his "greatest pleasure in the midst of all this praise" was to imagine how his success would delight his father and sisters. "It is happy for me that ambition—the fiercest and most devouring of all passions—has in my mind been softened into a kind of domestic feeling."[47] Ambition, that most political and thus public of emotions, is not just softened by domesticity. It is mediated by the domestic, performatively routed through the intimate act of letter writing.

The Macaulays enlisted even bureaucratic paperwork as props of graphomaniacal intimacy. In Calcutta, Charles Trevelyan wooed Hannah by slipping her policy documents about Indian educational reform. Soon, they were chatting about "oriental alphabets" and falling in love.[48] Tom, meanwhile, considered his penal code an appropriate gift for friends and family. He promised Ellis a copy. He also said he would bring one home to his middle sisters, Selina and Frances—although, he conceded, "it will have no interest for ladies."[49]

Macaulay's ungainly physique made him an odd presence at Parliament. He was, in the words of a contemporary, "a little man of small voice, and affected utterance, clipping his words and hissing like a serpent."[50] Presumably he appreciated oratory's power to distract from his body, making him a creature of words alone. His sisters played an active role in this transmutation. Margaret kept a scrapbook of her "poetic conversations" with her brother to record his brilliant but ephemeral speech for posterity.[51] Hannah became Tom's primary posthumous redactor and interpreter, editing and publishing multiple editions of his works later in the century. The public figure "Macaulay" was a family production.

So too was the intimate figure "Tom," who emerged through a different literary genre: the letter. In the early nineteenth century, letter writing was an aesthetic activity governed by printed style manuals, which recommended a spontaneous tone that, ironically, took several drafts to achieve.[52] Tom's letters are certainly literary in flavor: one precedes an account of a dinner party with a list of *dramatis personae*; another uses the *Odyssey* to frame his Indian exile.[53] They were also written at a transitional moment in postal history. The private letter as we now understand it is the historically contingent outcome of postal reforms of the late 1830s; where once letter recipients had to retrieve their mail from the local post office (and often read it aloud there), henceforth it would be delivered to the residential privacy of home.[54] Those reforms further banned the practice of franking, or sending letters for free under parliamentary privilege—as Tom did when writing to his sisters.[55] During the 1830s, systematizing Benthamites in India were enacting their own set of reforms, shutting down private letter carriers and integrating regional postal systems into a single colonial network.[56] The imperial mail conjoined these postal worlds, shuttling paper and ink between London and Calcutta on a sea voyage that took around six months.

Franz Kafka once described letter writing as a "dislocation of souls," a "communication of specters."[57] The time lag in the imperial mail meant that Tom experienced this dislocation with jarring literalness. His sisters were, in some very real sense, paper phantoms, their physical being displaced onto epistolary relics that structured a distanced intimacy predicated on the implied possibility of posthumous reading.

Letters were thus structurally akin to literature, with its more explicit promise of posthumous life. The two collided in the February 1835 letter to Ellis, where Tom confessed to being unmanned by Margaret's death. "I labor under a suppression of Greek," he wrote. Old books were a way to "converse with the dead," to "live amidst the unreal," to forget the funeral relic of the letter, to forget Margaret. They were the physical objects through which Tom tried to regain his status as independent man, to free himself from sweet bondage. And not just any books. Greek and Latin meant Oxbridge, upper classness, and male homosociality. They also, for Macaulay, had become the secularized carriers of a print-mediated Protestant ethic.

BOOKS BECOME EVERYTHING

In his "Minute on Education," Macaulay measured civilizations by their bookshelves. He also amassed quite a bookshelf of his own. Toward the end of his life, he counted more than seven thousand volumes in his personal library, including a few hundred inherited from his father.[58] At least some of these must have traveled with him to Calcutta (where he worried white ants would devour his library).[59] Books were Tom's most intimately physical of loves. Blood and soap still stain the copy of Thucydides he would read while being shaved in his Calcutta mornings.[60]

The Christmas that Hannah married, Tom wrote the dead Margaret to tell her about the "alteration" inside him. "My affections are shutting themselves up and withering.... My intellect remains and is likely, I sometimes think, to absorb the whole man.... Books are becoming everything to me. If I had at this moment my choice of life, I would bury myself in one of those immense libraries that we saw at the universities and never pass a waking hour without a book before me."[61] An ascetic's tool for dulling emotion, books sealed Macaulay inside a sort of paper tomb, making him the most independent man in the world.

Literary Orientalism, as is well-known, tends to encase "the East" in textual projections.[62] Macaulay was no Orientalist, at least not in the narrow sense of the term. He did, however, fortify himself against the colonial world with literature. He disliked India's streets ("the dark faces and bodies with white turbans and flowing robes, the trees not our trees, the very smell of the atmosphere.... I was quite stunned").[63] He disliked its colonial parties ("the conversation is the most deplorable twaddle that can be conceived").[64]

What he liked were the "good books for a library" he had bought at bookstalls before leaving London.[65] Homer, Virgil, Horace, Dante, Cervantes, Gibbon, Voltaire—the closest he got to India was James Mill.[66] Perversely, he used his subcontinental sojourn to pick up a reading knowledge of Portuguese; Hannah learned more Hindustani than her brother ever did.[67]

Macaulay's "Minute on Education," written in January 1835 in the throes of his grief about Margaret, sought to extend his bookish cloister to elite Indians, immunizing them against India too. This procedure could only ever partly succeed, of course. Indians could, in Macaulay's terms, become English in "taste," "opinions," "morals," and "intellect," but never in "blood" or "colour." The resulting gap between bodies and their cultivated moral acquirements would structure a historically specific formation of race and, with it, write the script for colonial mimicry.[68]

The ascetic labor of using physical books to place the physical fact of Indianness under textualized erasure was also a labor of secularization. If, as Viswanathan suggests, English literary education worked to create "non-Hindu Hindus" and "non-Muslim Muslims," it did so partly via reading, as a printed-mediated moral labor of self-cultivation.[69] By this account, Macaulay could be said to have used books to transform himself into a non-Christian Christian. His "secularizing genius," as Sullivan explains, lay in his ability to articulate a "Protestantism minus Christianity," an evangelical Indophobia "minus God and Bible."[70] This Bible-shaped hole was certainly apparent in his reading practices. Every day, during the three or four hours prior to breakfast, Tom religiously read the Greek and Roman classics. That was the precise period that his father had devoted to Bible study.[71] If the classics implied male friendship, biblical reading implied paternal authority. While at university, Tom wrote his father a letter promising that "if my life be a life of literature, it shall certainly be one of literature directed to moral ends."[72] He kept that promise, after a fashion.

His "Minute" moralized literature, reinventing Englishness as a moral property that could be extended even to non-English bodies—thus simultaneously solving a problem for Company secularism and also opening a conceptual space or gap within Englishness that colonial mimics would later widen (showing how the English failed to coincide with themselves).[73] "It is the duty of the British government in India to be not only tolerant but neutral on all religious questions," wrote Macaulay in the "Minute." By substituting Shakespeare for the Bibles used in Britain to mold the character of the working classes (or the Greek and Latin used to mold Oxbridge elites), English literary education appeared a religiously neutral means of converting Indians to colonial modernity. A "learned native" steeped in Milton, Locke, and Newton instead of the "sacred books of the Hindoos" will naturally abandon Hindu "hieroglyphics" for English and French science, the "Minute" proclaims.[74] Literature, Macaulay wrote his father, will redeem "idolaters" without "the smallest interference with religious liberty."[75] This refiguring of Englishness as a moral (i.e., juxta-religious affective) force emerged from within a particular formation of the secular.

As winter 1835 turned into spring, Tom turned from literature to law, from the "Minute on Education" to the Indian Penal Code. Were his legal labors also shaped by his literary asceticism, his post-Protestant readerly ethic? Perhaps. Macaulay did not just have a feeling for books. He used books to control feelings, both his own and others'. What better way to control emotion than with a penal code? His was certainly designed to suppress the "religious excitement" of Hindu and Muslim multitudes. It seems reasonable to suppose that he also used it to dampen his own feelings—laboring under a suppression of law to forget his grief.

Macaulay was not the only person in colonial India to develop a distinctive askesis of the book.[76] His print asceticism was distinctive, however, in its intersection with law and codification. As we saw in the previous chapter, early nineteenth-century legal codes participated in a sort of legal Protestantism, fetishizing the printed book's ability to hold the fundaments of law between tidy covers. They were secular-legal "bibles", sometimes displacing actual Bibles. In Macaulay's case, this bookish drama had a semi-Oedipal charge. He used law and literature to oust the father.

FATHER, SON, AND SECULAR EMPIRE

Secular empire was, for Macaulay, an oddly domestic project. Raised in the evangelical stronghold of south London's Clapham Common, Tom drifted from Christianity while at Cambridge (as by siding with blasphemers like Richard Carlile). By 1823, he was speaking gingerly of his family's "rigidly religious sentiments," especially his father's "utmost" evangelicalism.[77] Years later in Calcutta, he complained about Hannah's new husband Charles by noting that his "religious feelings" were "ardent . . . even to enthusiasm," "perhaps too much so for my taste."[78] The phrase "religious feelings" would recur in Macaulay's public writings, including the Indian Penal Code. The resonance is striking. It seems he was managing religious feelings at both an intimately familial and grandly political scale.

The Macaulay clan was shaped by empire long before Tom was born. His uncle Colin, a general in India, fought against Tipu Sultan and Hyder Ali in the Mysore Wars and was taken prisoner at the 1799 Siege of Seringapatam (a ten-year-old Tom wrote a poem for him).[79] For the Macaulays, however, empire mostly meant the Black Atlantic, that birthplace of modernity as "civilizational assemblage of race and religion."[80] This was certainly the case for Zachary Macaulay, reborn at sea. The son of a Scottish Calvinist minister, teenaged Zachary fell in with heavy-drinking Glasgow freethinkers. "David Hume was now my Oracle," he later lamented in an autobiographical fragment, and "to profane the sacred name of God, to prostitute His word to the purpose of exciting licentious merriment ... was my pastime."[81] Still young, Zachary moved to Jamaica to work as a bookkeeper on a sugar plantation. There, he was further corrupted by an innately wicked system of slave labor. "And yet so very a wretch was I, as to love and hug my Chains." It was only on his voyage home, as he sank into a gambling addiction, that he "heroically" resolved to "break the chain."[82] Following a common pattern, the white Atlantic traveler takes the chains of the enslaved as a metaphor for his spiritual redemption, his movement from sin to freedom.

Upon arriving back in Britain in 1789 and meeting his sister Jean's new husband, Thomas Babington, Zachary had an intense conversion experience. Hall describes the change as a sort of recivilization. The rustic Scot, further roughened by Jamaica, was born anew through the genteel Christianity of an English country house.[83] These English gentlefolk seem to have viewed Scotland as a colonial hinterland: when Babington married Jean Macaulay, his family compared him to an Arctic explorer returning home with "an Esquimaux bride"; he compensated by assiduously "improving" her savage brother.[84] It was Babington who introduced Zachary to the members of the Clapham Sect, a group of elite Anglicans orbiting William Wilberforce. And it was Clapham that introduced Zachary to his future wife, the Bristol Quaker Selina Mills, then studying under prolific tract-writer Hannah More.[85] Zachary and Selina remained apart while he campaigned for the abolition of slavery and served as governor of Sierra Leone, a colony for formerly enslaved persons. He wrote love letters to Selina while aboard the slave ships he was investigating, musing that though physically separated, the two were one in Christ and met "as often we go into His presence."[86]

These multiples histories of race and religion were inscribed on Zachary's eldest son from the moment of his birth. Thomas Babington Macaulay bore the name of the man in whose house he was born, the man who had civilized his father. He spent his childhood at Clapham, with its crisscrossing households, domestic affections, and voraciously intellectual children—children who spawned longstanding intellectual clans (a direct line connects Clapham to modernist Bloomsbury).[87] At age thirteen, Tom was sent off to school in what at first felt like exile. Hannah's earliest memories were of the "intense happiness" she felt on finding him home for Christmas.[88] Tom called the holiday "the festival not only of our religion, but of civilization, of morals, of toleration, of domestic happiness, of social courtesy." It encapsulated Christianity's "beneficial influence" on the world.[89]

As that description implies, Clapham was simultaneously an intimate and a geopolitical space, its domesticity a model for empire's civilizing mission. "The truth is that from that little knot of men emanated all the Bible Societies and almost all the Missionary Societies in the world," Tom later reflected.[90] "The Saints," as they were teasingly known, helped found the British and Foreign Bible Society and the Church Mission Society, and one of them (Charles Grant) authored an influential treatise urging the East India Company to allow Protestant missionaries into its territories.[91] The Claphamites were also fierce abolitionists, with Wilberforce now mostly remembered as Britain's great emancipator—the oratorical titan driving the 1833 abolition of slavery throughout the British empire (minus India, where caste-based agrestic slavery remained officially legal into the 1840s and was practiced for much longer).[92]

Abolition and civilizational missionizing went hand in hand. "God Almighty has set before me two great objects," Wilberforce wrote in a 1787 diary entry: "the suppression of the Slave Trade and the Reformation of Manners."[93] Freedom meant little without moral reform (as Zachary's narrative of spiritual redemption implied), such that these twinned objectives came to articulate one shared politico-moral and religio-racial field of action. When Tom broke with Clapham, he also abandoned the sect's antiracist commitments, as suggested by the overtly racist language in his letters and his recommendation that the Irish be "extirpated" like Indigenous Americans.[94] He did not, however, abandon Wilberforce's second objective—the reformation of manners. His "Minute on Education" may have used different nouns (taste, opinions, morals), but this was, in a sense, precisely its project. Macaulay simply secularized Wilberforce. Ever the Claphamite, he was still civilizing subjects.[95]

Tom too had once been forcibly civilized. In 1814, his namesake, Thomas

Babington, published a tract on Christian education that explained how schools should correct the "natural propensity of man to evil." Unlike Enlightenment optimists with their cheery belief in childhood innocence, Babington thought education should "crucify the flesh with its affections and lusts."[96] When this tract was published, Tom was already away at school. Still, it seems likely that some version of these ideas played a role in his Clapham upbringing. Wilberforce also believed that humanity was "tainted with sin" to the "very core," as demonstrated by Indigenous America's "barbarism."[97]

At Clapham, "the minutest faults of temper, manner, and social habits" were noticed and corrected.[98] Discipline and domesticity were inseparable, and this was perhaps especially true of Zachary. A model of Protestant punctiliousness and regimented routine, he enforced strict educational discipline on his children, perhaps anxious about his provincial family's class status.[99] Whatever the reason, he was the sort of father who wrote things like "unless you are thus docile and obedient, you cannot expect, my dear children, that Jesus Christ shd. [sic] love you."[100] A parent, he once wrote Selina, should apply "regular and constant discipline" to a child, correcting its "bad dispositions."[101] The child should emulate Jesus, a model (as he wrote Tom) of "self-denial and resignation and holy and cheerful obedience."[102]

Tom's manners were, reportedly, impeccable. At age four, a friend's servant spilled hot coffee on the tot, dressed in white trousers and a frill-throated green coat. When the hostess tried to console him, Tom dissuaded her: "Thank you, madam, the agony is abated."[103] At age six, when Selina explained that he should not expect bread and butter while at school, he swiftly replied, "No, mamma, industry shall be my bread and application my butter."[104] These hilarious tales are probably more family lore than historical fact; in actuality, Tom seems to have been an unhappy student who begged his mother to let him come home for lunch.[105] Still, precisely as lore, they are informative: the Macaulays, they suggest, placed a strong value on mannered words' power to suppress bodily pain.

Young Tom was a budding bibliophile. Hannah More first encouraged him to build a library ("you will one day, if it please God, be a man: but long before you are a man I hope you will be a scholar").[106] He "read incessantly, for the most part lying on the rug before the fire, with his book on the ground, and a piece of bread and butter in his hand." The parlor maid recalled his "expounding to her out of a volume as big as herself." He spoke in "quite printed words."[107] (Even as an adult, an acquaintance once described him as "a book in breeches.")[108] Tom's first publication, at age eleven, was an extract from Foxe's *Book of Martyrs*, printed in his father's journal, the *Christian Observer*.[109] At age thirteen, he wrote to his father to say he was "very much pleased that the nation seems to take such interest in the introduction of Christianity into India."[110]

Tom's childhood habitus—that is, his very flesh—was shaped from within by the dreams of a Christian empire. The savage child had been reformed in evangelical virtue, and thus in a civilizational assemblage of race and religion. Tom's boyhood schoolteacher came to Clapham to teach "Western civilization" to "African youths." Only when that project failed did he switch to educating white pupils.[111] There were, to be sure, other practices of the self that would have swirled around Clapham—not least class-based practices of politesse, civility, and good etiquette.[112] Still, Clapham had clearly honed its civilizing pedagogies through the racial capitalism of the Atlantic world. Its families were crucibles not just of sexuality, but also of religio-racial virtue—technologies for the conduct of self and others that could then circulate globally.

Macaulay tried to use empire to become an independent man, financially free of his father. He could never, however, be free of the disciplinary grooves that his father had, long before, etched into his disposition. His efforts at self-government simply dug those grooves deeper. It may be going too far suggest that Macaulay was more governed than governing. Still, precisely because his sense of manly self-rule always required external props and norms, it always involved him in the things he tried so hard to disavow: dependence, sentiment, sweet bondage. Tom was always already unmanned. He could not be otherwise.

CONCLUSION: THE ART OF SELF-GOVERNMENT

According to Jeremy Bentham, "the art of self-government" is the "private art" whereby a man directs his own actions, and it is necessarily linked to the parallel art of legislation, the art of governing others.[113] Ethics, or the principled practice of the self, is, in other words, intrinsically linked to law, an ethics generalized to the population. These are not just complementary tactics for ensuring the greatest happiness of the greatest number; they are constitutively intertwined.

Bentham's evangelical contemporaries were similarly "obsessed with conduct," both "their own and others," seeing personal influence as integral to the larger work of morally reforming society.[114] For them, one might say, personal relations were the matrix of all governmentalities, the register at which the "conduct of conduct" necessarily unfolded.[115] If the personal was political in each of these cases, the shape of this connection varied. For Bentham, ethics was the obverse face of legislation. For Wilberforce, it was the disciplinary complement to political freedom. For Macaulay, it was a crux of colonial governmentality, both in India and the Atlantic world.

In his 1837 draft Code, Macaulay wrote that "it is not to our virtue that the penal law addresses itself." The world, after all, would not require "penal laws if men were virtuous."[116] By suggesting that law regulates behavior where virtue fails to do so, Macaulay would seem to position law and virtue as distinct but complementary registers of governance. He thus understates the extent of their entanglement. The Macaulay Code did indeed address itself to virtue, and in at least two different ways. First, and most obviously, it set out to reshape Indian subjectivity, reforming manners to create a class of little Englishmen. Second, and much less obviously, Macaulay addressed the Code to his own virtue. During the two years he labored on it, it would have become incorporated into his practice of self-government, his bibliophilic suppression of pain. While it is impossible to know precisely what "use" Macaulay put this legal document to, one can cobble together a rough account by reconstructing the documents surrounding it on his bookshelf: Bibles, Greek and Latin classics, English literature, evangelical tracts, family letters. The Code was a public document, an instrument of the art of legislation. It was also part of the private self-government of Tom, its author and first reader.

This secret history of the Indian Penal Code found an epilogue of sorts in 2018, when the Supreme Court decisively modified jurisprudence around Section 377—which prohibits "carnal intercourse against the order of nature"—by exempting from its scope consensual intercourse between individuals of the same sex. Arguments against 377 drew on contemporary legal concepts (individual dignity, right to privacy, constitutional guarantee of equality before the law) that made the section seem like a fusty artifact of Victorian sexuality—as of course it is.[117] The section dates to the 1860 version of the Code, which lightly revised Macaulay's pre-Victorian 1837 language about "unnatural lust."[118] That language, meanwhile, as Hall suggests, strongly echoes Macaulay's epistolary confession of three years earlier: he had made "war on nature" in loving his sisters.

The question thus arises: In laying down the law on Indian sexuality, was Macaulay also laying down a law for himself? If so, did his attempted repression of desire actually function, as commonly happens, to incite more desire? These questions unsettle the public status of law, perhaps radically. They imply that the Indian Penal Code was a tool in a very intimate erotic game, a personal history concealed within its official prose. Would it then follow that any person whose sexuality is later regulated by the Code becomes implicated in that game too? Does law start to appear as the perverse extension of a long-dead family affair?

Whatever one makes of such open-ended questions, it bears noting that Macaulay's war on nature was not just the product of family desire. It was also, at least arguably, shaped by his era's reformist impulses—at once secular and religious, pressed deep into bodily habitus. For Macaulay, "nature" indicated not just that which must be obeyed, a biopolitical "law" implicit in the unchanging, ancient constitution of human bodies (as suggested in the 1834 letter to Margaret). Nature was also that which must be tamed. It was constitutively opposed to religion, or so suggested Thomas Babington in 1814, describing "religion [as] that which is, beyond all things, repulsive to the nature of man."[119] By this account, the whole point of evangelical Christianity is to make war on nature, especially in children, by disciplining nature toward virtue. If we take Macaulay as having transposed this model of pedagogy to India, then would it follow that the Indian Penal Code too made war on nature—seeking to civilize rustic bodies and thus replaying Macaulay's personal and family history at a geopolitical scale?

To pose such questions is by no means to suggest that this Macaulayan project succeeded. It is simply to try to find ways of rendering law's public documents strange unto themselves, more weirdly intimate than they appear at first glance. A gestalt shift of this kind is arguably necessarily if we want to get a clearer view of the history of secularism—a political project rooted in the reorganization of the intimate and articulated around the modern public/private distinction, which secularism works to naturalize and thus partly occlude. That distinction's historical contingency is explored in greater depth in the next chapter.

6

LIBELING RELIGION

Secularism and the Intimacy of Insult

BLASPHEMY, OBSCENITY, SEDITION, SLANDER—to open a reference work on libel law is to confront a rainbow of possible word crimes, and perhaps to wonder how this modern taxonomy of verbal offense came to be. The curious reader soon learns that the Latin word *libellus* denotes a small book. Entering common English usage in the early modern period, it indicated scandalous writing, both printed and handwritten.

Today, one can still correctly use the term in this broad sense by referring to "blasphemous libel," "seditious libel," "obscene libel," and more. If those phrases have an antiquated feel to them, however, that is because the primary meaning of *libel* shifted during the nineteenth century. So did the focus of libel law, which came to center paradigmatically on private defamation—slanders against the personal or professional reputation of individuals. (In most common-law jurisdictions today, libel is the written form of defamation and slander the oral form. This distinction was not firmly established until the early nineteenth century, and it was rejected by the Indian Penal Code. Here, to emphasize the historical plasticity of these concepts, I use the terms *libel*, *slander*, and *defamation* loosely and at times interchangeably.)

This remapping of libel law was implicated in the larger history of secularism. By distinguishing between blasphemy and sedition, libel law became one site for the conceptual disarticulation of the "religious" from the "political."[1] By criminalizing defamation and obscenity, it restricted the entry of "private" matters into "public," thus participating in the gendered demarcation of those separate spheres.[2] The history of blasphemous libel, then, spans the conjoined terrains of sex and secularism.

Circling around this unstable territory, this chapter sketches a concept history for an unholy quadrivium of word crimes (blasphemy, sedition, obscenity, and defamation), moving from early modern England to late nineteenth-century India to explore how a persistent set of "legal affinities" thwarted the efforts of treatise writers and colonial bureaucrats to keep these concepts distinct.[3] Where the previous chapter told a story about the intimacy of law by digging into a stash of private letters, this chapter pursues a complementary project, asking how the legal regulation of blasphemous speech extricated itself from the intimate in the first place—or, at least, how it tried to.

TOWARD A GENEALOGY OF BLASPHEMOUS LIBEL, OR, A DRUNKEN COMMUNION

"To create an offence is to make a law," observed Jeremy Bentham in 1782.[4] That is, the philosophical work of crafting concepts necessarily precedes the practical work of legislation and jurisprudence. This maxim serves as a useful epigraph for the history of libel law, wherein concepts can appear to be in a perpetual process of uncreation—rising, falling, merging, splitting, and otherwise contorting themselves for three centuries before finally settling down into the taxonomy of offenses familiar today.

There is not yet, to my knowledge, a comprehensive history of libel law from the sixteenth to the nineteenth century. The inquisitive scholar must thus consult a series of largely siloed literatures on blasphemy, sedition,[5] obscenity,[6] and personal defamation.[7] Taken together, these literatures reveal a tangle of antiquated crimes with exotic names (e.g., *scandalum magnatum*, the slander of great men) prosecuted across an interlocking warren of equally antiquated court chambers (ecclesiastical, Crown, Star Chamber, etc.). They also suggest at least two key periods of historical change.

The early modern period, especially the seventeenth century, saw a substantial remapping of libel law's conceptual landscape. This was the moment when Justice Matthew Hale redefined blasphemy, literally secularizing this ecclesiastical crime by claiming it for the Crown courts (see chapter 1). Nor was blasphemy alone in shifting from spiritual to worldly jurisdiction. Crown courts of this period were busily laying claim to an assortment of spiritual offenses (sodomy, witchcraft) and thus positioning themselves as sites for the moral regulation of the people.[8] One can see this pattern in the history of defamation law. Prior to around 1600, defamation was typically tried in ecclesiastical courts, where it was considered a crime for much the same reason it was considered a sin: it harmed the soul of the speaker. As defamation trials shifted to secular courts, their conceptual basis also shifted. The harm in defamation was increasingly understood to be to the honor or good name of the defamed. This was a gradual change—as late as 1662, a treatise writer could still denounce slander as a spiritual "disease" ("the iniquity of the Tongue, that little Member"), the recent preponderance of which was a clear sign of coming apocalypse.[9] And it was not yet a shift to a nineteenth-century notion of "reputation" as a form of property in self; early modern "honor" was hierarchical, even quasi-feudal.[10]

These seventeenth-century changes, articulating a historically specific formation of the secular, were linked to the rise of the printing press. New legal concepts and tools (such as registered authorship) were a means of regulating a proliferation of printed tracts and pamphlets criticizing the state.[11] Thus, in the seventeenth century, the old legal notion of treason was supplemented with a novel notion of "seditious libel." By the 1720s, the notion of "obscene libel" had also emerged as a means of restricting bawdier forms of writing—seeming to signal an epochal shift in Britain's sense of bodily decorum, tipping toward the Victorian.[12]

The crime of blasphemous libel kept shifting location during this period. It sometimes appeared as a quasi-political word crime, as in a 1678 treatise that defined blasphemy as "Treason against the Heavenly Majesty."[13] At other times, it seemed akin to defamation, as in a 1647 treatise that defined blasphemy as to "detract from God the honour due to him."[14] At still other times, blasphemy joined hands with obscenity. We have already encountered John Taylor, whose description of Jesus as a "whore-master" landed him in court in 1676 (see chapter 1). One might further consider a case like *Rex v. Curl* (1727), which hinged partly on the question of whether common-law courts had jurisdiction over the moral/spiritual crime apparently committed by the English publishers of *Venus in the Cloister* (1683), a classic of French anticlerical convent pornography.[15]

To see just how indistinguishable politics, religion, and the obscene body could be during this period, however, there is perhaps no case more illuminating than that of Charles Sedley. In 1664, this poet and two of his friends climbed drunkenly onto the balcony of a London tavern, pulled down their breeches, and "excrementized in the street." Stripping naked, Sedley then delivered a "mountebank sermon" and performed a mock communion in which he dipped his penis in a glass of wine, drank it, and then poured another to toast the health of the king. Somewhere in the process, he also enacted "all the postures of lust and buggery that could be imagined." Upon seeing this performance, the gathered crowd tried to break down the tavern door. When the door held, they instead pelted Sedley and friends with projectiles. Eventually, the trio were dragged to Westminster and fined. Sedley quipped that he was the first man in history "that paid for shitting."[16]

Sedley's phallic communion is often mentioned in histories of obscenity law. It could just as easily feature in histories of blasphemy or even sedition. A clear burlesque of the ritual theater of sovereign power by a noted court poet, Sedley's impromptu performance happened dangerously soon after the English Civil War, at a moment when the royal palace was rumored to be a den of rakish licentiousness.[17] Sedley was thus parodying the royal body and its Anglican liturgies to scandalous effect. In this sexual-scatological-theologico-political theater, there is no point in trying to distinguish between blasphemy, sedition, and obscenity, or, by extension, between the religious and political or the public and private. In this communion, these domains are most emphatically fused—a fusion that, to early nineteenth-century writers, would seem like a problem.

"THE LAW OF LIBEL! THERE'S NO SUCH THING."

"The law of libel! There's no such thing," complained an 1815 book reviewer after reading a flurry of recent treatises on the topic. Libel, he insisted, was just a "circumlocution-saving phrase," not "a description of an entity."[18] During the eighteenth century, libel law had apparently come to constitute what seemed like a single legal sphere, if an incoherent one. It was also a sphere under increasing pressure. The Crown leaned on libel law to suppress revolutionary sentiment and other forms of political dissent. Parliament eventually pushed back, passing Fox's Libel Act of 1792, which granted juries more power in libel cases.[19] Courts too started scrutinizing and clarifying libel law. Most notably, *Thorley v. Kerry* (1812) cemented the distinction between libel and slander—provoking the flurry of publications that exasperated our complaining critic.[20]

Although he did not realize it, our book critic was witnessing the emergence of a new configuration of libel law. The books he was reviewing, by "Messrs. George, Holt, Starkie, & Jones," were not the first libel treatises (that honor probably goes to a book from 1647).[21] They did, however, mark an important transitional moment in the history of libel law. In 1825, James Mill could still complain that there was "no definition of libel," with autocratic judges defining it however they pleased.[22] By 1881, when W. Blake Odgers published his *Digest of the Law of Libel and Slander*, Mill's complaint would have been less tenable. Modern defamation law had been born.[23] (Government authorities had also, starting around 1819, changed legal tactics, realizing that unlawful assembly was easier to prove than libel. By the early 1820s, they were charging famed blasphemer Richard Carlile with attracting nuisance crowds outside his shop window.)[24]

Treatises do not make law, but they do help make concepts or offenses. Notably, then, the flurry of libel treatises published after 1812 define and structure their topic in a motley multiplicity of ways. One sorts libel into seven categories, starting with libels against private character and then moving across the state, Christianity, and the public at large before finally arriving at the dead.[25] Another specifies ten different kinds of libel—against Christianity, morality, nations, the king, courts, magistrates, and more, before ending with private persons.[26] Some get quite philosophical. What is libel? asks one writer. A "medium of detraction." Libelous words work by "detracting from any given object." This includes not just the objects they describe, but the audiences they describe them to. Obscenity constitutes a libel on "the public at large" because it implies the public will "take pleasure" in smut. Blasphemy works similarly, presuming the public delights in sacrilege.[27]

Most of these treatises are now historical obscurities. The only one to have outlived its moment is Thomas Starkie's *Treatise on the Law of Slander and Libel* (1813), a standard reference work well into the twentieth century. Unlike his contemporaries, Starkie imposed a stark binary on libel law, dividing it into two branches: private wrongs, injuring the reputation of individuals, and public wrongs, attempting to "produce disorder in society."[28] Starting his book from the private, he arguably granted it implicit priority. In 1823, Starkie was elected Downing Professor of Law at Cambridge. From 1833 to 1849, he served on Henry Brougham's commission for the codification of English criminal law.[29] Perhaps because of this professional prominence, his treatise on libel became a classic. By 1844, it was being lauded as a "comprehensive and philosophical" survey of its topic.[30] In 1883, Lord Chief Justice Coleridge explicitly cited and praised Starkie (whom he had known personally) in *Ramsay*, taking Starkie's *Treatise* as the basis for his redefinition of blasphemous libel as a stylistic crime.[31] That citation, however, was possibly unusual in its attention to blasphemy. Other

Starkie fans followed his *Treatise* in presuming that "communications affecting public interests alone are not very accurately included under the law of defamation," and thus noting them only "cursorily" in surveys of this reputation-obsessed field.[32]

If Starkie pioneered the systematic bifurcation of libel into private and public, Odgers's 1881 *Digest* consolidated the job, joining Starkie as standard reference text. Although conceding that libel remains "practically impossible to define," Odgers does not seem particularly worried about this ambiguity.[33] Taxonomy, it seems, had made definition redundant. Odgers opens his *Digest* with the confident declaration that "no man may disparage or destroy the reputation of another."[34] Like Starkie, he prioritizes the personal. Thus, although the seven-hundred-plus pages to follow do include substantial chapters on sedition, obscenity, blasphemy, and *scandalum magnatum*, it would be difficult for a reader to see these public offenses as anything but vestigial inclusions. If, in the seventeenth century, blasphemy (i.e., "religion") cut across various discursive fields, it was in the 1880s contained to a single chapter of a book—a print-mediated formalization of the cultural logic of secularization-as-differentiation.

LIBEL IN THE COLONIES

Odgers's sidelining of public libels was not, however, the end of the story. To examine the history of statutory libel law in the nineteenth century is to discover a more complex picture—one where colony and metropole are, once again, thoroughly entangled. After the 1810s, reformers kept demanding more changes to libel law. Some of these demands were realized in Lord Campbell's Libel Act of 1843, which allowed for the prosecution of authors as well as publishers. Others shaped the Obscene Publications Act of 1857, which cemented the criminalization of pornography (and, in 1868, became the basis for the "Hicklin test," which defined obscenity around reader reception, not authorial intention—with *Regina v. Hicklin* holding that a work of anti-Catholic convent erotica from British-colonial Montreal would corrupt morals despite its publishers' insistence that their intention had been to reform them).[35] As usual, however, legal reformers had more success in the colonies, as seen in the strongly reformist defamation law that New South Wales enacted in 1847.[36]

The Indian Penal Code was part of this transcolonial process. In keeping with the recommendation of an 1843 House of Lords committee on libel reform, the 1860 Code eliminated the distinction between libel and slander—which Macaulay had already, in 1837, derided as "indefensible."[37] In fact, Macaulay mostly avoided using the word *libel*, preferring *defamation*. He parsed the harm in the latter in loosely Benthamite terms as the "pain" a person experiences when he "knows himself to be the object of the unfavorable sentiments of his fellow-creatures."[38] Disaggregating libel, Macaulay sorted word crimes according to their objects and arrayed them in a descending scale of publicity, from the state to the private individual. He also, in keeping with reformist proposals, allowed for justification in cases where defamatory claims are both true and in the public good and offered wide protection to criticisms of "a public servant in the discharge of his public functions" (inverting the logic of the older concept of *scandalum magnatum*, which had protected public men).[39] Law commissioners of the late 1850s then added the newly visible crime of obscenity to their revised Indian Penal Code (as Sections 292–4), with the final version of that document thus integral to the British empire's larger efforts at the moral regulation of medicalized, racialized, and gendered bodies.[40]

As an implicitly moral crime, obscenity was difficult to reconcile with the dictates of colonial secularism. The Code cued obscenity's conceptual proximity to religion by transitioning directly from the former (at the end of the chapter on "Offences affecting the Public Health, Safety, Convenience, Decency, and Morals") to the latter. It also carefully carved out special exemption within obscenity law for sexually explicit religious images in Hindu temples.[41] Obscenity law, with its biopolitical regulation of public morals, was part of the same Victorian formation of secularism that reframed blasphemy as a crime against decency (see chapter 1). In this formation of secularism, the lines separating the political, the religious, and the moral were quite murky. "There is as much difference between *religion* and *politics* as there is between *religion* and *morality*, and that is merely none at all," insisted one late-century conservative in arguing against permitting atheists to sit in Parliament.[42] He was, in a certain sense, right: religion, politics, and morality were porous cultural fields. Their continued interpenetration indicated not a failure of Victorian secularism, but the secret to its success—fueling the extension of what Hussein Ali Agrama calls secularism's questioning power, its insistent efforts to disentangle the religious from the secular. As new controversies arose in both Britain and India, these lines had to be continually renegotiated.

There are all kinds of stories to be told about religion and libel law in colonial India. The most famous trial is surely the Maharaj Libel Case (1862), which cited some of the Victorian libel treatises mentioned above.[43] To this, one might add historical episodes involving slandered Presbyterians,[44] defamed Parsi priests,[45] missionaries rumored to have abused orphans,[46] or perhaps even allegations of religio-racial impurity leveled at whole communities, like the Rangoon Parsis.[47] The archive of libel is an intimate archive, bringing gossipy tales about bodies, sexuality, and personal relations into luridly public light. It also (as case law tends to do) points in multiple directions not reflected in the relatively tidy realm of statutory legal codes and printed treatises.

Still, even that tidy world contains more mess than might be evident at first glance. Old legal concepts never really went away. They lurked in the wings, waiting to emerge—with early modern conceptual confusions resurfacing in the nineteenth century to fuel secularism's questioning power.

AMENDING THE CODE: FROM SEDITION TO BLASPHEMY

Or that, at least, is one way to narrate the fin de siècle history of the Indian Penal Code. After the Code became law in 1862, colonial officials quickly realized that its typology of word crimes was inadequate to the task of rule. They thus set about amending it. What followed was a tale of three amendments, each begetting the next in genealogical sequence: 124A (sedition, 1870) begat 153A (class hatred, 1898) begat 295A (religious feelings, 1927).[48] Especially in 1898, lawmakers found themselves retreading the early modern conceptual murk that early nineteenth-century libel theorists worked so hard to eliminate.

Our story begins with a clerical error. A hapless clerk allegedly lost the piece of paper on which the 1850s law commissioners had written their revision of Macaulay's 1837 sedition law, which was why the 1860 Code had no such section.[49] This was a problem. Throughout the 1860s, British bureaucrats were paranoid that seditious writing might spark a repeat of the 1857 "Mutiny." The very first round of amendments to the Code, in 1870, thus added a sedition law, appending it to a section about assaulting the governor-general (124). Championed by James Fitzjames Stephen, the new 124A's core language echoed Macaulay's ("to excite feelings of disaffection to the Government").⁵⁰ The limits of this language became evident, however, during prominent sedition trials of the 1890s. Judges and lawyers kept pressing at the word *disaffection*. What kind of emotion was this, precisely? Should it be construed as including "every form of bad feeling" toward the colonial state?[51]

In 1898, bureaucrats proposed adding the phrase "hatred or contempt" to 124A, hoping more emotion words might resolve the law's verbal ambiguity.[52] They had a hard time seeing an arguably more fundamental problem: a great deal of political speech in late nineteenth-century India was also religious speech, with consequently dubious legal status. In 1870, Stephen advocated for 124A by describing a man going from village to village "preaching a *Jehád* or holy war against Christians in India" (thus invoking the specter of the "phantom Wahhabi").[53] Paranoid government officials feared that Indian Muslims felt "bound in conscience to rebel against the Queen."[54] By the 1890s, imperial anxiety had partly shifted to Hindus, as seen in the legal prosecution of B. G. Tilak's *Kesari* and J. C. Bose's *Bangobasi*, which had both accused British colonialism of (as the *Bangobasi* put it) undermining "Hindu civilization and the Hindu religion."[55] The core conceptual quandary, however, remained much the same. Were such comments political or religious? Did dislike of British Christians imply disaffection toward British government? How could the colonial state prosecute such statements without seeming to infringe on religious liberty?

Colonial bureaucrats tried to resolve these quandaries by adding a new section to the Code, spun out of 124A. "It is a regrettably frequent practice," one explained, for Indian controversialists "to make violent assertions against classes of persons, and against classes of public officers, which would amount to gross defamation if made against individuals."[56] In Britain, these slanders would be prosecuted as defamation, which was once possible in India too, as seen in the 1861 *Nil Darpan* case (concerning the defamation of indigo planters as a class). Courts had recently confused the issue, however, making it advisable to create a new law protecting "a class or community" from injurious speech. Our bureaucrat described this offense as "general defamation" and "sectarian defamation" (we might now call it group defamation or even hate speech), and recommended appending it to Indian Penal Code Section 499, concerning the defamation of individuals.

When London responded to this Calcutta memo, the Secretary of State for India (George Hamilton) endorsed the idea of a group defamation law but proposed that it be added instead to Section 124A, as it seemed closely akin to sedition. In English law, Hamilton explained, "stirring up racial or class animosity" is treated as "a species of seditious libel" and the same principle should hold for India.[57] The Calcutta bureaucrats did as instructed. They put forward a bill amending 124A to penalize not just words that "excite hatred, contempt, or disaffection" toward the Queen, but also those that "promote feelings of ill-will between different classes" of her subjects.

The game of conceptual pinball was, however, just starting. When the expanded 124A was sent to committee, its members objected that it conflated two distinct offenses—a direct crime against the state and a crime that affects the state only indirectly by stoking breaches of the peace. The committee also rejected the analogy to English law, suggesting that common law's conflation of sedition and group defamation "is probably due to historical causes and has nothing to do with logical arrangement." They thus decided to create an entirely new section within the Code's chapter on "Offences against the Public Tranquility." The new 153A, appended to a section about provoking riots (153), would stipulate punishment for promoting the riot-adjacent feelings of class enmity or hatred.[58] Some committee members cautioned that 153A was a "dangerous" threat to free speech. Others objected that it was redundant with the Code's religion chapter.[59]

AN INSTINCT TO THRASH

They were likely right on both counts. Twenty-five years later, these issues surfaced yet again when the failed prosecution of Mahashe Rajpal under 153A prompted the creation of 295A. Retreading much the same conceptual ground as 153A but from within the legal domain of "religion," this law too was immediately decried as a danger to free speech.

It would have been far better, argued legal scholar Hari Singh Gour, to have fashioned the new law as an addendum to 153A or even 124A rather than 295. The Indian Penal Code was, he said, a "most unscientific enactment" in that it delineated four distinct types of defamation (of the state, a class, religion, and a person) and dispersed them across its entire length when it should have grouped them into a single chapter so as to more effectively set limits on their prosecution.[60] Nineteenth-century Benthamites would have bristled at being called unscientific. Gour tried to outscientize them, effectively replaying nineteenth-century reformist debates to produce a more rational arrangement of libel law—a doomed endeavor insofar as the cultural field of injurious speech necessarily exceeds the ability of legal categories to describe it and thus prompts ongoing renegotiation of those legal categories.

Popular discussion of the 1920s reflected the persistent porousness of legal concepts. Section 295A, objected one newspaper, created "in the field of religion a new offence analogous to that of sedition in politics."[61] It would, in the words of a member of the Legislative Assembly, result in people getting charged "with sedition against many modern gurus and saints."[62] A likely malapropism, this comment makes the personal political in a comically literal way, with slander, sedition, and blasphemy fully fused.

The legal affinity between blasphemy and personal defamation was front and center during the Rajpal affair. In acquitting Rajpal under 153A, the Lahore High Court held that the *Rangila Rasul* was a slander against the Prophet Muhammad in his private (or, as the Hindi press translated, *niji*) capacity but not therefore also a slander against Islam or Muslims.[63] Rajpal was guilty of personal defamation, and that was all. Although this decision overturned lower court rulings, it also in a sense followed their conceptual lead. In 1924, a local magistrate decided to permit "evidence showing that the pamphlet was based on historical facts and was published for the public good"—contributing to the protracted length of the trial by allowing expert testimony about Muhammad's life.[64] Such testimony would, presumably, have been of dubious relevance to a 153A case centered on class enmity. It would certainly have been relevant to a libel case. The magistrate was, in effect, trying to assess whether the libel was justified.

Libel law also remained an important framework for public discussion in the months after the Lahore court ruling. The Legislative Assembly, for instance, considered adding libel-style language about truth and the public interest to 295A, or perhaps scrapping 295A entirely and instead adding a new defamation section to the Code.[65] In a suggestively comparative move, the Lahore and Karachi papers pointed to a recent British court case as offering a potentially useful analogy to *Rajpal v. Emperor*.[66]

The case, *Wright v. Gladstone* (1927), concerned a book that revived old rumors that former prime minister William Gladstone had fathered an illegitimate child, romanced a Russian spy, and otherwise pursued "every sort of woman" under cover of his morally upright public image. The late Gladstone's sons were incensed, but because defamation of the dead was not a crime in Britain, they could not file a libel suit against the book's author, Peter Wright. Instead, they libeled him so thoroughly that he had no choice but to bring a suit against them. The resulting trial cleared their father's good name and ruined Wright.[67] In reporting on this case, the Lahore *Muslim Outlook* and Karachi *New Times* drew an implicit analogy between Gladstone and Muhammad, a "political" figure and a "religious" one, conjoined around the intimacy of family feeling. When one of the Gladstone sons took the witness stand in court, he was handed a passage from Wright's book. As the *Muslim Outlook* reported, he "flushed and clenched his fist," exclaiming, "It is a revolting passage which angered me, almost to an ungovernable extent."[68] This scene closely echoes the accounts of offended readers like Muhammad Daud Ghaznavi (see chapter 2) reported by the Indian press that summer. On the witness stand, Gladstone and Ghaznavi experienced similarly "ungovernable" affects. They were overcome by emotion.

To compare *Rajpal* to *Wright v. Gladstone* is to think across the line separating religious feelings from political ones. It is also to confront an important legal difference between 1920s India and Britain. Was it a crime to defame the dead? In early modern Britain, legal authorities like Edward Coke and William Blackstone held that it was: libel was criminal insofar as it risked breaches of the peace, and libeling the dead could certainly provoke living family to revenge. Nineteenth-century legal theorists thought differently. "The dead have no rights and can suffer no wrongs," proclaimed James Fitzjames Stephen in 1887. They thus, he reasoned, cannot be libeled.[69] Critics immediately noted the emotional weirdness of this claim; the dead, after all, are intrinsically connected to the living.[70] Nonetheless, Stephen's claim set precedent for decades to come—in Britain anyway. The Indian Penal Code, by contrast, did in certain cases criminalize defaming the dead. The 1837 version explicitly stated that "a deceased person may be defamed," even as its appendices expressed discomfort with using breach of the peace as defamation's conceptual basis (suggesting that a shift in legal concepts was underway).[71] The 1860 Code cemented this shift by rejecting breach of the peace as its standard and instead defining defamation around reputation. Nonetheless, it still criminalizes defamation of the dead in instances where it is "intended to be hurtful to the feelings of his family or other near relatives."[72] It said nothing about the dead's religious devotees.

Comparing to *Wright v. Gladstone* to *Rajpal v. Emperor* raises the question, however, of whether slanders of the familial dead and slanders of the holy dead are similarly hurtful to the feelings of the living. Are these similarly intimate emotions, with the Prophet Muhammad functioning as a kind of kin, written into the very body of the devout subject? Such parallels were certainly drawn in 1927. Justice Dalip Singh, after all, had given his proposed law the number 297A—appending it to the section about trespassing on burial places, disrupting funerals, and performing "indignities" on corpses. The essence of offense, he would thus have implied, is desecration of the dead.

This comparison could potentially pull "religious feelings" in several different directions. One of them, in the 1920s, was increased privatization—a further reframing of religious affect via the classed and gendered domain of bourgeois domesticity. Perhaps the *Muslim Outlook*'s and *New Times*'s implicit comparison of devotional to filial feeling tended in this direction. A slightly earlier comparison certainly had.

As it happens, the judge who presided over *Wright v. Gladstone*, Justice Horace Avory, also presided over the trial of the last man in Britain jailed for blasphemy—the 1921 trial of John Gott. There, Avory explicitly reframed blasphemy via personal defamation. To ensure that even a "lukewarm Christian" could understand the harm in blasphemous speech, Avory asked the gentlemen of the jury to imagine "you received by post some abominable libel upon yourself. . . . What is your first instinct? Is not the instinct of every man who is worthy of the name of a man—the instinct is to thrash the man or the woman who has written a libel on him?"[73] Painting a scene of privatized media reception, Avory described a libelous publication arriving by post to impugn gentlemanly honor and thus disrupt the self-enclosure of the bourgeois home. Like libel, Avory implied, blasphemy is personal. It gets under the skin.

Avory's redescription of blasphemy as personal libel totally altered the classed and gendered specificity of Gott's alleged crime. He and other members of the Socialist Freethought League had been carrying rationalist placards and distributing birth control pamphlets in the streets of east London while fending off mixed-sex hecklers ("Disgusting! Disgusting!" "You ought to be ashamed of yourself").[74] The transposition from public street to bourgeois privacy, then, is key to how Avory redefined religious feeling, a minor reworking of Coleridge's crime against decency. A theologico-political offense had already become a sentimental offense, linked to the cultural regulation of emotion. Now it was reterritorialized yet again, routed through personal defamation.

The crime of blasphemous libel, as we have seen, spills outward into a historical game of conceptual pinball in which an interconnected cluster of mobile legal terms (blasphemy, sedition, obscenity, defamation) keep bouncing off one another, recombining component parts in the process. Nor did this game end in the 1920s. In the 1970s and '80s, for instance, Pakistani judges reinterpreted blasphemy law once again, this time via trademark and copyright law—making Islam a kind of neoliberal intellectual property.[75]

Avory's words—an "instinct to thrash"—are a fitting place to close this discussion. Blasphemous speech, he implied, elicits ungovernable affect. This feeling is simultaneously secular and religious, public and private, British and Indian. It also fuses bodies to printed texts in ways that will be explored further in part III.

III

POLEMICS AS ETHICS

SECTION 295A WAS NEVER QUITE SURE what kind of law it was. It was definitely not a blasphemy law, as Hari Singh Gour and M. R. Jayakar reminded their Legislative Assembly colleagues in 1927. Since the 1830s, after all, the Indian Penal Code had been a site for reconceptualizing this common-law crime as a purely secular offense. It was also not a personal defamation law, extending special legal protections to prophets, avatars, saints, gurus, godlings, founders, reformers, and other sacred personalities—much to the frustration of those who rallied behind the "Respect for All Prophets" movement. We now, coming out of part II, can see the state's misrecognition of this movement's demands more clearly. Insults to sacred persons produce intimate affects. They are not quite blasphemy, as public crime. Neither are they quite like libel, as private offense. Rather, they hover uneasily in the liminal space between the two.

To more clearly see the intimacy of such insults, we need to leave law behind—opening the doors of the 1927 Legislative Assembly to explore the world outside. There, in Shimla's lower bazaar, one would have found a thriving branch of the Arya Samaj, the religious society that published the *Rangila Rasul* or "merry Prophet." Established in 1882, the Shimla Samaj had, by the 1920s, attracted several hundred members, a roster of doctors, bankers, and traders that ran a temple and two schools and played a prominent role in local politics.[1] To understand the affective force of secular law, we need to presume that the history of "political" bodies like the Assembly is constitutively intertwined with the history of "religious" bodies like the Samaj.

The Rajpal affair was a bad romance, a dance between two texts, one "legal" (295A), the other "religious" (*Rangila Rasul*). Where part II constructed a history of the former, part III does so for the latter, diving deep into Arya Samajist polemics between the 1870s and 1920s. Rather than trying to provide a comprehensive account of the Samaj, I approach the Aryas as integral to the history of Indian secularism (thus building on Cassie Adcock's pioneering work).[2] This Arya history might strike some readers as excessively local or particular. Only by attending to the particular, however, can we as scholars begin to invert the abstracting impulses of Benthamite law. What would it look like, I ask, to take the *Rangila Rasul* as a text truly parallel to 295A, its import (theoretical, not practical-legal) just as general as that of its counterpart?

To pose this question is to ponder the relationship of law to other normative mechanisms for shaping or governing human behavior. It is to ask about law and culture (in the early nineteenth-century sense of self-cultivation) or law and ethics. In the nineteenth century, the seemingly depoliticized domain of ethics was often a repository for forms of law denied official status by colonial-modern states busily delegitimizing the legal pluralisms that preceded them. Ethics was also a site for generating new forms of politics. To gesture to the breadth of this scene, I use the word *ethics* capaciously and in a loosely Foucauldian sense to indicate a structured practice of the self that spills outward into networks of governmentality (i.e., the conduct of conduct, both of oneself and others) wherein the modern state apparatus is just one node.

In developing this notion of ethics, part III extends part I's argument about low or governmental secularism. Because governmentality as modern political rationality proliferates lines of governance that crisscross "state" and "society" (resulting in a societalization of the state and statification of society), a governmental secularism cannot be adequately studied from the vantage of the state alone. Rather, one needs to ask how state power becomes salient from within society. One would thus, for instance, trace how the quasi-physical force implicit in legal words combines with other types of quasi-physical verbal forces—like the force of affect. In pursuit of such questions, I argue that religious polemics in late colonial India can be productively understood as a mode of ethics. That is, polemics exerted an affective force that was intrinsically connected to the work of moral reform and that overlapped with the pedagogic-behavioral regimes of colonial law.

My use of the term *ethics* thus departs slightly from Michel Foucault's oft-cited discussion of ethics as a practice of freedom, not only in emphasizing how the ethical subject is necessarily situated within larger structures of governance (a fully Foucauldian point) but also in approaching this set of problems via affect theory (which becomes a means of partially reframing a Foucauldian account of subjectivation). The ethical self is shot through with lines of force, making the subject of ethics a fissiparous subject. Whether we describe this force as moral force (recalling M. K. Gandhi and J. F. Stephen) or whether we call it affect, it often was carried by traveling words that, in turn, were integral to the "moral languages" (Arya Samaj, Singh Sabhas, Ahmadiyya, etc.) taking off in Punjab in the late nineteenth century.[3] This affective force's history is thus also a history of media forms. Force lines established power relations, structuring a capillary micropolitics that could enter into assemblage with the macropolitical structures of colonial rule—which likewise relied on moral force, as through the "gospel of law" (see chapter 1).

To see these fields as constitutively intertwined is, in concrete terms, to work toward the following argument. The *Rangila Rasul* was not just an object of governance, the target of legal secularism. It was also an instrument of governance, a paper tool devised to govern the behavior of a Vedic nation.

The arc of part III runs as follows. Chapter 7 develops an account of the Aryas' aptitude for insult, asking how libidinally cathected print media became carriers of moral or affective force. (As in chapter 5, media theorist Friedrich Kittler is a subterranean presence.) Chapter 8 asks how the affective force conveyed by religious polemics conjoined with the force of law, or a culturalized version thereof, with Samajists crafting a sort of Arya doppelgänger of the Indian Penal Code. In Arya controversies, the political became personal in a quite specific way: legal force was used to produce shifts in the field of personal relations (the decisive field for shaping the conduct of conduct, and thus the matrix of all governmentalities). Chapter 9 continues this archaeology of personalist slander by reconstructing a slightly different historical archive—that of comparative prophetology, the condition of possibility for both the *Rangila Rasul* and the "Respect for All Prophets" movement. With attention to the transnational circulation of middlebrow texts and popular images, I suggest that the cultural formation "world religions" was a structure of feeling predicated on sacred personalities. Across all three chapters, I work to uncover a cultural history of secularism that emerges from the printed word, the graphomaniacal body, and the popular practice of comparative religion.

This cultural history of secularism is, crucially, closely connected to practices of controversial speech. My argument on this front is connected to my somewhat atypical presentation of the Arya Samaj. Typically, the Aryas appear in scholarship primarily as progenitors of Hindu nationalism. That is not incorrect. Still, to foreground that lineage is potentially to flatten a more complex historical landscape. To restore some of this complexity, I resuscitate minor scenes of Arya life often sidelined by political histories (Cantonese cobblers, quick-witted colonels). I also ask how the microhistoriographical problem of Arya religion indexes a larger theoretical problem about the conceptualization of "excessive" or "fanatic" religious speech.

To typecast the Aryas as fundamentalist demagogues is to risk reinscribing a classically liberal bifurcation of speech into the good and the bad (persuasion vs. coercion, deliberation vs. polemic) that, in turn, relies on an implicit bifurcation of speech and bodies. By presuming that all words necessarily produce something like physical force, I mean to shift the ground of this liberal problem-space so that new and more productive questions can come into view. Rather than "fanatic" speech appearing as liberalism's constitutive other, we see how a certain form of secular subjectivity emerged via gendered, racialized, and caste bodies and their intimate relations with print and other media objects.

7

PRINTING PAIN, RULING SENTIMENT

A Brief History of Arya Insult

SOMETIME AROUND 1910, AN INDIAN SOLDIER bested his white lieutenant in a round of wits. Annoyed, the lieutenant reported the insubordination to his colonel, who then summoned the offending Indian. "Well, Badmash [scoundrel] Arya Samajist, why did you speak rudely to the sahib?" "[But] I am a Mussulman, Sir!" the soldier protested. He could hardly, that is, be a member of a Hindu organization known for its anti-Muslim rhetoric. This deflection should have sidetracked his opponent. Yet the colonel—not one to be bested at badinage—persisted, unfazed: "Well then! You are a Mussulman Arya Samajist!"[1]

A sort of Arya urban legend, this narrative has the streamlined quality of a twice-told tale, culminating in a comic punchline. Its lesson, our storyteller explains, is that "nowadays a plain outspoken man and an Arya are considered to be synonymous terms." Arya Samajists used this story and others like it to demonstrate how the British colonial state routinely persecuted their religious society, thus violating its own principle of noninterference in religion. The joke, however, has a doubled edge in that it implicates Aryas too—which is why the punchline lands. By 1910, Samajists were so infamous for their aptitude at insult that it seemed comically plausible to use the word *Arya* as a kind of meta-insult, denoting serial insulters.

A single instance of Arya insult sits at the center of this book's account of religiously injurious speech. To understand the *Rangila Rasul*—or merry Prophet, the 1924 tract written anonymously by one Arya Samajist (Pandit Chamupati) and published by another (Mahashe Rajpal)—we need to situate it within the Aryas' larger penchant for pugnacious speech. In doing so, we should also reconsider standard narratives about "fanatic" or "excessive" religion. Too often, Arya insult has been read as evidence of antisecular or even fundamentalist religious intolerance, a handy synecdoche for communalist hate speech as such.[2] The Aryas themselves told a different story. Their polemics, they said, demonstrated truth-seeking plainspokenness. There was, to be sure, some irony in a society dedicated to the Vedas (texts not known for their verbal transparency) championing plain speech.[3] Still, the Aryas were not wrong. Their insults were as much in the tradition of Enlightenment raillery and Victorian freethought as of religious fundamentalisms. Or, at least, Arya insult forces us to confront our tendency to separate the "secular" from the "religious" by sorting speech into two tidy piles, the rationalist and the fanatic.

To explore a different model, I argue that Arya polemics were a mode of ethics. That is, Aryas used bellicose (*polemikós*) words to shape the character (*ethos*) of self and others. Words exert force. Aryas used this force relationally to direct human conduct in the name of social, cultural, and religious reform. This spiritual-semiotic governance acted on and through human bodies implicated in structures of caste, gender, and sexuality, as well as religion. The Aryas sought to reshape this intimately corporeal terrain, and they used lampoons on prophets, saints, and other sacred personalities to do so.

A VEDIC MODERNITY

A central factory of global religious modernity, nineteenth-century India produced a plethora of new religious movements that eventually spanned the world—spreading from Cairo to Tokyo, Fiji to Berlin, Johannesburg to Los Angeles. The Arya Samaj (Noble Society) was a major player on this transnational scene. Founded in 1875 by Swami Dayananda Saraswati, a wandering Hindu ascetic, the Samaj taught that present-day Hinduism was a debased corruption of humanity's original Vedic religion. India's religious decline prompted a parallel political decline, allowing invading Muslims and later the British to conquer the subcontinent. To fashion a shining future, India would thus have to disavow its gods and goddesses, its temples and pilgrimages. What others saw as the eternal religion, or *sanatana dharma*, the Aryas dismissed as so much "Brahmanic balderdash."[4]

Although founded in Bombay, the Samaj rose to prominence further north in Punjab, which Dayananda (Saraswati is his religious order, not his surname) first visited in 1877.[5] (By the 1920s, people joked that "nearly all of

Punjab's educated Hindu population is Arya Samaji, whether their names are in the Arya Samaj's register or not.")[6] Over the following decades, it established itself across north India and, starting in the late 1890s, in diaspora locations from Fiji to Trinidad. Aryas managed this geographic sprawl with an institutional structure that mirrored the bureaucratic divisions of the modern state—and, like the state, produced bureaucratic paperwork, such as manuals of procedural bylaws.[7] Local samajes were federated into regional Arya Pratinidhi Sabhas (representative assemblies) that were in turn coordinated by a Sarvadeshik Arya Pratinidhi Sabha, an international Arya assembly.[8] Like most new religious movements, the Arya Samaj fractured as it grew, with the major break happening in 1893 between two factions that came to be known by the names of the educational institutions that they ran: the "College Party" (associated with meat, English, and the Dayanand Anglo-Vedic College in Lahore) and the "Gurukul Party" (associated with vegetarianism, Hindi, and the Gurukul Kangri in Haridwar).

The Samaj succeeded, the historians tell us, because it appealed to culturally discombobulated urbanites who were grateful to find Hindu tradition and colonial modernity wrapped in a single sacred package.[9] Discombobulation, however, was not so easily resolved. Aryas dreamed of Vedic antiquity erupting into the colonial present to redeem India from its more recent past. Its Vedic modernity was thus founded on anachronism and temporal rupture, with ancient steampunk sages wielding Victorian technology and Krishna traveling to America by steamboat.[10] The disjunctive temporality of this archaic modernity can be seen quite literally on the title pages of Arya publications, torn among competing calendars—Christian, Vikrami-Hindu, and Shrishtisamvat, dating to creation itself (e.g., 1888, 1945, and 1,960,852,988).[11]

The Aryas and their archaic modernity were important progenitors of the Hindu right that coalesced in the 1920s.[12] V. D. Savarkar, the author of the *Essentials of Hindutva* (1923), was an avid reader of Dayananda, probably first encountering his work at London's India House, run by the Arya Samajist radical Shyamji Krishnavarma.[13] One should not, however, reduce the Aryas to that inheritance. They can just as plausibly be claimed for the Hindu left.[14] Consistent critics of caste and advocates for women's education, the Aryas' most visible legacies in contemporary India are their myriad schools and their reinvented Hindu wedding ceremony (a ritually minimalist event sometimes described as the Hindu equivalent of a secular wedding).[15] The Aryas were key players in radical political networks that stretched from Punjab to California and linked Indian anticolonial revolutionaries to socialists, anarchists, and leftist intellectuals worldwide.[16] Some used this transnational frame to critique caste injustice at home, as by comparing brahman "supremacy" to the white retrenchment of the Reconstruction-era United States.[17] Maybe some Aryas managed to resolve the society's political contradictions. More likely, the Samaj provided an ideologically flexible space wherein bomb-wielding anarchists could hobnob with celibate pandits. It is important, I think, to preserve this complexity, lest we make Hindu nationalism seem more historically ineluctable or ideologically coherent than it actually is.

The Samaj's eclecticism could surprise even Aryas themselves, perhaps especially at the local level. In 1924, one ordinary Arya—a Ferozpur lawyer named Vishnudutt—traveled to Dalhousie, another then-Punjabi town (now in Himachal Pradesh), to attend the local Samaj's anniversary celebration or *varshikutsav* (the Arya calendar was dotted with these events). Staying afterward for a short holiday, Vishnudutt was surprised to hear rumors of a "Chinese Arya" who could be seen every morning performing ablutions in a local canal before doing the *sandhya* ritual. One morning, he went to investigate and was delighted to find that the rumors were true. There the man was, sacred thread and all. Vishnudutt convinced Aishashan (as Vishnudutt wrote his name) to sit for an interview later that day. Aishashan explained that he had come to Punjab from Canton in 1907 to work as a bootmaker. After a shopkeeper friend invited him to join the Arya Samaj, he started wearing Indian clothes, including a turban, and learning Sanskrit mantras (although he remained anxious about his pronunciation). He even became vegetarian. An excited Vishnudutt hoped that Aishashan's story augured well for the Aryas, indicating that Vedic religion could spread in China. He closed the interview by pelting Aishashan with questions: Are there printing presses and books in China that report on India and other countries? (A: Yes, of course.) What religions are in China? (A: Mostly Buddhists.)[18]

To find a Chinese Arya living in Punjab was, of course, unusual. It also resonated with the Arya Samaj's globalist aspirations. Pandit Chamupati, the *Rangila Rasul* author and editor of the Arya monthly that printed Vishnudutt's interview, would himself travel to British East Africa a year later, in 1925. There, he promoted Vedic religion to diaspora Indians as well as, apparently, Maasai, Kikuyu, and other African audiences who might be persuaded to join the Samaj in its Vedic modernity. Chamupati's celebration of Dayananda as a "cosmopolitan sage" was caught up with this globalist project.[19] So too was his polemic demotion of Muhammad to a status beneath that of the celibate swami.

VEDIC PUBLICITY: MEDIATING THE ARYA PUBLIC

If such polemics provoked controversy, there was nothing new in this. Vedic modernity had been contentious from the start. To build up the Vedas was to tear down everything else, and the Aryas were heavily invested in both projects, *mandan* and *khandan*. Thus, Dayananda's magnum opus, the *Satyarth Prakash* (*Light of Truth*, 1883) spends ten chapters explicating Vedic texts and describing the ideal Vedic society before, in its final four chapters, polemically attacking the major anti-Vedic sects (*vedviruddh mat*): the *purani*, *jaini*, *kirani*, and *kurani* religions—Puranic Hinduism, Jainism, Christianity, and Islam. Note the order. The book's polemic against Hinduism comes first and, in sheer size, dwarfs everything to follow. The chapters on Christianity and Islam were literally an afterthought.[20] Although they later became famous for anti-Muslim rhetoric, the Aryas sharpened their tongues on traditionalist Hindus, whom Dayananda railed against at pilgrimages like the Kumbh Mela and in traditional centers of learning like Banaras. Even the word *Arya* implies an argument: it displaces the word *Hindu*, marking a religious identity defined by its polemic departure from the Puranic past.

Aryas talked about their polemic activities in various ways, but if there was an organizing term for their efforts, it was *vedprachar*. They tended to translate this as "Vedic propaganda," presumably echoing propaganda's longstanding association with Christian missions rather than the more "sinister meaning" (to quote a 1929 source listed in the *Oxford English Dictionary*) that attached to it in the early twentieth century. I opt for the more neutral "Vedic publicity," thus stressing the resonance between the etymology of *prachar* (going forth) and a classic account of media publics as collectivities defined by the diffusive circulation of texts.[21] Vedic publicity, I suggest, organized a historically distinct discourse network or inscription system—that is, a tangle of technologies for recording and reproducing words and other signs. These technologies include the speaking human body (refracted through race, caste, and gender) as simultaneously a condition and an effect of shifting media networks.[22]

For millennia, Vedic hymns had been oral-only, transmitted from father to son within particular brahman families through highly disciplined (and remarkably accurate) recitation practices.[23] Although speech (*vach*) was sometimes figured as female, Vedic speech acts were inseparable from brahman male mouths.[24] The brahmanical body was a communications medium and its specific affordances were crucial to defining the sanctity of the Vedas. By restricting their circulation, it safeguarded them from the ritual pollution associated with other kinds of mouths, whether female or subordinated caste. Indeed, the brahman was arguably defined around an ideal of pure speech that took the unspeaking body (associated with Dalits, as figure for pure physicality) as its extimate other—with writing, or touchable speech, thus occupying an ambivalent site within the brahmanical sensorium.[25]

Dayananda upended this discourse network by transposing the Vedas into what, in 1870s India, was still a novel medium—the printed book. Aware of this novelty, Aryas often featured stacks of Vedic books in their visual art, a key iconographic attribute of Dayananda's saintly body as recorded in photographs and then reproduced in other lithographed images. Oral "texts" become paper objects, stacked neatly on an ornate side table (see figure 5). Indian scribes and pandits had, of course, cherished manuscripts for centuries, and in some ways print simply intensified this old affection.[26] Still, printed books were different. Print inscribed the Vedas onto paper, turning them into machine-made objects that anyone, in principle, could touch. At first, efforts to print *shruti* verses ("that which is heard," the most sacred class of Hindu "texts" or "scriptures") discomfited traditionalists, who worried that cheap paper might pollute or demean these sacred sounds.[27] Even as religious traditionalists embraced print, they continued to view it as conspicuously modern, surrounded by such novel literary genres as the preface.[28] Print was tinged with empire. Since the 1810s, Protestant missionaries had been proliferating print artifacts at an astonishing pace. In the 1860s, a single missionary group in Punjab, the US-based Ludhiana Mission Press, printed 1.3 million books, distributing twenty-five thousand at the Kumbh Mela alone.[29] Orientalist scholars pushed print too, synergizing with the missionaries. Tellingly, Dayananda probably first encountered the *Rig Veda* in book form in 1866, when a missionary showed him Max Müller's translation. He later, in the *Satyarth Prakash*, lambasted Müller. Still, Orientalist bookishness was hard to resist: the Gurukul Kangri went on to collect multiple volumes of Müller's *Sacred Books of the East* series.[30]

Aryas proliferated paper—books, tracts, pamphlets, magazines, news-

श्रीमद्दयानन्दचिववावलौ

गुरुवर
महर्षि श्रो स्वामी दयानन्द सरस्वतो ।
(इस चित्रका फोटो महाराजा शाहपुरा से प्राप्त)

(यज्ञळम)　　　　　　　　　　　(क)

FIGURE 5. "Maharishi Shri Swami Dayanand Saraswati" (Is Chitra ka Photo Maharaja Shahpura se Prapt) (Maharishi Shri Swami Dayananda Saraswati, based on a photo taken by the Maharaja of Shapura). Shitalprasad Vaidya, *Shrimaddayanand Chitravali* (Calcutta: Vedic Pustakalaya, 1925). © The British Library Board. Shelfmark Hin.D.1519.

papers, leaflets, handbills, letters, telegrams, and more, only a fraction of them literally "Vedic." They also made and circulated lithographed and other images, including magic lantern slides.[31] Their built environment was adorned with words, with gold-lettered banners festooning mandir (temple) walls and reading rooms adjoining these ritual spaces.[32] These texts were notably multilingual. The Aryas famously advocated for Hindi and Sanskrit, but they seem to have published at least as heavily in Urdu and English. They also sometimes published in Panjabi, Gujarati, and other regional languages.

Arya books were never separable from the bodies that used them.[33] The most paradigmatic Arya bodies were perhaps the itinerant speakers who, starting in the 1880s, fanned out across the villages and cities of north India to do Vedic publicity. Many were volunteers. Some were paid.[34] A few were unwanted (in the early years, unidentified sadhus seem to have wandered around claiming to speak for the Samaj).[35] *Pracharak*s usually preached alone or in small groups. Sometimes they formed massive processions and marched through city streets, chanting printed hymns, reciting printed texts, and raising *aum* flags, emblazoned with that sacred syllable—a multisensory display with a predictable tendency to annoy the neighbors.[36]

Especially in urban settings, acoustics were a challenge. To project over a crowd, *pracharak*s sometimes stood on each other's shoulders.[37] At other times, persistence paid off. One Arya recalled how on his first day in the Jalandhar bazaar only two dozen men gathered on the carpet he had laid before him, while all around shopkeepers chatted and smoked their hookahs. To compensate, he upped the volume, shouting his Sanskrit mantras before explicating them in Panjabi. More men trickled over. The next day the crowd swelled to a hundred and, by the fourth, to two hundred fifty. Eventually, listeners even left their hookahs behind.[38]

That outdoor crowd would have been overwhelmingly male, although likely mixed in terms of caste and community. Indoors, at rented lecture halls and Arya Samaj mandirs, *pracharak*s could better accommodate mixed-gender audiences, while otherwise restricting attendance.[39] At the 1879 celebration of the Lahore Samaj's anniversary, for instance, a crowd of men gathered on blankets while women sat in an upstairs gallery, keeping purdah. All gazes, male and female, converged on the lecture platform near the *havan-kund* (ritual fire altar) where male speakers held forth in Hindi and English on social reformist topics.[40] Some years later, at the 1886 anniversary celebration, a woman—Mai Bhagavati (see figure 6)—also gave a lecture, speaking with propriety from behind a screen. Hidden from sight but not verbally constrained, she explained to her audience that abusive husbands would be reborn as dogs and then "kicked and beaten." Male listeners reportedly met her claims with "incredulous smiles."[41]

If Vedic publicity was a mode of speech paradigmatically defined around, but not restricted to, bourgeois adult men, its internal contradictions perhaps came into clearest view around the figure of the Vedic girl,

PRINTING PAIN, RULING SENTIMENT 149

श्रीमती माई भगवतीजी ।

FIGURE 6. "Shrimati Mai Bhagavati-ji." Shitalprasad Vaidya, *Shrimaddayanand Chitravali* (Calcutta: Vedic Pustakalaya, 1925). © The British Library Board. Shelfmark Hin.D.1519.

educated in Sanskrit and modern-standard Hindi at Arya schools. Take, for example, Ved Kunwar, an Arya Kanya Pathshala (girls' school) student who in 1896 delivered a lecture to the Meerut Arya Samaj. As a "slight girl," she demurred, she could add very little to the "charming and quite long" speeches already delivered. She then politely reprimanded her "dear fathers and brothers." "Are you going to reform the country through little 'lectures'?" she demanded, using the English word. "Can the mouth become sweet just by saying 'sugar, sugar'?" Even schoolgirls laugh at the hypocrisy of Arya gentleman who throw their children weddings in "a wholly Vedic style" after having educated them mostly in English and Urdu. They should be doing more to promote Sanskrit, and girls are the key. Real reform will remain impossible until "Arya dharma sprouts in women's hearts." Stop building college after college for boys and invest seriously in women's education.[42]

Boys' schools were indeed central to the Aryas' educational mission, cultivating specific styles of Vedic masculinity. Language training in Sanskrit and Hindi happened alongside yoga, team sports, and even Boy Scouting, with control of speech and of the male body (e.g., through restraining from masturbation) seen as constitutively intertwined.[43] The key to the "Aryan ideal of education," as Pandit Chamupati explained in 1927, was sexual "continence."[44] Combined with the fresh mountain air of a place like the Gurukul Kangri, it could restore the vigor of dissipated colonial youth. Dayananda was a model of both modes of self-control, of tongue and flesh: a lifelong celibate, he was famed for speaking only truth.

The Arya network of girls' schools articulated a different set of gendered ideals. Even as institutions like Jalandhar's Kanya Mahavidyalaya or women's college (established in 1890) and Dehra Dun's Kanya Gurukul (established in 1923) educated a generation of prominent Indian feminists, they also idealized bourgeois women as physical embodiments of tradition sequestered in the inner sphere of the home.[45] Arya women and girls thus occupied a doubled position, both in and out of public view.

Ved Kunwar seems to sense this doubleness, exploiting the internal contradictions of her rhetorical situation by simultaneously laying claim to and disavowing the colonial public's established speech genres. By presenting public speech as something men have and girls want, she casts herself as a liminal subject, both public and not. She reads the newspapers and is perfectly capable of giving lectures, yet she remains marginal to these anglophile cultural forms—which is precisely why she is able to speak from and for the feminized "heart" of the nation. This Vedic girl is doing the work of Vedic publicity, preaching to hypocritical men who "have raised a ruckus giving lectures but, in terms of action, have zero to show."[46] She is just not using the term *prachar* to describe her speech. Her lecture is further contained in its printed version (edited by a Doctor Ramchandra Varma), to which is appended an advertisement for powdered soap ("cheap," "good for all purposes," and "lard-free") that would seem directed at a female readership. The advertisement literally domesticates this not-quite-public text.

I do not know whether Ved Kunwar or Dr. Varma gave the printed version its title, *Chota Munh, Badi Baat* ("little mouth, big talk"). Still, the Hindi idiom (indicating speaking above one's station) is suggestive, underlining Ved Kunwar's diminutive stature and thus the human body as semiotic apparatus. Her grand words exceed her slight frame yet remain irreducibly physical, acting upon bodies of various kinds. Although Ved Kunwar draws a distinction among mental (*manasa*), verbal (*vacha*), and effective (*karmana*) action, praising deeds over mere words, her lecture undermines her speech typology. It is a demonstration of how to do things with words, taking speech itself as a form of action—a means of exerting force on human bodies.

FORCE OF WORDS: POLEMICS AND THE PRACTICE OF TRUTH

In this, Ved Kunwar's words are typical of polemics more generally. Etymologically, these are bellicose or fighting words, words analogized to war. A certain strand of liberal theorizing about speech has tended to see polemics as illegitimate precisely because of their implicit physicality: deliberative reason should work on the mind alone, eschewing physical coercion as well as sensuous, flowery rhetoric.[47] (Liberalism, as key semiotic ideology of secularism, likely owes something here to Protestantism, with its constitutive mistrust of material signs.)[48] Yet this occlusion of affective materiality distorts our understanding of actual speech. Surely all forms of verbal persuasion exert physical force, or something like it.[49] If we want to understand religious polemics, we need to ask how this force works.

Where classically liberal speech theory presents deliberative reason as constitutively removed from power (dismissing polemics as illegitimate speech because they are so obviously shot through with power relations), a nonliberal speech theory might take power as constitutive of all discussion, both good and bad. Thus, by one influential account, polemics are defined by their antirelationality. Polemical speech is speech that tries to cancel or destroy the opponent, foreclosing relationship and immuring the self within a wall of words. Dialogue, by contrast, establishes a verbal power relation in which both parties submit to the truths that emerge immanently through conversation, risking that they will be changed by those truths: the self that exits a dialogue might not be identical to the self that entered. This scenario is quite different from the liberal scene of self-contained individuals freely entering and exiting debates. Here, dialogue is an agonistic process of mutual subjectivation. It is a force relation.[50] Surely something similar could be said for polemics too: rather than being purely antirelational, they simply establish force-relations of a distinctive kind. If this is true in one way for face-to-face communication, it is true in another way when speech is disseminated through media technologies that might, at first glance, appear constitutively nonrelational—a sort of speaking into the air.[51] To explore these varieties of verbal force, let us turn to the archive of Arya polemic.

Aryas, to be clear, routinely denied that they were engaged in polemics. In the *Satyarth Prakash*, Dayananda insisted that "the purpose of a human birth is to judge between truth and untruth and to help others do the same, not to engage in debate [*vadvivad*] and conflict"; he then promptly commenced a hundred-page diatribe against Puranic Hindus.[52] Similarly, before an 1877 debate with Deobandi Muslims and Protestant missionaries, he rejected the Deobandis' proposal to join forces against the Christians, explaining that "hostile opposition to anyone" is "always inappropriate" and insisting that debaters should strive to "decide truth" while "dispensing with partisanship."[53] These ideals faltered when debate began: participants reportedly mocked each other's religious doctrines, clambered shouting onto tables while still wearing shoes, and dispersed before the planned event concluded. Why these disavowals of polemic intent, when polemic was so clearly occurring? There were perhaps legal reasons, linked to the Indian Penal Code (see chapter 9). Dayananda was also probably aware of classical Sanskritic norms that valorized "truth-directed" debate over "victory-directed" and "destruction-directed" debate.[54] He purported to be doing the first of these, while excelling at the latter two.

Aryas did, however, understand speech as exerting a kind of force. They wrote about Vedic publicity as a set of techniques for the tandem governance of self and others—ideally reshaping both in the process. "What is a *pracharak* like?" asked a 1945 article. He should be like a good doctor, one who studies his patient before offering treatment rather than mindlessly applying formulas from books. "It is absolutely necessary to take the measure of the place, time, and situation" before preaching to a public, and it is equally necessary to calibrate the *pracharak*'s own character, ensuring that he stays "established in truth and good conduct." "For the preacher, the endlessly difficult and endlessly necessary thing is this: to be able to thoroughly study the situation in which he wants to do publicity and to be able to alter himself [*apne ko parivartit karna*] in accordance with it."[55] The self bends toward its rhetorical situation, with speech an occasion for the disciplined inhabitation of truth—a relational force extending between speaker and listener, changing both in the process.

Actual *pracharak*s struggled to live up to these high ideals. Rushing from town to town, their dreary third-class-carriage lives severed the outward work of *prachar* from the inward work of self-improvement (*atmoddhar*) and thus prevented *pracharak*s from providing a model of how to lead a spiritually "new life year-round."[56] Because men pinballed haphazardly from one local Samaj anniversary celebration to another, they became "speech-giving machines," as one experienced *pracharak* put it. The harried traveler would neglect his own physical and ritual health and further forget to tailor his message to particular audiences, as by asking "Has my instruction had any effect? What is the real situation of the members? Who among them needs to have particular topics explained?" This is why, the article suggests, audiences treat *pracharaks*' lectures as fleeting entertainments, akin to songs in a theater hall. It has become impossible "for a relationship to form between student and instructor, *pracharak* and public [*janata*]," just as in modern schools where the traditional bond between guru and disciple is severed.[57] This last claim rhetorically links Vedic publicity to Arya educational institutions, which tried to reestablish the guru-disciple bonds of ancient ashrams. Yet can a lecturer ever establish individualized, durational bonds of this sort? He exists within the more diffuse cultural space of the public, necessarily experimenting with the creation of new and perhaps more ephemeral kinds of force lines.

Consider the following anecdote from the so-called golden age of Vedic publicity. In 1879, young Munshiram's atheism had his father worried. Father drags son to a public debate featuring Dayananda. Booming words have the desired effect. Son draws toward swami. After attending several debates on his own, Munshiram approached Dayananda: "My lord, your powers of argumentation are very strong. You have silenced me, but not given me the belief that God exists." Dayananda laughed in reply: "When did I promise that I would give you faith in God? Your faith in God [*parameshvar*] will happen when God himself makes you a believer."[58] What we see happening here is something other than liberal persuasion. Argumentation does not itself provoke a change in opinion or belief. Rather, Dayananda's words exert an almost physical force, silencing Munshiram (*unko chup to kara diya*) until God himself—an inward affective force—can transform his mind. If Dayananda appears here as a kind of guru (a title he disavowed), his guru-dom unfolds from within the bustling spaces of public speech.

Transformation took time. Munshiram did not officially join the Arya Samaj for another five years. At his final induction ceremony, he was asked to deliver an impromptu speech. The request, he later recalled, hit him like a lightning bolt. Although he had spoken in classrooms and courts (he was a lawyer), he had never "given a speech before a large gathering of the general public [sarvasadharan]. . . . As I got up, it seemed as though I would just reveal my inner feelings." He then found himself lecturing about how no one should become an Arya preacher if he cannot fashion his life strictly on Vedic principles. To do the "sacred work of religious publicity," the publicist's "thoughts" and "deeds" must perfectly align.[59] His lecture performatively enacted that very principle. Because Munshiram discovers his inner state (*andar ki bhav*) through the act of speaking, inside and outside seamlessly coincide. Encounter with the public changes him, with the lecture a technology for elucidating his own inner truth. Did his lecture shape any of his listeners as Dayananda's lecture once shaped him? If so, this speech event would have established a clear force line between subjects, realigning embodied religious selves via public oratory. This is polemics as ethics, a means of shaping self and other.

THE SPIRITUAL GOVERNMENT OF ALL AND EACH: REFORMING THE HINDU RACE

These Arya others were multitudinous, linked to a colonial imaginary of number. In a 1925 paean to Dayananda, Pandit Chamupati wrote that "he multiplied numbers, and made it his special business to reform each individual internally. Without numbers his idea of reform should have remained only an idea; without individual reform the very numbers he had gained should have proved his stumbling block."[60] That is, and in rigorously Foucauldian terms, the spiritual governmentality of the Arya Samaj necessarily operated simultaneously at two distinct registers—that of the population and of the individual, of all and of each—with these registers remaining in persistent tension, an irreducible dialectic at the very center of Vedic publicity.

Numbers were always important to the Aryas. The first all-India census was conducted in 1871, four years before the Samaj was founded. Over the following decades, census and Samaj developed in tandem. The census played a pivotal role in the reorganization of religion in late colonial India, allowing "Hindu" and "Muslim" to re-emerge as statistically determinable populational identities.[61] The Aryas had a vexed relationship to these categories, insisting in 1891 that they be listed in the census as "Aryan" not "Hindu," then flipping positions in later censuses to claim a Hindu identity ("They cannot have it both ways," complained a census administrator in 1931).[62] Their obsession with numbers elicited criticism on several fronts. In 1893, a prominent Samajist complained that the "Arya Samaj has recognized the principle of numbers somewhat too freely" in its internal governance, deferring to "universal suffrage" instead of wisdom in decision-making.[63] In 1927, the *Muslim Outlook* complained that the Samaj understood democracy overly simplistically as "government by the counting of heads."[64]

Counting was central to the work of Vedic publicity. Take, for instance, an essay on *dharm prachar* by Pandit Lekhram, the prominent polemicist murdered in 1897 for his slanders of the Ahmadis. In it, Lekhram tries to awaken "our Arya *jati* [race, nation, caste]," still "sleeping the sleep of Kumbhakarna" (the drowsy giant in the *Ramayana*) while its "dharma is being destroyed" and its "children are becoming barbarians [*mlecch*]." "Brothers, open your eyes for God's sake. Awake from sleep!" His fellow Aryas needed to be alert in order to solve a mathematical word problem: If, in the eight centuries since the coming of Islam, the Hindu population has, through conversion, decreased from two hundred forty million to two hundred million, how many years will it take to zero out? Four thousand years, Lekhram tells us. That might seem like a long time, but Christian missionaries will accelerate the decline. Fortunately, there is a solution. The ancient philosopher Shankaracharya brought a quarter billion Buddhists and Jains back to the Vedic fold, making them do penance (*prayaschit*) before investing them with the sacred thread. Modern Aryas should do the same, joining with their "lost brothers after putting them through a purification ritual."[65]

Vedic publicity might begin with words. But especially when directed toward Muslims and Dalits, it would end with a ceremony that inscribed religious change into the body. Arya *shuddhi* or purification ceremonies built on forms of ritual penance with a long history.[66] The Aryas put that penance to a new and controversial use. Their earliest *shuddhi* ceremonies, in the 1870s and '80s, were performed on individual converts. In the late 1890s, they began doing *shuddhi* en masse, with hundreds or even thousands of bodies "purified" (a term dripping with caste ideology) in a single go.[67] Some ceremonies were highly publicized. Others were homespun affairs, like the ritual hosted in 1903 by an Amritsar lawyer for a bureaucrat acquaintance whose father had converted to Christianity; guests included Muslims and Christians, all of whom sat on a carpet in the lawyer's home and received sweets from the convert.[68]

The Aryas wanted to correct for caste injustice, yet they never quite managed to break free of their privileged-caste presumptions.[69] Their attitude toward Dalits was frequently paternalistic, or at least parental (one 1926 article imagined Dalit multitudes crawling into the Samaj's "mother-shaped lap").[70] The very idea of *shuddhi*, moreover, reinforced the symbolic hegemony of caste by implying that Dalit and Muslim bodies were impure. (Dalit intellectuals noticed these hypocrisies: Swami Acchutanand, the erstwhile Arya who later founded the Akhil Bharatiya Acchut Mahasabha and Adi Hindu Movement, described the Samaj, in 1912, as a "deceit of the Vedic religion devised to protect Brahmanism.")[71] The Aryas did create avenues for subordinated-caste mobility—prodded by subordinated-caste groups impatient with Arya indecision. But that mobility, in turn, provoked dominant-caste resistance, with subordinated-caste Aryas bearing the brunt of the backlash. Dominant-caste Aryas sometimes sprang to their defense; for example, when brahman cooks at a Samaj school refused to serve subordinated-caste students, their dominant-caste peers protested and got the cooks fired, if only temporarily.[72] Perhaps more often, attempts at caste mobility ended in tragedy. In 1903, a group of Dalit converts in Punjab, their heads newly shaved from a *shuddhi* ceremony, entered a dominant-caste shop and were promptly beaten for their transgression.[73]

The Arya Samaj was shadowed by such violence, especially when plying its politics of number. In the early 1920s, Aryas substantially expanded their *shuddhi* campaigns, targeting entire communities like the Malkanas, a north Indian Muslim Rajput caste. To some, this seemed like a "collective political attack by Hindus on Muslims," creating so much "ill-feeling" that the communities were "ready to cut each other's throats."[74] The immediate context for the *Rangila Rasul*, this ill-feeling also foreshadowed the horrors of Partition some twenty years later.

Furthermore, Arya rhetoric of the 1920s and '30s had clear parallels with and empirical connections to the Hindu-Aryan myth gaining traction in Germany.[75] Both stoked fear of small numbers.[76] In *Hindu Sangathan: Saviour of the Dying Race* (1926), Swami Shraddhananda—Munshiram, whom we met above, now under a renunciant name—recounted how, after seeing the 1911 census, he tried to tabulate the rate of decline of the "Indo-Aryan race" and failed. He then resolved to become a "mere student of statistics," his ascetic-religious discipline absorbing mathematical discipline.[77] What *race* means here is something of an open question: at times, Shraddhananda seems to use the term as a near-synonym for *samaj*; it may be an English calque on *jati* or another word indicating "community" or "nation." Still, Shraddhananda's book clearly echoes the racialized ideas about numeric nationhood gaining currency elsewhere in the world.

These religio-racial ideas were biopolitical ideas, understood via the gendered, reproductive capacity of populations. They were also, in the case of the Aryas, semiotic ideas. *Ved* or *dharmprachar* linked words to bodies, purifying the flesh by retraining its speech. If *shuddhi* was one means of ritually rewriting the religio-racial caste-Hindu body, then Vedic education was another. "A pious and righteous person who has correctly read and understood the Vedas and who never deviates from their teachings in his practice is a Brahman, be he or she the native of America, Europe or Aryavarta itself," explained an Arya pensioner in 1902.[78] Caste, in other words, was to be based not on biological-familial inheritance, but on acquired virtue.

This meant that caste reform implied a parallel restructuring of the family and, with it, gender and sexuality.[79] Much of this reengineering was meant to happen at neotraditional ashrams like the Gurukul Kangri. Its ascetic teachers would become like parents, displacing biological family to remake the pupil's body as twice-born (i.e., *dvija*, dominant-caste Hindu). It takes "a philosopher to handle an infant," explained one 1902 document, with the male teacher like a second mother, the medium or "means of bringing forth or giving birth to . . . the spiritual, the emotional, the intellectual element" in the child.[80] According to Chamupati, these philosopher-ascetics were "literally parental. The Veda places the *brahmachari* [celibate student] in the womb of the Acharya, meaning that the latter should be as solicitous of the welfare of the disciple as the pregnant mother is of the embryo."[81] Here, "the Veda" (that nebulous noun, never quite equivalent to the four actual *samhitas*) produces a gender inversion, both feminizing the philosopher and turning language education (whether in Sanskrit or Sanskritized Hindi, as *Arya bhasha* or Aryan language) into a ritual of purification, of rebirthing biological bodies into the symbolic order of an ostensibly meritocratic caste system.

PRINT AESTHETICS, BODILY AESTHETICS

The gendered, religio-racial caste body was on fulsome display in late colonial tracts and pamphlets, which strongly foregrounded physicality. Even their titles were colorfully corporeal: "A Slap on the Face of Dayananda Saraswati," "A Slap on the Face of Critics of Pilgrimage," "A Nose Ring in Arya Samaj's Nose," "Pandit Buddhdev's Foot on Rishi Dayananda's Head," "The World's Foot on the Arya Samaj's Head."[82] This litany of physical assaults suggests a performative truth: print can seem to deliver a physical blow, transmitting pain to its readers. This was not a new phenomenon; such titles were also common in early modern polemics.[83] Inevitably, however, it assumed historically specific contours.

Late colonial print polemics invoked bodies frequently and in grotesque ways, with routine references to sexual acts and scatology. Sanatanists, for instance, were described as "eaters of night soil."[84] Such rhetoric could create legal trouble under the Indian Penal Code, as when the *Arya Musafir* (Arya traveler), a journal associated with Lekhram, alleged that the Prophet Muhammad prescribed to his followers the medicinal ingestion of his own and also camel urine, as well as asking them to drink from a basin of water in which he had washed his hands and expectorated. Another *Arya Musafir* article alleged that a premodern *qazi* told his tax collectors to spit in the mouths of non-Muslims while levying *jizya*. Obviously offensive, this somatic imagery presumably played on caste-Hindu anxieties about saliva as carrier of ritual pollution.[85] It may also have recalled Ayurvedic notions of auto-urine therapy. It was certainly, in context, a means of deflecting a charge that Muslim-owned publications had apparently leveled at Aryas: that participants in *shuddhi* ceremonies were required to ingest all five sacred products of the cow, including urine and dung, so that the Samaj could later blackmail them about having undergone this indignity.[86]

Even if all such claims were bogus, this obscene exchange succinctly captures an important literary register of nineteenth- and early twentieth-century religious polemics. Polemic was not an ethereal domain of theological disputation. It was a bawdy arena of embodied being. "Aesthetics is born as a discourse of the body," the literary theorists tell us, recalling the word's Greek etymology.[87] In this sense, late colonial religious polemics were aesthetic texts. They took the body as both message and medium, writing about the flesh to produce strongly visceral effects on the bodies that read and circulated them. Affectively supercharged, these tracts tactically transgressed caste, gender, and religious norms to position the porous human body as a site of public contestation.[88] They developed an aesthetics of disgust (*ghrna*) that relied on the affective dispositions of the caste-Hindu body—at times working to reform the caste-based distribution of the sensible toward a more equitable affective order, at other times clearly operating in excess of reformist imperatives or in service of communalist rhetoric. Aryas often redirected *savarna* disgust away from Dalits and toward Muslims.[89]

If religious polemics had a bawdily carnival sensibility, this was perhaps because they poached on festivals and fairs, adapting the aesthetic of open-air debate to the printed page. A raucous form of outdoor entertainment—often the best show in town—public debates were sometimes explicitly described as "fairs" (*mela*), and their carnival conditions implicitly granted debaters a "license to insult," as Usha Sanyal suggests.[90] There were no clear rules governing most debates, nor in many cases even a clear way to decide the winner. A certain degree of chaos thus reigned—with, for instance, a speaker dwelling at length on the meaning of the word *virgin* in the Christian scriptures to titillate his audience.[91] While the Aryas mistrusted fairs—they tried to discipline and desexualize traditional festivals like Holi by devising wholesome holidays like the Gurukul Mela, a sort of ascetic anti-carnival—it is hard not to feel the carnival impulse in Arya writing.[92] Aryas delighted in topsy-turvy debasements of the sacred.

How actual readers reacted to any of these printed texts is mostly impossible to know. Reception happens off the record. The print archive does, however, contain clues about what Arya readers may have been doing, which—as is often the case—probably departed from what writers imagined. Or so, at least, one is inclined to speculate upon seeing the dedication page that prefaces a 1928 edition of Pandit Lekhram's collected works (see figure 7). This book invites its buyer to bestow it as a "gift of love," bequeathed "in service"—presumably to the Arya cause. Given Lekhram's bloody legacy, love might not be the first emotion one would associate with his writings. Still more jarring is the woodcut baby Krishna at the bottom of the page—not only a cardinal instance of Puranic religion, but also one thought to induce in viewers an affective state (*vatsalya bhava*, relating to God as cute child) that would seem flatly at odds with fiery religious polemics.

These are probably rote words and symbols, common on dedication pages of the period. That they appear here suggests the difficulty Aryas faced in extricating themselves from the visual economy of Hindu material culture. Perhaps a few readers did what this page invited them to do. Perhaps none did. Either way, the page cues the necessarily speculative question of how printed words enter social life, becoming embedded in social relations. The work of Vedic publicity persisted as friends passed books from hand to hand, nudging one another toward religious reform by deploying printed paper as a tool of microscopic affective governance, transmitting lines of verbal force.

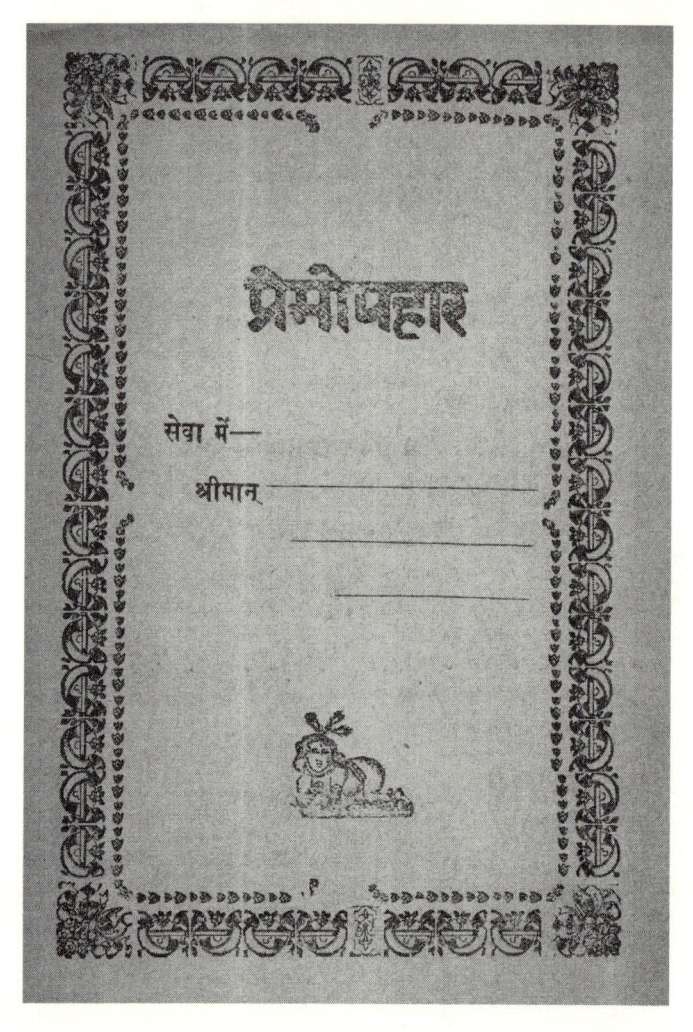

FIGURE 7. Dedication page in Lekhram, *Aryapathik Granthavali*, trans. and ed. Premsharanji Pranat (Agra: Arya Publishing Depot, 1928). © The British Library Board. Shelfmark Hin.B.7654.

SLANDERING THE PRIEST

This capillary field of personal relations was a persistent concern not just for the Aryas, but also for late colonial socio-religious reformism more broadly. "Personal animosity," as one historian notes, peppered Aryas' criticisms of other religions "from the very beginning."[93] There was a good reason for these personalist insults: they were a key means by which Arya polemicists sought to reshape the moral character of the nation. Personalist slander was a tool of ethics, targeting allegedly unethical behavior and exposing it to public view so that the print public would become an instrument of moral reform. Ad hominem attack was not a gossipy side show to the work of religious reform, as expressed in theological disquisitions. It was integral to that work, the site where reform's interest in ethical subjectivation was most evident.

In late colonial India, religious authority was in flux. Old institutions were reinventing themselves and their associated sacred bodies (pirs, purohits, 'ulama, sannyasis, etc.). New institutions were also emerging, and with them a new set of charismatic figures: Madame Helena Blavatsky, Keshub Chunder Sen, Shiv Narayan Agnihotri, Mirza Ghulam Ahmad, Dayananda Saraswati, and more. These personalities were objects of gossip, speculation, and slanderous accusation, with defamation a tactic for dimming their charisma. Agnihotri, the controversial founder of Lahore's Dev Samaj, was especially active in this regard. Dubbing Dayananda a "Vedic Maha-Pope," he also condemned Keshub Chunder Sen for declaring himself a prophet or *paigambar*—a rich claim coming from a man who would soon don ocher robes and announce he was a god.[94]

Agnihotri took the term *pope* from Dayananda, who used it in public speeches to describe false brahmans and subsequently incorporated it into the *Satyarth Prakash*'s narrative of how those same brahmans had buried the Vedas under priestly lies. Dayananda's mission was to eliminate what he called "pope-*lila*," a translation of the English term *priestcraft*.[95] Dayananda was ecumenical in his allegations of religious imposture. If brahmans had set up mechanical contrivances (a bubble-blowing icon, a self-propelling chariot) to produce false miracles, so too had Madame Blavatsky, an erstwhile ally whose theosophical "humbuggery" he publicly denounced in 1882.[96] Similarly, he accused Jesus of using magic-trick miracles (e.g., multiplying fishes and *rotis*) to dupe savages (*jangli log*) just as any bogus sorcerer (*siddha*) or illusionist (*indrajali*) would.[97] He derided Muhammad as a hypocritical impostor (*pakhandi*) who faked miracles to catch the gullible in his magician's net (*jal*).[98]

The pope trope remained a staple of Arya rhetoric in the decades to come, from Lala Mulraj's *Pope Nash Mala* (Rosary of the destruction of popes, 1890) to Manasaram Shastri's *Pauranik Pope par Vaidik Top, arthat Sanatan Dharm ki Maut* (A Vedic cannon on the Puranic pope, or the death of the Sanatanist religion, 1933).[99] By dismissing certain religious authorities as fraudulent "popes"—that is, "wealth-stealing promoters of false religion" like brahmans and Christian missionaries—Aryas were able to position themselves as "true teachers."[100] They also clearly delighted in the verbal play the term allowed. One described how India had become a *"pop samaj"* (or popish society), which was why it now needed to be remade as an Arya Samaj. Another rhymed "Mister Pope" with *"angrezi top"* (English hat) to suggest the changeable superficiality of subordinated-caste conversion to Christianity.[101]

Allegations of fraud were frequently paired with sexual slander. Once, at a public lecture, British attendees made the mistake of laughing at a joke Dayananda had cracked about the moral corruption of the Puranas. He turned scathingly in their direction to say that "if this is the *lila* [here, trickery] of the Puranis, then listen to the *lila* of the Christians," who are so debased they no longer even feel shame at attributing sin to God by suggesting a "virgin" became pregnant.[102] Such comments created the rhetorical space into which the *Rangila Rasul* would later be launched. In the *Satyarth Prakash*, Dayananda accused Muhammad not just of priestcraft but also of *vishayasakti ki lila*, "the play of sensuality."[103]

If the trope of priestcraft gestured toward a general framework for understanding the history of religions, it also at the same time aided in the circulation of extremely local gossip. These were intertwined projects, the twinned faces of moral reform. With small print runs and clearly demarcated audiences, late colonial tracts and periodicals were not always as impersonal as media as one would tend to assume. In many towns and cities, an accusatory publication could be all but guaranteed to find a particular reader: the accused, thus functioning more like a letter than a "public" document. Gossipy divulgence of private matters could thus be marshaled for both tactical and moral ends. In Jalandhar, Munshiram and associates so antagonized local brahmans that traditional authorities decided to outcaste all of the city's Samajists; when the Samajists retaliated by threatening to publicly expose prominent brahmans' gambling habits and secret mistresses, the brahmans backed down.[104] Sanatanists, meanwhile, were turning moral scrutiny back on Arya behaviors, as when the *Sanatan Dharm Gazette* reported that a Gurukul graduate had been caught performing a "bestial act" and demanded that Munshiram divulge the facts in his *Sat Dharm Pracharak*.[105] In such contestations, print emerged as an arena for negotiating the moral boundaries of the colonial public, or for using that public to regulate private or intimate life.

VIOLENCE AND THE GOVERNANCE OF RELIGIOUS AFFECT

If the Arya project of moral reform revolved around the force of words, reform was inseparable from the potential intensification of force in acts of physical violence. Violence goes back to the earliest days of the Samaj. In the 1870s and '80s, audiences reportedly pelted Dayananda with stones and other objects. He would wipe the blood off his forehead with a handkerchief and keep speaking, or simply smile and say that one day people would throw flowers instead—or so later Aryas recalled.[106] The verbal violence that Aryas inflicted on others sometimes induced those others to commit acts of physical violence. Aryas then used accounts of these attacks to depict themselves as persecuted champions of free speech, with a sense of collective identity forming around Arya martyrs like Pandit Lekhram.

To read government files about the Aryas from the 1920s and '30s is to be confronted with horrific acts. In 1926, an Arya living in a block of laborer's quarters in Rajasthan verbally abused a Muslim neighbor for months, until said neighbor "finally lost control of himself" and shot his tormentor.[107] One assumes that the abused party's violent act brought more violence upon him, with tragedy begetting tragedy. In 1938, a Samajist was murdered for helping Dalits gain entry to Hindu temples and government schools in the princely state of Indore. "They first took out his eyes by means of nails, severed his hands and feet and then broke his head with sticks," members of the Delhi Samaj reported to the Maharajah.[108] It seems likely that an equal or greater violence was inflicted on Indore Dalits. There is no minimizing such horrors. Then as now, the most acute forms of violence in India seem reserved for Muslims and Dalits. The Aryas are interesting partly because of their ambivalent position within these persistently unequal social structures—simultaneously fostering violence and bringing it, if selectively, onto their own bodies.

I will close this discussion by considering a tract that encapsulates the Aryas' late colonial rhetorical moves: their ongoing conflict with Sanatanist Hindus, their persistent commitment to a sexual-scatological aesthetic, and their use of print media to finesse the gap between words and bodies. In *Mere Pacchis Minet* (My twenty-five minutes, 1936), Manasaram Shastri (a.k.a. the "Vedic Cannon") explained how, at a recent Sanatana Dharma Conference, he was denied his allocated speech time by angry Sanatanists, who silenced him by beating him with *lathis* (heavy bamboo sticks). Their violent censorship incited more speech, prompting Shastri to switch mediums and bring his planned rebuttal of Sanatanist claims to a print audience instead. His published tract opens by refuting sexual slanders of Dayananda. It then goes on to detail the salacious contents of the Puranas: beef consumption, divine ejaculate, sex workers, and Krishna transforming Arjuna into a woman before "sporting with him in the forest and taking pleasure with him in accord with desire."[109] Although it depicts the Aryas as tolerant victims of violent fanaticism, Shastri's tract is, unmistakably, a weapon. Indeed, its martial metaphors commence on the title page, which describes its author, the "Vedic Cannon," as a "debate warrior" (*shastrarth maharathi*). This paper weapon works by physically effacing and thus silencing the bodies of opponents. To write is to monologue, with Shastri's tract circulating independently of any possible Sanatanist response.

Notably, government censors banned *Mere Pacchis Minet*. They also retained a copy, now housed in the British Library's India Office collection of proscribed publications. The force of the state apparatus was greater than Shastri's verbal force. Indeed, one might suggest that this legal force was already implicit in Shastri's tract, circulating within the same field of social relations that religious controversialists were contesting. The force of law, in its social life, was an immanent force that could be turned to various ends—as we shall see in the next chapter.

CONCLUSION: THE ONE ABOUT THE QUICK-WITTED COLONEL (REPRISE)

We thus return to where this chapter began: the tale of the quick-witted colonel and sharp-tongued soldier, men well-matched in banter but otherwise quite differently positioned. Only the white colonel's words are backed by the force of the state. This difference helps to explain what would otherwise seem a problem with the joke's implicit logic. If all excessively witty persons qualify as Aryas, then surely the colonel counts as an Arya too. That this does not even seem to occur to our storyteller suggests a corollary rule. *Arya* was a racializing term, structured by state imperatives such that only the speech of the colonized would qualify as excessive, pungent to the point of requiring policing.

A better reading of this scene would notice the implicit excess in the colonel's words. White violence was, after all, routine in colonial India.[110]

A posse of drunken Britons strolling down a train platform at night might reach into the window of a passing sleeper car to give a dozing passenger a "violent slap" on the head—as happened to Munshiram in 1911.[111] Such minor indignities scaled upward into horrifically violent events like the 1919 Jallianwala Bagh Massacre. Counterviolences were similarly distributed between large and small. For an example of the latter, consider an Arya threatening publicly, in 1912, to kick the viceroy if he ever saw him in person.[112] Taken together, these violent words and acts produced a volatile forcefield.

The colonel's retort channels such violence, literally silencing the soldier by bringing the joke to a close. It also renders the man the object of police suspicion. Why do we not notice the force in the colonel's words? The colonel downplays and disavows this force by pointing to the excessiveness of Arya speech, an act of rhetorical displacement that indicates an arguably pervasive tactic. By reifying the distinction between state and society, and thus occluding how the state was coconstitutive of the social conflicts it purported to externally manage, the British were able to disavow state violence and displace it onto the colonized.

Pushing past that paradigm, this chapter has shown how the colonial state was not the only bureaucratic entity trying to rule religious sentiments in late colonial India. The Arya Samaj and other religious organizations developed a complementary project of affective governance, a set of mediated techniques for regulating conduct. Directed simultaneously at the individual and the population, Arya words were, ideally, relational—establishing embodied networks of power, whether in schools or, more expansively, in the anonymous relations established by *prachar*, the dissemination of the Vedic message through lectures and print publications. Even in print, that seemingly anonymous or impersonal medium, Aryas and their contemporaries engaged in highly personalist forms of insult, calling out individuals living and dead. Polemic tracts were physical objects that acted on bodies, bringing those bodies into new moral-affective relations. In this, they were perhaps not so different from legal texts.

08

THE ARYA PENAL CODE

Law and the Practice of Documentary Religion

IN 1862, THIRTEEN YEARS BEFORE the Arya Samaj was founded, the Indian Penal Code became law. It was thus always a structuring condition of Vedic publicity, a forcefield shaping the mobile trajectories of the Aryas' forcefully polemic words. Aryas were accused of various word crimes under the Code: sedition (Section 124A), obscenity (292–4), religious offense (295–8), and defamation (499–500). They also, in 1927, triggered the addition of a new word crime, Section 295A.

The Aryas incorporated the Code's concepts into their polemic lexicon, vocally alleging that their "religious feelings" had been "injured," "hurt," or "offended" by opponents.[1] In doing so, they made the Code their own, creating a sort of "Arya Penal Code," a popular reflection of the official document. The story of this Arya Code is not a tale of "law's religion" (i.e., secular law's ideas about what counts as religion, constituting something like a form of religion within law). It is, rather, a tale of religion's law (i.e., modern religion's notion of secular law, as seen in popular citations of legal terms, constituting something like a form of law within religion).[2] Like other such tales, it suggests that the history of a document like the Indian Penal Code cannot be written independently of the various cultural doppelgängers that circulated alongside it and shaped its social effects.

Law was an arrow in the controversialist's quiver, with the threatened prohibition of alleged word crimes a tactic for exciting more speech. The Aryas were hardly alone in invoking the Code. When, in 1904, residents of the Rajasthani town of Khandela tried to stop the local Samaj from holding a *nagar-kirtan* (public hymn-singing) procession, they alleged that Arya songs would endanger the peace, thus intimating a 153A offense. The Aryas countered by insisting that any such restriction would infringe on "religious liberty" and "deeply wound the feelings of the members of the Arya Samaj," pairing a 298 offense with infringement on religious freedom as overarching colonial-secularist ideal.[3] Law, it seems, was anyone's to use.

Consistently savvy secularists, Aryas knew how to use secularism's constitutive language game—its irresolvable effort to demarcate the categorical boundaries of religion—to their strategic advantage, deploying "religious liberty" as a shield against state interference.[4] It is perhaps ironic that such invocations rhetorically inscribe the state's symbolic power into religious practice, such that the state becomes so-called free religion's very ground and condition of being. Intrapolemical citations of law work similarly. To quote the law in silencing a religious rival is to claim for oneself a slice of governmental authority, mobilizing the symbolic force of the state to reshape one's rhetorical situation. Extralegal legal words cannot, by definition, exert legal force. They can, however, exert a kindred force, poaching on and partly redistributing the power of law, and thus intertwining state and society in a shared field of governmental power wherein the state's censorial function is widely distributed.

This redistribution of legal power was grounded in material practices, including print-cultural practices. The Aryas' Vedic dharma was, one could say, a paper religion—mediated by a proliferation of books, tracts, pamphlets, broadsheets, posters, telegrams, letters, and bureaucratic documents, from membership rosters to subcommittee minutes to manuals of rules and regulations. This paper had symbolic as well as practical importance. Documents in modern South Asia have often seemed to possess an almost-magical quality, as Akhil Gupta notes, embodying and congealing state power by concretizing its "aura."[5] This was perhaps especially true under Britain's *Kaghazi Raj*, or paper empire, with its proliferate documentary practices.[6] The period's religious movements mirrored empire by proliferating bureaucratic paper and even—in the case of the Theosophical Society, once an Arya Samaj ally—investing documents with explicitly occult qualities.[7]

The bureaucratic document that emitted the strongest aura for late colonial secularists was surely Queen Victoria's 1858 proclamation of Crown rule, guaranteeing noninterference in Indian religions. Aryas cited this text to fend off state surveillance, sometimes imagining it as an actual piece of paper. A 1909 article in the Arya journal *Indar*, for instance, reported that police had barged into a Samaj mandir, interrupting the singing of hymns. When the surprised Aryas cited Victoria's proclamation, the police demanded to see a copy. Not having one, the Aryas grabbed their musical instruments and dashed out the door, later grousing that the police "dogs" were too illiterate to have read it anyway.[8] I am drawn to the counterfactual scene that this article seems to imply—what the Aryas evidently wished they had been able to do, which is brandish a bureaucratic document to keep the police at bay. This imagined document exudes the auratic authority of the Crown, benevolently presiding over the rancorous actualities of colonial governance.[9] It is a quasi-ritual object, part of the devotional scene of the mandir itself.

What about the Indian Penal Code, a colonial-secular document enacted two years after Victoria's proclamation? How did the Aryas imagine it? The following series of vignettes responds to that question. Each implies a microargument, building toward the macroargument of the mosaic whole: Paperwork is never just official. It is also intimate, enabling new associational forms or forms of social life.[10] To study Arya encounters with the Indian Penal Code is to get a sense for this intimacy, seeing how the legal governmentality of the colonial state intersected with religious governmentality. Indeed, it is to see how the colonial-secular state was less a bounded entity, discrete from society, than a constellation of social practices that blurred the line between the intimate and the official.

THE MACAULAY CODE AND THE ARYA "BIBLE"

Swami Dayananda Saraswati's *Satyarth Prakash* or *Light of Truth* is sometimes described as the "bible" of the Arya Samaj. That label would probably have surprised Dayananda himself, who arduously promoted the Vedas as quasi-biblical texts, comparable to Christian missionaries' printed Bibles. The elevation of the *Satyarth Prakash* to biblical status seems to have happened mostly in the early twentieth century. It was a savvy rhetorical tactic. To call a book a bible is to immunize it against state censorship. Bibles, by definition, are beyond the reach of secular law, meaning that if the *Satyarth Prakash* was the Arya bible, the British could not ban it.[11]

This rhetorical move, however, elides an inconvenient fact. Colonial law was inside the *Satyarth Prakash* in the most literal way: the book quotes the Indian Penal Code. "No statement has been put in this book with the intention of causing anyone emotional pain or injury [*kissi ka man dukhana va kissi ki hani*]," wrote Dayananda in the preface to the revised 1883 edition of the original 1875 text. He reiterated this disclaimer a few hundred pages later, when transitioning to the book's polemical second half, and yet again in a prefatory note to the chapter on Islam.[12] If Dayananda's language here recalls Section 298, with its talk of "wounding the religious feelings of any person," there is a good reason. A few months earlier, he had been threatened with a 298 lawsuit.

In June 1882, the swami received a letter from the Bombay law firm Smith and Frere alleging that he had written the first edition of the *Satyarth Prakash* with "the deliberate intention of wounding and offending the religious feelings of our client and other followers of the Jain religion," and thus "grossly insulted and offended their religious feelings." The client in question, Lala Thakurdas Moolraj, demanded that Dayananda either prove his injurious claims in court or issue an apology.[13] Dayananda did neither. Instead, he hired another law firm, Payne and Gilbert, to reply on his behalf, explaining that he had never intended to wound anyone's feelings but would voluntarily amend any errors in a second edition.[14] In August 1882, while staying at the garden palace of the Maharaja of Udaipur, Dayananda wrote the new edition's preface, with its quasi-legal disclaimer—a near-direct quotation of Smith and Frere's paraphrase of Section 298.[15] This legal resonance grew louder when Aryas began translating the *Satyarth Prakash* into English, with Dayananda now professing (posthumously, in 1906) that he had not meant "to hurt anyone's susceptibilities" or (in 1908) to "hurt the feelings of any person, either directly or indirectly."[16]

It could be objected that a legal disclaimer in a book's preface is ultimately extraneous to that book. Perhaps. And yet prefaces and other seemingly marginal matter can have a way of revealing the performative conditions under which a book was written with particular clarity. There are, in any case, other traces of colonial law in the *Satyarth Prakash*, including a probable echo of the Maharaj Libel Case in Dayananda's chastisement of the Vallabhacharya *sampradaya*.[17] Any religious text written in this period could probably be shown to have a few such traces.

Let us take Dayananda's paraphrase of Section 298 as a sort of first chapter in the "Arya Penal Code." It provides crucial insight into the social life of legally actionable religious feelings in the 1880s, highlighting the tight imbrication of law with more personal forms of affect.

Law here was literally a letter—one of many. Thakurdas, a Jain from the Punjabi town of Gujranwalla, had first written Dayananda in 1881.[18] Initially, he was polite, kindly requesting that the worthy swami provide the name of a Jain shastra he had quoted in the *Satyarth Prakash* that was, apparently, not Jain at all. When Dayananda failed to reply, Thakurdas sent a second, much testier letter, the very first sentence of which threatens to drag the swami to court. Dayananda still did not answer. Instead, his assistant Anandilal Mantri responded for him, and less than diplomatically. "From your writing, we can tell that you have no learning, nor have you spent time with learned people, which is why you can't understand the meaning of Swami-ji's text." While it true that Thakurdas was not as learned as Anandilal and was less than careful with his prose—he mixes Hindi with Gujarati so thoroughly that he sometimes ends a Hindi sentence with a Gujarati verb—Anandilal might still have refrained from ending his response with a chart detailing the errors in Thakurdas's Sanskrit quotations.[19] Thakurdas, predictably, was not pleased. He dashed off one angry letter and then another, chiding Dayananda for relying on a middleman of such "ignorant stock." "If I have something to write, it is to you, if something to ask, it is of you, and the legal action that I will bring will be on you, so why are you answering me via somebody else?" Anandilal responded again to accuse Thakurdas of failing to understand his previous letter. All that is the swami's is his, and all that is his is also the swami's, mused the secretarial medium.[20]

As the months rolled on, letters piled up. Thakurdas enlisted the help of a prominent Jain scholar to support his arguments. Local Samaj secretaries from Gujranwala to Dehra Dun assured Thakurdas that they bore only "friendly feelings" (*mitrabhav*) toward him. (He seems to have shown up at the Gujranwala Samaj demanding that somebody give him Dayananda's personal address.)[21] Dayananda, meanwhile, remained silent. Eventually, Thakurdas issued a public notice stating that Dayananda had caused "harsh dishonor" to "our religion" and noting that the punishment for this crime under Section 295 of the Indian Penal Code is two years in prison (the legal citation is dubious: 295 is about defiling places and objects).[22] In August 1882, the very month that Dayananda was writing his new preface, Thakurdas published the complete correspondence as a printed tract, titled *Dayanand Sarasvati Mukh Chapetika* (A slap in the face of Dayananda Saraswati). This is perhaps the ultimate act of postal reappropriation, a redirection of unwanted mail to the prying eyes of the print public.

The conflict between Dayananda and Thakurdas was a conflict about, among other things, linguistic and documentary practices. All sorts of languages jostle for space here, from learned Sanskrit to vernacular Hindi and Gujarati to legal English (reproduced in florid cursive in the printed text). So too do different notions of textual address. Thakurdas assumes that a letter addressed to an individual will be read by that individual. Dayananda speaks through his secretary, as human communications medium. Thakurdas responds with an escalating series of public genres—a notice, a lawyer's letter, a printed book—two of which by definition hail multiple readers at once. No matter how public they get, however, these documents still ooze personal animus, trying to inflict a reciprocal pain on their intended recipient: Dayananda.

The swami responded eventually—in public. His legal disclaimer, paraphrasing Section 298, clearly addresses all possible readers of the *Satyarth Prakash*. It also arguably, and perhaps inevitably, addresses Thakurdas in particular, although it mentions neither him nor the fracas he caused. All printed texts have an ambiguous or indeterminate addressee; they speak to all potential readers and yet somehow also to *you* specifically.[23] Some texts call attention to this ambiguity of address through devices that test the limits of public speech to reveal its underlying rhetorical structure ("I bet you think this song is about you"). The disclaimer in the preface of the *Satyarth Prakash* was indeed about Thakurdas. In its way, it was the letter he had been waiting for.

When invoking the Indian Penal Code, Thakurdas was keen to allege that Dayananda had offended not just him but also "other followers of the Jain religion." This offense was a collective, and thus legally actionable, injury. Without denying that other Jains may have been offended by Dayananda's writings, I would suggest that we should slow our impulse to jump-cut from the individual, Thakurdas, to the abstract collectivity, Jains. In late colonial India, "religious feeling" was a presumptively populational affect. It pulled away from the contingent particularity of a given situation and toward the abstraction of bureaucratically legible "classes." Legal professionals participate in this logic when they impose taxonomic gridlines, identifying certain feelings as religious while ignoring others. Scholars should not follow suit. Such taxonomic procedures replicate, in fractal miniature, the semantic boundary-work of secularism itself.[24]

Whatever religious affect might be, it emerges in and through a larger swirl of feelings, many of them quite particular. Thakurdas's sense of injury was intensely personal, fueled by Anandilal's classed condescension and Dayananda's vexing silence as much as by anything Dayananda had written. His wounded religious feelings cannot be readily separated from this social context. Nor can they be readily separated from their media. A letter is a physical object that, when opened, can feel like a "slap in the face."

This holds for lawyers' letters too—here, put to personalized effect. You can almost feel Thakurdas trying to get a rise out of Dayananda through legal paperwork.

AN IMPOSTOR UNVEILED

The Aryas also liked making private matters public, especially in their moralizing exposés of rival religious leaders. From Dayananda forward, they took slander as a tool of moral reform, framing their exposures of hidden sin as part of a war on "priestcraft" or "pope-*lila*."[25] This was the broad literary context of the *Rangila Rasul* (an exposé of Muhammad), as well as other Arya texts of the 1920s like the *Risala-i-Vartman*'s "Sair-i-Dozakh" (A trip to hell). Its author, Devi Sharan Sharma, protested that "his intention was only to warn everyone concerned against the evils of reposing faith in *Pirs* and *Gurus*."[26]

The Aryas' opponents engaged in similar tactics. Thus, in *Pandit Dayanand Unveiled* (1891), Shiv Narayan Agnihotri quoted the Gospel of Luke: "Whatsoever ye have spoken in darkness shall be heard in the light; and that which ye have spoken in the ear in closets shall be proclaimed upon the housetops."[27] Such divulgences were manifold. Some were minor—in 1890, Agnihotri accused Lala Hansraj (a prominent Arya) of habitually eating pickled boar's flesh and having once, as a youth, posed as his brother's servant so he could ride a cross-country train for free.[28] Others were significant enough to land the parties involved in court.

Such was the story of *Pandit Gopi Nath v. Lala Munshi Ram and Others* (1901). Munshiram, the Arya polemicist whom we met in the previous chapter, was the editor of the newspaper *Sat Dharm Pracharak* (which later became the *Risala-i-Vartman*) and, in this role, had subjected Pandit Gopinath, a Sanatanist, to uncomfortable public scrutiny.[29] He alleged, first, that Gopinath's father was not a Kashmiri brahman (as Gopinath had claimed when arriving penniless in Lahore decades earlier) and, second, that Gopinath had used the prominent Urdu newspaper his father founded, the *Akhbar-i-Am*, to inflame communal feelings after the 1897 murder of Pandit Lekhram. He allegedly published anti-Muslim content to court a Hindu readership and then, when Muslim readers canceled their subscriptions, published pro-Muslim content to recoup them.[30] Reading these allegations, Gopinath turned to the courts to clear his good name.

He was disappointed. The British magistrate ruled that his father was an "adventurous upstart" and Gopinath himself "an impostor who has persistently played on the Hindu public for the sake of his own aggrandizement."[31] The only question was whether "the exposure of this impostor" was justifiable under the defamation sections of the Indian Penal Code (499–502). The magistrate decided it was. Unlike in England, where criminal libel is defined by its potential to breach the peace, the Code defined it around damage to reputation and exempted libels that correct a public misrepresentation of the public acts of a public man. Gopinath was indeed "a public man," and the public had a "right to learn the truth" about him.[32]

Munshiram celebrated his newspaper's courtroom victory by publishing a complete account of the trial in Urdu and Hindi, thus revealing "the hidden secret of Pandit Gopinath's public life" to the "public." He transliterated that English word into both Hindi and Urdu, as though to indicate his books' participation in a self-consciously modern print sphere.[33] "Truth is stranger than fiction," he explained, comparing his exposé to "novels" and "romances" (*upanyasom* and *fasanom*). Unlike such mere entertainments, however, true stories spur social reform. To "read this story [*kahani*] from beginning to end" is to realize that charlatans like Gopinath must be purged from all religious organizations.[34] A printed exposé opens a private life to the reading public—which is to say, to the intimate lives of those who encounter the text and perhaps reshape their lives around it.

What kind of a public is this? Calvert, the magistrate, seems unsure. Thinking from within libel law, he appears to refer to a general public that stands in structural opposition to private individuals, with reputation the mediating term between them. In closing his judgment, however, Calvert pauses around another sense of the public—worried that condemnation of Gopinath might be misconstrued as implicating "the Sanatan Dharma Sabha or the ancient religion which it upholds."[35] Does libeling a pandit necessarily imply a libel of his community? In colonial India, could privatized libel law adequately parse what it meant to be a "public man"? Did sacred personalities serve a representative function, standing in for populations? With such questions flickering in the background, Calvert vacillated momentarily, worried that Indian libel law did indeed need to consider potential breaches of the peace.

Nor was this an isolated worry. A decade later, in 1911, the Agha Khan's wazir wrote to the viceroy alleging that, in directing "defamatory and libelous language" at his boss, the Aryas were guilty of "publishing articles likely to cause a breach of the peace."[36] Did this letter allege an act of libel, or one of inducing the interreligious "enmity," described by 153A? Is this slander personal or public?

THE CASE OF THE PURLOINED PAPERS

Sometimes the shift between private and public was quite abrupt, as documented in *Amar Singh v. Dharmpal* (1909).[37] It is easy to imagine Amar Singh's horror when, in November 1907, he opened the Arya journal *Agni* to discover that his sexual confession to his guru had been reprinted in its pages. There for all Lahore to read was his description, drenched in self-loathing, of his frotteuristic pleasure in brushing up against women on a packed Punjabi train.

His words had been meant for a single reader, Shiv Narayan Agnihotri—the Lahore ex-Brahmo who had been jousting with the Aryas since the 1870s and who, after founding the Dev Samaj in 1887, began restyling himself as Bhagwan Dev Atma.[38] In the late 1900s, it was apparently standard practice for Dev Samajis to write confessional letters to Agnihotri. Some letters were anonymized and published in the society's newsletter, the *Jivan Tat*, for the moral benefit of readers. Others were circulated in the Samaj's inner circle. A few were labeled "secret and confidential" and filed in a locked cabinet. Amar Singh's had been in this last category.[39]

As official secretary of the Dev Samaj, Amar Singh had access to the locked cabinet, and one imagines him rushing to open it that November—only to find that his letter had been stolen, along with three others also reprinted in *Agni*. He headed to the police station to report the theft, pointing police toward the obvious culprit: Dharmpal, the *Agni*'s editor. Dharmpal was a colorful local figure. Né Abdul Ghafur to a Muslim and possibly subordinated-caste family, he had joined the Dev Samaj in 1898 and even worked at the Dev Samaj high school in the town of Moga alongside the author of another of the purloined letters (Gurmukh Singh). After moving to Lahore in 1902, he joined the Arya Samaj, becoming, from 1903, one of its most fearsome polemicists—until, in 1911, he converted back to Islam under the name Ghazi Mahmud.[40] Dharmpal's Arya writings lean on tropes of exposure, describing Moses as a trickster "magician" (*jadugar*) and outing the hidden moral corruption of the Prophet Muhammad.[41]

How did Dharmpal get the letters? Provenance was murky—and legally, that was a problem. Amar Singh filed suit against Dharmpal under Section 411 of the Indian Penal Code, concerning dishonest reception of stolen property. The local magistrate, clearly annoyed, advised him to bring charges instead under Section 499 (defamation) or 153A (class hatred), as the issue at stake was clearly "discredit, ridicule, and damage to reputation with respect to the Dev Samaj."[42] Amar Singh seems to have thought theft would be easier to prove. He was wrong. Had Dharmpal asked a clerk in the Dev Samaj office to steal the letters for him? Had the clerk, Mansa Ram, shown him the originals or copies? Did Agnihotri's wife give Mansa Ram the letters, such that Dharmpal could plausibly claim not to have known they were stolen? There were just too many empirical ambiguities. The trial took more than a year and, at the end of it, Dharmpal was acquitted. The magistrate's advice was apparently warranted: practically speaking, theft was the wrong charge.

At another level, however, it was precisely the right one. Amar Singh's sense of intimate injury had as much to do with the medium as the message. The physicality of stolen paper was affectively important, with the letter an eroticized object:

> I did not like this, but was obliged to do so. I could not help touching her. After a while I began to feel a sort of satisfaction and my mind seemed to draw some enjoyment from this (contact). At intervals I separated my body (from that of the woman) by force of will, so as to avoid contact with her, but at times my heart feeling hungry for this low pleasure and enjoyment (derived from contact) felt drawn (towards the woman) and I used to bring my body into contact with hers. The effect of this was very harmful both on my body and soul.

After a few hours of this, Amar Singh "found how weak I still was" and "how little strength I had to resist such temptations," such "unlawful lust." Only his guru could save him. "Oh my Bhagwan, who purifies the fallen. I bow before your blessed feet. . . . It is only through you that it is possible for me to be completely freed from this degradation."[43]

Amar Singh's confession letter, reopened here for the eyes of twenty-first century readers, is likely to produce an acute visceral response precisely because such nonconsensual scenes remain queasily common today. I quote his words so that we might better see how the affective materiality of Arya paper drew its intensity from broader cultural currents that included sexuality, in its manifold forms. I would also propose using the frotteuristic tactility of paper to read this heteroerotic scene against the grain.

Amar Singh's confession letter is not just a constative document describing a sexual experience. It is a performative document, producing and extending that experience. Prohibition, of course, frequently incites and structures desire in this way. Here, that structuration is oriented around the letter's addressee: Bhagwan Dev Atma, the very form of divine law. It is via the guru's body that the disciple's "lust" becomes "unlawful," with Singh's verbal performance of sexual degradation working to underscore the hierarchical relation between the two men. Further, the structuration of desire takes physical form in the material act of letter writing. A libidinally cathected object, the confession letter becomes a medium for establishing a religio-erotic relation between men. Importantly, it is an object of touch, moving semi-anonymously from hand to hand in Dev Samaj circles and thus partly replicating the scene of public tactility that took place on the train—or at least ferrying that scene's visceral charge into a differently located (yet still physical) paper-public milieu. Indeed, one might well insist that the scene of letter writing was in a crucial respect prior to the train scene, with its touching bodies. Amar Singh presumably knew all along he would be reporting these events, with his consequent sense of shame infusing his actions; his guru-Bhagvan was implicitly present as Singh enlisted unwilling female passengers as tools for affectively supercharging his prior relationship. One could take this case of erotic triangulation as revealing displaced or disavowed desire. I would read it instead as a demonstration of both the mobility of affect and the deep entanglement of late colonial print polemics with the embodied practice of gender and sexuality, in all its socially located ambivalence. Like religion, sexuality was never quite interior or private, but rather emerged across various kinds of public spaces.

These spaces included courtrooms and the print media that buzzed around them. The confession letter would seem to court publicity, putting secret thoughts onto pages that, by definition, are prone to circulate. Dev Samaj procedure seems to have maximized this uncertainty: letters could end up in the locked cabinet—or in print. Dharmpal's theft was a postal reappropriation, producing a sense of injury in Amar Singh by violating the public/private distinction. Yet, in doing so, it perhaps perversely fulfilled the implicit desire of this confessional text, one always already at risk of being published. If the act of publication fulfills the letter's erotic structure, then Dharmpal's theft is implicated in its sacred game. So too, by extension, are reading public and secular court. Law does not just govern the intimate; it is harnessed by the intimate toward intimate ends, becoming an arena for the further circulation of libidinally cathected paper artifacts.

THE USES OF OBSCENITY

Amar Singh's confession was tame compared to religious publications prosecuted for obscenity, a legal category designed to keep intimate matters out of public view. The Indian Penal Code's obscenity sections were, as we have seen, crafted in the shadow of Britain's 1857 Obscene Publications Act and interpreted via subsequent common-law jurisprudence, especially *Regina v. Hicklin* (1868)—a case concerning the resale of *The Confessional Unmasked* (1836), anti-Catholic convent erotica from British-colonial Montreal with the ostensibly high moral purpose of reforming priestly sexuality and redeeming fallen nuns. What came to be known as the "Hicklin test," articulated by Chief Justice Alexander Cockburn, brushed this justification aside. Henceforth, intention would be irrelevant to obscenity, a crime Cockburn defined around reception. Obscenity rests in a text's potential to "deprave and corrupt the minds" of readers.[44]

This conceptual ground, defined around Protestant smut, was retread in late colonial India in cases like *Empress v. Arya Samaj* (1890).[45] The case concerned an 1888 Arya tract, *Aj Kal ke Sadhuon ke Kartut* (The deeds of sadhus these days) that narrated a probably fictional debate with traditionalist sadhus. When the sadhus try to prove that image-worship is Vedic by citing Mahidhara's late-medieval commentary on the *Yajur Veda*, the Aryas respond by quoting sections of that commentary which refer to sex between a horse and a human woman (the wife of the *yajurman* or sacrificial presider), with notably explicit descriptions of the relevant human and equine anatomy.[46] The cheaply priced tract apparently proved popular with Lahore schoolboys.[47] In court, the Aryas' lawyer insisted his clients had published the questionable passages "for the benefit of the educated public" with no intention of causing offense; they thus could not be found guilty of obscenity.[48] The judge, citing the Hicklin test, rejected this argument. The text would necessarily tend to corrupt morals. It was therefore obscene.

Potentially obscene texts could also be prosecuted under Section 153A of the Code, added in 1898. The Aryas were involved in a 153A case just a few years later—as the injured party. *King Emperor v. Ala Ram Sanyasi* (1902) concerned an ex-Arya who, now an *upadeshak* or preacher of the Sanatan

Hindu Dharm Sabha, had been giving incendiary lectures around north India. One provoked a Shahjahanpur listener to physically assault an Arya. Another prompted Kanpur Aryas and Sanatanists to band together against the reckless orator. In publications, Ala Ram called Aryas buffoons, butchers, cannibals, liars, asses, dogs, prostitutes, and pimps, as well as monkey-faced, cow-eating, incestuous traitors. One article described in detail how Aryas should be executed (a process involving shoes, dogs, and a donkey). Another depicted Dayananda in the court of heaven; sentenced to a prison term of 432 billion years, he is beaten with shoes and force-fed urine and feces. Yet another article describes Aryas as children of Bhangis (a sweeper caste) and states that they have "mouths like latrines" because they eat "the ordure of Sudra men and women." As the court laconically noted of this last comment, "the simile is expanded in a most disgusting manner with regard to Dayanand himself." The judge ruled against Ala Ram, noting that his speech had already resulted in class enmity and violence. Aryas celebrated by publishing a transcript of the ruling.[49]

Ala Ram's writings remind us, once again, just how thoroughly a *savarna* imaginary of bodily purity informed late colonial religious polemics. Possibly in response to the Aryas' widely publicized outreach to Dalit communities in the preceding years, Ala Ram used obscenity to suggest that the Vedic mouth is constitutively impure. His insults thus not only impugn the Aryas. They also reinforce social hierarchies, with the structural violence of caste almost painfully implicit in his rhetorical imagery.

Even colonial officials seem to have had strongly visceral responses to such rhetoric. When, in 1915, Lahore's *Arya Musafir* forfeited its Rs. 2000 security deposit for having published articles that made vividly Islamophobic use of human urine and saliva (see chapter 7), the bureaucrat who processed the file scrawled in the margin that the articles in question violated "decency" and were clearly "calculated to give intense offense."[50] You can almost feel him bristling over the page. Wittingly or not, he also invoked the concept (decency) that had, since the 1880s, rendered blasphemy and obscenity law close neighbors.

THE SWAMI'S OFFICE

Blasphemy and obscenity also remained conceptually proximate to sedition. From the 1880s forward, but especially after the 1907 agrarian uprisings in

Punjab, the Arya Samaj was put under police surveillance for suspected sedition against the British Raj. In response, the Samaj invoked the political semantics of secularism by protesting that it was a "much maligned church" persecuted by an inquisitorially intolerant state.[51]

Sedition law had undergone several important changes in the preceding decades, not least the 1898 splintering of class enmity (153A) out of sedition proper (124A). In practice, however, keeping these offenses separate was apparently not a priority. Aryas, at least, were often charged under both, as happened in Patiala in 1909 when the Maharaja had all of his state's Aryas arrested for anti-British propaganda.[52] Government officials too tended to confuse these offenses, as when Lord Minto in a 1907 letter to John Morley veered suddenly from talking about sedition to talking about Aryas "wickedly" stirring up "racial ill-feeling."[53] The political offense and the religious or group defamation offense were hard to keep separate.

Sedition talk could also sometimes verge into private defamation, as happened with Lajpat Rai, the prominent Arya anticolonial leader. Deported to Burma in 1907 under sedition charges and then released due to insufficient evidence, Rai filed libel suits against newspapers that continued to impugn his good name (Calcutta's *Englishman* and London's *Daily Express*) and was, in 1909, awarded over £1000 in damages.[54] In 1912, when novelist Edmund Candler published a fictionalized account of these events with the provocative title *Siri Ram, Revolutionist*, Rai threatened its publishers with another libel suit.[55]

I want to pause for a moment on a scene from Candler's novel, a text brimming with imperial anxieties about a racialized Indian other—as suggested by its 1912 cover art, with its dark and glowering mutineer (a stand-in for Rai, see figure 8).[56] At one point in the novel, Siri Ram visits a Himalayan cave where a sadhu named Narasimha Swami is hoarding anticolonial literature. The cave floor is littered with letters postmarked in Paris, Dublin, Seattle, Portland, and Los Angeles—all nodes in India's anticolonial network. "Shiva's mansion," writes Candler, had become "the Swami's office," an epicenter of an oxymoronically clerkish religion. As though to dramatize the juxtaposition, a letter flutters onto an ice lingam as Siri Ram enters.[57]

This literary scene is not so different from others of its era (Rudyard Kipling's *Kim*, with its fakir-spies, was published in 1901). And while it is suffused with paranoid imperial fantasy, it also dramatizes the social life of late colonial documents with some acuity. Anticolonial letters were indeed sites where religion and politics intertwined or fused—and thus occasions for

FIGURE 8. Original cover of Edmund Candler's *Siri Ram, Revolutionist* (London, 1912). © The British Library Board. Shelfmark T 7903.

the colonial-secular state to cement and extend its authority by insisting on the distinction between them, exposing "politics" concealed in "religious" robes. Letters were also mobile objects, circulating readily across national and imperial borders—and finding new and perhaps unlikely readers along the way.

UNCOMMON READERS

By the 1890s, Aryas were experimenting with mailing books to India's princely states (which, taken together, occupied around a third of the subcontinent's landmass). Dayananda had hoped Hindu princes would become key patrons of his Vedic modernity. While that hope never fully materialized, there were notable successes. In the 1910s, for instance, the Maharaja of Kolhapur—a social reformist ally of Ambedkar—invited the Aryas to administer education in his state as part of a general assault on "Brahmin Bureaucracy."[58] Other princes, meanwhile, were wary. The Muslim Nizam of Hyderabad ejected Aryas more than once in the 1890s and 1900s for their anti-Muslim rhetoric.[59] In 1910, the Sikh Maharaja of Patiala ejected them for anti-British sedition.[60] The Maharaja of Dholpur caused a minor scandal in 1919 when he appropriated an Arya temple only to face rumors he meant to convert it into a latrine.[61] Nepal seems to have banned Aryas outright from 1926 to 1933 (leading Aryas to argue that this infringement on their religious liberty violated the Nepali king's treaty with the British).[62]

Monarchs could stop Aryas from crossing borders. It was harder to stop the mail. Consider two parcels sent in the 1890s. In 1891, the Afghan emir Abdur Rahman Khan received a copy of Pandit Lekhram's *Takzib-i-Barahin-i-Ahmadiyya* (Falsification of the Ahmadiyya arguments, 1887), sent by Muslims in the British-Indian city of Peshawar. They apparently hoped he would use his influence to get the book banned in India. Although the Afghan emir did feel "very much grieved" by the book and its "impertinent expressions," as he explained to his kingdom's British Agent, he decided not to intervene directly. Instead, he advised the Peshawar Muslims to file a complaint in British courts, showing his letter to British authorities if they liked. Afghanistan had carefully crafted its independence at the intersection of British, Russian, and Ottoman empires.[63] The emir presumably decided that it was more strategic to let legally actionable feelings stay on the other side of the British border.

In 1896, the Begum of Bhopal opened her mail to find another copy of the *Takzib*, plus an additional Lekhram title. Whoever sent them (likely Lekhram himself) had also sent copies to one of her ministers and several of her subjects. The Begum decided to read the books, marking objectionable passages in red ink. She then sent her copies to her state's British Agent, with a letter explaining how they "grossly insulted all the Prophets of Islam and the Christians and the Holy God" in order to "to wound the religious feelings" of Muslims. The agent agreed that the books were "undoubtedly calculated to offend" but was unsure what to do about it, seeing as Section 298 of the Indian Penal Code pointedly omitted printed texts. While he and his fellow bureaucrats dithered—asking, among other things, whether this might be pursued as a defamation case instead, given its libels on individuals like Muhammad—Pandit Lekhram was murdered. They decided to drop the matter.[64]

"I wonder why these books have been sent to me to wound my religious feelings and embitter my life," sighed the Begum.[65] Why indeed. Her query provides a fitting end to our discussion of Arya insult as a postal and print-mediated practice. What kind of affective work did such circulatory paper objects do?

Without an explicit statement by Lekhram as to why he sent these texts (if it was indeed him who sent them), one is left speculating about motive. His books were part of a much larger campaign of anti-Muslim invective, organized around Mirza Ghulam Ahmad (whose claims to have been a prophet like Muhammad made him a controversial figure among Muslims too).[66] In *Barahin-ul-Ahmadiyya* (Proofs of the Ahmadiyya, 1880–84), Ahmad had invited rebuttals but asked that critics refrain from "uncivil and derogatory language" and undue disparagement of "holy personages."[67] (He also included a requisite genuflection to colonial law, asserting that his intention in writing the book was "not to injure anyone's feelings or provoke unnecessary controversy."[68]) In his decidedly uncivil response, Lekhram ignored this request. Calling Ahmad a "defrauder" and "mad dog," he depicted the principal Islamic prophets as adulterers, murders, and idolators and concluded by comparing the Prophet Muhammad unfavorably to Dayananda Saraswati. The official government translator said that Lekhram's language was so "intemperate" it was almost as though he "does not understand what sober language means." He was drunk on insult.[69]

Between 1887 and 1896, Lekhram was threatened with lawsuits under various sections of the Indian Penal Code—often several at once, as in 1896, when he was charged with obscenity, religious offense, and personal defamation (292, 293, 298, 500, 501, and 502) in a Delhi case.[70] If his "falsification" of Ahmad's "proofs" was, as the official translator suggested, clearly "calculated to wound deeply and stir up violently the feelings of the people thus railed at and ridiculed," surely Lekhram also calculated the likelihood of legal blowback—an engine for further publicity.[71]

When print polemics traveled, they carried the forcefield of colonial law with them. The Indian Penal Code applied in princely states, and the princes used it, as seen in the Begum's appeal to her British Agent. Print also drove law into the domain of sentiment. An unwanted parcel arrives in the mail, eliciting a bitter sigh from an exasperated monarch. If that sigh is coded as an instance of "religious feelings," it comes to express the cultural force of law. Even a royal body can be hailed as an exemplum of an administered population in need of affective management.

CONCLUSION: TO READ OR NOT TO READ

"It appears to be a silly production, but I can't make out that it is criminal," wrote a British official in 1891, apropos of Lekhram's migratory text. "The simplest plan for a Mahomedan appears to be not to read the book."[72] This was dubious advice. A book like Lekhram's exerts a force on potential readers even with its covers closed.

It does this precisely because it can hail even a nonreader as a "Mahomedan," with comments like that of our bureaucrat overdetermining the conditions of reader reception. The comment puts the Mahomedan nonreader in a precise form of double bind, pulled between the public and the population (see chapter 2). By refusing to read a book, a person opts out of its public, or at least would seem to. A population cannot escape so easily. It remains tethered to a given text by the historically determinate forces that situate them both, allowing that media text to hail a populational public, simultaneously open edged and bound to an enumerable religious group. By describing his nonreader as a Mahomedan, then, the bureaucrat reinforces and performatively reconstitutes this larger set of discursive structures, ensuring that his Mahomedan nonreader remains tied to Lekhram's text whether or not she chooses to open its covers.

In this chapter, we have encountered Arya words as material presences, working on historically situated bodies in localized ways. Their intimately physical force arrogated and combined with the force of law, turning that force to unexpected ends—above all, perhaps, to moral or affective ends, shaping subjects. Personal animus was central to this era's culture of religious controversy, with capillary personal relations often appearing as the matrix of all governmentalities, the most effective arena for reshaping the conduct of self and others. To be efficacious, then, the legal needed the personal as much as or more than the personal needed the legal.

When we move too quickly to talking about collective or communal feelings, we lose site of the microhistorical scale at which affect can be most properly said to emerge. The Aryas' paper insults were simultaneously political (i.e., about the production of state sovereignty), communal (i.e., about the production of administered populations), and personal (i.e., inseparable from capillary social networks and the intimate production of gender, sexuality, and bodily virtue), and should be studied at all these registers at once.

09

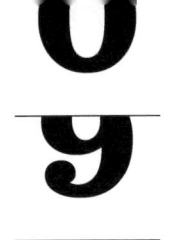

THE SWAMI AND THE PROPHET

Slandering Lives, Conducting Character

GIVEN THEIR FREQUENTLY LIBELOUS POLEMICS against allegedly corrupt sacred persons, it is perhaps unsurprising that Arya Samajists were behind the *Rangila Rasul*—the scandalous 1924 pamphlet that, by mocking the Prophet Muhammad, prompted the addition of Section 295A to the Indian Penal Code. The *Rangila Rasul* was many things: a print artifact, a communalist polemic, a libel on the dead. It was also, in a way that has mostly gone unnoticed in scholarship, an ethical treatise—or rather a precise inversion of the ethical. At several key points in the tract, its author, Pandit Chamupati, compares the alleged sexual profligacy of the Prophet Muhammad to the sexual restraint of Swami Dayananda Saraswati. The tract's prophet is a model of what not to do with sex, a reverse image of its implied swami.

Published in the lead-up to the February 1925 centennial celebration of Dayananda's birth, the *Rangila Rasul* needs to be read in relation to the many hagiographic books, tracts, plays, and images circulating among Aryas at the time—sold at bookstalls to the thousands of pilgrims who flocked to the "Dayanand Shatabdi" (centenary) celebrations at Mathura and distributed at schools and gardens parties in regional centers like Haridwar and Lahore. Nor were these books the only hagiographic texts circulating in early twentieth-century India. The *Rangila Rasul* also brought Arya hagiography into polemic proximity with printed *sira* literature (i.e., biographies of Muhammad), shoehorning *sira* into the quadrangle of classical Hinduism's four *ashrama*s, or life phases. Part of a larger biography boom in late colonial India, it also circulated alongside printed lives of historical figures from Abraham Lincoln to Rammohun Roy, Sita to Christopher Columbus.

In such works, biography was routinely positioned as a tool for national uplift, its printed lives serving as moral templates. Print biography was thus shadowed by a perhaps irresolvable question: Can a life reduced to writing be successfully replicated once again in a different medium, the body of the reader?

Exploring that question both theoretically and empirically, this chapter maps a cultural history for the *Rangila Rasul* and its polemic prophetology, situating it both as an Arya Samajist text and a transcolonial one. The chapter builds toward an analysis of the tract's rhetorical structure, thus bringing *Slandering the Sacred* full circle. We can now see how the *Rangila Rasul*, as "religious" tract, was a paper tool for the governance of affect, functioning in parallel with Section 295A, the "secular" law, in a shared field of pedagogic governmentality. My discussion concludes by asking how this chapter's history of comparative prophetology might be used to revisit more recent scandals about sacred slander.

REPRINTING THE SWAMI: AFTERLIVES OF A HINDU REFORMER

In late 1883, after a public career spanning more than a decade, Dayananda Saraswati suddenly fell ill. Some said it was poison. Food-borne sickness seems at least as likely. Whatever the cause, Dayananda died that October after a month of agony. Ordering all the doors and windows of his sickroom opened, he uttered his final words ("God, you have done a good *lila*") and began "his pilgrimage to the realm of the immortals."[1]

On earth, a different type of immortality awaited. In 1886, Lala Lajpat Rai published an article in the *Arya Patrika* calling for a "systematic biography" of the swami. "Great and noble souls," he explained, are "lighthouses in the great ocean of human progress," and nothing—not pictures, shrines, or even their published writings—can "bring them home to us" like a good biography.[2]

Would-be biographers were confronted with a substantial problem, however. Dayananda's early life remained cloaked in mystery. Although he often recounted personal stories and even published an autobiographical essay in *The Theosophist*, his self-narrative tended toward the spare and the symbolic—how, as a boy, he realized the error of image worship when he saw a rat scramble across a Shiva lingam; how he resolved to renounce the world after a sister's and an uncle's deaths; how he fled home, defying his father.[3] He never revealed his birth name; "Dayananda" was the moniker bestowed when Purnananda Sarasvati of the Shringeri Math initiated him as a renunciant.[4] A proper biography would, in its way, reverse this renunciation, returning Dayananda to the life he left behind.

It would also require serious research. In 1888, the Punjab Arya Pratinidhi Sabha nominated Lekhram, the editor of the *Arya Gazette*, to travel India collecting relevant oral histories. He pursued the project for nearly eight years prior to his 1897 murder. Meanwhile, a Bengali researcher named Devendranath Mukhopadhyay was also hard at work; he too died prematurely, publishing only a preliminary sketch of his planned opus. Years later, these two bodies of research were compiled into a single biography by Ghasiram, whose text remains the authoritative empirical source on Dayananda's life.[5]

Hagiographic chronicles of the swami's deeds also began to appear by the late 1880s. A steady textual trickle widened to a rushing stream during the Dayanand centenary of 1924–25, during which more than two dozen biographies were published in Hindi, Sanskrit, Urdu, Bengali, English, Marathi, Gujarati, and Punjabi.[6] By this time, Arya hagiography had emerged as a distinct genre within the wider field of modern Hindu hagiography, and one with clear literary conventions.[7] These narratives typically begin in ancient India, with the battle of Kurukshetra, then glide quickly across the millennia to Dayananda's 1824 birth. Most conclude with a summary of the swami's teachings. "Without this part," explained Ghasiram, "no biography can be said to be complete."[8]

Arya hagiography was diverse, spanning sundry media and literary genres. There were Hindi biographies composed in poetic forms like *doha*, *lavni*, and *ghazal*, as well as Sanskrit biographies that tendentiously disavowed the voluptuous "poetry of contemporary times" to imitate the Vedas.[9] There was at least one hagiographic play, written to wean Punjabi audiences away from their stock diet of "indecent" theater; its first Urdu edition sold out in six months and was followed by a Hindi reprint.[10] Tantalizingly, one pamphlet mentions a Bioscope film about Dayananda's boyhood encounter with the temple rat.[11]

Clearly Aryas were using images, although most do not survive. To get a sense for their iconography, we might leaf through the pages of Shitalprasad Vaidya's *Shrimaddayanand Chitravali* (Dayananda picture album, 1925). There, we find depictions of major biographical episodes in glossy black-and-white prints alongside a handful of color images. One of the latter

FIGURE 9. "Bharat Mata" (Mother India). Shitalprasad Vaidya, *Shrimaddayanand Chitravali* (Calcutta: Vedic Pustakalaya, 1925). © The British Library Board. Shelfmark Hin.D.1519.

shows Mother India striding across a map of the subcontinent with an Aum flag in one hand and a cameo portrait of Dayananda in the other (see figure 9). A second depicts Dayananda sitting cross-legged on an animal skin in an idealized Himalayan setting, his frontal gaze recalling the composition of devotional bazaar art (see figure 10). Here, ironically, the notorious iconoclast has become an icon in the style of mass-produced pictures common in the period.[12]

Nonetheless, "Yogi-Raj" is an icon with a difference. Although obviously referencing Shiva posters, his ascetic body is depicted as stripped of the usual divine accoutrements, suggesting an iconoclastic impulse. It further

FIGURE 10. "Yogi-raj: Maharishi Dayananda Saraswati." Shitalprasad Vaidya, *Shrimaddayanand Chitravali* (Calcutta: Vedic Pustakalaya, 1925). © The British Library Board. Shelfmark Hin.D.1519.

disciplines visual Hinduism by submitting it to the dictates of photorealism: the image is clearly modeled on a commonly reproduced photograph of Dayananda and possibly even painted overtop it (as suggested by the odd foreshortening of the hands). "Mother India" works similarly. More secular woman than Hindu goddess, she adheres to a realist aesthetic, from the drapery of her sari to the topographic detail of her map to her individuated facial features—likely based on a photograph. The cameo portrait in her hand is almost certainly based on one, probably the photo of Dayananda sponsored by the Maharaja of Shapura and reproduced elsewhere in the *Chitravali* (see figure 5).[13]

Arya iconoclasts may have mistrusted images, but they sometimes carved out an exception for photography. As an 1889 Arya catechism explains, the "idolatry" evident in Ramlilas and other popular performances is wrong—a "sin" and a form of "fetishism" (invoking the anthropological category derived from colonial West Africa)—because it creates a visual likeness of a divine entity that has no visual form. Photographs, by contrast, are grounded in visual reality, so it is permissible to use them in various "remembrance" practices.[14] The problem with pictures, then, is not their visuality per se, but rather their dishonest semiotics, their bad ontology.

The 1924 *Dayanand Chitravali* exists in this space of photographic exception, enacting a remembrance of the Arya past. Loosely replicating the structure of a photo album, its pages are packed with black-and-white portraits of Arya leaders, students, and martyrs, standing alone and in groups, variously clustered on the page. These two-toned photos represent ordinary Aryas. The color images of Dayananda are different in kind, jumping out from the rest of the *Chitravali*. Closer to bazaar art than to the photo album, they create a kind of two-way traffic between disciplined photorealism and calendar-art iconicity—and thus between two distinct modalities of modern religion.[15]

These images also point to a larger paradox of Arya devotion. When Dayananda founded the influential Lahore chapter of the Samaj in 1877, he refused to be named the society's guru, explaining that his mission was to eradicate the "stink of gurudom" (*gurupan ki bu*) from the world.[16] Later Aryas pointed to this foundational disavowal of sacred authority as emblematic. This was the gesture that "made the Arya Samaj a democratic [*prajasattatmak*] organization," as one society historian put it in 1949.[17] If revering Dayananda as a guru was bad, deifying him was definitely worse. Arya hagiography was therefore a constitutively fraught genre. As one 1914 writer confessed, he had "no desire to carve a place for Dayananda in the Hindu Pantheon. It is already too full. And the task will be a thankless one. It will be a direct violation of his injunction and the spirit of his work to set him up for a God."[18]

These tensions were particularly acute in retellings of the definitive fable of Arya iconoclasm, the tale of the Shivaratri rat: A boy and his father go a Shiva temple to keep the all-night Shivaratri vigil, and the father falls asleep. Awake and alone, the boy sees a rat clamber over the *shivalingam*. This sight produces a critical disenchantment, wherein the boy suddenly perceives the impotence of religious icons (see figure 11). Dayananda's published account of this story in *The Theosophist* is sparse in its details. Nor do later retellings

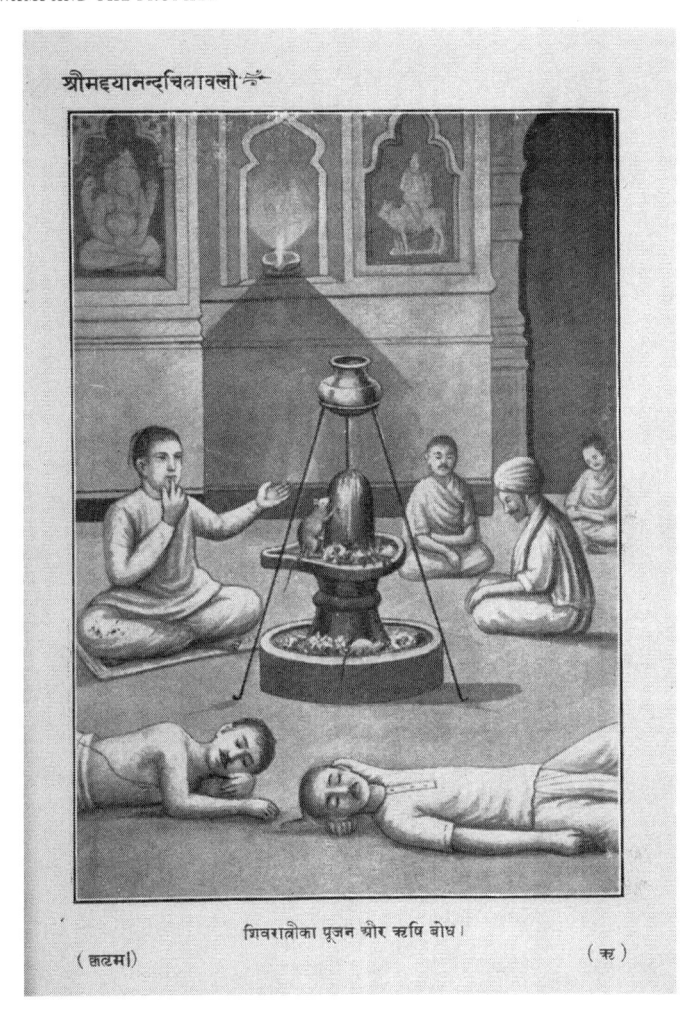

FIGURE 11. "Shivaratri ka Pujan aur Rishi Bodh" (Shivaratri puja and the rishi's realization). Shitalprasad Vaidya, *Shrimaddayanand Chitravali* (Calcutta: Vedic Pustakalaya, 1925). © The British Library Board. Shelfmark Hin.D.1519.

ever quite clarify what it is about the rat, as animal, that provokes disenchantment. (One is left to speculate: Is this an Oedipal drama, underscored by the rat's association with Ganesh? Is it referencing and then rejecting *bhakti* stories in which rats become accidental devotees? Does it connote filth or even ritual pollution?) Later retellings do, however, embellish the story by adding detail (e.g., the foods used for *prasad*).

Several, notably, insert supernatural elements. By the late 1890s, the booming voice of Shiva was addressing young Dayananda in his moment of disillusionment.[19] By the 1920s, hagiographers were implying that Dayananda was an avatar of Vishnu, with his birthplace of Morvi listed alongside Rama's Ayodhya and Krishna's Mathura.[20] Most vivid in this regard is perhaps Sudarshan's *Dayanand Natak* (Dayananda: The play, 1917). The production begins with Mother India standing before the closed stage curtain, mournfully recalling the golden days of her sons Ram and Lakshman. Krishna then steps in from the wing to explain that the present darkness is just a passing rainstorm. He riffs on the verse from the *Bhagavad Gita* promising that Vishnu will incarnate whenever (in this play's words) "dharma is disgraced in all the bazaars"; divine lightning flashes at the moment of greatest darkness. Cue an offstage firecracker. The curtain opens onto our boy-hero praying and singing to a Shiva *murti*. The offstage sound of Shiva's supernatural voice soon follows.[21]

A late 1920s pamphleteer called this story the Samaj's "seed" or "guru-mantra," underlining its succinct distillation of Dayananda's critique of Puranic Hinduism.[22] But of course that phrase also underscores the extent to which this story had been used to position Dayananda as the guru he so emphatically refused to be. Arya hagiography was, it seems, an inherently unstable genre, one predicated on a tension between enchantment and disenchantment, iconophilia and iconoclasm.

A SAINTLY CENTENNIAL

It was also a genre that operated on the flesh, with biographical paper pressing on readers and their bodies in a variety of ways, many of them evident during the centennial celebration of Dayananda's birth in February 1925.

The Gurukul Kangri had been celebrating a *rishi utsav* or festival on Dayananda's death anniversary since at least the 1910s, and its leader Swami Shraddhananda (a.k.a. Munshiram) took a leading role in conceiving the 1925 *janmshatabdi* (birth centenary), sketching a plan in his diary in 1922.[23] An All-India Dayanand Centenary Committee, chaired by Narayan Swami of the Sarvadeshik Pratinidhi Sabha, was then appointed to organize the festivities.[24] Committee members hoped to use the celebration to promote the cause of Hindi. They also wrote the Government of India requesting that Arya employees be granted official leave to fulfill their "religious duties" during the centennial; Delhi demurred, referring them to local governments.[25]

More than two hundred thousand people reportedly traveled by train and other transport to Mathura, the centennial's epicenter, where Dayananda had studied under the blind sage Virajananda. They formed a temporary city, or Arya Nagar, where massive crowds attended lectures and *havan* rituals. Students won medals in the "Shatabdi games." A "Conference of Religions" showcased Jain, Christian, and Bahai delegates. Pilgrims strolled past Virajananda's dilapidated house. As a reporter from the *Leader* noted, these events had an air of "austerity" about them. Shops sold none of the sacred knickknacks common at Hindu festivals, only books and food. The food, moreover, was shared, in defiance of caste norms, with Dalits and women milling about freely in significant numbers. Traditionalist Hindus seem to have disapproved. When festivalgoers visited nearby Vrindavan, they found some temples closed and others with signs saying no Aryas allowed. Nonetheless, when thousands of Aryas processed through the streets of Mathura, locals reportedly gathered on rooftops to shower them with flowers.[26]

Festivities extended around the Arya world. In Mauritius, Aryas celebrated for two full days. In Durban, they celebrated for a week, holding South Africa's first "Vedic Conference."[27] At Lahore's Dayanand Anglo-Vedic College, the Young Men's Arya Samaj organized tournaments, debates, lectures, and a massive parade. "The air was full of Great Swami in those days," the school principal later recalled. Students felt his "living presence" in their dorms and playing fields, until their enthusiasm was "screwed . . . to the highest pitch."[28]

Print helped publicize the holiday. As early as November 1924, the Punjab-based journal *Arya* was stoking excitement for a special "Dayananda Centennial Issue" by soliciting essays, poems, and pictures about the swami.[29] By February, the centennial was getting coverage in more obscure periodicals like *Vaidik Dharm*, published from the Maharashtrian princely state of Aundh.[30] Print was also integral to the festivities. Those Mathura bookstalls, surely, were selling Arya hagiographics. In Lahore, meanwhile, the DAV College block-printed ten thousand copies of a biography on "art paper," distributed booklets with Dayananda's photo and a list of his principles at a garden party, and printed a centennial message on handkerchiefs that were used to wrap sweets for schoolchildren.[31] Print spilled off the page, by design.

The *Rangila Rasul* was published in the lead-up to the centennial festivities, in May 1924. This context matters. Whether or not it was actually written as retribution for a Muslim-authored travesty of Dayananda's life, the

Rangila Rasul clearly emerged from a polemic literary field in which lives of Dayananda and the Prophet were closely intertwined.[32] Not only does the *Rangila Rasul* explicitly compare the two men, but in 1923, its anonymous author, Pandit Chamupati, also published a series of biographical essays on Dayananda in the *Vedic Magazine* that he later collected into a centennial book, *Glimpses of Dayananda* (1925).[33] (As late as 1948, it was said that Rajpal had taken the secret of the author's name to his grave.[34] A decade later, that secret had outed. The author was Chamupati.[35]) These texts are pinned to their moment of publication—extending into 1926, when Aryas organized a follow-up celebration at Dayananda's birthplace or *janmbhumi* in Morvi.[36]

The back cover of the *Rangila Rasul* effectively maps the literary constellation that presided over this historical moment, advertising books available at "moderate" prices from Mahashe Rajpal, manager of the Arya bookstore on Lahore's Hospital Road.[37] These include an Urdu version of the *Satyarth Prakash*; tracts by Arya polemicists like Lekhram and Dharmpal; Arya hagiographies with titles like *Dayanand Anand Safar* (Dayananda's blissful journey), *Rishi Jivan* (A life of the rishi), and *Dayanand Prakash* (The light of Dayananda); and a biography of Napoleon Bonaparte.[38] Taken together, these texts—including the Napoleon biography—situate the Aryas' polemicized prophet and reveal the range of his textual connections.

PROPHETIC BIOGRAPHY IN A POLEMIC AGE

Or, at least, they do if read alongside the *Rangila Rasul*'s footnotes, which offer a rough-and-ready survey of modern *sira* literature, the genre that the tract so viciously spoofed. Major references include William Muir's *Life of Mahomet* (1861–1878), Shibli Numani's *Sirat un-Nabi* (1914), and Syed Ameer Ali's *The Spirit of Islam* (published in 1891, with an amplified and revised edition issued in 1922).

"Probably more lives of Muhammad appeared in every one of the years between the two World Wars than in any of the centuries between the twelfth and nineteenth," speculated Wilfred Cantwell Smith in the 1940s while teaching at Lahore's Foreman Christian College.[39] In the 1920s, provincial schoolmaster Abd al Majid Qarashi announced what he called a "Sirat Movement," distributing biographies of the Prophet and modernist tracts by thinkers like Rashid Rida to middleclass readers. Twenty years later, Smith borrowed Qarashi's term to describe the wave of publications in several languages (Urdu, Sindhi, English, etc.) that arose around the 1890s.[40] The *Rangila Rasul* rode this cresting wave, harnessing it for its own ends.

Although the *sira* was a classical genre, it had been reframed around a distinctly modern set of concerns, giving rise to a new subgenre: the polemical *sira*.[41] Keen to defend the Prophet from Western critics like Muir, Muslim writers proliferated new biographies. The more they responded to criticisms, however, the more Muslim and non-Muslim lives of the Prophet became interdependent—until, at least by one scholar's assessment, they ceased to constitute discrete literary traditions altogether.[42] The polemical *sira* was thus, in its very emergence, a globalizing genre intertwined with English. It was also linked to Hindi and other South Asian vernacular languages, where the Prophet was becoming a figure of parody and satire. Sometimes, as in Bharatendu Harishchandra's 1873 essay on "Shri Hazrat Honorable Mr. Double White Sucking Prophet [*chusa paigambar*], the Destroyer of the Universe," satire was directed at the British (Harishchandra's prophet is a barbarian "guru" who uses religion as a ruse for "sucking" wealth).[43] Probably more often, as in Jagganath Das's *Muhammad Jivan Charitra* (1887), moral scrutiny was directed at the Prophet himself, lacing his life narrative with libelous imputations.[44]

Good character was this literature's key leitmotif. Muir weighed Muhammad's virtues (e.g., "magnanimity") against his alleged flaws (e.g., "cruelty").[45] Numani insisted that, where earlier "religious personalities" had embodied only particular virtues, Muhammad offered an integrated vision of the moral life. His religious mission was primarily ethical: "to reform and perfect the morals and culture [*akhlaq o tarbit*] of human beings."[46] Modern *sira*'s ethicized Prophet participated in a larger literary field, linked to a nineteenth-century efflorescence of Urdu tracts on the "polishing of morals" (*tahzib ul-akhlaq*). These tracts both revived an early modern genre and overlaid it with Victorian values like frugality, cleanliness, and self-improvement, as seen in texts like Hali's *Musaddas* (1879).[47]

This late colonial rearticulation of ethics was constitutively intertwined with questions of gender and sexuality. The Prophet's wives, lampooned by the *Rangila Rasul*, were sites for the articulation of shifting gender norms in a series of moral panics in the nineteenth and twentieth centuries—with Khadijah, for instance, rising to prominence alongside the ideal of companionate marriage.[48] They were thus linked to a set of nineteenth-century social reformist impulses that Aryas also helped carry into the early twentieth century, as with an Arya Marriage Validation Bill ratifying inter-caste and interreligious marriages proposed in 1928 and enacted in 1937.[49] In addition to advocating inter-caste marriage, Aryas also—still more scandalously—endorsed *niyog* (a temporary sexual liaison, in cases of infertility, between a married woman and a man other than her husband).

As part of the archive of late colonial sexuality, the *Rangila Rasul* circulated alongside sexology manuals and pornographic literature, weaponizing smut for communalist ends.[50] The controversy around it overlapped with the controversy around Katherine Mayo's *Mother India* (1927) and thus also with the newly nationalized feminist politics that coalesced in the shadow of that text.[51] If Mayo refitted nineteenth-century reformist discourses about Indian women to the emergent geopolitics of the US empire, the *Rangila Rasul* gestured to a different historical trajectory, hewing closer to a nineteenth-century cultural formation. By submitting the Prophet to a sexualized "trial [*pariksha*] by fire" (as the *Arya* wrote in 1926), it echoed earlier tracts like *Rampariksha* (An examination of Rama, 1867), wherein American Presbyterians compared Rama to the celibate Jesus, or *Muhammad Pariksha* (1888), wherein a Hindu pandit assessed the Prophet just as he would any guru, pir, fakir, prophet, or avatar. He began by comparing Muhammad's wives to Krishna's gopis—a move that flatters neither sacred man.[52]

In such texts, women are (to recall Lata Mani's formulation) neither subjects nor objects but rather the ground on which men conduct their culture wars.[53] The real objective of these tracts was the regulation of male heterosexuality. Using textualized women to triangulate relations among men, they establish a print-mediated regime of homosocial sexual governance.[54] "The Vedic man is a rougher sort of person than the modern Hindu. He is more manly," opined a prominent Arya in 1893.[55] Such muscular Hinduisms were a riposte to the trope of the "effeminate Hindu," used to justify India's subordination to "manly" Victorians.[56] Positioning the male body as a site for contesting colonial rule, Vedic masculinity became an idiom of geopolitics.

Sexual self-control is the key theme here. Consider Chamupati's *Glimpses of Dayananda*, the *Rangila Rasul*'s companion text in its author's oeuvre. Each chapter introduces a different view or "glimpse" of the swami—the warrior, the iconoclast, the mystic, the patriot, the physical colossus, and so on. The key to the whole, however, is arguably the chapter on the "brahmachari," a term that Chamupati imports into English as simultaneously untranslatable and central to Dayananda's status as a universal figure—a "cosmopolitan sage" and "apostle" to humanity at large. (The global-cosmopolitan was, for the Aryas, almost always accessed through English, even when English was made to carry the linguistic marks of Indian national or Hindu difference.)[57] Sexual continence powered Dayananda's other virtues, including his famed physical strength (dramatically displayed when he hitched himself to a pull-cart, outmuscling two horses). It was also prescribed for his followers—who, even if unable to join the celibate elite, could practice continence within marriage, elevating sex from "animal necessity" to "sacred duty."[58]

When the *Rangila Rasul* presents its title character as unable to control his sexual impulses, it implicitly casts him as weak and feminized. Unsurprisingly, we meet a very different figure in Muslim-authored lives of the Prophet from the 1920s. Take, for example, Muhammad Ali's *Muhammad the Prophet* (1924), written while its author was imprisoned for sedition and modeled on Numani's *Sirat un-Nabi*.[59] Ali's Muhammad is a "complete master of his passions," immune to the allure of "worldly things."[60] The Prophet of Syed Ameer Ali's *Spirit of Islam* (1922) is similarly ascetic. He first appears in a novelistic passage as a "quiet thoughtful man" sauntering through the streets of Mecca "heedless of the gay scenes around him ... yet withal never forgetful to return the salutation of the lowliest."[61] Although living in sensualist times, he keeps his house unheated and often subsists only on dates and water—the very antithesis of "a self-indulgent libertine."[62]

If we translate *rangila* as a "rake" or "sybarite" (following John Platts's 1884 Urdu dictionary), the very title of Chamupati's tract is a precise inversion of Ameer Ali. Its inverse valuation of celibacy is also quite precise. Where Ameer Ali describes the Hindu, Buddhist, and Christian ideal of absolute celibacy as a "perversion of nature," Chamupati hails celibacy as what makes Dayananda, the Buddha, and Jesus superior to Muhammad.[63] Ameer Ali and Chamupati agree on the value of ascetic self-restraint; they diverge on how to reconcile asceticism to sexuality.

SACRED AND SECULAR BIOGRAPHY: PRINTED LIVES, IMITABLE VIRTUES

There is one last text on the back cover of the *Rangila Rasul* that needs explaining: the biography of Napoleon. Although I have not managed to track down that exact title, it is still possible to reconstruct its general context—suggesting the historically specific connections between "secular" political biography and "religious" biography in the late colonial period.

Early twentieth-century India witnessed a veritable biography boom.

Life writing surged across languages and genres—an important literary carrier of this moment's larger ethical turn, its interest in refashioning the self to refashion the nation.[64] Late colonial biography was notably eclectic. Looking at Hindi alone, one finds lives of religious reformers like Rammohun Roy; nationalist leaders like M. G. Ranade and Lajpat Rai; precolonial kings like Maharaja Chhatrasal; and North Atlantic luminaries from Christopher Columbus to Dan Breen.[65] Men predominate, but alongside them one finds the occasional life of Sita or compendium of biographical sketches of "brave and learned" Hindu women.[66] Aryas were enthusiastic contributors to this literary scene, authoring numerous biographies and autobiographies of Samaj members both renowned and obscure.[67]

Late colonial biography was a medium for ethical reproduction, for the replication of the printed life in the life of the reader. "The worthy man will attempt to write his [Dayananda's] biography not just on paper pages but also on the book of his heart," wrote one Arya hagiographer in 1925.[68] Or, as another opined in the same year, "I am pouring Swamiji's biography [*jivani*] into my life [*jivan*]."[69] Similar claims are found in secular biographies. In his preface to a 1928 Hindi translation of Benjamin Franklin's *Autobiography*, for instance, one writer says that biographies will guide India's youth onto the "path of self-improvement and service of country" by presenting "imitable" (*anukaraniya*) virtues like Franklin's industriousness.[70] Some biographers highlighted a specific virtue that their subject ostensibly exemplified (Columbus's courage, Lajpat Rai's charity).[71] Others offered more general advice about how to read their books, as by explaining that Sita's life was "not just a novel or entertaining story, but a treasury of ethics [*niti*] and instruction."[72] Throughout, life writing appears as an exercise in ethics, with narrative exerting normative force on its readers.

In this ethical field, even political figures could assume an aura of sanctification. Anyone who sacrifices himself for the good of the nation should be considered a *sadhu*, as a biographer of Abraham Lincoln argued in 1917, with any assembly of such persons an instance of *sant-samagam*, a gathering of holy men. There is, moreover, no need, our biographer argues, to insist on "face-to-face meeting" (*pratyaksh samagam*), as books facilitate a similar ethical imitation.[73] To read hagiographies is to commune with saints gathered on bookshelves. "There is no difference between *satsang* [associating with good people] and reading true biographies," concurred a 1918 biographer of Lajpat Rai, except the accident of medium. One happens face-to-face, the other via a book.[74] Other writers disagreed with this easy equation. In 1914, for instance, Shibli Numani insisted that though print might be the "modern method" of perfecting morals, it remains inferior to the morally upright person, "every movement of whose lips does the work of thousands of books."[75] Bodies are better than books—but to argue the point is perhaps to concede the analogy between these media.[76]

A WORLD OF WORTHIES: HERO-ANTHOLOGIES AND THE GLOBAL CARLYLE

To better understand this print-mediated gathering of saints, I want to underline its connections to global-anglophone literature of the same period. It is well-known that hero worship, or what Rabindranath Tagore termed "*charitra-puja*," was commonplace in late colonial India.[77] It is also well-known that Thomas Carlyle's *On Heroes, Hero-Worship and the Heroic in History* (1840) was a standard reference point for this hero worship. What has gone largely unnoticed is how "Carlyle" indicated a literary genre as much as an author function. To speak of Carlyle in late colonial India was to conjure lists of great men, anthologies of heroic lives at once political and moral, national and cosmopolitan.

Wildly popular in Victorian Britain, Carlyle's *On Heroes* argues that "Universal History" is "at bottom" the history of "Great Men." It also dusts off the old euhemerist claim that religion arose from the mistaken deification of heroes. "Hero-worship, heartfelt prostrate admiration, submission, burning, boundless, for a noblest godlike Form of Man—is not that the germ of Christianity itself?"[78] This Carlylean religion is a manly affair. Odin, Muhammad, Dante, Shakespeare, Luther, Knox, Rousseau, Cromwell, Napoleon—heroes band together in a world-historic brotherhood. With these heroes' eclecticism so obviously integral to the book's appeal, one might plausibly suggest that Carlyle's argument about universal history is just a narrative MacGuffin, a device facilitating the pleasurable stringing together of capsule biographies into a sort of Victorian *sant-samagam*, a garland of heroes.

Whatever the reason, *On Heroes* went global. Carlyle's sympathetic account of Muhammad made him a useful ally for Muslim defenders of the Prophet.[79] He also showed up in Arya hagiographies, most notably in Lajpat Rai's five-volume 1890s series Great Men of the World, which cites "Carlyle sahib" routinely, even while lionizing an entirely different set of heroes: Giuseppe Mazzini, Giuseppe Garibali, Shivaji, Krishna, and Dayananda.

While not every late colonial reference to a "great man" or *mahapurush* was an allusion to Carlyle, the Scotsman does seem to lurk behind this term with remarkable regularity—from an 1898 Arya biographer's claim that "the history of the world's progress is always made ready by the blood of great men," to a 1908 Delhi newspaper article on "Hero Worship," to a 1929 book on *Kangres ke Mahapurush*, "the great men of the Congress."[80]

Even in English, the Carlylean obsession with great men was always part of a larger cultural field. Earlier texts continued to circulate, as seen in Aryas' routine quotation of Henry Wadsworth Longfellow's "Psalm of Life" (1838), with its "great men" leaving "footprints on the sands of time."[81] So did later texts, including historical ephemera. To discover one of the latter, we might trace a quotation about men of "genius and strength" (men, that is, like Dayananda) that features in a landmark 1893 speech on the future of the Arya Samaj by Munshiram.[82] Munshiram does not name his source. Digital search tools, however, make it easy to find—an article on Martin Luther from *Ward & Lock's Worthies of the World: A Series of Original Biographical Sketches of the Great Men of All Countries and Times*, complete with cameo portraits on the cover. The series also featured a life of Napoleon (see figure 12).[83]

Ward & Lock's Universal Instructor was a multivenue British publishing enterprise with the motto "Self-Culture for All." It was not difficult reading: advertisements for *Worthies of the World* focused on the fact that the book had pictures.[84] The *Universal Instructor* was a quintessentially middlebrow publication, marketed to readers hungry for aspirational self-improvement.[85] Its great men are thus also middlebrow, their greatness defined against the middlingness of their readers. Conspicuously male, these worthies circulated alongside conduct manuals and housekeeping guides marketed to Victorian women—including *Sylvia's Home Journal*, also published by Ward & Lock and advertised with the *Worthies*.

Middlebrow British publications, including novels, were commonplace in colonial India.[86] Some could be described with only a little anachronism as self-help books—referencing Samuel Smiles's *Self-Help* (1859), the Victorian bestseller that propelled its title phrase to global fame through translations into Japanese and Arabic, as well as (in combination with Smiles's other works) Gujarati, Marathi, Hindi, and Urdu.[87] *Self-Help* collected inspiring, up-by-the-bootstraps biographies into a single volume so that readers might commune with these lives and reform their own indolent behavior. Like many of its contemporary texts, it was a moralizing biographical anthology.

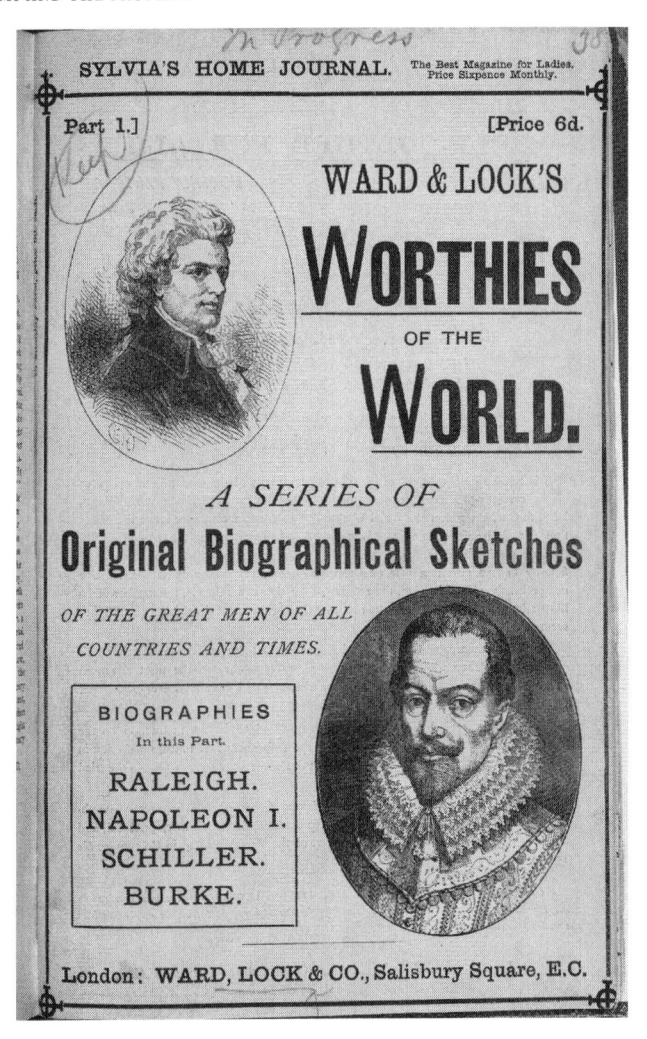

FIGURE 12. *Ward and Lock's Worthies of the World* (London: Ward, Lock, 1881). © The British Library Board. Shelfmark 10604.ee.14.

As these texts circulated, a key affordance of the anthology form became apparent. Anthology is flexible. It allows for abridgment, serialization, and outright substitution. This meant that Carlyle and company traveled well, with writers like Lajpat Rai able to use "Carlyle sahib" to authorize (i.e., to extend his author function to include) an entirely different set of great men. "Carlyle" indicated not so much an author as a discursivity.[88] Or, perhaps better, it indicated an open-ended literary genre.

This genre could then be combined with other genres in creative ways. Consider Rai's vacillation around what to term great men, men whose "name never dies." "They are called avatars by some, prophets by others . . . as well as rishis, maharishis, [and] great men."[89] This list of nouns is also a list of lists. Each of these words (avatar, prophet, rishi) implies its own anthology form or aesthetic genre: *dasavataram*, prophet tree, rishi mandala, and so on. This was not the first time these anthology forms overlapped; the trope of the "Muhammadan avatar" goes back centuries.[90] Still, such overlaps seem to have intensified in the late colonial period.

Arya hagiographers were certainly happy to mix and match list types. They continued to develop the notion of the *sattpurush* or "man of truth" that Dayananda had introduced in the *Satyarth Prakash*, a "chain of great men" in which Dayananda himself was "the last link."[91] They then interleaved this list with Vaishnava avatars or rishi mandalas, tracing a line from Dayananda back to Valmiki.[92] Sometimes Aryas used terms loosely, as in a 1924 article on "Mahapurush Lenin" published in the Arya women's magazine *Jyoti* that, in praising Lenin, Tolstoy, and Gandhi, uses "great man" (*mahapurush*), "great soul" (*mahatma*), and "great sage" (*mahamuni*) almost interchangeably.[93] At other times, they developed firmer taxonomies, as when a 1926 *Arya* article distinguished among "great men" who launch a "new age" (Buddha, Jesus, Muhammad, Dayananda), those who revivify old traditions (Luther, Shankaracharya), and mere holy men (Nanak, Kabir).[94]

COMPARATIVE PROPHETOLOGY

Such formal experimentation lay behind the emphatically global lists of sacred personalities seen around the Dayananda centennial. In 1924, the *Dayanand Chitravali* claimed Dayananda as the culmination of a long line of "holy souls" that included Rama, Krishna, Moses, Jesus, Zarathustra, Buddha, Shankaracharya, Muhammad, and Luther.[95] In 1933, Har Bilas Sarda's life of Dayananda expanded this list to include Rama, Bhishma, Ashoka, Vikramaditya, Alexander, Caesar, Akbar, Charlemagne, Napoleon, Valmiki, Kalidasa, Homer, Virgil, Shakespeare, Goethe, Vyasa, Shankaracharya, Plato, Aristotle, Kant, Herbert Spencer, Shivaji, William Tell, George Washington, Garibaldi, Robert Bruce, and Kamal Pasha Ataturk, among others. These heroes, Sarda tells us in a paraphrase of Carlyle, are "fire-pillars in the dark pilgrimage of mankind." Hovering above this heroic scrum is a still-higher

"Elect": Krishna, Jesus, Buddha, and Dayananda.[96] The Prophet Muhammad is a conspicuous omission.

This kind of list making was not limited to the Arya Samaj. It lay behind Sarojini Naidu's "Respect for All Prophets" movement, contributing to a certain cultural logic of the Indian secular (see chapter 3). It also overlapped with list making among South Asian Muslims, including the Ahmadiyya, as well as that of more conservative Hindu figures like M. M. Malaviya. "Every religion has somebody or some person at its head," Malaviya explained to the members of the 1927 Legislative Assembly. It is because such persons sit atop a "mountain of feelings" a "thousand times greater" than filial love that criticism of them must always be "reverential."[97]

This speech, complained one of Malaviya's colleagues, amounted to "a dissertation on religion."[98] The complainer had a point. Since the Victorian period, scholars of comparative religion had tended to assume that all so-called world religions had a sacred text like the Bible, plus a "founder" like Jesus. They thus created a Christianity-shaped template to which any aspiring world religion would need to conform.[99] The popular practice of comparative prophetology emerged alongside of and in tandem with this scholarly practice. Both, moreover, were thoroughly entangled with the cultural politics of empire. When, around 1905, Punjabi fakir Rama Tirtha categorized Muhammad, Jesus, the Buddha, and Krishna together as "prophets" and "saints of the world," he was asserting Hinduism's parity with its peers. It was not a mere "ethnic" or regional religion but a universal or world religion.[100]

These lists drew on the aesthetic logic of Hindu eclecticism pioneered by the Brahmo Samaj—and then later reworked, by Naidu and others, into a defining aesthetic idiom of Indian secularism.[101] In 1880, for instance, Keshub Chunder Sen instructed his followers to make mental pilgrimages to "saints," "prophets," and "great men" including Moses, Socrates, the Buddha, the Vedic rishis, Jesus, Mohammad, Chaitanya, Galileo, Isaac Newton, Michael Faraday, Ralph Waldo Emerson, and Thomas Carlyle.[102] What appeared as pluralist inclusion was often, however, a means of rearticulating Hindu hegemony. Thus, in 1869, Kedarnath Dutt gave a lecture about "great reformers" at a Brahmo venue, constructing a list spanning Valmiki, Vyasa, Plato, Jesus, Mahomed, Confucius, and Chaitanya—an eclectic assemblage wherein the Bengali Vaishnava saint is given pride of place.[103] In an 1866 lecture on "Great Men," Sen insisted on "honouring" all great men without "sectarian bigotry." "It is the evil of awarding honor to particular prophets, that has filled the religious world with jealousies, hatred, and sanguinary strife."[104] His noun choice is notable: this paean to religious inclusion is constructed around what certainly feels like an Islamophobic jab. All religions are equal, but some are more equal than others.

These rhetorical patterns persisted into the 1920s, when Arya Samajists danced around the figure of the Prophet Muhammad in various ways. He could be included in the category "great men" by being interpreted through Hindu categories, as when a *Jyoti* article suggested that Dayananda, Jesus, Muhammad, and the Buddha were "great men" because they were also "karmayogins."[105] Alternately, the term *prophet* could be rejected entirely as a "Semitic" imposition on Vedic dharma, which had not prioritized "personal religion." The Vedas were authorless.[106]

If the popular devotional practice of comparative prophetology emerged partly through lists and literary genres like "Carlyle," it also relied on the aesthetic procedures of popular visual culture. As Kajri Jain suggests, bazaar art was an important site for developing the aesthetic procedures of religious commensuration. Its interchangeable, mass-produced squares fitted heterogeneous religious worlds into a standardized aesthetic template so that they might appear functionally equivalent. Creating a kind of miniparliament of world religions within the everyday realm of iconopraxis, the aesthetic logic of commensuration correlated to the biopolitical logic of enumeration and the liberal-constitutional logic of parliamentary representation—three distinct, if mutually reinforcing, means of producing religious difference.[107]

Pictures of so-called founders lent themselves readily to this aesthetic project, easily circulating even beyond the lithographed page. Consider, for example, the Temple of Religion in the main entry hall of the Theosophical Society's Adyar headquarters, its construction between 1885 and 1911 overseen by Henry Steel Olcott and Curuppumullage Jinarajadasa.[108] The temple walls feature representations of nearly twenty sacred men in bas-relief white plaster set against a pink background. Large images of the "five founders" of the "great religions" (Jesus, Buddha, Krishna, Zoroaster, and, in place of Muhammad, the *shahada*) occupy arched niches. Above them, the ceiling is ringed by small ovals containing abstract symbols of more minor prophets, including Moses, Mahavira, Mithra, Orpheus, Confucius, Quetzalcoatl, and Baha'u'llah.[109] This spatial arrangement preserves difference even while performing unity: each religion is literally ringed off from the others. Perhaps surprisingly for a society founded on the dream of reconciling religion and science, all these men are straightforwardly "religious" figures.

Two of these bas-reliefs appear to have been modeled on widely circulated images of Zoroaster and Jesus (see Figures 13 and 14). (The Krishna and Buddha also echo mass-produced images, but without clear specific referent.) The Zoroaster image, based on a misidentified Persian relief sculpture, had become commonplace in Parsi circles by the 1880s and circulated in a variety of forms, including the "excellent" color print that Olcott obtained in Bombay in 1882.[110] Reproductions of William Holman Hunt's *The Light of the World* also circulated in South Asia, including as the frontispiece to Edwin Arnold's 1891 book of the same title (reissued in Bombay in 1903). This poetic life of Christ was the sequel to Arnold's popular 1879 life of the Buddha, *The Light of Asia*, with the geographic discrepancy of these twinned titles articulating a clear hierarchy: only Christianity is a world religion.[111]

Aesthetic form—including both literary list making and visual list making—determined the distribution of the sensible, thus shaping the ground on which religious comparison could occur.[112] Even when it seemed to produce equivalence, it could reinforce difference. This was particularly clear when it came to the question of who founded Hinduism—and thus also the related question of whether "Hinduism" was a discrete "religion."[113] Without a clear founder, Hinduism certainly did not quite fit the world religion template. What seemed like a shortcoming could, however, be recast as a virtue. It was certainly the case, as Vivekananda explained in Madras in 1897, that Hinduism was exceptional: "every other religion depends on some person or persons."[114] But that lack was to Hinduism's advantage. "No religion built upon a person can be taken up . . . by all the races of mankind," because persons are irreducibly local and particular. This is why Hinduism is the only "universal religion." It has "persons by the score" (indeed, room for "millions" of them, including Krishna), but they are always "embodiments" or "illustrations" of higher doctrines. Hinduism "teaches principles and not persons."[115]

Vivekananda's argument here is starkly different from Malaviya's claim, thirty years later, that all religions, including Hinduism, have a person at their head. The difference can perhaps be explained by what appears in Vivekananda's lectures as a distinctively fin de siècle anxiety: the epistemological uncertainties created by new historical methods. The "great founders" had a way of evaporating in the hands of historians, Vivekananda explained, so by insulating Hinduism against them, he was also insulating it against history itself.

FIGURE 13. Dosabhai Framji Karaka, *History of the Parsis*, vol. 2 (London: Macmillan, 1884). Public domain.

HISTORY AS A MORAL PROBLEM, OR, THE ETHICS OF DISENCHANTMENT

That strategy would not work for the Aryas, who were firmly committed to a historical figure. For them, history posed both an epistemological and a moral problem. As we have seen, Dayananda's biographers fretted about the implications of inserting supernaturalisms into the swami's story. Some

FIGURE 14. William Holman Hunt, *The Light of the World*, as reproduced in Edwin Arnold, *The Light of the World* (London and Bombay: Longmans, 1903 [1891]). Courtesy of the Royal Ontario Museum © ROM.

of these implications were ethical. "The purpose of reading biographies of great men is to improve the reader's behavior. But, if the biography is of an omnipotent god, imitation becomes impossible," explained Durga Prasad in 1913. This is why inserting miracles into the "lives of great souls," or interpreting those souls as avatars or prophets, is dangerous. It leads to "idiot devotionalism" (*murkhta ki bhakti*).[116] In a 1924 essay on "the rishi's miracle," Chamupati made a similar point. Miracle, he says, is the "basis of fools' religion." All intelligent people agree that religion's proper foundation is not *chamatkar* but *achar*, not miracle but right conduct. The latter (i.e., ethics) is the "highest miracle."[117]

This ethicization of religion went well beyond the Aryas. We can see it in M. G. Ranade's proposal that "biographies" of *bhakti* saints emphasize not miracle but "moral law."[118] We can see it in modern *sira* texts that strip the Prophet's life of miracles such as the splitting of the moon, presenting him as an ethico-political figure whose real miracle was civilizational reform.[119] The Aryas were notably crisp, however, in how they framed miracle as a moral problem. "Man is essentially an imitative being, individually and collectively," wrote the *Arya Patrika* in 1891, and the "Hindu nation" has had only "bad models" in Krishna and other "heroes" of "Puranic mythology."[120] To critique miracle was to reform classical Hinduism by checking its euhemerist impulses. "Even though Shri Krishna was not an incarnation of God but only a human being, he was a model human being. He was a great teacher, a great warrior, and a man of great learning. His life is an ideal for us," wrote Lajpat Rai in the 1890s.[121] In 1883, Dayananda had argued that Rama and Krishna were not gods but "great kings and emperors"; in 1886, Bankimchandra Chatterjee similarly tried to recuperate Krishna as the "ideal man."[122] Rai built on this project, incorporating an ethicized Krishna into the globalist framework of Carlylean anthology and then redirecting anthology toward nationalist ends. Sequence and selection imply argument. Mazzini and Garibaldi give Rai's Shivaji a nationalist hue that then paints his Krishna and Dayananda in "political," not "religious," tones.

A persistent tension between miracle and morals, enchantment and disenchantment, cut across many literary genres in the nineteenth century. Indeed, it could be plausibly suggested that the dialectic of disenchantment dates to precisely this period, a literary corollary to Victorian secularisms.[123] If, in India, the realist novel was one aesthetic coordinate for the disciplining of miracle, the generic tension between hagiography and biography was another.[124] Biography was simultaneously a mechanism of epistemic discipline, ensuring veridiction of fact, and a mechanism of ethical discipline, restraining writers' impulses to indulge in miracle tales.

Late colonial biography was shaped profoundly by the evidentiary norms of the new scientific history that percolated outward from Leopold von Ranke's Berlin, becoming fashionable among South Asian intellectuals around the 1880s and leading to the establishment of the subcontinent's first graduate-level history program in 1919.[125] The new academic history seriously challenged earlier traditions of popular history writing—the world of Carlyle's *Heroes* and Macaulay's *History of England*—without ever fully displacing them. It posed a similar challenge to religious life writing. Muslim biographers of the Prophet had to reckon with Muir's expertise in "original sources" (as advertised in the title of his book). Modern Hindu hagiographers were likewise grappling with the evidentiary norms of scientific biography as a rival genre.[126] These norms are likely what drove the Aryas, in the 1880s, to amass a primary source base for reconstructing Dayananda's life. They also seem to have inflected Ghasiram's 1912 remark that the Samaj had yet to produce "a true biographer of the rishi, in the full sense of that word"—that is, a sympathetic yet impartial writer with exhaustive knowledge of his topic based on primary source research.[127]

By bracketing miracle, biography opened the history of religion to new political uses. History writing was never far from nationalist politics, as seen in Arya texts like Ramdev's multivolume *Bharatvarsh ka Itihas* (History of India, 1910), or Rai's juxtaposition of Garibaldi with Dayananda.[128] But history also became political when rendered as a moral battleground, a contest over the character of the nation. In a 1924 Dayananda centennial essay, the anticolonial thinker Har Dayal noted that he was neither an Arya nor even interested in religious debate, but rather came to Dayananda through the lens of "history and sociology" (*samajik shastra*). His disciplinary goggles showed religious personalities to be ethical exemplars, communicating universal virtues like sacrifice and charity such that even an anarcho-leftist could extend "respect" to "all of the world's great men, rishis, and sages, whether they are Hindu, Christian, Parsi, or Arya Samaji or Brahmo."[129] Ethics neutralizes sectarian difference, opening the way to a cosmopolitan politics.

THE RHETORIC OF THE *RANGILA RASUL*

Although he did not know it, Har Dayal was echoing a core rhetorical move of the *Rangila Rasul*, a text published five months earlier that was heavily invested in the sort of religious debate he himself had disclaimed. It too introduces conceptual space between life and ethical teachings, turning personalist slander toward polemic ends. To the twenty-first-century reader, the tract's smutty titillations will seem quite restrained. Its hypersexualization of Muslim men and panic about interreligious marriage will, meanwhile, seem drearily familiar, a dispiriting reiteration of Islamophobic tropes still current today.

To me, two features of the *Rangila Rasul* have seemed most interesting, most in need of critical elaboration. The first is the text's emphatic positioning of its Prophet within a comparative list of sacred personalities. It opens by contrasting Muhammad with the Buddha, Jesus, and Dayananda. Midway through, it proffers a much more irreverent list, placing Muhammad ("the wives guy" or *biviyon-wallah*) alongside Krishna ("the flute guy"), Rama ("the archery guy"), Guru Gobind Singh ("the plume guy"), and Dayananda ("the Veda guy") (the Americanism "guy" captures some of the disparaging irreverence of "wallah" here).[130] Pandit Chamupati, our pamphleteer, has taken the established genres of hero-worship as an opportunity for parody or farce in a blasphemous inversion of comparative prophetology. He also underscores this genre's maleness: Khadijah, Ayesha, and company are reduced to adornments of the male body, of a kind with plume, flute, bow, and book.

The second key feature of the *Rangila Rasul* is its rhetorical structure. The tract is a parody self-help book, a joke hagiography that guides its presumptively male reader toward sexual virtue. It is written in the voice of a semifictitious first-person narrator who identifies himself as a devotee of Muhammad, a "chela" to the Prophet's "guru." This spiritual seeker has compared multiple sacred personalities and chosen Muhammad, finding greatness in the fact that he was a "householder prophet" (*grihast paigambar*). Where many Muslims have seen this status as a mark of virtue, indicating an ability to integrate spiritual and worldly life, the *Rangila Rasul*'s narrator is more cynical in his assessment: a married prophet appeals to human weakness. Like Jesus and the Buddha, "Dayananda was a lifelong celibate. He was a god [*devata*], but since I am just an ordinary human how could I ever attain his kind of celibacy [*brahmacharya*]? I have neither the desire for such saintliness [*sadhuta*] nor the courage to choose it," he confesses.[131] This, of course, was the precise problem that Arya hagiographers had been formulating. If Dayananda seems too godlike, then ordinary readers will fail to emulate his virtues, presuming them to be inimitable. The *Rangila Rasul* plays this (here sexualized) anxiety for polemic purposes, implying that a deified Dayananda would propel Hindus toward Islam.

Delivered with snarling insincerity, these opening remarks foreshadow what follows. The narrator veers in and out of character (like most polemic literature, the *Rangila Rasul* was probably written in a hurry). Sometimes he engages in comic duplicity, as by saying he would never accuse Muhammad of marrying selfishly and then immediately comparing him to Henry VIII. At other times, his insults are implicit, as with feminizing the Prophet by describing his "bashful eyes" or his subordination to Khadijah.[132] At no point could any reader of this tract be deluded as to its purpose.

Repeatedly, the narrator frames Muhammad's life via the Hindu ideal of the four *ashramas*, or life stages. Muhammad, we learn, mostly kept to the shastric ideal until age fifty. He was celibate until twenty-five and subsequently lived virtually as an "Arya householder" with Khadijah. The problems came when he should have entered *vanaprastha*, leaving householder life behind to become a semi-ascetic forest dweller. Instead, he married profligately, flouting the "Arya *dharmashastras*."[133]

The divergence of human life from moral ideal emerges as the tract's defining preoccupation. In the opening section, the narrator describes Muhammad as an "experienced prophet" (*anubhavi paigambar*), probably with sexual innuendo. Repeated in the closing section, this phrase also does considerable conceptual work for the tract as a whole. The *Rangila Rasul* is a sort of polemical *Bildungsroman*, using its protagonist's errors to direct its reader toward moral truths. Or, to take the term that the tract itself uses on its title page, it is an "instructive history" (*shikshaprad itihas*), transmuting events (*itihas*, that which happened) into moral lessons (*shiksha*). Its protagonist turns bitter experience into a sweet drink "for everyone's benefit."[134] Muhammad's wives, with their names serving as section headings, become the textual ground from which this experience grows. If he could live again, the text's prophet admits, he would cover his ears at the very mention of polygamy; his followers should cultivate the "moderation" at which he failed.[135] His "life is instructive, filled with lessons, and filled with warnings; truly Muhammad is the one who shows the right path."[136] This last phrase, a parodic rendering of the Qur'anic motif of the straight path, would suggest that this polemic tract is a sort of rival scripture, guiding its readers toward unattained virtue.

The *Rangila Rasul* culminates in a section called "The Rainbow," which reaffirms its protagonist's instructive value. "Reader! You have seen some colors of the life of the colorful [*rangila*] prophet." The narrator then lists seven lessons, one for each of the rainbow's hues. Take only one wife. Keep *brahmacharya* until the age of twenty-five. Do not marry an old lady of forty but make her your mother. And so on.

This bifurcation of norm and narrative provided Justice Dalip Singh of the Lahore High Court with the basis for his controversial 1927 ruling. He could find no passage in the *Rangila Rasul*, he wrote, indicating that the tract "was meant to attack the Muhammadan religion as such or to hold up Muhammadans as objects worthy of enmity or hatred. On the contrary, the pamphlet expressly says the people should do as Mohammad advised but should not act as Mohammad himself acted."[137] The Lahore public, as we have seen, decried this argument as convoluted nonsense. Whatever its demerits, the ruling did stick close to the text of the *Rangila Rasul*, which went out of its way to produce precisely this division.

It seems likely that Chamupati understood the legal context within which he was writing and finessed his tract accordingly. Still, this conceptual structure did not come out of nowhere. As Ghasiram said, no biography of Dayananda is complete without a list of the swami's teachings—often a list of the ten rules of the Arya Samaj. The seven colors of Chamupati's rainbow echo this Arya convention.

CONCLUSION: CODE AND LIFE

"Our Prophet's life is a code in itself," declared a Peshawar group in response to the Lahore High Court's ruling.[138] That is, in classical terms, *sira* contains *sunna*.[139] Here, the sacred life sets an example, becoming an ethical paradigm such that life and rule fuse together in sacred indistinction.[140]

Can a sacred body stand in for a religion? Are textualized faiths separable from the lives of their founders? Like so many of their contemporaries, the Aryas kept coming back to these questions. From Dayananda forward, they were obsessed with sacred personalities, using personalist slander as a tool for moral reform and sometimes sidelining doctrine in the process. Principles and persons came to occupy parallel streams of Arya thought, each vying for preeminence. The resulting tension between rule and life, text and body can be seen quite clearly in an October 1924 image (see figure 15). Illuminated by a heavenly Aum, a loincloth-clad Dayananda holds up a tablet with his ten commandments, "The Rules of the Arya Samaj." Despite the prominence of doctrine in this composition—literally foregrounded, the tablet text is printed in eye-grabbing red ink—the ascetic body insistently asserts its iconic presence. The beams lead the viewer's eye straight toward Dayananda's frontally directed gaze. Text and body compete for visual attention, each implicated in the other to exert a doubled normative force.

Religion here is about books, bodies, and the spaces in between. Aryas traversed these spaces using a historically specific network of media technologies. The virtuous body was a site of inscription, a kind of media text, with printed biography (*jivani*) "pouring" into life (*jivan*) (to recall the

FIGURE 15. "Arya Samaj ke Niyam" (Rules of the Arya Samaj). Cover of *Prakash* (Lahore), Rishi Birth Centennial Issue, October 26, 1924. © The British Library Board. Shelfmark 14154.c.40.

Dayanand Chitravali) through concrete media practices. In 1914, the Lahore Young Men's Arya Samaj held a contest on Shivaratri for the best student essay about Dayananda's biography.[141] None of the submissions survive. Still, one can imagine the scene. Young men pick up pens, their disciplined bodies hunched over desks while inscribing onto paper a life that makes a moral claim, etching itself into their flesh through their gendered identification with the boy who once saw a rat.

EPILOGUE: INSULTING ALL PROPHETS

Such minor scenes have major effects, shaping not just the ethical practice of the self in late colonial India but also, arguably, the twenty-first-century politics of religious offense. In her widely read essay on the 2005–2006 Danish cartoon affair—wherein caricatures of Muhammad published in an Aarhus newspaper sparked global protests—the anthropologist Saba Mahmood demonstrates how most policy and scholarly discussions of religiously injurious speech rely on a culturally provincial set of liberal presuppositions. As Mahmood explains, religion is not, as the liberal fiction has it, a set of beliefs or propositions chosen by a fundamentally autonomous subject. It is, rather, a habitation of the subject that shapes the emergence of the embodied self well before the fictive moment of liberal choice. To develop a theoretical vocabulary for describing such religious subjectivity, Mahmood excavates an Aristotelian language of *schesis* (translated into Latin as *habitus*), which she presents as in some sense internal to Islamic tradition (with Arastu appearing as Islamicate philosopher). For Mahmood, *schesis* indicates the disciplined inhabitation of an external norm that becomes the prior condition of the self as subject of virtue. When the devout Muslim models his or her life on the Prophet, then, Muhammad becomes inscribed into the virtuous subject's bodily habitus, existing in "intimate proximity" with the self. No wonder insults to him get under the skin.[142]

This chapter's cultural history of comparative prophetology would seem to indicate two important adjustments to Mahmood's account of religious subjectivity. First, this disciplined inhabitation of ethical models—this veneration of religious heroes—was also a media practice, emerging from within historically specific assemblages of media technologies (print, lithograph, etc.). Second, it was not just about Muslims. Popular devotion to the Prophet Muhammad in the late nineteenth and early twentieth centuries was part of a transcolonial and transreligious cultural field, wherein great men appeared central to various world religions, and religious heroes were continuous with political ones.

"Why this modern religious interest in a person?" wondered Wilfred Cantwell Smith in 1943. Smith's answers to this question are still persuasive: Liberalism and capitalism fetishize the individual. Urban atomization leads people to invest feeling in larger-than-life personalities rather than each other, giving rise to a newly deinstitutionalized politics of the heart.[143] To this, we might add that sacred personalities help mediate historic shifts in the structure of religious institutions.

If religious "authority is constantly a work in progress" (as one scholar puts it), this was especially true in colonial India, where ʿulama, pirs, pandits, gurus, and more were scrambling to reinvent themselves in an age of rapid social and technological change.[144] The old networks of monastic governmentality were, in short, being rewired.[145] When a figure like Ahmad Riza Khan Barelwi situated his embodied devotion to the Prophet (e.g., kissing his thumbs and touching them to his eyes whenever the Prophet was mentioned in prayer) by teaching that the Prophet is the culmination of a chain of authority that runs through other men (pir, shaikh, etc.), he linked ethical emulation of the Prophet to shifting networks of governmental power.[146] Something similar could be said for other religious movements. The networked field of religious governmentality was shifting, and devotion to prophets (and swamis, avatars, founders, reformers, great men, etc.) helped mediate these shifts. Representations of these men entered into assemblage not just with each other, but also with living human bodies of various kinds.

I gesture to this broadened history to de-exceptionalize Islam—and thus counter a potent strand of Islamophobic rhetoric that routinely positions Islam as a unique symbol of excessive religious feeling. The modern religious interest in sacred personalities was never just Islamic. It was also never just "religious."

Thinking with Mahmood, we might ask how Arya *schesis*—an ethical emulation of Dayananda Saraswati—was predicated on a remarkably diffuse cultural field. Hagiography put Aryas into intimate proximity not just with Dayananda's virtuous flesh, but also with all of that saintly body's eclectic connections. If their comparative prophetology was frequently polemical, using the popular practice of comparative religion to produce and control religious difference, its end result, perhaps, was to inscribe that very difference into Arya bodies, a side effect of absorbing the swami's saintly virtues. Difference was the precondition of the polemical-ethical self—a trace of the other under Arya skin.

10

CONCLUSION

A Feeling for "Religion"

THEY SAY "DEAD SCANDALS FORM good subjects for dissection."[1] The Rajpal affair may not be entirely dead. Somebody maintains a Facebook page under the name "Pandit Chamupati M.A.," and #rangeelarasul is now a Twitter hashtag for Islamophobic remarks like "your prophet is gay" (repurposing an adjective used in 1920s translations in its earlier meaning of "carefree"). There are even sporadic rumors about a *Rangila Rasul* movie. Still, precisely in its undead state, this historical scandal offers a clarifying window onto our present—a view onto the transcolonial history of secularism as global political form. I return to what it shows us below, where I reprise and further develop this book's core arguments. First, however, I draw my historical narrative to a close with what amounts to a public service announcement.

"WE SAFEGUARD AN HONEST MAN"

Amid all the disagreement of the 1927 Legislative Assembly debates, one point comes through quite clearly—and it bears stressing for readers interested in the contemporary application of 295A. Its framers emphatically exempted two types of writing from this law's scope: scholarship and reformist critique.

It was "fundamental" to 295A that "historical works" and "bona fide and honest criticisms" be protected, as the committee charged with revising the law explained, which is why they added the phrase "deliberate intention" to the central government's draft language. With this phrase, one committee member said, "we safeguard an honest man."[2] Another committee member put the matter more colorfully. Section 295A was written to protect the "sly skeptic," the "doughty doubter," the "diligent sociologist," the "absent-minded philosopher," and even "the apparently merciless satirist" who applies his "knife" for the "good of society."[3] There were those, like Lajpat Rai, who wanted these protections made clearer. He proposed an amendment explicitly protecting "historical research" and "legitimate criticism."[4] Other legislators, like Pandit Thakur Das Bhargava, asked for language protecting "the comparative study of religion." James Crerar, the British home member, rejected these proposals by insisting that such protections were already implicit in the existing text. New language would be redundant.[5]

Crerar also shot down a proposal to write a sundown clause into 295A, making it expire automatically on December 31, 1930.[6] If this was "emergency" legislation tailored to the "special circumstances" of the Rajpal affair, it would be foolish to render emergency permanent by converting a temporary crisis into a general rule, Lajpat Rai argued.[7] Crerar denied the point. A general rule, he argued, is precisely what 295A was. Soon it was time for a vote. The bill passed, 61–26.[8] It was then sent to the Council of State, the upper house, which adopted the motion on September 21.[9] Section 295A has been protecting "religious feelings" ever since.

The Legislative Assembly did not, as one of its members reminded the room, have a "monopoly of the best brains of the country."[10] That someone even felt the need to argue this point underscores the assembly's intellectual firepower. These lawmakers' strong reservations about 295A might well give pause to those who would invoke this law today.

AFTER THE AFFAIR

Once enacted, Section 295A was immediately greeted with howls of disapproval. The press described it as "savage and irrational," "worse than the disease," an "engine of repression" that would turn religious reformers like Rammohun Roy and Dayananda Saraswati into outlaws.[11] "Save Us from Our Friends!" cried the *Muslim Outlook*, protesting a law ostensibly made for Muslims that many Muslims did not want.[12]

It was hoped the new law would end the controversy over the *Rangila Rasul*. That did not happen. In September 1927, Mahashe Rajpal was stabbed in his bookshop. He survived. Then, in 1929, he was stabbed again—fatally. Offensive texts, meanwhile, kept circulating. In September 1927, a new Hindi edition of the *Rangila Rasul* came to official notice, with all copies declared forfeit to the Crown.[13] A few weeks later, the book was reportedly still circulating, with rumors of a Gujarati edition on the way. The government's response was scattered. Bengal did nothing. Bombay police confiscated pamphlets without initiating legal proceedings. The United Provinces filed a suit under 153A, the very law 295A had been meant to replace.[14] Two years later, a government report found that only seven 295A trials had been conducted to date, with just two of them resulting in convictions under the section.[15]

Perhaps 295A was destined to fail. The Legislative Assembly, after all, had not been optimistic about its success. To them, it seemed a "spider's web, in which the warp of intolerance has been crossed by the woof of fatuous reasoning."[16] It was "repressive legislation" serving "no useful purpose whatever."[17] Or perhaps its purpose was all too clear: it augmented the authoritarian powers of the colonial state, the latest in a growing "catalogue" of repressive measures.[18]

It certainly did not seem likely to end religious conflict. Religions, one legislator insisted, are inherently at odds, with one person's cherished belief another's outrage.[19] Worse, censorship just incites desire. "Forbidden fruit has always tasted sweet," and "one stupid fanatical man in jail does not solve the problem" if a "book goes on circulating . . . passed from hand to hand."[20] For all these reasons and more, it seemed probable that 295A would create "greater discord between communities," functioning to "increase fanaticism because it creates a new offence."[21] (Many scholars would agree that this is exactly what it has done.) "Personally I feel that neither religions nor their founders should require any legislative protection," remarked Lajpat Rai.[22] He would have preferred 295A never existed. Many people today feel the same. They would like to abolish this troubled law.

In twenty-first-century India, the problem of 295A is tightly intertwined with Hindu nationalism and its hold on contemporary public culture. In a dark irony (but globally a common one), a law initially devised to protect a minority group has since been co-opted as a tool of aggrieved majoritarianism. The historical complexity of this aggrievement should, at this point, be evident. In invoking the Indian Penal Code, Hindu nationalists become Macaulay's children. They speak in his words, channeling affect into the narrative grooves of colonial-secular law.

I am certainly sympathetic to 295A's would-be abolishers. Yet, as I hope this book has shown, the section stands in for a larger set of problems that admit no easy solution. We are still, in a sense, replaying the scene of indecision that unfolded in 1927. What kinds of limits can a liberal state place on free speech without ceasing to be liberal? What kinds of protections should a secular state afford to something called "religion"? What, after all, is the harm in religiously injurious speech, and do legal systems devised to decrease that harm actually intensify it?

ON PENAL SECULARISM

Blasphemy, as excessive religious semiosis, sits at the intersection of "free speech" and "fanaticism," in one of liberalism's aporetic blind spots. It pulls liberal speech theory in two directions at once, appearing both as a practice of freedom and an atavistic threat to the rationally autonomous individual. Blasphemy poses a parallel problem for secularism. (While not all secularisms are liberal, liberalism has been the dominant idiom of secularism in the global Anglosphere, so I partly conflate them here.) It activates both secularism's promise of freedom and its regulatory impulse (to recall Saba Mahmood). Or, put differently (recalling Partha Chatterjee), it activates both the modern state's liberal-constitutional rationality, which takes religion as a site of rights, and its ethnographic-governmental rationality, which takes religion as an empirical object requiring documentation and technical management.

In colonial India, this ethnographic-governmental secularism took a variety of forms. One of them was what I am calling penal secularism— that is, a secularism that approaches religion as a potentially criminal object, requiring policing and rehabilitation. Penal secularism's religion is conceived from within the logic of security, population, and territory. It is the religion of (to use the jargon of several distinct historical periods) enthusiasm, fanaticism, and terrorism. This penal secularism is—more or less by definition—the secularism implied by the Indian Penal Code, a self-consciously secular document that approaches religion as a source of potential violence. Its "religious feelings" indicate a given class or population's propensity to breach the peace. They are an affective proxy for violence, violence *in potentia*.

No less an authority than William James concluded, in 1902, after an exhaustive survey of the relevant scholarly literature, that there is no specifically "religious feeling." Instead, a feeling like "religious love" is simply ordinary love "directed to a religious object."[23] A feeling, one might paraphrase, is a directionality, orienting a subject toward some object in the world. Section 295A orients via "outrage." It finds its "religious" object in the law's populational "classes"—classes that the law, in turn, orients around outrage in an affective-conceptual loop. "Religion" here is less an object than a router word or transponder node, connecting the colonial state to the ostensibly excitable feelings of its racialized subjects.

If 295A and related laws increase rather than decrease violence (a perverse outcome, given their ostensible aims), it is partly because they inscribe the potential for violence into law—and, with it, the cultural script of communal conflict. Law becomes a technology for structuring and even eliciting outrage, a relay in the ongoing transmission of affect. It bears asking whether sustaining rather than dampening violence served the ends of the colonial state—justifying continued intervention in Indian society and thus reinforcing the state's symbolic power.[24]

ON "RELIGIOUS" PAIN

If a feeling is a directionality orienting a body toward an object, a body oriented toward the modern concept of religion is an odd body indeed. It is a body oriented by an abstraction, a generalized, administrative category. Nobody cares about insults to "religion," the general-order anglophone concept. People care about insults to beloved particularities: Krishna, crucifix, Qur'an. The category "religion" works to mediate among these affectively charged particularities. It is a router word—an especially dense transfer point for the circulation of affect.

Secular law, we might say, speaks the language of Bentham, not Burke. It describes legal feelings that are phenomenologically thin but meant to regulate the phenomenologically thick world of tradition or prejudice (i.e., untaught feeling). Secular law's structural exclusion of tradition (in the Burkean sense—or what could, moving deeper into the nineteenth century, be called culture) creates a standing reserve of dissatisfaction among those who see their lifeworlds as inadequately captured by law's language. Because a legal code (that austerely philosophical print genre, linked to the Benthamite-rationalist currents of Atlantic-world Enlightenments) speaks in the order of the general, its emotional lexicon is necessarily incommensurate with the intimate particularities of human life.

The emotional mismatch between legal and lived religion was especially visible when the Legislative Assembly's select committee clarified the terms of 295A. In the section, they explained, the phrase "religious beliefs" was meant to include "founders" like Muhammad. What a strange reduction. Persons are not beliefs, abstract propositions to which one assents; they invite much more intimate and affectively intense forms of identification. This reduction of religion to belief is, however, a routine feature of modern secular governance, as is the related reduction of belief to cognitive assent to propositions (sidelining the forms of social trust long integral to the word).[25] Such reductions abstract religion from the body and its ritual and social practices. Law's religion comes to look like law itself, consisting of rules, books, bureaucracy.

Codified law is not therefore, however, purged of emotion—as leeched of life as Bentham's taxidermized corpse. Rather, law becomes a site for the production of new species of sentiment. These might include class feelings, affects articulated around enumerable identities anchored in the administrative rationality of the modern state. They might also include the procedural effervescence that burbles up in civic meetings, those paradigms of liberal deliberation. In both cases, religious affect emerges from within the institutional structures of the modern state and its affiliate organizations. It thus takes on some of the tenor of those structures.

This is perhaps especially clear when affective claims are made via the term *religion*. What is it to feel for, or through, this modern concept? The answer will vary depending on context, of course. In many cases, however, it is to feel via an abstraction, entangling affect with the transcolonial histories of secular law.

ON SPIRITUAL GOVERNMENTALITY

To see any of these feelings clearly, we need to think past the reified distinction between state and society, those abstract categories. Toward that end, this book has framed its arguments via a postcolonial-Foucauldian notion of governmentality that blurs the line between law and culture, public and private, the official and the intimate, the bureaucratic and the embodied (especially when governmentality is refracted through affect theory, as it has been here). The preceding chapters have traced crossings between seemingly disparate registers of power. They asked, for instance, how Macaulay upscaled Claphamite reformism when he wrote the Indian Penal Code, and how Arya Samajists downscaled that document by harnessing its legal concepts to their polemical-ethical project of moral reform. I hope such analytic exercises have thrown the public/private distinction into productive confusion, in sympathy with scholars like Lisa Lowe and Joan Wallach Scott—especially the latter's argument that the history of secularism cannot be written independently from the history of gender and sexuality. The history of Indian secularism also cannot be written independently of the history of caste, with the structural transformations of the late colonial public inseparable from the ongoing rearticulation of the caste sensorium.

Legal religion is not lived religion, just as law, by definition, cannot coincide with life.[26] We might take this claim as axiomatic for critical secular studies. Still, one should be careful about how one configures this axiom. Lived religion, after all, is not life itself. Religion is a means of governing life, of bringing life into closer alignment with a set of ethical or even legal norms. It is thus, in some sense, functionally analogous to law and can enter into assemblage with it.

To study the history of what could be called religious or spiritual governmentalities is to see how such assemblages emerge. In late colonial India, legal and spiritual governmentalities emerged in tandem, as complementary mechanisms for managing feeling. Occasionally, somebody would try to pull them into tighter relationship, as with the 1927 "Respect for All Prophets" movement. Its proponents asked the colonial state to create a law mandating respect for all religions—a law that would have ratified a social norm by turning it into a legal one (thus abridging the nominal distinction between state and society preserved by 295A, and perhaps revealing that distinction's constitutive artificiality). The lost law would have knit the colonial state more deeply into South Asia's crisscrossing, capillary networks of spiritual governmentality (monastic governmentality, guru governmentality, 'ulama governmentality, and so forth).[27] Its critics argued that granting legal protection to all such sacred personalities would be both socially corrosive and preposterously impractical. With the conceptual difficulties alone almost comedically insurmountable, the "Protection for Prophets" law never got off the ground.

Even so, the lost law points to a more pervasive political impulse. Many people in late colonial India were trying to better coordinate legal and spiritual governmentalities. We have already, in chapter 3, encountered the Legislative Assembly select committee proclaiming that "the inculcation of peace is an essential principle of all the great religions"; any religion that departs from it is not "religion" at all but criminal "fanaticism." This claim works to position the folk practice of tolerance as a correlate of state secularism. Religions too, or at least those worthy of recognition, work to preserve public order. They function in tandem with law.

The law that the committee helped craft was perhaps, then, more like the religions it sought to govern than one might at first expect. Section 295A, as another assembly member put it, was "necessary to educate people into tolerance."[28] It too would inculcate peace. It was not just a legal decree, stipulating rules in the style of juridico-sovereign power. It was a pedagogic governmental tool, training the colonized in the norms of good citizenship. If the *Rangila Rasul* was an instrument of governmentality, a printed tool designed to alter the flow of words and feelings, so too, in a sense, was 295A.

ON THE GOVERNMENT OF WORDS AND FEELINGS

Liberal states strive to govern by governing less, especially when it comes to speech. Yet even the most liberal of states cannot help but govern the circulation of signs, becoming involved in the project of what could be termed "semiotic governance." With this phrase, I mean to invert the notion of "free speech," both semantically and conceptually, by suggesting that in matters of speech, governance is primary and freedom a secondary effect.

When a person declares that she is engaging in free speech, she marks her speech as receiving the implicit protection of the state, as guarantor of fundamental rights. This rhetorical inscription of the state within the "free" speech act thus produces a sort of paradox, at least if one takes *free* to indicate total independence from external constraint. By marking her speech as "free," the speaker works to situate her speech within a larger structure of political sovereignty, in which she is but one node; dependent on and shaped by that larger structure, her speech is, by a certain definition, not free at all. She also, at the same time, uses the marker *free* to reshape her immediate rhetorical situation, as by insisting that some other person should not be trying to restrain her speech. The word *free* becomes a means of inverting this perceived restraint, flipping the power relation to restrict the actions available to her interlocutor through invocation of the state's symbolic authority. The rhetorical marker *free* thus, counterintuitively, works to proliferate constraint. It shapes a field of power relations in which the state is a palpable symbolic presence, mediated through the social.

Free speech might well remain an important tactical concept in a variety of political struggles. It is, however, a poor tool of social and cultural analysis. Among other things, it tends to abstract speech from the body and its practices. So, for example, when free-speech purists in the US defend what they experience as repugnant speech (e.g., a neo-Nazi rally)—even going so far as to seek that speech out, intentionally exposing themselves to injurious words—they are engaging in what one media theorist has presented as a quasi-spiritual bodily exercise, a practice of secularized asceticism centered on a neo-Stoic cultivation of indifference to pain.[29] In this, these free-speech ascetics are perhaps not so different from a late colonial figure like M. K. Gandhi, who also exposed himself to painful speech so that he could cultivate an attitude of tolerance. Such speech ascetics force us to think past the presumptions of most free-speech talk. Speech here functions as an occasion for self-negation, not self-expression. It is a mode of force, a means of acting on bodies with words—perhaps producing generative constraint, with the ascetic body directing force toward new ends. This is not news, exactly. Liberalism is an embodied practice, and a historically variable one.[30] Secularism is also necessarily a formation of the flesh, acting in and on bodies. We simply do not typically think of either liberalism or secularism in that way.

To see speech as shot through with embodied power relations is both an argument for, and a recognition of the limits of, "hate speech"—the notion that emerged in the 1980s and later became ubiquitous in discussions of injurious words. Hate speech law correctly recognizes that speech exerts force. It often fails, however, to recognize the full performative force of legal speech itself.[31] For related reasons, hate speech law tends not to foreground its core concept's multilayered history. To begin to peel back these layers, we might revisit the 2006 Racial and Religious Hate Speech Act that allowed Britain to finally abolish the common law of blasphemy in 2008. This act echoed a long history of colonial-secular governance, for which race and religion had appeared as twinned administrative objects (see, for instance, Bulwer-Lytton's remarks in chapter 1), while also retailoring these objects to the new governance paradigms of multicultural Britain.[32] Meanwhile, the act's critics, in mounting neo-Millian defenses of free speech, were literally quoting an East India Company employee, bringing Victorian liberalism into the twenty-first century.[33]

The post-1980s notion of hate speech built on and repackaged an older set of legal ideas. Its archive included such documents as the 1966 International Covenant on Civil and Political Rights, which prohibits advocacy of "national, racial, or religious hatred."[34] Behind that text, one can feel the influence the 1948 Universal Declaration of Human Rights (emerging from the same moment of decolonization as the postcolonial Indian constitution).[35] Still further back are the transcolonial legal codes discussed in chapter 1. It is not, I think, unreasonable to presume that the legal concept of hate speech derives from the same set of entangled histories as the Indian Penal Code.

Section 153A was certainly a hate speech law *avant la lettre*, criminalizing the incitement of "enmity or hatred" between classes. It is about group defamation, or at least something like it (in chapter 6, we saw one 1898 bureaucrat calling it "sectarian defamation"). Section 295A is also a hate speech law of a kind, delineating an offense substantially redundant with 153A. In it, "enmity" becomes "outrage," rerouted through the discursive object *religion*.

What is it to defame a religion? This question was—and remains—a source of persistent confusion. In 1927, the Lahore High Court distinguished among insults to Islam (a religion), Muslims (a class), and the Prophet Muhammad (a deceased individual) and thus, by extension, among three possible word crimes: blasphemy, or slanders of the sacred; group defamation; and personal defamation. The court then immediately muddied its nonce taxonomy of offense. So does 295A, with its circuitous syntax. It references the crimes of blasphemy and sacred libel while also grammatically subordinating them to outrages on class-based religious feelings (outrages that are akin to, but not quite the same as, group defamation). It is a secularized blasphemy law, a law that is no longer blasphemy. Nonetheless, from the 1920s to the 2020s, it has remains persistently blasphemy-adjacent. People keep on describing 295A as a blasphemy law—with the concept of blasphemy thus overdetermining this not-blasphemy law's reception and cultural effects.

To see the continuities between the 1920s and the 2020s is to get a clearer view of our perpetually offended present. We now live in the era of the governmentalization of the globe, routinely discussing populations and their "sentiments, proclivities, and passions" as social facts requiring technical administration.[36] In the 1920s, Walter Lippmann saw the public awakening to the realization that its sovereignty was a fiction, its opinions massaged and manufactured by media professionals and other technocrats. That realization has since hardened into jaded acceptance.

The media infrastructures of public speech, meanwhile, keep shifting. Once upon a time, liberals insisted that the cure for "bad speech" was always "more speech." Now, the ease and consequent profusion of digital communication has so fundamentally altered our information economy that more speech appears a surefire tactic for drowning out not just critical voices, but reality itself.[37] The old-fashioned tools of juridico-legal power are still around (with India, for instance, regularly using censorship laws like 124A, 153A, and 295A). Increasingly, however, newfangled tools of digital governmentality (e.g., "the nudge") seem to have displaced or absorbed these older tools of semiotic governance. Hate speech is met with "hate spin," a rhetorical technique that inverts the usual rhetorical structure of verbal aggression by rendering aggrievement itself an aggressive act—a means of hurling sticks and stones onto unsuspecting speakers.[38] This kind of affective inversion has certainly happened with 295A, a mere mention of which can alter the flow of words and feelings. Law, in such cases, has become something else: a cultural idiom or rhetorical tool, used in extralegal semiotic governance. This phenomenon is not, in itself, new. Law was already shadowed by cultural doppelgängers in the late colonial period (see chapter 8). It seems, however, to have intensified with the digital expansion of controversial speech.

RELIGION AS GEOPOLITICAL FEELING

Where would one begin a history of religious offense after Rajpal? In December 1927, when Ambedkar burned a copy of the *Manusmriti* to protest caste-Hindu oppression of Dalits? In 1928, when a Bombay publishing house printed a Marathi-language life of Krishna under the cheekily reappropriated title *Rangila Rasul*?[39] In 1931, when the *Rangila Rasul* itself popped up in Fiji alongside a tract called the *Rangila Rishi*, mocking Dayananda Saraswati?[40] In 1933, when *Angarey* (Embers), a founding text of the Progressive Writers Movement, was banned under 295A?[41]

Such a history would ideally be global in scope. The Rajpal affair was, after all, global from the start. So was the Indian Penal Code, with versions implemented across the British-colonial world. Section 295A was a relative latecomer on the scene, and so it only extends to the four countries of former British India. In Myanmar, for instance, it was recently invoked against a Yangon nightclub poster depicting the Buddha as a headphone-clad disc jockey.[42]

In 1980s Pakistan, Sections 295A and 298 spawned several new amendments to the Code during a period of national desecularization.[43] These new sections restricted speech about the Qur'an (295B), Muhammad and other prophets of Islam (295C), and additional holy personages (298A), as well as limiting the ability of Ahmadis to call themselves Muslim (298B and C).[44] By Jayakar's definition (see chapter 1), these new sections would count as blasphemy laws. They are not, however, some kind of atavistic eruption of medieval religion, as global media coverage has sometimes implied. Rather, they are blasphemy rebooted from within the terms of colonial secularism. In Pakistani debates about blasphemy, Islamic law and Macaulayan law are fully fused.[45]

Studies of blasphemy should keep this geopolitical field in view to better see how transnational structures determine the rhetorical situation of blasphemy's critics in any given national context. For example, it bears asking whether secularist critics of 295A in contemporary India implicitly invoke the specter of Pakistan (wittingly or not) when they disapprovingly describe 295A as a blasphemy law. Pakistan's blasphemy laws are, after all, much better known than the nineteenth-century British blasphemy trials that were 295A's actual historical background. If so, these critics would be implicitly contrasting "secular" India with "fundamentalist" Pakistan, thereby reinscribing Islamophobia as a defining condition of Indian secularism.[46]

Similarly, if we are to understand how twenty-first-century consternation around any of these South Asian laws plays into global debates about "religious freedom," we need to ask how those debates are shaped by the ongoing life of empire in its mutating forms. For the contemporary global politics of religious freedom, the US empire has been especially determinative.[47]

The incipient US empire was already evident on the margins of the Rajpal affair. The *Rangila Rasul* was not the only outrageous book circulating in India in summer 1927. It was accompanied by Katherine Mayo's *Mother India*, which by August had generated a "storm of indignant protest" all its own.[48] Gandhi dubbed it a "drain inspector's" report; Annie Besant accused it of "slandering the whole Indian people."[49] *Mother India* punched many of the same buttons as the *Rangila Rasul* (religion, gender, and sexuality). It is thus unsurprising that it was mentioned in the Legislative Assembly debates that September—with the same representative who had expressed alarm over insults to "his" women and religion accusing Mayo of "blasphemy of things too holy for her American brain to fancy."[50] His mention of Mayo's nationality is important. As Mrinalini Sinha has argued, her book presaged an interwar shift toward increasing US hegemony, including in British India.[51]

A whiff of Mayo looms over the series of 295A scandals that erupted starting in the 1990s around white US American scholars of Hinduism like

Wendy Doniger.[52] One needs to be careful here, however. By definition, these controversies unfolded from within a global assemblage of race and religion. But the geopolitical structures of the early twenty-first century were not the same as those of the early twentieth. To pretend otherwise is rhetorical obfuscation. For example, when Dinanath Batra accused Doniger, a secular Jew, of attacking Hinduism with "Christian missionary zeal,"[53] his jarring anachronism (overlaying a quintessentially nineteenth-century foe onto a decidedly twenty-first-century writer) deflected from contemporary political realities—not least the imperial dependencies of Hindu nationalism.

Hindu nationalism emerged via empire. Conceived from within the late colonial apparatus of the populational public, it has, in the twenty-first century, become increasingly parasitic on US empire as a globalized economic formation.[54] Certainly, the transmission of outraged religious feelings in contemporary India relies on US-based media platforms like Facebook, Twitter, and WhatsApp. Then there are the Americanisms like "Hinduphobia"; the financial flows circulating through Silicon Valley; and even the managerial rhetoric of American-style business "gurus" who naturalize Hinduism by presenting it as pop psychology rather than religion.[55] I do not mean to overstate the US connection. The Hindu right has also, for example, deployed geopolitics by defending the *Charlie Hebdo* blasphemers (and thus tacitly affirming the Islamophobic rhetoric surrounding them).[56] My point is simply that wounded religious sentiments are not some kind of autochthonous outgrowth of organic Indian tradition. They are hypermediated global affects, fully imbricated with empire in its mobile forms. They are, after all, articulated from within the terms of 295A, a colonial-secular law. The Whig-liberal narrative of blasphemous modernity crumples in the face of such complexities. It fails at parsing the politics of the Hindu right, just as it fails at mapping a more global structure of feeling centered on wounded attachment.[57]

To see these global affects in action, we might consider a controversy from early 2021. The Indian subsidiary of the US technology firm Amazon released a web series called *Tandav*, starring film actor Saif Ali Khan. With its title referencing the god Shiva, the show seemed almost to solicit controversy. The 295A charges filed against it in several states pointed to one scene in particular as having outraged religious feelings. In it, a student actor performs the role of Shiva in a lightly satirical university play, wherein the sage Narada advises the deity to up his social media presence to compete with Rama. At one point, Shiva says, in English, "What the . . ." The omitted expletive elicits a laugh from the student audience.

If courting sacrilege was, by the 2020s, a familiar entertainment industry strategy for boosting ratings and profits (cf. Madonna), this strategy provoked equally familiar resistances—now digitalized. Mobilization against the show thrived on Twitter (#BanTandavNow), and the director ultimately issued a formal apology, with Amazon altering or cutting contested scenes. The contours of this controversy were also shaped profoundly, however, by the politics of contemporary India. The actor who played the student playing Shiva, Mohammad Zeeshan Ayyub, was Muslim. The controversy thus fueled the further production and circulation of Islamophobic sentiment.[58] These are scandals with very real and tragically violent consequences for Indian Muslims.

What becomes visible through such events is perhaps best described as a palimpsest of empires—a sedimented accretion of histories that refract and produce the affectively charged space of the national present. Twitter, Amazon, Indian Penal Code—these are the half-seen infrastructures of "religious feeling" as legally actionable affect.

Empire was (and is) an affective force, ordering bodies by ordering their feelings, and the emotions it structures are thus both intimate and geopolitical. They dig deep into particular bodies while also coursing around the world. As a charter text of colonial secularism, the Indian Penal Code has become part of the scaffolding of world religions as both global cultural form and global structure of feeling. The trick is in seeing these feelings in all their registers at once.

ACKNOWLEDGMENTS

THIS BOOK TOOK SHAPE OVER MANY YEARS and was, consequently, shaped by a large number of people and places—more, I fear, than can be acknowledged here. None of them, it bears stating, have any responsibility for claims made herein.

My interest in Section 295A was kindled by a panel on the Doniger affair at the 2014 meeting of the American Academy of Religion, organized by Brian Pennington and featuring presentations by Cassie Adcock, Rupa Viswanath, Elaine Fisher, Chad Bauman, Thomas Blom Hansen, P. Pratap Kumar, Gerald Larsen, and Laurie Patton, all of whom made the history of this troubled law irresistible. My research was then supported by grants from Montana State University, the University of Toronto, and the Social Science and Humanities Research Council of Canada. I am indebted to each of these institutions, as well as to the generous staff at libraries and archives including the British Library, University College London, National Archives of India, Nehru Memorial Museum and Library, Gurukul Kangri University Special Collections, Royal Ontario Museum, and University of Toronto Libraries.

At an early phase of the writing process, Brian Hatcher and Nada Moumtaz each patiently perused a sprawling chapter plan and helped me see what needed cutting. The manuscript then took shape while I was a scholar-in-residence at NYU's Center for Religion and Media, buoyed by the hospitality of Angela Zito, Janine Paolucci, and Adam Becker. The enthusiasm of Katie Lofton and John Modern at Class 200 brought the project to the University of Chicago Press, where I have been very happy to work with editor Kyle Wagner and editorial associate Kristin Rawlings. The press's two blind readers offered incisive feedback that made the book immeasurably better. So did Cassie Adcock, who generously read the entire manuscript and applied just the right mix of frank criticism and enthusiastic insight. Ridhima Sharma gave the manuscript a final incisive read, sharpening key arguments and drawing out crucial connections with intellectual generosity and precision.

Then there are the more diffuse debts. David Gilmartin first kindled my interest in colonial law, with Mitra Sharafi offering wisdom at various points along the way. Adnan Naseemullah cheered this book along from beginning to end, a stalwart compatriot in all things writerly. Yves Latreille lightened the writing with love and laughter. Yurou Zhong gamely listened as I blathered on about a dozen different iterations of this project (one day I will write "Oceanic Associations"!) and joined me in the Kittlerian trenches. Kajri Jain geeked out over Arya images. Echoes of Daniel Elam are audible throughout this book, especially in its discussions of rhetoric and print culture: can a monograph be a letter?

Many colleagues and friends helped me think through key topics or find essential references: John Cort, Dan Guadagnolo, Jack Hawley, Deana Heath, Brannon Ingram, Jaby Matthews, Farina Mir, Azfar Moin, Karuna Nundy, Luther Obrock, Shruti Patel, John Durham Peters, Sarah Qidwai, Enrico Raffaelli, Torrey Shanks, Youcef Soufi, Julia Stephens, Randall Styers, SherAli Tareen, Aparna Vaidik, and Jade Werner. Many more helped make Toronto a happy academic home: Kyle Smith, Ted Sammons, Nada Moumtaz, Margaret Boittin, Miguel de Figueredo, Emily Nacol, Ruth Marshall, Pamela Klassen, Walid Saleh, Ritu Birla, Arti Dhand, Andreas Bendlin, Duncan Hill, Sharon Marjadsingh, Shabina Moheebulla, Michael Twamley, and Fereshteh Hashemi. Particular thanks are due to members of the South Asia working group, who commented on a portion of the manuscript and also provide a model for what scholarly community can and should be: Ajay Rao, Malavika Kasturi, Kajri Jain, Srilata Raman, Christoph Emmerich, Karen Ruffle, Rijuta Mehta, Frank Cody, Bhavani Raman, Sarah Richardson, Waqas Butt, Julie Vig, and Kristin Plys.

Audiences at various venues responded to early versions of the ideas presented here, to the great benefit of the book before you: Columbia University, Dalhousie University, Macalester College, National Academy of Legal Studies and Research–Hyderabad, University of Göttingen, University of Victoria, University of Wisconsin–Madison, Yale University, and the University of Toronto's Comparative Political Theory Reading Group. I thank those involved in these events, especially Neilesh Bose, Rohit De, Susanna Drake, Krista Kesselring, Jim Laine, Lawrence Liang, Karuna Mantena, Colin Mitchell, Manisha Sethi, Mitra Sharafi, Gauri Viswanathan, Rupa

Viswanath, and Matt Walton. To write as a scholar is to be shaped profoundly by people one has not met—other scholars, as credited in endnotes. Sometimes the influence of a scholar on a given book goes beyond the credit visible there, as is the case for Asad Ali Ahmed's influence on this book, which is in its way just a footnote to his formative work on blasphemy.

Finally, nothing would have been written without the lifetime's worth of friends and loved ones who, though far-flung, kept me going through it all. They are the condition of possibility for everything. Even a dry and dreary scholarly book rests on mountains of unseen feeling.

NOTES

CHAPTER 1

1. For a snapshot, see Sumathi Ramaswamy, ed., *Barefoot across the Nation: Maqbool Fida Husain and the Idea of India* (London: Routledge, 2011). For contemporary jurisprudence, see Gautam Bhatia, *Offend, Shock, or Disturb: Free Speech under the Indian Constitution* (Delhi: Oxford University Press, 2016).
2. Surbhi Karwa and Shubham Kumar, "A Blasphemy Law Is Antithetical to India's Secular Ethos," *Economic and Political Weekly* 54, no. 37 (September 14, 2019), https://www.epw.in/engage/article/blasphemy-law-antithetical-indias-secular-ethos.
3. Joss Marsh, *Word Crimes: Blasphemy, Culture, and Literature in Nineteenth-Century England* (Chicago: University of Chicago Press, 1998).
4. Christopher Grenda, Chris Beneke, and David Nash, introduction to *Profane: Sacrilegious Expression in a Multicultural Age* (Berkeley: University of California Press, 2014), 1–24.
5. Clifford Geertz, *Interpretation of Cultures* (New York: Basic Books, 1973), 87–125. For a critique, see Talal Asad, *Genealogies of Religion: Discipline and Reasons of Power in Christianity and Islam* (Baltimore: Johns Hopkins University Press, 1993), 27–54.
6. Salman Rushdie, *The Satanic Verses* (New York: Henry Holt, 1997 [1988]), 353.
7. While I have learned a great deal from the following books, I think we need to question their geographic circumscription insofar as they function within the scholarship not as narrow area studies but as studies of blasphemy per se: Leonard Levy, *Blasphemy* (New York: Knopf, 1993); David Lawton, *Blasphemy* (Philadelphia: University of Pennsylvania Press, 1993); Alain Cabantous, *Blasphemy: Impious Speech in the West from the Seventeenth to the Nineteenth Century*, trans. Eric Rauth (New York: Columbia University Press, 2002 [1998]); and David Nash, *Blasphemy in the Christian World* (Oxford: Oxford University Press, 2007).
8. Talal Asad, "Reading a Modern Classic: W. C. Smith's *The Meaning and End of Religion*," *History of Religions* 40, no. 3 (2001): 205–22, at 221. For an overview of relevant scholarship, see Brent Nongbri, *Before Religion: A History of a Modern Concept* (New Haven, CT: Yale University Press, 2013).
9. Lucia Hulsether, "The Grammar of Racism: Religious Pluralism and the Birth of the

Interdisciplines," *Journal of the American Academy of Religion* 86, no. 1 (2018): 1–41, at 11.

10. "Charlie Hebdo: Macron défend «la liberté de blasphémer» en France," *Le Figaro*, September 1, 2020, https://www.lefigaro.fr/flash-eco/charlie-hebdo-macron-defend-la-liberte-de-blasphemer-en-france-20200901.

11. Elizabeth Shakmun Hurd and Nadia Marzouki, "Is There a Right to Heresy?," *Boston Review*, March 5, 2021; Mayanthi Fernando, *The Republic Unsettled: Muslim French and the Contradictions of Secularism* (Durham, NC: Duke University Press, 2014).

12. T. S. Eliot, *After Strange Gods: A Primer of Modern Heresy* (New York: Harcourt, 1933), 55–56.

13. Rajeev Bhargava, "The Distinctiveness of Indian Secularism," in *The Future of Secularism*, ed. T. N. Srinivasan (New Delhi: Oxford University Press, 2007), 20–53, at 25.

14. J. Barton Scott, "Review of *Reason* (*Vivek*) (dir. Anand Patwardhan, 2018)," *Journal of Religion & Film* 22, no. 2 (October 2018), https://digitalcommons.unomaha.edu/jrf/vol22/iss2/13.

15. "Extract from the Legislative Assembly Debates, Vol. IV," in National Archives of India (henceforth NAI)/Home/Political/1927/F.132/I. (Henceforth *LAD*.) I follow the printed pagination, which is organized by date. Citations for the above quotations are thus M. R. Jayakar (Bombay City), *LAD*, September 5, 26–28, and Sir Hari Singh Gour (Central Provinces), *LAD*, September 19, 22–24.

16. For subtraction stories, see Charles Taylor, *A Secular Age* (Cambridge, MA: Belknap, 2007).

17. Compare Talal Asad, *Secular Translations* (New York: Columbia University Press, 2018).

18. Talal Asad, *Formations of the Secular* (Stanford, CA: Stanford University Press, 2003), 1.

19. Hussein Ali Agrama, *Questioning Secularism: Islam, Sovereignty, and the Rule of Law in Modern Egypt* (Chicago: University of Chicago Press, 2012).

20. Winnifred Fallers Sullivan, *The Impossibility of Religious Freedom* (Princeton, NJ: Princeton University Press, 2018).

21. Henry Maine, *Ancient Law*, 4th ed. (London: John Murray, 1870), 23. See also James Mill, *History of British India* (Cambridge, UK: Cambridge University Press, 2010), 3:341.

22. C. S. Adcock, "Sacred Cows and Secular History: Cow Protection Debates in Colonial North India," *Comparative Studies of South Asia, Africa, and the Middle East* 30, no. 2 (2010): 297–311.

23. Hla Tun Pru (Burma), *LAD*, September 5, 29.

24. William Blackstone, *Commentaries on the Laws of England*, ed. Ruth Paley (Oxford: Oxford University Press, 2016), 4:39.

25. Tomoko Masuzawa, *The Invention of World Religions: Or, How European Universalism Was Preserved in the Language of Pluralism* (Chicago: University of Chicago Press, 2005).

26. Carl Ernst, "Blasphemy," in *Encyclopedia of Religion*, ed. Lindsay Jones (Detroit: Macmillan, 2005), 2:974–77; Talal Asad, "Reflections on Blasphemy and Secular Criticism," in *Religion: Beyond a Concept*, ed. Hent de Vries (New York: Fordham University Press,

2008), 580–609; Ebrahim Moosa, "Muslim Political Theology," in Grenda, Beneke, and Nash, *Profane*, 169–88.
27. See, for instance, Vidyut Aklujkar, "Maharashtra: Games with God," in *Krishna: A Sourcebook*, ed. Edwin Bryant (Oxford: Oxford University Press, 2007), 205–22, at 219.
28. Valerie Stoker, *Polemics and Patronage in the City of Victory* (Berkeley: University of California Press, 2016); Elaine Fisher, *Hindu Pluralism* (Berkeley: University of California Press, 2017).
29. Compare Jeremy Waldron, *The Harm in Hate Speech* (Cambridge, MA: Harvard University Press, 2014).
30. *Trial of George Jacob Holyoake* (London: Thomas Paterson, 1842).
31. George Jacob Holyoake, *English Secularism: A Confession of Belief* (Chicago: Open Court, 1896).
32. Melissa Mohr, *Holy Shit: A Brief History of Swearing* (New York: Oxford University Press, 2013), 124–25.
33. Sarah Apetrei, "The 'Sweet Singers' of Israel," *Reformation & Renaissance Review* 10, no. 1 (2008): 3–23.
34. Taylor's Case, (1676) 1 Ventris 293.
35. Elliot Visconsi, "The Invention of Criminal Blasphemy: Rex v. Taylor (1676)," *Representations* 103, no. 1 (2008): 30–52.
36. Nash, *Christian World*, 46, 150–57.
37. Marsh, *Word Crimes*, 3–17.
38. Regina v. Ramsay and Foote, (1883) 48 LT 733.
39. Marsh, *Word Crimes*.
40. Marsh, *Word Crimes*, 47. See J. Lorand Matory, *The Fetish Revisited: Marx, Freud, and the Gods Black People Make* (Durham, NC: Duke University Press, 2018).
41. Regina v. Hetherington, (1840) 4 St. Tr. N.S. 563, at 565–66.
42. Regina v. Bradlaugh, (1883) 15 Cox C.C. 217, at 219.
43. Compare Tisa Wenger, *Religious Freedom: The Contested History of an American Ideal* (Chapel Hill: University of North Carolina Press, 2017).
44. For the "religio-racial," see Judith Weisenfeld, *New World A-Coming: Black Religion and Racial Identity During the Great Migration* (New York: NYU Press, 2016).
45. See Nash, *Christian World*, 71.
46. Walter Arnstein, *The Bradlaugh Case* (Columbia: University of Missouri Press, 1965); Mytheli Sreenivas, "Birth Control in the Shadow of Empire: The Trials of Annie Besant, 1877–1878," *Feminist Studies* 41, no. 3 (2015): 509–37.
47. *Ramsay*, 739.
48. Rex v. Gott, (1922) 16 Cr App R 87, as quoted in David Nash, *Blasphemy in Modern Britain* (London: Routledge, 2019), 189–90.
49. Whitehouse v. Lemon, (1979) AC 617, HL.
50. Law Com. No. 79: *Offences against Religion and Public Worship* (London: Her Majesty's Stationary Office, 1981); Law Com. No. 145: *Criminal Law: Offences against Religion and Public Worship* (London: Her Majesty's Stationary Office, 1985).
51. Regina v. Chief Metropolitan Stipendiary Magistrate, ex parte Choudhury, (1990) 3

WLR 986, 1 QB 429; Clive Unsworth, "Blasphemy, Cultural Divergence, and Legal Relativism," *Modern Law Review* 58, no. 5 (1995): 658–77; Eliza Filby, *God & Mrs. Thatcher* (London: Biteback, 2015), 185–89; Nash, *Christian World*.

52. Russell Sandberg and Norman Doe, "The Strange Death of Blasphemy," *Modern Law Review* 71, no. 6 (2008): 971–86; David Nash and Chara Bakalis, "Incitement to Religious Hated and the Symbolic," *Liverpool Law Review* 28, no. 3 (2007): 349–75.

53. Munshi Iswar Saran (Lucknow), *LAD*, September 19, 19; Srinivasa Iyengar (Madras City), *LAD*, September 16, 24; India Office Records (henceforth IOR)/L/PJ/6/1941-F.1513/pp.131-2; *Indian National Herald* (Bombay), August 9, 1927, clipping in NAI/Home/Political/F.132&KW/p.11.

54. Controversy centered on the appeal, *Rajpal v. Emperor*, AIR 1927 Lah 590, but see also the original case, *King-Emperor v. Rajpal*, AIR 1926 Lah 196. Notably, the Lahore High Court's judgement cites Hari Singh Gour, *The Penal Law of British India*, 3rd ed. (Calcutta: Butterworth, 1925), thus presumably enhancing his prestige at the Legislative Assembly some months later.

55. IOR/L/PJ/6/1941/1513.

56. *LAD*, September 5, 15–17.

57. For contrapuntalism, see Edward Said, *Culture and Imperialism* (New York: Vintage, 1993).

58. Gauri Viswanathan, *Outside the Fold: Conversion, Modernity, Belief* (Princeton, NJ: Princeton University Press, 1998); Peter van der Veer, *Imperial Encounters: Religion and Modernity in India and Britain* (Princeton, NJ: Princeton University Press, 2001).

59. Bhargava, "Distinctiveness"; Rajeev Bhargava, ed., *Secularism and Its Critics* (Delhi: Oxford, 1997).

60. William Elison, Christian Lee Novetzke, and Andy Rotman, *Amar Akbar Anthony: Bollywood, Brotherhood, and the Nation* (Cambridge, MA: Harvard University Press, 2016). For modernist painting as a site of secularist cultural production, see Karin Zitzewitz, *The Art of Secularism: The Cultural Politics of Modernist Art in Contemporary India* (London: Hurst, 2014).

61. Viswanathan, *Outside the Fold*, 4.

62. Saba Mahmood, *Religious Difference in a Secular Age: A Minority Report* (Princeton, NJ: Princeton University Press, 2015), 10.

63. Nathaniel Halhed, *A Code of Gentoo Laws, or, Ordinations of the Pundits* (London: 1776), ix; Penelope Carson, *The East India Company and Religion, 1698–1858* (Cambridge, UK: Cambridge University Press, 2012).

64. Proclamation by the Queen in Council to the Princes, Chiefs, and People of India, IOR/L/PS/18/D154.

65. Bernard Cohn, "Representing Authority in Victorian India," in *The Invention of Tradition*, ed. Eric Hobsbawm and Terence Ranger (Cambridge, UK: Cambridge University Press, 1983), 101–210.

66. J. Talboys Wheeler, *History of the Imperial Assemblage at Delhi* (London: Longmans, 1877), 111.

67. Nicholas Dirks, *Castes of Mind: Colonialism and the Making of Modern India* (Princeton, NJ: Princeton University Press, 2001); Peter Gottschalk, *Religion, Science, and Empire:*

Classifying Hinduism and Islam in British India (New York: Oxford University Press, 2013).
68. Partha Chatterjee, *The Politics of the Governed: Reflections on Popular Politics in Most of the World* (New York: Columbia University Press, 2006).
69. Mahmood, *Religious Difference*, 21.
70. Homi Bhabha, *The Location of Culture* (London: Routledge, 1994).
71. See especially Asad Ali Ahmed, "Specters of Macaulay: Blasphemy, the Indian Penal Code, and Pakistan's Postcolonial Predicament," in *Censorship in South Asia*, ed. Raminder Kaur and William Mazzarella (Bloomington: Indiana University Press, 2009), 172–205.
72. *A Penal Code Prepared by the Indian Law Commissioners* (Calcutta: G. H. Huttmann, 1837), 72.
73. W. Blake Odgers, *Digest of the Law of Libel and Slander*, 2nd ed. (London: Stevens and Sons, 1887), 338. Absent in the first edition of 1881, this 1887 definition clearly emerged from *Ramsay*.
74. IOR/L/PJ/6/1941-F.1513/p.34.
75. For a development of this Foucauldian argument, see Kaur and Mazzarella, *Censorship*; Judith Butler, *Excitable Speech: A Politics of the Performative* (New York: Routledge, 1997).
76. Walter Bagehot, *Physics and Politics* (Boston: Beacon, 1956 [1867]).
77. Elizabeth Kolsky, *Colonial Justice in British India: White Violence and the Rule of Law* (Cambridge, UK: Cambridge University Press, 2009).
78. J. S. Mill, *On Liberty* (Cambridge, UK: Cambridge University Press, 1989 [1859]), 13–14; J. F. Stephen, *Liberty, Equality, Fraternity* (New York: Holt, 1873), 28.
79. Elizabeth Pritchard, *Religion in Public: Locke's Political Theology* (Stanford, CA: Stanford University Press, 2013).
80. Stephen, *Liberty, Equality*, 17.
81. Stephen, *Liberty, Equality*, 112–15.
82. Stephen, *Liberty, Equality*, 45–46.
83. Stephen, *Liberty, Equality*, 31–32, 179–81.
84. J. F. Stephen, "Legislation under Lord Mayo," in *A Life of the Earl of Mayo*, 2nd ed., by W. W. Hunter (London: Smith, Elder, 1876), 2:168–69.
85. For an overview, see Melissa Gregg and Gregory Seigworth, eds., *The Affect Theory Reader* (Durham, NC: Duke University Press, 2010); Donovan Schaefer, *Religious Affects: Animality, Evolution, and Power* (Durham, NC: Duke University Press, 2015); John Corrigan, ed., *Feeling Religion* (Durham, NC: Duke University Press, 2017).
86. C. P. Tiele, *Elements of the Science of Religion* (Edinburg: William Blackwood, 1899), 2:15.
87. Thomas Dixon, *From Passions to Emotions: The Creation of a Secular Psychological Category* (New York: Cambridge University Press, 2006), 98–134.
88. Margrit Pernau, *Emotions and Modernity in Colonial India* (New Delhi: Oxford University Press, 2019), 29, 171–94. See also Elizabeth Chatterjee, Sneha Krishnan, and Megan Robb, eds., "Feeling Modern: The History of Emotions in Urban South Asia," special issue, *Journal of the Royal Asiatic Society* 24, no. 4 (2017): 539–680.

89. C. S. Adcock, "Violence, Passion, and the Law: A Brief History of Section 295A and Its Antecedents," *Journal of the American Academy of Religion* 84, no. 2 (2016): 337–51.
90. Ann Cvetkovich, "Public Feelings," *South Atlantic Quarterly* 106, no. 3 (2007): 459–68.
91. Sara Ahmed, *Cultural Politics of Emotion* (London: Routledge, 2004); Teresa Brennan, *The Transmission of Affect* (Ithaca, NY: Cornell University Press, 2004).
92. Joan Wallach Scott, *Sex and Secularism* (Princeton, NJ: Princeton University Press, 2017).
93. William James, *Writings, 1902–1910* (New York: Library of America, 1987), 36.
94. James, *Writings*, 435.
95. Partha Chatterjee, *The Nation and Its Fragments* (Princeton, NJ: Princeton University Press, 1993).
96. Faisal Devji, "Gender and the Politics of Space," *South Asia* 14, no. 1 (1991): 141–53; Usha Thakkar, "Puppets on the Periphery: Women and Social Reform in Nineteenth-Century Gujarati Society," *Economic and Political Weekly* 32, nos. 1/2 (1997): 46–52; Shefali Chandra, *The Sexual Life of English: Languages of Caste and Desire in Colonial India* (Durham, NC: Duke University Press, 2012)
97. Sumanta Banerjee, *The Parlour and the Street: Elite and Popular Culture in Nineteenth-Century Calcutta* (Chicago: University of Chicago Press, 2018 [1989]).
98. On the phenomenology of caste, see Gopal Guru, "Aesthetic of Touch and Skin: An Essay in Contemporary Indian Political Phenomenology," in *Bloomsbury Research Handbook of Indian Aesthetics and the Philosophy of Art*, ed. Arindam Chakrabarti (London: Bloosmbury, 2016), 297–315; Sundar Sarukkai, "Phenomenology of Untouchability," *Economic and Political Weekly* 44, no. 37 (2009): 39–48; Joel Lee, "Odor and Order: How Caste is Inscribed in Space and Sensoria," *Comparative Studies of South Africa, Asia, and the Middle East* 37, no. 3 (2017): 470–90. On brahmanical patriarchy, see Sunaina Arya and Aakash Singh Rathore, eds. *Dalit Feminist Theory: A Reader* (London: Routledge, 2020).
99. Kajri Jain, *Gods in the Time of Democracy* (Durham, NC: Duke University Press, 2021), 81–119.
100. See Charu Gupta, *Sexuality, Obscenity, and Community: Women Muslims and the Hindu Public in Colonial India* (New York: Palgrave, 2002) and *The Gender of Caste: Representing Dalits in Print* (Seattle: University of Washington Press, 2016).
101. *LAD*, September 16, 42. Compare Mrinalini Sinha, *Specters of Mother India: The Global Restructuring of an Empire* (Durham, NC: Duke University Press, 2006), 8.
102. For the larger British-imperial legal scene, see Thomas Metcalf, *Imperial Connections* (Berkeley: University of California Press, 2007), 16–45, and Wing-Cheong Chan, Barry Wright, and Stanley Yeo, eds., *Codification, Macaulay, and the Indian Penal Code* (London: Ashgate, 2011).
103. "The Codification of Law," *Morning Post*, November 13, 1872, in *Public Opinion: A Comprehensive Summary of the Press Throughout the World* 22, no. 582 (1872): 613–14; J. F. Stephen, *Digest of the Criminal Law* (London: Macmillan, 1877).
104. Barry Wright, "Criminal Law Codification and Imperial Projects: The Self-Governing Jurisdiction Codes of the 1890s," *Legal History* 12, no. 1 (2008): 19–47; *Acts of the Parliament of the Dominion of Canada*, vol. 1, *Public General Acts* (Ottawa: Samuel Dawson,

1892); Jeremy Patrick, "Not Dead, Just Sleeping: Canada's Prohibition on Blasphemous Libel as a Case Study in Obsolete Legislation," *University of British Columbia Law Review* 41, no. 2 (2008): 193–248

105. Apirat Petchsiri, "A Short History of Thai Criminal Law Since the Nineteenth Century," *Malaya Law Review* 28, no. 1 (1986): 134–50; G. Glover Alexander, "The Egyptian Draft Penal Code, 1919," *Journal of Comparative Legislation and International Law*, 3rd series 1, no. 3 (1919): 244–47.

106. *Palestine Gazette* (Jerusalem), September 28, 1936.

107. Thomas Macaulay to James Mill, August 24, 1835, in *Letters of Thomas Babington Macaulay*, ed. Thomas Pinney (Cambridge, UK: Cambridge University Press, 1976), 3:146–51.

108. K. J. M. Smith, *Lawyers, Legislators, and Theorists: Developments in English Criminal Jurisprudence, 1800–1957* (Oxford: Clarendon, 1998), 121–72.

109. "Blasphemy," *Westminster Review*, July 1883, 1–11.

110. W. Blake Odgers, "The Law Relating to Heresy and Blasphemy," *Modern Review* 4, no. 15 (1883): 586–608.

111. J. F. Stephen, *History of the Criminal Law of England* (London: Macmillan, 1883), 3:312–13; J. F. Stephen, "Blasphemy and Blasphemous Libel," *Fortnightly Review*, March 1, 1884; Lindsey Aspland, *The Law of Blasphemy: Being a Candid Examination of the Views of Mr. Justice Stephen* (London: Stevens & Haynes, 1884).

112. Stephen, *Digest of Criminal Law*, xxxv, 97–98, and *History of Criminal Law*, 2:396–497. See also K. J. M. Smith, *James Fitzjames Stephen: Portrait of a Victorian Rationalist* (Cambridge, UK: Cambridge University Press, 1988).

113. "Appendix C," in Odgers, *Digest of the Law of Libel*.

114. Courtney Kenny, "Evolution of the Law of Blasphemy," *Cambridge Law Journal* 1, no. 2 (1922): 127–42, at 135.

115. Levy, *Blasphemy*, 505.

116. AC 617, HL.

117. Law Com. No. 79.

118. Select Committee on Religious Offences in England and Wales, House of Lords Paper 95, vol. 1 (2002–3).

119. Levy, *Blasphemy*, 238–71, 506–33; Sarah Barringer Gordon, "Blasphemy and the Law of Religious Liberty in Nineteenth Century America," *American Quarterly* 52, no. 4 (2000): 682–719. For a recent case, see Samuel G. Freedman, "A Man's Existentialism Construed as Blasphemy," *New York Times*, March 20, 2009, https://www.nytimes.com/2009/03/21/us/21religion.html.

CHAPTER 2

1. *Muslim Outlook* (Lahore) (henceforth *MO*), June 17, 1927. Henceforth all press dates 1927 unless otherwise specified.

2. *MO*, June 17.

3. National Archives of India (NAI)/Home/Political/F.132/ Serials Nos.1-39/p.4.
4. John Platts, *A Dictionary of Urdu, Classical Hindi, and English* (Oxford: Oxford University Press, 1974 [1884]), 601.
5. *MO*, June 30, 1.
6. For a full recounting of events, see Gene Thursby, *Hindu-Muslim Relations in British India* (Leiden: Brill, 1975), 41-71, and Richa Raj, "A Pamphlet and Its (Dis)contents: A Case Study of *Rangila Rasul*," *History and Sociology of South Asia* 9, no. 2 (2015): 146-62. In taking the affair as an episode in the history of secularism, I build on Neeti Nair, "Beyond the 'Communal' 1920s: The Problem of Intention, Legislative Pragmatism, and the Making of Section 295A of the Indian Penal Code," *Indian Economic and Social History Review* 50, no. 3 (2013): 317-40; and Julia Stephens, *Governing Islam: Law, Empire, and Secularism in South Asia* (Cambridge: Cambridge University Press, 2018), 132-54.
7. NAI/Home/Political/1927/132/III/p.45; *MO*, July 27, 5, and August 21, 3-4.
8. 209 Parl. Deb., H.C. (5th ser.) (1927) 1649; *Tribune* (Lahore), July 30, 16; *Manchester Guardian*, July 26, 8, and August 8, 3.
9. India Office Records (IOR)/L/PJ/6/1941/F.1513; *MO*, July 30, 5.
10. Kṛṣṇdev Kapil, "Afrīkā Deś meṃ Isāiyat aur Ārya Samāj," *Ārya: Ārya Pratinidhi Sabhā Pañjāb kā Māsik Patra* (Lahore) (February 1926): 9-12; Kṛṣṇdev Kapil, "Īṣṭ Afrīkā meṃ Āryasamāj," *Ārya* (June 1926): 2-6.
11. John D. Kelly, *A Politics of Virtue: Hinduism, Sexuality, and Countercolonial Discourse in Fiji* (Chicago: University of Chicago Press, 1991), 208, 217-18.
12. Thomas Macaulay, "The Government of India," in *Works of Lord Macaulay*, ed. Hannah Macaulay More Trevelyan (London: Longmans, Green, 1866), VIII:139-42.
13. Partha Chatterjee, *The Politics of the Governed* (New York: Columbia University Press, 2006), 34-38.
14. Nicholas Dirks, *Castes of Mind* (Princeton, NJ: Princeton University Press, 2001); Gyan Prakash, "Colonial Genealogy of Society," in *The Social in Question*, ed. Patrick Joyce (London: Routledge, 2002), 81-96.
15. *Proceedings of the Council of the Governor-General of India* (Calcutta: Superintendent Government Printing, 1910), 48:171.
16. H. H. Risley, "The Study of Ethnology in India," *Journal of the Anthropological Institute of Great Britain and Ireland* 20 (1891): 235-63.
17. Thomas Trautmann, *Aryans and British India* (Berkeley: University of California Press, 1997), 198-204.
18. Walter Lippman, *Public Opinion* (New Brunswick, NJ: Transaction Publishers, 1991 [1922]), 52-53, 14; Timothy Mitchell, *Rule of Experts: Egypt, Techno-Politics, Modernity* (Berkeley: University of California Press, 2002).
19. Arun Mukherjee, "B. R. Ambedkar, John Dewey, and the Meaning of Democracy," *New Literary History* 40, no. 2 (2009): 345-70; Scott Stroud, "What Did Bhimrao Ambedkar Learn from John Dewey's *Democracy and Education*?," *Pluralist* 12, no. 2 (2017): 78-103; B. R. Nanda, ed., *Collected Works of Lala Lajpat Rai* (New Delhi: Manohar, 2004), 5:74-75.
20. See Brannon Ingram, J. Barton Scott, and SherAli Tareen, eds., *Imagining the Public in Modern South Asia* (New York: Routledge, 2016); and Brian A. Hatcher, "From Court

NOTES TO PAGES 37–42

to Court: Religious Polities and the Modern South Asian Public," *Religion Compass* 14, no. 8 (August 2020), https://doi.org/10.1111/rec3.12367.

21. Compare David Gilmartin, "Democracy, Nationalism, and the Public," *South Asia: The Journal of South Asian Studies* 14, no. 1 (1991): 123–40.

22. I build on Benedict Anderson, *The Spectre of Comparisons* (London: Verso, 1998), and William Mazzarella, *Censorium: Cinema and the Open Edge of Mass Publicity* (Durham, NC: Duke University Press, 2013). For further discussion, see J. Barton Scott, "Aryas Unbound: Print Hinduism and the Cultural Regulation of Religious Offense," *Comparative Studies of South Asia, Africa, and the Middle East* 35, no. 2 (2015): 294–309.

23. Although now most often associated with Michael Warner, *Publics and Counterpublics* (Cambridge, MA: Zone, 2002), this term has a longer history in German (*Gegenöffentlichkeit*) and then English, as seen in Oskar Negt and Alexander Kluge, *Public Sphere and Experience* (London: Verso, 2016 [1972]), and Nancy Fraser, "Rethinking the Public Sphere," *Social Text* no. 25–26 (1990): 56–80.

24. Warner, *Publics and Counterpublics*, 120.

25. Thursby, *Hindu-Muslim Relations*, 41–43.

26. M. K. Gandhi, "Inflammatory Literature," *Young India*, June 19, 1924, in *Collected Works* (Ahmedabad: Navjivan Trust, 1967), 24:261.

27. Compare Isabel Hofmeyr, *Gandhi's Printing Press: Experiments in Slow Reading* (Cambridge, MA: Harvard University Press, 2013).

28. Abul Wafā Sanāullāh Amritsarī, *Muqaddas Rasūl, Bajawāb Rangīlā Rasūl* (New Delhi: Al-Kitab International, 2011 [ca. 1924]), 7–9, 19–21.

29. *Leader* (Allahabad), May 27, 1928, clipping in NAI/ Home/Political/1927/10/50/p.29.

30. *MO*, July 17, 6. For further description of the activities of Mohammad Daud Ghaznavi of Amritsar, see Henry Craik, "Muhammadan Agitation against the High Court," in NAI/Home/Political/1927/132/III/pp.41–7.

31. *Tribune* (Lahore), July 31, 2; *MO*, July 31, 2, and August 7, 3.

32. *Tribune*, July 19, 2.

33. *MO*, July 30, 6.

34. *Tribune*, August 10, in NAI/Home/Political/1927/132&KW/p.6.

35. Gayatri Chakravorty Spivak, "Can the Subaltern Speak?," in *Marxism and the Interpretation of Culture*, ed. Cary Nelson and Lawrence Grossberg (Urbana: University of Illinois Press, 1988), 271–313.

36. Compare Charu Gupta, *Sexuality, Obscenity, Community: Women, Muslims, and the Hindu Public in Colonial India* (New York: Palgrave, 2002).

37. IOR/L/R/5/205. For further discussion, see Stephens, *Governing Islam*, 135.

38. Joel Lee, *Deceptive Majority: Dalits, Hinduism, and Underground Religion* (Cambridge, UK: Cambridge University Press, 2021).

39. Compare Arjun Appadurai, "Number in the Colonial Imagination," in *Orientalism and the Postcolonial Predicament*, ed. Carol Breckenridge and Peter van der Veer (Philadelphia: University of Pennsylvania Press, 1993), 314–40.

40. *Alārm Bel, arthāt Khatre kā Ghaṇṭā*, 6th ed. (Ajmer: Ārya Sāhitya Maṇḍal, 1924), iii.

41. Dharmdev Siddhāntālaṅkār, "Ārya Samāj kā Bhaviṣya," *Ārya*, May 1924, 19–22; T. L.

Vāsvāni, "Bhāratīya Itihās kī Sākṣī," *Ārya*, May 1924, 38–43; Mahātmā Gāndhī, "Svāmi Dayānand aur Ārya Samāj," *Ārya*, June 1924, 38–39; "Kyā Pratyek Musalmān Arya Banāyā Jā Saktā Hai?" *Ārya*, June 1924, 41–42.

42. Ishita Pande, "Loving Like a Man: The *Colourful Prophet*, Conjugal Masculinity, and the Politics of Hindu Sexology in Late Colonial India," *Gender & History* 29, no. 3 (2017): 675–92; Pandey Bechan Sharma, *Chocolate and Other Writings on Male Homoeroticism*, trans. Ruth Vanita (Durham, NC: Duke University Press, 2009).

43. See, for instance, Shiv Sharma, *Strī Śikṣā* (Bareli: Vidyābhūṣaṇ Śarma, 1927). The above discussion leans heavily on Gupta, *Sexuality, Obscenity*.

44. [Camupati], *Rangīlā Rasūl: Mūl Pustak Urdu kā Hindī Rūpāntar*, ed. Baldev Śarma (Banaras: Baldev Sharma, ca. 1927), 22, 25. To my knowledge, the Urdu original has not been preserved in government archives.

45. Amritsarī, *Muqaddas Rasul*, 79–84. For more on Zainab, see SherAli Tareen, *Defending Muhammad in Modernity* (Notre Dame, IN: University of Notre Dame Press, 2020), 179–223.

46. Gupta, *Sexuality, Obscenity*, 151–62.

47. *MO*, July 13, 3, and July 15, 5.

48. *MO*, June 21, 4; telegraph from Aziz-ur-Rahman, May 14, in NAI/Home/Political/1927/132/III/p.2.

49. IOR/L/PJ/6/194/F.1513/pp.215–6.

50. Émile Durkheim, *The Elementary Forms of Religious Life*, trans. Karen Fields (New York: Free Press, 1995).

51. For a dialectic Durkheim, see William Mazzarella, *The Mana of Mass Society* (Chicago: University of Chicago Press, 2017), 63–100.

52. NAI/Home/Political/1924/F.44/VII.

53. Motilal Nehru to Jawaharlal Nehru, July 7, 1927, quoted in Stephens, *Governing Islam*, 139.

54. On *joś* as cultivated feeling, see Margrit Pernau, *Emotions and Modernity in Colonial India* (New Delhi: Oxford University Press, 2019), 219–33.

55. *Abhyudaya* (Allahabad), July 2, 1, and July 9, 5.

56. *Hindu Sansar* (Delhi), July 1, 1.

57. *Hindu Punch* (Calcutta), July 21, 19–20.

58. *Abhyudaya*, July 2.

59. *Hindu Sansar*, June 21, 5; July 2, 1.

60. *MO*, June 24, 5; *Tribune*, June 24, 6; *The People*, June 26, 502. For context, see Martin Hewitt, "Aspects of Platform Culture in Nineteenth-Century Britain," *Nineteenth-Century Prose* 29, no. 1 (2002): 1–31, at 10; N. Gerald Barrier, "The Punjab Disturbances of 1907," *Modern Asian Studies* 1, no. 4 (1967): 353–83, at 366; and, for petitions, Rohit De, "Cows and Constitutionalism," *Modern Asian Studies* 53, no. 1 (2019): 240–77.

61. Arjun Appadurai, *Fear of Small Numbers* (Durham, NC: Duke University Press, 2006). Walter Lippmann, *The Phantom Public* (New Brunswick, NJ: Transaction Publishers, 1993 [1927]), 145. On crowds, see especially William Mazzarella, "The Myth of the Multitude" *Critical Inquiry* 36, no. 4 (2010): 697–727. On crowd theory in South Asia, see Pernau, *Emotions and Modernity*, 171–94.

62. *Tribune*, May 10, 1.
63. G. D. Ogilvie to Henry Craik, June 29, in NAI/Home/Political/1927/F.132/III/p.7.
64. NAI/Home/Political/1927/132/III/pp.43–5; *Tribune*, July 1, 1; *The People*, June 26; *Abhyudaya*, August 13, 2.
65. *MO*, July 6, 6.
66. I summarize from the decidedly unsympathetic *Hindu Sansar*, July 2, 1.
67. *MO*, June 24, 5. See also June 30, 1, and July 2, 2.
68. *MO*, June 18, 6.
69. Gabriel Tarde, "The Public and the Crowd," in *On Communication and Social Influence: Selected Papers*, ed. Terry N. Clark (Chicago: University of Chicago Press, 1969), 277–96.
70. I use this event as metaphor for crowd violence, in the manner diagnosed by Shahid Amin, *Event, Memory, Metaphor: Chauri Chaura, 1922–1992* (Berkeley: University of California Press, 1995).
71. Gail Minault, *The Khilafat Movement: Religious Symbolism and Political Mobilization in India* (New York: Columbia University Press, 1982).
72. *Tribune*, July 21, 2.
73. *Hindu Sansar*, July 1, 1.
74. "The Moral Teachings of Hussain" and "Husain and Humanity," *MO*, July 19, 2; July 26, 1. For context, see Syed Akbar Hyder, *Reliving Karbala: Martyrdom in South Asian Memory* (Oxford: Oxford University Press, 2006), 137–202.
75. Compare Faisal Devji, *The Impossible Indian: Gandhi and the Temptation of Violence* (Cambridge, MA: Harvard University Press, 2012).
76. *Tribune*, May 21, 1; IOR/L/PJ/6/1932.
77. IOR/L/PJ/6/1977/F.1113/p.12.
78. IOR/L/PJ/6/1941/F.1513/p.90.
79. On Ilm ud-din's martyr cult, see Farhat Haq, *Sharia and the State in Pakistan: Blasphemy Politics* (New York: Routledge, 2019).
80. "Śrī Svāmī Śraddhānandjī Mahārāj Dharmvedī par Balidān Hue!," *Vaidik Dharm* (Aundh), January, 20–22.
81. Pandit Muniśvarprasād Avasthī, "Hamārā Śraddhānand!," *Hindu Punch*, January 20, 974–75.
82. *The People*, September 29, 239.
83. Kama Maclean, *A Revolutionary History of Interwar India: Violence, Image, Voice, and Text* (London: Hurst, 2015); Chris Moffat, *India's Revolutionary Inheritance: Politics and the Promise of Bhagat Singh* (Cambridge, UK: Cambridge University Press, 2018).
84. Tapati Guha-Thakurta, *The Making of a New "Indian" Art: Artists, Aesthetics, and Nationalism in Bengal, c.1850–1920* (Cambridge, UK: Cambridge University Press, 1992); Kajri Jain, *Gods in the Bazaar: The Economies of Indian Calendar Art* (Durham, NC: Duke University Press, 2007), 133. My thanks to Kajri Jain for discussing this image with me.
85. Satyakām Vidyālaṅkār, "Vedvarṇit Balidān yā Ātmasamarpaṇ," *Balidān* (Lahore) 2, no. 1 (April 1935): 13–16.
86. Ajay Kumār, "Śahīd," *Balidān* (Lahore) 2, no. 1 (April 1935): 31.

87. Satyavrat Siddhāntālaṅkār, "Mṛityu meṃ Jīvan," *Balidān* (Lahore) 2, no. 1 (April 1935): 23–25.
88. IOR/L/PJ/6/1977-F.1113/pp.10–4; Stephens, *Governing Islam*, 151.
89. Svatantrānand, *Āryya Samāj ke Mahādhan* (Delhi: Sārvadeśik Ārya Pratinidhi Sabhā, 1948), 164.
90. Achille Mbembe, *Necropolitics* (Durham, NC: Duke University Press, 2019).
91. Joseph Alter, "Yoga at the Fin-de-Siècle," *International Journal of the History of Sport* 23, no. 5 (2006): 759–76.
92. "Caturvidh Puruṣārth kā Sādhan: Śārīrik Bal Baṛhāne ke Upāya," *Vaidik Dharm*, June, 98–99.
93. *MO*, June 14, 3; June 29, 5; August 16, 1; *Tribune*, July 20, 2.

CHAPTER 3

1. "Extract from the Legislative Assembly Debates, Vol. IV," in National Archives of India (NAI)/Home/Political/1927/F.132/I. (Henceforth *LAD*.) I follow the printed pagination, which is organized by date. Citation for the above quote is thus D. V. Belvi (Bombay Southern Division), *LAD*, September 16, 8.
2. Compare Asad Ali Ahmed, "Adjudicating Muslims: Law, Religion, and the State in Colonial India and Postcolonial Pakistan" (PhD diss., University of Chicago, 2006).
3. Dane Kennedy, *Magic Mountains: Hill Stations and the British Raj* (Berkeley: University of California Press, 1996).
4. Vipin Pubby, *Shimla, Then & Now*, 2nd ed. (New Delhi: Indus Publishing, 1996), 88.
5. Pubby, *Shimla*, 93.
6. M. K. Gandhi, "Five Hundredth Storey," *Collected Works* (Ahmedabad: Navajivan Trust, 1966), 20:115–18.
7. Thomas Metcalf, *Ideologies of the Raj* (Cambridge, UK: Cambridge University Press, 1995).
8. For late colonial security discourse, see Durba Ghosh, *Gentlemanly Terrorists: Political Violence and the Colonial State in India, 1919–1947* (Cambridge, UK: Cambridge University Press, 2017), 15–19, 31–32.
9. N. Gerald Barrier, *Banned: Controversial Literature and Political Control in British India, 1907–1947* (Columbia: University of Missouri Press, 1974), 16–17. For further context, see C. A. Bayly, *Empire and Information: Intelligence Gathering and Social Communication in India, 1780–1870* (Cambridge, UK: Cambridge University Press, 1996), and Devika Sethi, *War over Words: Censorship in India, 1930–1960* (Cambridge, UK: Cambridge University Press, 2019).
10. Pandit Thakur Das Bhargava (Ambala), *LAD*, September 5, 19.
11. Bhubananda Dass (Orissa), *LAD*, September 16, 35.
12. M. K. Acharya (South Arcot cum Chingleput), *LAD*, September 16, 41.
13. *The Hindu* (Madras), as quoted in *Muslim Outlook* (henceforth *MO*), September 23, 1927, 1–2. Henceforth all press dates 1927 unless otherwise specified.

14. *Bombay Chronicle*, as extracted in *MO*, September 24, 2
15. *MO*, September 8, 3; September 18, 3.
16. *MO*, September 23, 2.
17. Sir Zulkifar Ali Khan (East Central Punjab), *LAD*, September 16, 5.
18. Ravi Bali, "Witness to Many a Glorious Moment," *Tribune*, February 12, 2000, https://www.tribuneindia.com/2000/20000212/windows/main2.htm.
19. Gayatri Chakravorty Spivak, "Can the Subaltern Speak?," in *Marxism and the Interpretation of Culture*, ed. Cary Nelson and Lawrence Grossberg (Urbana: University of Illinois Press, 1988), 271–313.
20. Partha Chatterjee, *The Nation and Its Fragments* (Princeton, NJ: Princeton University Press, 1993).
21. *LAD*, September 16, 42.
22. Mrinalini Sinha, *Specters of Mother India: The Global Restructuring of an Empire* (Durham, NC: Duke University Press, 2006).
23. Act No. XXV of 1927, in *A Collection of the Acts of the Indian Legislature for the Year 1927* (Calcutta: Government of India, 1928), in India Office Records (IOR)/V/8/72.
24. "Report of the Select Committee," Serials Nos. 1–39, pp. 38–41, in NAI/Home/Political/1927/F.132/I.
25. *LAD*, September 16, 26.
26. *Abhyudaya* (Allahabad), August 27, 1927, 5
27. Allan Octavian Hume and Kour Luchman Singh, *Hindee Version of the Indian Penal Code, or Act XLV of 1860* (Etawah: Hukeem Jowahir Lall, 1861), 202–3.
28. Shabnum Tejani, *Indian Secularism: A Social and Intellectual History, 1890–1950* (Ranikhet: Permanent Black, 2007).
29. Ronojoy Sen, *Articles of Faith: Religion, Secularism, and the Indian Supreme Court* (Delhi: Oxford University Press, 2018).
30. For context, see Anupama Rao, *The Caste Question: Dalits and the Politics of Modern India* (Berkeley: University of California Press, 2009), and Joel Lee, *Deceptive Majority: Dalits, Hinduism, and Underground Religion* (Cambridge: Cambridge University Press, 2021).
31. On the emergence of the communal question, see Sandria Freitag, *Collective Action and Community: Public Arenas and the Emergence of Communalism in North India* (Berkeley: University of California Press, 1989); Gyanendra Pandey, *The Construction of Communalism in Colonial North India*, 3rd ed. (New Delhi: Oxford University Press, 2012).
32. Khalid Anis Ansari, "It's Not Just Religion, It's Also Caste," *Indian Express*, March 29, 2018, https://indianexpress.com/article/opinion/columns/hindu-muslims-the-minority-space-caste-system-in-india-5115108/.
33. C. S. Adcock, *The Limits of Tolerance: Indian Secularism and the Politics of Religious Freedom* (New York: Oxford University Press, 2014).
34. B. P. Naidu (Guntur cum Nellore), *LAD*, September 16, 13–14; S. D. Nadakarani, "Religion-mongering," *The People* (Lahore), May 8, 364–65; Abdul Haye (East Punjab), *LAD*, September 5, 3.
35. Ahmad Ali Amir to Governor of Punjab, telegram of July 27, IOR/L/PJ/6/1941/F.1513/pp.287–90.

36. "Wanted: A Secular Party," *Tribune* (Lahore), July 27, 1; "What Is a Secular Party?," *Tribune*, July 28, 1; Lajpat Rai, "Religionism vs. Secularism," *The People*, September 8. Cf. Julia Stephens, *Governing Islam: Law, Empire, and Secularism in South Asia* (Cambridge, UK: Cambridge University Press, 2018), 16, 149–50.
37. S. D. Nadakarani, "Gleanings from a Rationalist's Notebook," *The People*, January 30, 83–85.
38. S. Srinivasa Iyengar (Madras City), *LAD*, September 5, 10–12.
39. James Crerar (Home Member), *LAD*, September 5, 30–31.
40. NAI/Home/Political/1928/217/Appendix 2.
41. J. Barton Scott, "Aryas Unbound: Print Hinduism and the Cultural Regulation of Religious Offense," *Comparative Studies of South Asia, Africa, and the Middle East* 35, no. 2 (2015): 294–309.
42. See Raminder Kaur and William Mazzarella, eds., *Censorship in South Asia* (Bloomington: Indiana University Press, 2009).
43. Compare Wendy Brown, *Regulating Aversion: Tolerance in the Age of Identity and Empire* (Princeton, NJ: Princeton University Press, 2006), 87.
44. *Forward* (Calcutta), quoted in *MO*, September 23, 1–2.
45. *MO*, May 25, 1.
46. *LAD*, September 16, 24.
47. *LAD*, September 5, 15.
48. "Report of the Select Committee."
49. *Tribune*, September 1, 9.
50. *The People*, May 29, 427–28.
51. NAI/Home/Political/1927/10/93/pp.4–17; *Tribune*, June 22, 1.
52. *MO*, July 13, 2. For more on Nariman, see M. R. Jayakar, *The Story of My Life* (Bombay: Asia Publishing House, 1959), 2:28.
53. *MO*, August 2, 7; *Indian Quarterly Register* 11, nos. 1–2 (Calcutta: Annual Register Office, 1927): 10.
54. On Ali and Naidu cooperating on "Respect for All Prophets," see *The People*, September 1, 166–67. On their cooperation in the Khilafat movement, see Padmini Sengupta, *Sarojini Naidu: A Biography* (New York: Asia Publishing House, 1966), 160.
55. *Leader* (Allahabad), July 23, extracted in NAI/Home/Political/1927/132&KW/p.46. For context, see Afzal Iqbal, *Life and Times of Mohamed Ali* (Lahore: Institute of Islamic Culture, 1974), 348–49; "Rangīla Rasūl ke Faisle par M. Muhammad Ali kī Rāy," *Abhyudaya*, July 2, 9.
56. *MO*, August 13, 6; *Hindustan Times* (Delhi), August 11, in NAI/Home/Political/1927/132&KW/p.20.
57. *Indian National Herald* (Bombay), August 9, and *Tribune*, August 10, in NAI/Home/Political/1927/132&KW/pp.11, 14; *Tribune*, August 18, 1.
58. *Tribune*, September 1, 9.
59. Lord Irwin, Viceroy, to Earl of Birkenhead, India Secretary, July 27, NAI/Home/Political/1927/10/93/p.20.
60. *Indian Quarterly Register*, 330–31.

61. *Tribune*, August 25, 6; *MO*, August 27, 7; NAI/Home/Political/1927/132/III/pp.125–9. For context, see Spencer Lavan, *The Ahmadiyah Movement* (Delhi: Manohar, 1974), 136–37.
62. Pandit Nilakantha Das (Orissa), *LAD*, September 16, 34.
63. Bhubanananda Das (Orissa), *LAD*, September 16, 34.
64. Abdul Haye (East Punjab), *LAD*, September 5, 3.
65. *The People*, September 1, 166–67.
66. M. R. Jayakar (Bombay City), *LAD*, September 5, 27.
67. Pandit Hirday Nath Kunzru (Agra), *LAD*, September 5, 13.
68. T. A. K. Shervani (Cities of United Provinces), *LAD*, September 5, 30.
69. Bhubanananda Das (Orissa), *LAD*, September 16, 35.
70. Talal Asad, *Secular Translations* (New York: Columbia University Press, 2018). For commensurability, see especially Kajri Jain, *Gods in the Time of Democracy* (Durham, NC: Duke University Press, 2021), 102.
71. *Hindu Punch* (Calcutta), July 21, 19–20; *Hindu Sansar* (Delhi), June 30, 1.
72. *Hindu Sansar*, June 29, 1.
73. *Abhyudaya*, August 6, 2.
74. Sarojini Naidu to M. K. Gandhi, August 7, 1928, in *Sarojini Naidu: Selected Letters, 1890s to 1940s*, ed. Makarand Paranjape (New Delhi: Kali for Women, 1996), 202–4.
75. Sengupta, *Sarojini Naidu*, 73; Paranjape, *Selected Letters*, 192–97; Tara Ali Beg, *Sarojini Naidu: Portrait of a Patriot* (New Delhi: Congress Centenary Committee, 1985), 45.
76. Sheshalatha Reddy, "The Cosmopolitan Nationalism of Sarojini Naidu, Nightingale of India," *Victorian Literature and Culture* 38, no. 2 (2010): 571–89.
77. Sarojini Naidu, *Speeches and Writings of Sarojini Naidu*, 2nd ed. (Madras: G. A. Natesan, 1925 [1918]), 6.
78. Naidu, *Speeches and Writings*, 102.
79. Meena Alexander, "Sarojini Naidu: Romanticism and Resistance," *Economic and Political Weekly* 20, no. 43 (1985): 68–71; Parama Roy, *Indian Traffic: Identities in Question in Colonial and Postcolonial India* (Berkeley: University of California Press, 1998), 136–37.
80. For "sensible infrastructures," see Jain, *Gods in the Time*.
81. *MO*, August 2, 7. Tantalizingly, Naidu had a productive two-month burst of poetic activity in July and August 1927, after having given up writing in 1917. However, none of those posthumously published poems matches the description quoted above. See Sarojini Naidu, *Feather of the Dawn* (New York: Asia Publishing House, 1961).
82. Sarojini Naidu, *The Bird of Time: Songs of Life, Death, and the Spring* (London: William Heinemann, 1912), 95–96, and Sarojini Naidu, *The Broken Wing: Songs of Love, Death, and Destiny* (New York: John Lane, 1917), 55–56.
83. Compare Tomoko Masuzawa, *The Invention of World Religions* (Chicago: University of Chicago Press, 2005).
84. Naidu, *Broken Wing*, 32; Jayakar, *Story of My Life*, 1:202; Mushiril Hasan, *Sarojini Naidu: Her Way with Words* (New Delhi: Niyogi, 2012), 24.
85. Naidu, *Speeches and Writings*, 87–88.
86. Naidu, *Speeches and Writings*, 43.

87. Sarojini Naidu, *The Golden Threshold* (London: William Heinemann, 1916 [1905]), 59–61.
88. Sarojini Naidu to William Heinemann, July 27, 1911, *Selected Letters*, 57–59.
89. Srinivas Aravamudan, *Guru English: South Asian Religion in a Cosmopolitan Language* (Durham, NC: Duke University Press, 2005).
90. Sengupta, *Sarojini Naidu*, 20–23; Roy, *Indian Traffic*, 146.
91. Brian A. Hatcher, *Eclecticism and Modern Hindu Discourse* (New York: Oxford University Press, 1999).
92. Sengupta, *Sarojini Naidu*, 13–16, 33–34, 64, 187; Beg, *Sarojini Naidu*, 3–4; Naidu, *Speeches and Writings*, 11.
93. Sengupta, *Sarojini Naidu*, 73; Beg, *Sarojini Naidu*, 12.
94. Naidu to Heinemann, August 17, 1911, *Selected Letters*, 59–61.
95. Sengupta, *Sarojini Naidu*, 134–35; Naidu, *Speeches and Writings*, 102.

CHAPTER 4

1. John Stuart Mill, "Penal Code for India," in *Writings on India*, ed. John M. Robson, Martin Moir, and Zawahir Moir (Toronto: University of Toronto Press, 1990), 17–30. For details on the other four commissioners, see George Rankin, *Background to Indian Law* (Cambridge, UK: Cambridge University Press, 1946), 201.
2. Thomas Babington Macaulay (henceforth TBM) to Macvey Napier, August 29, 1836, in *Letters of Thomas Babington Macaulay*, ed. Thomas Pinney (Cambridge: Cambridge University Press, 1976), 3:189–90. (Henceforth cited as *L*, followed by volume number.)
3. TBM, "The Government of India," in *Works of Lord Macaulay*, ed. Hannah Macaulay More Trevelyan (London: Longmans, Green, 1866), 8:111–42. (Henceforth *W8* or other volume number.)
4. James Mill, February 21, 1832, in *Minutes of Evidence Taken before the Select Committee on the Affairs of the East India Company: I. Public* (London: House of Commons, 1832), 46.
5. James Mill to Henry Brougham, August 27, 1834, in Alexander Bain, *James Mill: A Biography* (London: Longmans, 1882), 372–75.
6. Emmanuelle de Champs, "Utility, Morality, and Reform: Bentham and Eighteenth-Century Continental Jurisprudence," in *Bentham's Theory of Law and Public Opinion*, ed. Xiaobo Zhai and Michael Quinn (New York: Cambridge University Press, 2014), 184–207.
7. Mario Rodriguez, "The Livingston Codes in the Guatemalan Crisis of 1837–1838," in *Applied Enlightenment: Nineteenth-Century Liberalism*, by Mario Rodriguez, Ralph Lee Woodward Jr., Miriam Williford, and William J. Griffith (New Orleans: Tulane University, 1972), 3–32.
8. Jeremy Bentham, *Constitutional Code: Volume 1*, in *Collected Works*, ed. F. Rosen and J. H. Burns (Oxford: Oxford University Press, 1983 [1830]), 3; David Lieberman, "Bentham on Codification," in *Jeremy Bentham: Selected Writings*, ed. Stephen G. Engelmann (New Haven, CT: Yale University Press, 2011), 460–77.

9. John Bowring, ed., *Works of Jeremy Bentham* (Edinburgh: William Tait, 1843), 10:589–92.
10. Eric Stokes, *English Utilitarians and India* (Oxford: Clarendon, 1959), 225–31; Gerald Postema, "The Soul of Justice," in Zhai and Quinn, *Bentham's Theory of Law*, 40–62; Jeremy Bentham, "Codification Proposal, or, Idea of an All-Comprehensive Body of Law," in Bowring, *Works*, 4:535–94, at 554.
11. David Skuy, "Macaulay and the Indian Penal Code of 1862," *Modern Asian Studies* 32, no. 3 (1998): 513–57; Rankin, *Background to Indian Law*, 204.
12. *A Penal Code Prepared by the Indian Law Commissioners* (Calcutta: G. H. Huttmann, 1837), 1.
13. Penelope Carson, *The East India Company and Religion, 1698–1858* (Cambridge, UK: Cambridge University Press, 2012); Nandini Chatterjee, *The Making of Indian Secularism: Empire, Law, and Christianity, 1830–1960* (New York: Palgrave, 2011).
14. Donald Eugene Davis, *India as a Secular State* (Princeton, NJ: Princeton University Press, 1963), 65–84.
15. Lata Mani, *Contentious Traditions: The Debate on Sati in Colonial India* (Berkeley: University of California Press, 1998).
16. Glenda Sluga and Timothy Rowse, eds., "Global Liberalisms," special issue, *Modern Intellectual History* 12, no. 3 (2015).
17. See especially Stokes, *English Utilitarians*, and Uday Singh Mehta, *Liberalism and Empire: A Study in Nineteenth-Century British Liberal Thought* (Chicago: University of Chicago Press, 1999). For a revisionist take, see Karuna Mantena, *Alibis of Empire: Henry Maine and the Ends of Liberal Imperialism* (Princeton, NJ: Princeton University Press, 2010), and Andrew Sartori, *Liberalism in Empire: An Alternative History* (Berkeley: University of California Press, 2014).
18. For entry into an immense literature, see Jörg Fisch, *Cheap Lives and Dear Limbs: The British Transformation of the Bengal Criminal Law, 1769–1817* (Wiesbaden: Franz Steiner Verlag, 1983); Scott Kugle, "Framed, Blamed, and Renamed: The Recasting of Islamic Jurisprudence in Colonial South Asia," *Modern Asian Studies* 35, no. 2 (2001): 257–313; Jon Wilson, "Anxieties of Distance: Codification in Early Colonial Bengal," *Modern Intellectual History* 4, no. 1 (2007): 7–23; Rosanne Rocher, "The Creation of Anglo-Hindu Law," in *Hinduism and Law: An Introduction*, ed. Timothy Lubin, Donald R. Davis, and Jayanth K. Krishnan (Cambridge, UK: Cambridge University Press, 2010), 78–88; Rachel Sturman, *The Government of Social Life in Colonial India: Liberalism, Religious Law, and Women's Rights* (Cambridge, UK: Cambridge University Press, 2012); Deepa Das Acevedo, "Developments in Hindu Law from the Colonial Period to the Present," *Religion Compass* 7, no. 7 (2013): 252–62; Julia Stephens, *Governing Islam: Law, Empire, and Secularism in South Asia* (Cambridge, UK: Cambridge University Press, 2018), 22–56.
19. James Mill, *History of British India* (Cambridge, UK: Cambridge University Press, 2010), 3:341.
20. TBM, "Government of India," 137–38.
21. Javed Majeed, *Ungoverned Imaginings: James Mill's The History of British India and Orientalism* (Oxford: Oxford University Press, 1992), 44.
22. Jeremy Bentham, "Place and Time," in *Selected Writings*, 152–219, at 180.

23. David Lemmings, editor's introduction to *Commentaries on the Laws of England: Book 1*, by William Blackstone (Oxford: Oxford University Press, 2016), xxii; Richard Posner, "Blackstone and Bentham," *Journal of Law & Economics* 19, no. 3 (1976): 569–606.
24. Gerald Postema, "The Expositor, the Censor, and the Common Law," *Canadian Journal of Philosophy* 4, no. 4 (1979): 643–70.
25. Jeremy Bentham, *A Fragment on Government*, ed. J. H. Burns and H. L. A. Hart (Cambridge, UK: Cambridge University Press, 1988), 21; Gerald Postema, *Bentham and the Common Law Tradition* (Oxford: Clarendon, 1986), 268.
26. David Lieberman, "Mapping Criminal Law: Blackstone and the Categories of English Jurisprudence," in *Law, Crime, and English Society, 1660–1840*, ed. Norma Landau (Cambridge, UK: Cambridge University Press, 2002), 139–61.
27. Robert Yelle, "Bentham's Fictions," *Yale Journal of Law and Humanities* 17, no. 2 (2005): 152–79.
28. Boyd Hilton, *Age of Atonement: The Influence of Evangelicalism on Social and Economic Thought, 1795–1865* (Oxford: Clarendon, 1992), 31.
29. Postema, "Expositor," 646.
30. Bentham, "Place and Time," 154.
31. For global context, see Janet Halley, "What Is Family Law: A Genealogy, Part I," *Yale Journal of Law and the Humanities* 23, no. 1 (2011): 1–109. For India, see Flavia Agnes, *Law and Gender Inequality* (Delhi: Oxford University Press, 2001), and Rina Verma Williams, *Postcolonial Politics and Personal Laws* (Delhi: Oxford University Press, 2006).
32. Carl von Savigny, *The History of the Roman Law during the Middle Ages*, trans. E. Cathcart (Edinburgh: Adam Black, 1829), 1:lxxii, 122. See Duncan Kennedy, "Savigny's Family/Patrimony Distinction and Its Place in the Global Genealogy of Classical Legal Thought," *American Journal of Comparative Law* 58, no. 4 (2010): 811–41; and Stephens, *Governing Islam*, 36.
33. For context, see Lauren Benton, *Law and Colonial Cultures: Legal Regimes in World History, 1400–1900* (Cambridge, UK: Cambridge University Press, 2001).
34. Walter Morgan and Arthur Macpherson, eds., *The Indian Penal Code (Act XLV of 1860), with Notes* (Calcutta: G. C. Hay, 1861), 4. (Henceforth *IPC*.)
35. Elizabeth Kolsky, *Colonial Justice in British India: White Violence and the Rule of Law* (Cambridge: Cambridge University Press, 2009), 19.
36. Robert Yelle, "The Hindu Moses: Christian Polemics against Jewish Ritual and the Secularization of Hindu Law under Colonialism," *History of Religions* 49, no. 2 (2009): 141–71.
37. My discussion here leans heavily on Stephens, *Governing Islam*, 57–85.
38. Mitra Sharafi, *Law and Identity in Colonial South Asia: Parsi Legal Culture, 1772–1947* (Cambridge, UK: Cambridge University Press, 2013).
39. Morgan and Macpherson, *IPC*, 118.
40. Morgan and Macpherson, *IPC*, 16.
41. See Brannon Ingram, J. Barton Scott, and SherAli Tareen, eds., *Imagining the Public in Modern South Asia* (New York: Routledge, 2016).
42. Allan Octavian Hume and Kour Luchman Singh, *Hindee Version of the Indian Penal Code, or Act XLV of 1860* (Etawah: Hukeem Jowahir Lall, 1861).

43. Nathaniel Halhed, *A Code of Gentoo Laws, or, Ordinations of the Pundits* (London: 1776), 5.
44. Halhed, *Code of Gentoo Laws*, 202–38.
45. *A Penal Code*, 71–73; Morgan and Macpherson, *IPC*, 217–21. For the amendment process, see *Copies of the Special Reports of the Indian Law Commissioners* (London: House of Commons, 1848), 51–57.
46. *A Penal Code*, "Note J," 49.
47. Kolsky, *Colonial Justice in British India*.
48. *A Penal Code*, 72.
49. *A Penal Code*, "Note J," 49–50.
50. TBM, "Jewish Disabilities," W8, 100–10, at 104.
51. TBM, "Minute on Education," in *Archives of Empire*, ed. Barbara Harlow and Mia Carter (Durham, NC: Duke University Press, 2003), 1:227–38.
52. *A Penal Code*, "Note B," 12. See also Asad Ali Ahmed, "Specters of Macaulay: Blasphemy, the Indian Penal Code, and Pakistan's Postcolonial Predicament," in *Censorship in South Asia*, ed. Raminder Kaur and William Mazzarella (Bloomington: Indiana University Press, 2009), 172–205.
53. Ahmed, "Specters of Macaulay," 178.
54. J. S. Mill, *Autobiography* (Oxford: Oxford University Press, 2018), 52.
55. See Leonard Levy, *Blasphemy* (New York: Knopf, 1993), 333–99.
56. J. S. Mill, *Newspaper Writings: December 1822–July 1831*, ed. Ann P. Robson and John M. Robson (Toronto: University of Toronto Press, 1986), 6–18, 21–24.
57. James Mill, "Liberty of the Press," in *Political Writings*, ed. Terence Ball (Cambridge, UK: Cambridge University Press, 1992), 95–136, at 135.
58. David Nash, *Blasphemy in Modern Britain* (London: Routledge, 2019), 84; Richard Carlile to Jeremy Bentham, January 22, 1824, in *Correspondence of Jeremy Bentham*, ed. Catherine Fuller (Oxford: Oxford University Press, 2000), 11:341.
59. Zachary Macaulay to Hannah More, October 28, 1820, in *Life and Letters of Zachary Macaulay*, ed. Margaret Jean Trevelyan Knutsford (London: Edward Arnold, 1900), 362.
60. TBM to Zachary Macaulay, September 1819, L1, 132–34; Robert Sullivan, *Macaulay: The Tragedy of Power* (Cambridge, MA: Belknap, 2009), 28.
61. TBM, "Scenes from 'Athenian Revels,'" W7, 586; Sullivan, *Macaulay*, 30–37.
62. Knutsford, *Life and Letters*, 204.
63. TBM to Hannah Macaulay, June 14, 1831, L2, 44.
64. Macaulay was, in a way, part of Marx's intellectual history. Bruno Bauer's writings on "Jewish emancipation" used a phrase that had been imported into German from English (presumably, as Bauer noted, for its strong emotional appeal) in 1828—Macaulay's moment. Marx then worked from within the problematic (in the Althusserian sense) of emancipation to develop his account of modern political subjectivity. To note this English-German connection is to see how nineteenth-century discourses on religious minority emerged contrapuntally across multiple overlapping geographies. It is also to wonder whether the British took the term *emancipation* from the Black Atlantic context, with notions of religious minority thus emerging from within a problematic of race that would, by extension, have shaped Marx as it had Hegel before him. See

Jacob Katz, "The Term 'Jewish Emancipation,'" in *Studies in Nineteenth-Century Jewish Intellectual History*, ed. Alexander Altmann (Cambridge, MA: Harvard University Press, 2013), 1–25; Patchen Markell, *Bound by Recognition* (Princeton, NJ: Princeton University Press, 2003), 123–51; Susan Buck-Morss, "Hegel and Haiti," *Critical Inquiry* 26, no. 4 (2000): 821–65.

65. Linda Colley, *Britons: Forging the Nation, 1707–1837* (New Haven, CT: Yale University Press, 1992).
66. Gauri Viswanathan, *Outside the Fold: Conversion, Modernity, Belief* (Princeton, NJ: Princeton University Press, 1998); Aamir Mufti, *Enlightenment in the Colony: The Jewish Question and the Crisis of Postcolonial Culture* (Princeton, NJ: Princeton University Press, 2007).
67. Saint Helena Act 1833, sections 87, 89, 102, at https://www.legislation.gov.uk/ukpga/Will4/3-4/85.
68. *Hansard's*, April 5, 1830, column 1307.
69. *Hansard's*, April 5, 1830, column 1303.
70. *Hansard's*, April 5, 1830, column 1305.
71. *Hansard's*, April 5, 1830, column 1325.
72. Tisa Wenger, *Religious Freedom: The Contested History of an American Ideal* (Chapel Hill: University of North Carolina Press, 2017).
73. TBM, "Civil Disabilities of the Jews," W5, 458–69, at 463.
74. Viswanathan, *Outside the Fold*, 5.
75. Saba Mahmood, *Religious Difference in a Secular Age: A Minority Report* (Princeton, NJ: Princeton University Press, 2015).
76. TBM, "Jewish Disabilities," 104.
77. TBM, "Civil Disabilities," 459.
78. Joss Marsh, *Word Crimes: Blasphemy, Culture, and Literature in Nineteenth-Century England* (Chicago: University of Chicago Press, 1998).
79. *Report of the Proceedings of the Court of the King's Bench in the Guildhall, London . . . Being the Mock Trials of Richard Carlile for Alledged Blasphemous Libels* (London: R. Carlile, 1822), 8, 13.
80. "Defeat of the Vice Society," *Republican*, July 19, 1822, 227, quoted in Levy, *Blasphemy*, 393.
81. Thomas Paine, *Age of Reason* (London: Freethought Publishing, 1889), 8. For context, see Franklyn Prochaska, "Thomas Paine's *The Age of Reason* Revisited," *Journal of the History of Ideas* 33, no. 4 (1972): 561–76.
82. TBM, "Jewish Disabilities," 104.
83. TBM, "Jewish Disabilities," 104–5.
84. C. B. Macpherson, *The Political Theory of Possessive Individualism* (Oxford: Oxford University Press, 2011).
85. TBM, "Government of India," 142.
86. *Hansard's*, April 5, 1830, column 1322. For a slightly different formulation from Mackintosh, who in 1818 advocated that Parliament should mirror social classes protosociologically, rather than giving over to number and mob rule, see Greg Conti, *Parlia-

ment the Mirror of the Nation: Representation, Deliberation, and Democracy in Victorian Britain (Cambridge, UK: Cambridge University Press, 2019), 20–21.
87. Hansard's, April 5, 1830, column 1313; TBM, "Civil Disabilities," 459.
88. TBM, "Jewish Disabilities," 52.
89. TBM, "Civil Disabilities," 459.
90. TBM, "Gladstone on Church and State," W6, 326–80.
91. TBM, "Civil Disabilities," 459.
92. A Penal Code, "Note J," 49–50.
93. Jeremy Bentham, Introduction to the Principles of Morals and Legislation, ed. J. H. Burns and H. L. A. Hart (Oxford: Clarendon, 1996 [1789]), 11.
94. Bentham, Introduction to the Principles, 158.
95. Michel Foucault, Birth of Biopolitics: Lectures at the Collège de France, 1978–1979, trans. Graham Burchell (New York: Palgrave, 2008).
96. Jeremy Bentham, Rights, Representations and Reform: Nonsense upon Stilts and other Writings on the French Revolution, ed. Philip Schonfield, Catherine Pease-Watkin, and Cyprian Blamires (Oxford: Oxford University Press, 2002).
97. Bentham, Introduction to the Principles, 174.
98. James Crimmins, Secular Utilitarianism: Social Science and the Critique of Religion in the Thought of Jeremy Bentham (Oxford: Clarendon, 1990), 314.
99. Bentham, Introduction to the Principles, 17.
100. Philip Beauchamp [Jeremy Bentham], Analysis of the Influence of Natural Religion on the Temporal Happiness of Mankind (London: R. Carlile, 1822), 33.
101. Jeremy Bentham, Deontology Together with a Table of the Springs of Action, ed. Amnon Goldworth and F. Rosen (Oxford: Oxford University Press, 1983), 243.
102. Bentham, Deontology, 79–86.
103. Bentham, "Place and Time," 158–59.
104. Bentham, "Offences against Religion," in "Place and Time," 37n.
105. Jeremy Bentham, Letters to Count Toreno (London: R. and A. Taylor, 1822), 103.
106. A Penal Code, "Note J," 49–50
107. TBM, "Government of India," 120.
108. TBM to John Hobhouse, January 6, 1836, L3, 164–66; TBM to Thomas Flower Ellis, June 3, 1835, L3, 146.
109. C. F. A. Marmoy, "The Auto-Icon of Jeremy Bentham at University College, London," Medical History 2, no. 2 (1958): 77–86.
110. Jennifer Pitts, A Turn to Empire: The Rise of Imperial Liberalism in Britain and France (Princeton, NJ: Princeton University Press, 2005), 103–22.
111. Jeremy Bentham, Panopticon Writings, ed. Miran Božovič (London: Verso, 1995).
112. Bentham, Introduction to the Principles, 10.
113. Bentham, Introduction to the Principles, 157, 167.
114. See for instance Andrew Sartori, Bengal in Global Concept History: Culturalism in the Age of Capital (Chicago: University of Chicago Press, 2009).
115. Bentham, "Place and Time," 174–75, 179.
116. TBM, "Government of India," 139.

117. Everett Zimmerman, "Pride and Prejudice in *Pride and Prejudice*," *Nineteenth-Century Fiction* 23, no. 1 (1968): 64–73.
118. Halhed, *Code of Gentoo Laws*, lxxi.
119. Robert Aspland, *An Inquiry into the Nature of the Sin of Blasphemy* (London: R. Hunter, 1817), 77.
120. *Hansard's*, April 5, 1830, column 1324.
121. Edmund Burke, *Reflections on the Revolution in France*, ed. J. G. A. Pocock (Cambridge, UK: Hackett, 1987), 76.
122. Mehta, *Liberalism and Empire*, 153–89.
123. Jeremy Bentham, "Essay on the Influence of Time and Place in Matters of Legislation," in *Works of Jeremy Bentham*, ed. John Bowring (Edinburgh: William Tait, 1843), 1:169–94, at 180. The "soaring" rhetoric does not appear in the critical Yale edition cited above, which is based solely on the manuscript text and not, as with Bowring, the French 1802 edition. See Stephen G. Engelmann and Jennifer Pitts, "Bentham's 'Place and Time,'" *Tocqueville Review* 32, no. 1 (2011): 43–66.
124. David Bromwich, *A Choice of Inheritance: Self and Community from Edmund Burke to Robert Frost* (Cambridge, MA: Harvard University Press, 1989), 59; Burke, *Reflections*, 7.
125. Burke, *Reflections*, 68, 75.
126. John Stuart Mill, *A System of Logic* (London: Longmans, 1961 [1843]), 567.
127. Mill, *Autobiography*, 64, 79–85.
128. TBM, "Warren Hastings," *W*5, 543–644, at 620.
129. TBM, "Mill on Government" and "Westminster Reviewer's Defense of Mill," *W*5, 239–300. For Mill's response, see *Political Writings*, 304–14.
130. Sullivan, *Macaulay*, 43–46.
131. Edward Gibbon, *History of the Decline and Fall of the Roman Empire* (London: W. Strahan, 1782), 1:34–35.
132. TBM, "Government of India," 139.
133. TBM to Thomas Flower Ellis, December 18, 1837, *L*3, 235–38.
134. Theodore Koditschek, *Liberalism, Imperialism, and the Historical Imagination: Nineteenth-Century Visions of a Greater Britain* (Cambridge, UK: Cambridge University Press, 2011), 99–150; Catherine Hall, "Macaulay's *History of England*," in *Ten Books that Shaped the British Empire*, ed. Antoinette Burton and Isabel Hofmeyr (Durham, NC: Duke University Press, 2014), 71–89.
135. Stokes, *English Utilitarians*, 190–93, 211–12, 239–40, 261; John Clive, *Macaulay: The Shaping of a Historian* (London: Secker and Warburg, 1973), 463–66.
136. "Administration of Justice in India," *Edinburgh Review* 73, no. 148 (July 1841): 425–60, at 457.
137. Much of this narrative seems to derive from J. F. Stephen, writing a few decades later. See Rankin, *Background to Indian Law*, 201–3, and Stokes, *English Utilitarians*, 258–59.
138. TBM to Hannah Trevelyan, October 1854, quoted in George Otto Trevelyan, *Life and Letters of Lord Macaulay* (London: Longmans, Green, 1881), 337.

CHAPTER 5

1. Thomas Babington Macaulay (henceforth TBM) to Thomas Flower Ellis (henceforth TFE), February 8, 1835, in *Letters of Thomas Babington Macaulay*, ed. Thomas Pinney (Cambridge, UK: Cambridge University Press, 1976), 3:129–33. (Henceforth cited as *L*, followed by volume number.)
2. Joan Wallach Scott, *Sex and Secularism* (Princeton, NJ: Princeton University Press, 2017).
3. Robert Sullivan, *Macaulay: The Tragedy of Power* (Cambridge, MA: Belknap, 2009); Catherine Hall, *Macaulay and Son: Architects of Imperial Britain* (New Haven, CT: Yale University Press, 2012).
4. TBM to Margaret Macaulay Cropper (henceforth MM), December 7, 1834, *L*3, 99–107.
5. See Asad Ali Ahmed, "Specters of Macaulay: Blasphemy, the Indian Penal Code, and Pakistan's Postcolonial Predicament," in *Censorship in South Asia*, ed. Raminder Kaur and William Mazzarella (Bloomington: Indiana University Press, 2009), 172–205.
6. TBM, "Warren Hastings," in *Works of Lord Macaulay*, ed. Hannah Macaulay Trevelyan (London: Longmans, Green, 1866), 6:543–644, at 555 (henceforth *W*6 or other volume number). For context, see Mrinalini Sinha, *Colonial Masculinity: The "Manly Englishman" and the "Effeminate Bengali" in the Late Nineteenth Century* (New York: Manchester University Press, 1995).
7. See especially Matthew McCormack, *The Independent Man: Citizenship and Gender Politics in Georgian England* (Manchester: Manchester University Press, 2005), as well as Stefan Collini, *Public Moralists: Political Thought and Intellectual Life in Britain, 1850–1930* (Oxford: Clarendon, 1991); John Tosh, *A Man's Place: Masculinity and the Middle-Class Home in Victorian England* (New Haven, CT: Yale University Press, 1999); William Barnhart, "Evangelicalism, Masculinity, and the Making of Imperial Manliness in Late Georgian Britain, 1795–1820," *Historian* 67, no. 4 (2005): 712–32.
8. TBM to Hannah Macaulay (henceforth HM), October 31, 1833, *L*2, 328.
9. MM, "Recollections of a Sister of T. B. Macaulay," in *Memoirs of the Clan "Aulay," Extracted from Public Sources and Family Papers*, ed. Joseph Babington Macaulay (Carmarthen: William James Morgan, 1881), 232.
10. Compare Susan Mendus, "Liberty and Autonomy," *Proceedings of the Aristotelian Society* 87, no. 1 (1986–7): 107–29.
11. Lisa Lowe, *The Intimacies of Four Continents* (Durham, NC: Duke University Press, 2015).
12. Anna Stoler, *Race and the Education of Desire: Foucault's History of Sexuality and the Colonial Order of Things* (Durham, NC: Duke University Press, 1995); Anne McClintock, *Imperial Leather: Race, Gender, and Sexuality in the Colonial Contest* (New York: Routledge, 1995).
13. Leela Gandhi, *Affective Communities: Anticolonial Thought, Fin-de-Siècle Radicalism, and the Politics of Friendship* (Durham, NC: Duke University Press, 2005).
14. Compare J. Barton Scott, "Only Connect: Three Reflections on the Sociality of Secularism," *Cambridge Journal of Postcolonial Literary Inquiry* 6, no. 1 (January 2019): 48–69.

15. Katherine Lemons, *Divorcing Traditions: Islamic Marriage Law and the Making of Indian Secularism* (Ithaca, NY: Cornell University Press, 2019), 24.
16. Hall, *Macaulay and Son*, xii–viii.
17. Sullivan, *Macaulay*, 19.
18. TBM to TFE, December 18, 1837, *L*3, 235–38.
19. TBM to TFE, August 25, 1835, *L*3, 152–55; TBM to TFE, December 30, 1835, *L*3, 157–60; TBM to Thomas Spring-Rice, February 8, 1836, *L*3, 166–71; TBM to TFE, July 25, 1836, *L*3, 180–83.
20. For aesthetic justification, see Patricia Meyer Spacks, *Gossip* (New York: Knopf, 1985).
21. TBM to Maria Kinnard Drummond, September 20, 1837, *L*3, 224–26.
22. MM, *"Recollections,"* 216, 189.
23. TBM to MM, August 18, 1832, *L*2, 184; Macaulay, *Memoirs of the Clan*, 171–72.
24. TBM to MM, November 26, 1832, *L*2, 203–4.
25. TBM to MM Cropper, January 26, 1833, *L*2, 226.
26. TBM to HM, December 23, 1833, *L*2, 367–68.
27. TBM to HM, December 12, 1832, *L*2, 210–11.
28. TBM to HM, June 1, 1833, *L*2, 246–47.
29. TBM to HM, July 11, 1833, *L*2, 268–69. The verb recurs in July 25, *L*2, 277–78.
30. On incest, see Adam Kuper, *Incest and Influence: The Private Life of Bourgeois England* (Cambridge, MA: Harvard University Press, 2009), and Leonore Davidoff, *Thicker Than Water: Siblings and Their Relations, 1780–1920* (New York: Oxford University Press, 2012). On firms, see Leonore Davidoff and Catherine Hall, *Family Fortunes: Men and Women of the English Middle Class* (London: Hutchinson, 1987).
31. TBM to HM, January 2, 1834, *L*3, 5–7.
32. Hall, *Macaulay and Son*, 129.
33. On Zachary's finances, see TBM to HM, August 17, 1833, *L*2, 297, and November 2, 1833, *L*2, 329–30.
34. Sullivan, *Macaulay*, 113–14.
35. Mary Jean Corbett, "Husband, Wife, and Sister: Making and Remaking the Early Victorian Family," *Victorian Literature and Culture* 35, no. 1 (2007): 1–19.
36. TBM to HM, August 17, 1833, *L*2, 300–1.
37. J. L. Adolphus to H. H. Milman, *L*3, 14n1.
38. HM to MM Cropper, February 16, 1834, *L*3, 25n4.
39. HM to MM Cropper, February 16, 1834, *L*3, 25n4.
40. TBM to HM, January 2, 1834, *L*3, 5–7.
41. TBM to MM Cropper, December 24, 1834, *L*3, 113–16.
42. TBM to MM Cropper, December 7, 1834, *L*3, 99–107, at 104–5.
43. Christopher Johnson and David Sabean, eds., *Sibling Relations and the Transformations of European Kinship, 1300–1900* (New York: Berghahn Books, 2011), 16.
44. Simon Goldhill, *A Very Queer Family Indeed: Sex, Religion, and the Bensons in Victorian Britain* (Chicago: University of Chicago Press, 2016).
45. Friedrich Kittler, *Discourse Networks: 1800/1900*, trans. Michael Metteer (Stanford, CA: Stanford University Press, 1990).

46. Hall, *Macaulay and Son*, 155; Sullivan, *Macaulay*, 82.
47. TBM to HM, July 6, 1831, *L*2, 62–63.
48. TBM to MM Cropper, December 7, 1834, *L*3, 99–107.
49. TBM to TFE, July 25, 1836, *L*3, 180–83; TBM to Selina and Frances Macaulay, December 13, 1837, *L*3, 232–35.
50. Hall, *Macaulay and Son*, 155.
51. MM, "*Recollections*."
52. Eve Tavor Bannett, *Empire of Letters: Letter Manuals and Transatlantic Correspondence, 1680–1820* (Cambridge, UK: Cambridge University Press, 2005); Rachel Scarborough King, *Writing to the World: Letters and the Origins of Modern Print Genres* (Baltimore: Johns Hopkins University Press, 2018), 92.
53. TBM to HM, June 10, 1833, *L*2, 253–54; TBM to Charles Macaulay, December 5, 1836, *L*3, 203–5.
54. Catherine Golden, *Posting It: The Victorian Revolution in Letter Writing* (Gainesville: University Press of Florida, 2009); King, *Writing to the World*.
55. MM, "*Recollections*," 194–95.
56. C. A. Bayly, *Empire and Information: Intelligence Gathering and Social Communication in India, 1780–1870* (Cambridge, UK: Cambridge University Press, 1996), 217.
57. Janet Altman, *Epistolarity: Approaches to a Form* (Columbus: Ohio State University Press, 1982), 2.
58. TBM to Frances Macaulay, March 2, 1850, *L*5, 95–97.
59. TBM to Macvey Napier, February 13, 1834, *L*3, 21–22.
60. For a facsimile, see Sullivan, *Macaulay*, 140. For the physicality of books, see Leah Price, *How to Do Things with Books in Victorian Britain* (Princeton, NJ: Princeton University Press, 2012). For an entry to the thriving field of Indian book history, see Swapan Chakraborty and Abhijit Gupta, eds., *New Word Order: Transnational Themes in Book History* (Delhi: Worldview Publications, 2011).
61. TBM to MM Cropper, December 24, 1834, *L*3, 113–16.
62. Edward W. Said, *Orientalism* (New York: Pantheon, 1978).
63. Hall, *Macaulay and Son*, 216.
64. Sullivan, *Macaulay*, 137.
65. TBM to HM, January 4, 1834, *L*3, 8.
66. TBM to TFE, July 1, 1834, *L*3, 59–64.
67. Sullivan, *Macaulay*, 113–21.
68. Homi Bhahba, *The Location of Culture* (London: Routledge, 1994).
69. Gauri Viswanathan, *Outside the Fold: Conversion, Modernity, Belief* (Princeton, NJ: Princeton University Press, 1998).
70. Sullivan, *Macaulay*, 141, 166.
71. Sullivan, *Macaulay*, 31–32, 130.
72. TBM to ZM, February 5, 1819, *L*1, 118–21.
73. Gauri Viswanathan, *Masks of Conquest: Literary Study and British Rule in India* (New York: Columbia University Press, 2014).
74. TBM, "Minute on Education."

75. TBM to ZM, October 12, 1836, *L*3, 192–93.
76. Compare Isabel Hofmeyr, *Gandhi's Printing Press: Experiments in Slow Reading* (Cambridge, MA: Harvard University Press, 2013).
77. TBM to Charles Knight, June 20, 1823, *L*1, 189–90.
78. TBM to MM Cropper, December 7, 1834, *L*3, 99–107; TBM to TFE, December 15, 1834, *L*3, 110–13.
79. George Otto Trevelyan, *Life and Letters of Lord Macaulay* (London: Longmans, Green, 1881), 25.
80. Tisa Wenger, *Religious Freedom: The Contested History of an American Ideal* (Chapel Hill: University of North Carolina Press, 2017), 17; Paul Gilroy, *The Black Atlantic: Modernity and Double Consciousness* (Cambridge, MA: Harvard University Press, 1993).
81. Charles Booth, *Zachary Macaulay* (London: Longmans, Green, 1934), 4–5.
82. Booth, *Zachary Macaulay*, 13, 17.
83. Hall, *Macaulay and Son*, 8.
84. Margaret Jean Trevelyan Knutsford, *Life and Letters of Zachary Macaulay* (London: Edward Arnold, 1900), 13, 17.
85. Knutsford, *Life and Letters*, 98.
86. Knutsford, *Life and Letters*, 135–36.
87. Christopher Tolley, *Domestic Biography: The Legacy of Evangelicalism in Four Nineteenth-Century Families* (Oxford: Clarendon, 1997), 24–50; Kuper, *Incest and Influence*, 135–58.
88. Trevelyan, *Life and Letters of Lord Macaulay*, 43.
89. TBM to ZM, January 2, 1822, *L*1, 168–69; TBM to ZM, January 4, 1823, *L*1, 182–84.
90. TBM to Frances Macaulay, July 10, 1844, *L*4, 206–7.
91. Ernst Marshall Howse, *Saints in Politics: The "Clapham Sect" and the Growth of Freedom* (Toronto: University of Toronto Press, 1952); Charles Grant, "Observations on the State of Society among the Asiatic Subjects of Great Britain, Particularly with Respect to Morals" (London: House of Commons, 1813). For the complexity of missionary politics, see Winter Jade Werner, *Missionary Cosmopolitanism in Nineteenth-Century British Literature* (Columbus: Ohio State University Press, 2020).
92. Rupa Viswanath, *The Pariah Problem: Caste, Religion, and the Social in Modern India* (New York: Columbia University Press, 2014).
93. Robert Wilberforce and Samuel Wilberforce, *Life of William Wilberforce* (London: John Murray, 1838), 1:149.
94. Hall, *Macaulay and Son*, 206–7; Sullivan, *Macaulay*, 7, 196.
95. Compare Catherine Hall, *Civilising Subjects: Colony and Metropole in the English Imagination, 1830–1867* (Chicago: University of Chicago Press, 2002).
96. Thomas Babington, *A Practical View of Christian Education in Its Early Stages* (London: J. Hatchard, 1814), 3–4, 8.
97. William Wilberforce, *A Practical View of the Prevailing Religious System of the Professed Christians in the Higher and Middle Classes of This Country, Contrasted with Real Christianity*, 3rd ed. (London: T. Cadell, 1797), 26–27, 30–31.
98. Knutsford, *Life and Letters*, 16–17.

99. Sullivan, *Macaulay*, 18.
100. Sullivan, *Macaulay*, 21.
101. ZM to Selina Mills Macaulay, November 25, 1820, in Knutsford, *Life and Letters*, 364–65.
102. ZM to TBM, August 15, 1813, in Knutsford, *Life and Letters*, 307–8.
103. Trevelyan, *Life and Letters of Lord Macaulay*, 20.
104. Trevelyan, *Life and Letters of Lord Macaulay*, 21; MM, "Recollections," 190.
105. Trevelyan, *Life and Letters of Lord Macaulay*, 19–21.
106. Trevelyan, *Life and Letters of Lord Macaulay*, 25.
107. Trevelyan, *Life and Letters of Lord Macaulay*, 19.
108. John Clive, *Macaulay: The Shaping of a Historian* (London: Secker and Warburg, 1973), 243.
109. [Nature of an Auto-da-Fé], *Christian Observer* (March 1811): 161–62. See Thomas Pinney, "Notes on Macaulay's Unacknowledged and Uncollected Writings," *Papers of the Bibliographical Society of America* 67, no. 1 (1973): 17–31; Tolley, *Domestic Biography*, 29.
110. Trevelyan, *Life and Letters of Lord Macaulay*, 32.
111. Trevelyan, *Life and Letters of Lord Macaulay*, 21.
112. Norbert Elias, *The Civilising Process*, trans. Edmund Jephcott (London: Blackwell, 2000); Marjorie Morgan, *Manners, Morals, and Class in England, 1774–1858* (New York: St. Martin's, 1994); Lawrence Klein, *Shaftsbury and the Culture of Politeness* (Cambridge, UK: Cambridge University Press, 1994).
113. Jeremy Bentham, *Introduction to the Principles of Morals and Legislation*, ed. J. H. Burns and H. L. A. Hart (Oxford: Clarendon, 1996), 282–93.
114. Morgan, *Manners, Morals, and Class*, 14.
115. Michel Foucault, *Security, Territory, Population: Lectures at the Collège de France, 1977–1978*, trans. Graham Burchell (New York: Palgrave, 2007).
116. "Notes," in *A Penal Code Prepared by the Indian Law Commissioners* (Calcutta: G. H. Huttmann, 1837), 20.
117. Navtej Singh Johar v. Union of India, AIR 2018 SSC 4321.
118. *A Penal Code*, 92; Walter Morgan and Arthur Macpherson, eds., *The Indian Penal Code (Act XLV of 1860), with Notes* (Calcutta: G. C. Hay, 1861), 326. For the extension of 377 to other British colonies, see Enze Han and Joseph O'Mahoney, *British Colonialism and the Criminalization of Homosexuality: Queens, Crime, and Empire* (London: Routledge, 2018).
119. Babington, *Practical View*, 2–3.

CHAPTER 6

1. Hussein Ali Agrama, *Questioning Secularism: Islam, Sovereignty, and the Rule of Law in Modern Egypt* (Chicago: University of Chicago Press, 2012).
2. Joan Wallach Scott, *Sex and Secularism* (Princeton, NJ: Princeton University Press, 2017).

3. Clive Unsworth, "Blasphemy, Cultural Divergence, and Legal Relativism," *Modern Law Review* 58, no. 5 (1995): 658–77, at 663.
4. Jeremy Bentham, *Of Laws in General*, ed. J. H. Burns (London: Athlone, 1970), 33.
5. John Lassiter, "Defamation of Peers: The Rise and Decline of the Action for Scandalum Magnatum, 1497–1773," *American Journal of Legal History* 22, no. 3 (1978): 216–36; Philip Hamburger, "The Development of the Law of Seditious Libel and the Control of the Press," *Stanford Law Review* 37, no. 3 (1985): 661–765; Michael Lobban, "From Seditious Libel to Unlawful Assembly: Peterloo and the Changing Face of Political Crime, c. 1770–1820," *Oxford Journal of Legal Studies* 10, no. 3 (1990): 307–52; Philip Harling, "The Law of Libel and the Limits of Repression, 1790–1832," *Historical Journal* 44, no. 1 (2001): 107–34.
6. Colin Manchester, "A History of the Crime of Obscene Libel," *Journal of Legal History* 12, no. 1 (1991): 36–57; Simon Stern, "*Fanny Hill* and the 'Laws of Decency': Investigating Obscenity in the Mid-Eighteenth Century," *Eighteenth-Century Life* 43, no. 2 (2019): 162–87.
7. R. H. Helmholz, *Select Cases on Defamation to 1600* (London: Selden Society, 1985); C. R. Kopf, "Libel and Satire in the Eighteenth Century," *Eighteenth-Century Studies* 8, no. 2 (1974–5): 153–68; Norman Rosenberg, *Protecting the Best Men: An Interpretive History of the Law of Libel* (Chapel Hill: University of North Carolina Press, 1986); Laurence M. Friedman, *Guarding Life's Dark Secrets: Legal and Social Controls over Reputation, Propriety, and Privacy* (Stanford, CA: Stanford University Press, 2007).
8. Unsworth, "Blasphemy," 77.
9. William Sheppard, *Action upon the Case for Slander* (London: Adams, Starkey, & Basset, 1662), iii.
10. Helmholz, *Select Cases on Defamation*; Lawrence McNamara, *Reputation and Defamation* (Oxford: Oxford University Press, 2007), 61–103; Robert Post, "The Social Foundations of Defamation Law," *California Law Review* 74, no. 3 (May 1986): 691–742.
11. Mark Rose, *Authors and Owners: The Invention of Copyright* (Cambridge, MA: Harvard University Press, 1995); Adrian Johns, *The Nature of the Book: Print and Knowledge in the Making* (Chicago: University of Chicago Press, 1998).
12. See, for instance, Melissa Mohr, *Holy Shit: A Brief History of Swearing* (New York: Oxford University Press, 2013), 173–226.
13. John Godolphin, *Reportorium Canonicum* (London, 1678), 559–61.
14. John March, *Actions for Slander* (London: Elizabeth Walbanck, 1647).
15. Rex v. Curl, (1727) 2 Stra 788. See Lobban, "From Seditious Libel," 312.
16. *Diary of Samuel Pepys*, ed. Robert Latham and William Matthews (Berkeley: University of California Press, 2000), 4:209–10; *The Life and Times of Anthony Wood*, ed. Andrew Clark (Oxford: Clarendon, 1891), 1:476–77.
17. John Brewer, *Pleasures of the Imagination: English Culture in the Eighteenth Century* (London: Routledge, 1997), 24–25.
18. *A Review of the Late Publication on Libel of Messrs. George, Holt, Starkie, & Jones, by a Barrister of the Inner Temple* (London: Reed and Hunter, 1815), 7–8.
19. Philip Harding, "The Law of Libel and the Limits of Repression, 1790–1832," *Historical Journal* 44, no. 1 (2001): 107–34.

20. "The Pre-*Thorley v. Kerry* Case Law of the Libel-Slander Distinction," *University of Chicago Law Review* 23, no. 1 (1955): 132–50.
21. March, *Actions for Slander*.
22. James Mill, "Jurisprudence," in *Political Writings*, ed. Terence Ball (Cambridge, UK: Cambridge University Press, 1992), 43–94, at 88.
23. My narrative loosely follows Paul Mitchell, *The Making of the Modern Law of Defamation* (Oxford: Hart, 2005).
24. Lobban, "From Seditious Libel," 310.
25. John George, *A Treatise on the Offence of Libel* (London: Taylor and Hessey, 1812).
26. Francis Ludlow Holt, *The Law of Libel*, 2nd ed. (London: J. Butterworth, 1816).
27. George, *Treatise*, 12–14, 41–50, 90–92, 355. Compare the claim that blasphemy corrupts the morals of the living in John Jones, *De Libellis Famosis, or the Law of Libels* (London: S. Rousseau, 1812), 8–9.
28. Thomas Starkie, *Treatise on the Law of Slander* (London: W. Clarke, 1813), 13.
29. Michael Lobban, "Starkie, Thomas," *Oxford Dictionary of National Biography*, September 23, 2004. https://www.oxforddnb.com/view/10.1093/ref:odnb/9780198614128.001.0001/odnb-9780198614128-e-26319.
30. George Wingrove Cooke, *A Treatise on the Law of Defamation* (London: Owen Richards, 1844), i.
31. Regina v. Ramsay and Foote, (1883) 48 LT 733.
32. Cooke, *Treatise*, 69.
33. W. Blake Odgers, *A Digest of the Law of Libel and Slander*, 2nd ed. (London: Stevens and Sons, 1887), 468.
34. Odgers, *Digest of the Law of Libel*, 73.
35. Colin Manchester, "Lord Campbell's Act: England's First Obscenity Statute," *Journal of Legal History* 9, no. 2 (1988): 223–41. For a helpful overview, see also the Lords' discussion of *Whitehouse v. Lemon* in AC 617, HL.
36. Paul Mitchell, "The Foundations of Australian Defamation Law," *Sydney Law Review* 28, no. 3 (2006): 477–504.
37. B. N. Mehrotra, *Law of Defamation*, 2nd ed. (Allahabad: Delhi Law House, 1980), 3.
38. "Notes," in *A Penal Code Prepared by the Indian Law Commissioners* (Calcutta: G. H. Huttmann, 1837), 84–85, 94–95.
39. Eric Stokes, *English Utilitarians and India* (Oxford: Clarendon, 1959), 232–33.
40. See Deana Heath, *Purifying Empire: Obscenity and the Politics of Moral Regulation in Britain, India, and Australia* (Cambridge, UK: Cambridge University Press, 2010), 172–73, as well as A. B. Shah, ed., *The Roots of Obscenity* (Bombay: Lalvani, 1968).
41. Walter Morgan and Arthur Macpherson, eds., *The Indian Penal Code (Act XLV of 1860), with Notes* (Calcutta: G. C. Hay, 1861), 216.
42. Thomas Barber, *Ought Charles Bradlaugh to Be an MP?*, quoted in Edward Royle, *Radicals, Secularists, and Republicans: Popular Freethought in Britain, 1866–1915* (Manchester, UK: Manchester University Press, 1980), 269–70.
43. *Report of the Maharaj Libel Case* (Bombay: Bombay Gazette Press, 1862), 76. For further discussion, see J. Barton Scott, *Spiritual Despots: Modern Hinduism and the Genealogies of Self-Rule* (Chicago: University of Chicago Press, 2016), 119–49.

44. *Mr. Buckingham's Defence of His Public and Private Character against the Atrocious Calumnies Contained in a False and Slanderous Pamphlet* (Sheffield: John Blackwell, 1832), 112.
45. *Parsee Priest Defamation Case* (Bombay: Dorabjee Eduljee Tata, 1870).
46. *The Pigot Case: Report of the Case Pigot vs. Hastie* (Calcutta, 1884).
47. Mitra Sharafi, *Law and Identity in Colonial South Asia: Parsi Legal Culture, 1772–1947* (Cambridge: Cambridge University Press, 2013), 276–85.
48. My account parallels Walter Donagh, *The History and Law of Sedition and Cognate Offences* (Calcutta: Thacker, Spin, 1911), and Siddharth Narrain, "The Harm in Hate Speech Laws," in *Sentiment, Politics, Censorship: The State of Hurt*, ed. Rina Ramdev et al. (New Delhi: Sage, 2016), 39–54. On the continuity of colonial and British sedition law, see Sunny Kumar, "Is Indian Sedition Law Colonial: J. F. Stephen and the Jurisprudence of Free Speech," *Indian Economic and Social History Review* 58, no. 3 (2021): 477–504.
49. I repeat the story of Barnes Peacock, told to Henry Maine in an 1869 letter that James Stephen read aloud to the governor-general's council in 1870. See *Abstract of the Proceedings of the Council of the Governor General of India, 1870* (Calcutta: Office of the Superintendent of Government Printing, 1906), 9:371–75, 437–54. The story seems a little fishy, as suggested by Aravind Ganachari, *Nationalism and Social Reform in Colonial Situation* (Delhi: Kalpaz Publications, 2005), 54–57.
50. For early criticisms of the Macaulay language, see "Second Report on the Indian Penal Code," in *Copies of the Special Reports of the Indian Law Commissioners* (London: House of Commons, 1848), 6. For the 1870 version of 124A, see Fendall Currie, *The Penal Code Act XLV of 1860*, 5th ed. (London: John Flack, 1875), 81.
51. Queen-Empress v. Jogendra Chunder Bose and others, (1892) ILR 19 Cal 35.
52. G. K. Roy, *Law Relating to Press and Sedition* (Simla: Station Press, 1915), 17–18.
53. *Abstract of the Proceedings of the Council of the Governor General*, 451–54. For context, see Julia Stephens, "The Phantom Wahhabi: Liberalism and the Muslim Fanatic in Mid-Victorian India," *Modern Asian Studies* 47, no. 1 (2013): 22–52.
54. W. W. Hunter, *The Indian Musalmans: Are They Bound in Conscience to Rebel Against the Queen?* (London: Trübner, 1871). For context, see Ilyse Morgenstein-Fuerst, *Indian Muslim Minorities and the 1857 Rebellion* (London: I. B. Tauris, 2017).
55. ILR 19 Cal. 35. For Tilak, see ILR 22 Bom. 112, as well as Raminder Kaur, *Performative Politics and the Cultures of Hinduism: Public Uses of Religion in Western India* (Delhi: Permanent Black, 2003).
56. *Parliamentary Papers: 1850–1908*, vol. 63, *Papers Relating to Amendments in the Law Relating to Sedition and Defamation* (London: 1898), 7.
57. *Parliamentary Papers*, 9–11.
58. *Parliamentary Papers*, 12–17.
59. *Parliamentary Papers*, 15.
60. "Extract from the Legislative Assembly Debates (*LAD*), Vol. IV," in National Archives of India (NAI)/Home/Political/1927/F.132/I. I follow the printed pagination, which is organized by date. September 5, 15.
61. *Muslim Outlook* (Lahore), September 24, 1927, 2.

62. Bhubanananda Das (Orissa), *LAD*, September 16, 34.
63. *Abhyudaya* (Allahabad), August 13, 5.
64. India Office Records (IOR)/L/PJ/6/1941/F.1513/pp.41, 145; NAI/Home/Political/1928/103; Home/Judicial/1928/195.
65. Hirday Nath Kunzru (Agra), *LAD*, September 5, 13; A. Rangaswami Iyengar (Tanjore cum Trichinopoly), *LAD*, September 16, 1.
66. *Muslim Outlook*, May 28, 3; *New Times* (Karachi), August 8, as extracted in NAI/Home/Political/1927/132&KW/p.8.
67. F. P. Walton, "Libel upon the Dead and the Bath Club Case," *Journal of Comparative Legislation and International Law*, 3rd series 9, no. 1 (1927): 1–14; M. R. D. Foot, *The Gladstone Diaries* (Oxford: Clarendon, 1968), 1:xxxiii–xxxiv; Anne Isba, *Gladstone and Women* (London: Continuum, 2006). For related Indian cases, see "Libel: Defamation of a Dead Person, Injury to Reputations of Surviving Relatives," *Columbia Law Review* 40, no. 7 (1940): 1267–72.
68. *Muslim Outlook*, May 28, 1927, 3.
69. Regina v. Ensor, (1887) 3 Times LR 366; David Lieberman, "Mapping Criminal Law: Blackstone and the Categories of English Jurisprudence," in *Law, Crime, and English Society, 1660–1830*, ed. Norma Landau (Cambridge, UK: Cambridge University Press, 2002), 139–61.
70. *Law Notes: A Monthly Magazine* 6, no. 3 (March 1887): 69.
71. *A Penal Code*, 124.
72. Morgan and Macpherson, *Indian Penal Code*, 439–40.
73. Rex v. Gott, (1922) 16 Cr App R 87 and *Freethinker* (London), January 8, 1922, as quoted in David Nash, *Blasphemy in Modern Britain* (London: Routledge, 2019), 189–90. See also "Twofold Aspect of the Law of Blasphemy," *Solicitors' Journal & Weekly Reporter* 66 (July 8, 1922): 629; "Prosecutions for Blasphemy," *Solicitor's Journal and Weekly Reporter* 66 (January 28, 1922): 228.
74. *Times* (London), January 17, 1922, 4.
75. See Asad Ali Ahmed, "Paradoxes of Ahmadiyya Identity," in *Beyond Crisis: Reevaluating Pakistan*, ed. Naveeda Khan (Delhi: Routledge, 2010), 273–314; Naveeda Khan, *Muslim Becoming: Aspiration and Skepticism in Pakistan* (Durham, NC: Duke University Press, 2012), 109–16.

PART III

1. Pamela Kanwar, *Imperial Simla: The Political Culture of the Raj* (Delhi: Oxford University Press, 1990), 156–58, 184, 192, 218–21.
2. C. S. Adcock, *The Limits of Tolerance: Indian Secularism and the Politics of Religious Freedom* (New York: Oxford University Press, 2014). For comprehensive accounts, see Kenneth Jones, *Arya Dharm: Hindu Consciousness in Nineteenth-Century Punjab* (Berkeley: University of California Press, 1976), and Satyaketu Vidyālaṅkār and Haridatt Vedālaṅkār, *Ārya Samāj kā Itihās*, 6 vols. (New Delhi: Ārya Svādhyā Kendra, 1982–6).

3. Bob van der Linden, *Moral Languages from Colonial Punjab: The Singh Sabha, Arya Samaj, and Ahmadiyahs* (Delhi: Manoher, 2008).

CHAPTER 7

1. Madan Mohan Seth, *The Arya Samaj, a Political Body* (Haridwar: Anant Ram Sharma, ca. 1910), 46. For the government's reception of this story, see National Archives of India (NAI)/Home/Political/April 1912/Deposit No. 4/p.17.
2. For instance, G. R. Thursby, *Hindu-Muslim Relations in British India* (Leiden: Brill, 1975), 9; J. E. Llewellyn, *The Arya Samaj as Fundamentalist Movement* (Delhi: Manohar, 1993).
3. The Aryas developed a distinct hermeneutic for solving the "riddle" of the Vedas including by reading deity names as common nouns (e.g., *agni*). See for instance Jaydev Śarmā Vidyālaṅkār, "Ved kī Paheliyāṃ aur Unkī Būjh," *Ārya: Ārya Pratinidhi Sabhā Pañjāb kā Māsik Patra* (Lahore), May 1924, 6–11.
4. Munshi Ram and Rama Deva, *The Arya Samaj and Its Detractors* (Dayanandabad: 1910), 1.
5. Scholars of the Arya Samaj often write "Dayananda" as "Dayanand" to reflect its Hindi pronunciation. Here, for the sake of consistency and with an eye to a nonspecialist readership, I retain the Sanskritic terminal vowel. The authoritative biography remains J. T. F. Jordens, *Dayānanda Sarasvati: His Life and Ideas* (Delhi: Oxford University Press, 1978).
6. Buddhdev Vidyālaṅkār, "Ved Pracār kī Varttamān Praṇālī," *Ārya*, May 1924, 11–17, at 13.
7. For nineteenth-century religion's sublimation of bureaucracy, see Gauri Viswanathan, "The Ordinary Business of Occultism," *Critical Inquiry* 27, no. 1 (2000): 1–20. For examples of Arya bylaws, see *Cār Upaniyamoṃkā Sangrah* (Meerut: Vidyādarpaṇ Yantralaya, 1887), and *Brahmārṣi-deś ke Ārya Samājoṃke Niyam aur Upaniyam* (Moradabad: Ārya Bhāskar Yantrālaya, 1897).
8. Jones, *Arya Dharm*, 121–24.
9. Jones, *Arya Dharm*.
10. Gyan Prakash, *Another Reason: Science and the Imagination of Modern India* (Princeton, NJ: Princeton University Press, 1999), 86–122. For the steamboat, see Mahārṣi Dayānand Sarasvatī, *Satyārth Prakāś* (Dehli: Arya Parivar Yojna, 2007 [1883]), 218–19.
11. See title page of Jvālāsahāya, *Āj Kal ke Sādhuoṃ kī Kartūt*, transliterated by Durga Prasad (Lahore: Virajanand Press, 1888). I take the term "archaic modernity" from Banu Subramaniam, *Holy Science: The Biopolitics of Hindu Nationalism* (Seattle: University of Washington Press, 2019).
12. Christophe Jaffrelot, *The Hindu Nationalist Movement in India* (New York: Columbia University Press, 1996); John Zavos, *The Emergence of Hindu Nationalism in India* (New Delhi: Oxford University Press, 2000).
13. Harald Fischer-Tiné, *Shyamji Krishnavarma: Sanskrit, Sociology, and Anti-Imperialism* (London: Routledge, 2014).

14. Ruth Vanita, "Whatever Happened to the Hindu Left," in *Gandhi's Tiger and Sita's Smile* (New Delhi: Yoda Press, 2005), 77–88.

15. Madhu Kishwar, "Arya Samaj and Women's Education: Kanya Mahavidyala, Jalandhar," *Economic and Political Weekly* 21, no. 17 (1986): 9–24; Sangeeta Sharma, *Women's Liberation: The Arya Samaj Movement in India* (Jaipur: Rawat, 2010); "Editorial Reflections: The Kanya Gurukla, Dehra Dun," *Vedic Magazine* (Haridwar), June 1928, 248–49.

16. Maia Ramnath, *Haj to Utopia: How the Ghadar Movement Charted Global Radicalism and Attempted to Overthrow the British Empire* (Berkeley: University of California Press, 2011); Chris Moffat, *India's Revolutionary Inheritance: Politics and the Promise of Bhagat Singh* (Cambridge, UK: Cambridge University Press, 2019).

17. Lala Hansraj, *A Lecture on the Arya Samaj, Delivered on the Occasion of the Last Anniversary of the Lahore Arya Samaj* (Lahore: Arcrbans Press, 1893), 3.

18. Paṇḍit Viṣṇudattjī Vakīl Fīrozpur, "Ek Cīnī Āryya se Vārttālāp," *Ārya*, October 1924, 21–23.

19. See J. Barton Scott, "Pandit Chamupati Goes to Africa: On World Religions as Global Structures of Feeling" (article in progress).

20. Dayananda added them while revising the original 1875 version toward what would become the definitive 1883 edition.

21. Michael Warner, *Publics and Counterpublics* (Cambridge, MA: Zone, 2002).

22. Friedrich Kittler, *Discourse Networks: 1800/1900*, trans. Michael Metteer (Stanford, CA: Stanford University Press, 1990).

23. For a study of this tradition in the present, see David Knipe, *Vedic Voices: Intimate Narratives of a Living Andhra Tradition* (New York: Oxford University Press, 2015).

24. André Padoux, *Vāc: The Concept of the Word in Selected Hindu Tantras* (Albany: SUNY Press, 1990).

25. Sundar Sarukkai, "Phenomenology of Untouchablity," *Economic and Political Weekly* 44, no. 37 (2009): 39–48, at 47.

26. For such continuities, see Brian Hatcher, "What's Become of the Pandit? Rethinking the History of Sanskrit Scholars in Colonial Bengal," *Modern Asian Studies* 39, no. 3 (2005): 683–723.

27. J. Barton Scott, *Spiritual Despots: Modern Hinduism and the Genealogies of Self-Rule* (Chicago: University of Chicago Press, 2016), 144.

28. John Cort, "History and Indology as Authoritative Knowledge," in *Trans-Colonial Modernities in South Asia*, ed. Brian Hatcher and Michael Dodson (London: Routledge, 2012), 137–61, at 155.

29. Jeffrey Cox, *Imperial Fault Lines: Christianity and Colonial Power in India, 1818–1940* (Stanford, CA: Stanford University Press, 2002), 56.

30. Jordens, *Dayānanda Sarasvati*, 39–40; John Robson, *Hinduism and Its Relations to Christianity* (Edinburgh: Oliphant, Anderson, & Ferrier, 1893), 217–20; Dayānand, *Satyārth Prakāś*, 229; *The Aims, Ideals, and Needs of the Gurukula Vishvavidyalaya Kangri* (Kangri: Gurukula Press, 1914), xxvi. For context, see Arie Molendijk, *Friedrich Max Müller and the Sacred Books of the East* (Oxford: Oxford University Press, 2016).

31. For the lantern slides, see India Office Records (IOR)/L/PJ/6/1899/F.643/March 1925, and the 1923 UP police file cited in Charu Gupta, *Sexuality, Obscenity, Community:*

Women, Muslims, and the Hindu Public in Colonial India (New York: Palgrave, 2002), 264–65.
32. For the gold-letter banner, see *Arya Magazine*, as quoted in John Campbell Oman, *Indian Life: Religious and Social* (London: T. Fisher Unwin, 1889), 103.
33. Compare Brannon Ingram, *Revival from Below: The Deoband Movement and Global Islam* (Berkeley: University of California Press, 2018), 22.
34. For a sample salary of Rs. 50/ month see NAI/Home/Political/April 1912/ Deposit No. 4, "Appendix"/p.6.
35. Jones, *Arya Dharm*, 47, 120–25.
36. Sandria Freitag, *Collective Action and Community: Public Arenas and the Emergence of Communalism in North India* (Berkeley: University of California Press, 1989), 139–60.
37. Svāmī Śraddhānand [Munshiram], *Kalyān Mārg kā Pathik*, in *Svāmī Śraddhānand Granthāvalī*, ed. Bhavānīlāl Bhāratīya (Delhi: Govindaram Hasanand, 1987), 1:162.
38. Śraddhānand, *Kalyān Mārg*, 187–88.
39. For the rentals, see Śraddhānand, *Kalyān Mārg*, 105.
40. Oman, *Indian Life*, 87–120.
41. Oman, *Indian Life*, 119.
42. Ved Kunwar, *Choṭā Munh Baṛī Bāt*, ed. Rāmcandra Varmmā (Mathurā: Mathurā Bhūṣaṇ Press, 1896). See also the companion speech: Shakuntala, *Cetāvanī*, ed. Rāmcandra Varmmā (Mathurā: Mathurā Bhūṣaṇ Press, 1896).
43. For the Scouts, see Nehru Memorial Museum and Library (NMML)/Manuscripts/DAV College Papers/Register F. No. 110/pp.29–30.
44. Chamupati, *The Aryan Ideal of Education* (Lahore: Bombay Machine Press, ca. 1927), 7–8.
45. Kumkum Sangari and Sudesh Vaid, eds., *Recasting Women: Essays in Colonial History* (Brunswick, NJ: Rutgers University Press, 1989).
46. Kunwar, *Choṭā Munh*, 1–2.
47. Torrey Shanks, *Authority Figures: Rhetoric and Experience in John Locke's Political Thought* (University Park: Pennsylvania State University Press, 2014).
48. Webb Keane, *Christian Moderns: Freedom and Fetish in the Mission Encounter* (Berkeley: University of California Press, 2007).
49. Elizabeth Pritchard, *Religion in Public: Locke's Political Theology* (Stanford, CA: Stanford University Press, 2013).
50. Michel Foucault, "Polemics, Politics, and Problematizations," in *The Foucault Reader*, ed. Paul Rabinow (New York: Pantheon, 1984), 381–90.
51. John Durham Peters, *Speaking into the Air: A History of the Idea of Communication* (Chicago: University of Chicago Press, 1999), 33–62.
52. Dayānand, *Satyārth Prakāś*, 226.
53. Bakhtāvar Sinha, ed., *Satyadharmvicār* (Kashi: Vedic Press, 1880), 1.
54. Jonardon Ganeri, *Philosophy in Classical India* (London: Routledge: 2001), 10–15.
55. "Pracārak Kaisā Hai," *Ārya*, May 13, 1945, 4.
56. "Sampādakīya: Jalsā Dharm," *Ārya*, May 1924, 43–45.
57. Vidyālaṅkār, "Ved Pracār kī Varttamān Praṇālī," 11–17.

58. Śraddhānand, *Kalyān Mārg*, 73, 77. Compare Mohinder Singh, "'A Question of Life and Death': Conversion, Self, and Identity in Swami Shraddhanand's Autobiography," *South Asia: Journal of South Asian Studies* 41, no. 2 (2018): 452–67.
59. Śraddhānand, *Kalyān Mārg*, 101. See also J. T. F. Jordens, *Swāmi Shraddhānanda: His Life and Causes* (Delhi: Oxford University Press, 1981), 17.
60. Chamupati, *Glimpses of Dayananda*, 2nd ed. (Delhi: Sharada Mandir, 1937), 124.
61. For entry onto a substantial scholarship, see for instance Arjun Appadurai, "Number in the Colonial Imagination," in *Modernity at Large: Cultural Dimensions of Globalization* (Minneapolis: University of Minnesota Press, 1996), 114–38; and Sumit Guha, "The Politics of Identity and Enumeration in India, c. 1600–1900," *Comparative Studies in Society and History* 45, no. 1 (2003): 148–67.
62. *Arya Patrika* (Lahore), September 23, 1890, 1–2; NAI/Home/Public/1931/F.45/154/p.2. For context, see Kenneth Jones, "Religious Identity and the Indian Census," in *Census in British India: New Perspectives*, ed. N. Gerald Barrier (Delhi: Manohar, 1981), 73–102.
63. Hansraj, *Lecture on the Arya Samaj*, 19.
64. *Muslim Outlook* (Lahore), September 25, 1927 1.
65. Lehkram, *Dharm-Pracār*, trans. Śānti Prakāś (Lucknow: Arya Upapratinidhi Sabha, 1975).
66. Rosalind O'Hanlon, "Narratives of Penance and Purification in Western India, c.1650–1850," *Journal of Hindu Studies* 2, no. 1 (2009): 48–75.
67. See James Reid Graham, "The Arya Samaj as a Reformation in Hinduism with Special Reference to Caste" (PhD diss., Yale University, 1943); R. K. Ghai, *Shuddhi Movement in India* (New Delhi: Commonwealth Publishers, 1990); Ramnarayan Rawat, *Reconsidering Untouchability: Chamars and Dalit History in North India* (Bloomington: Indiana University Press, 2011), 120–54; Adcock, *Limits of Tolerance*, 115–42; Joel Lee, *Deceptive Majority: Dalits, Hinduism, and Underground Religion* (Cambridge, UK: Cambridge University Press, 2021), 77–120.
68. *Singh Sahai Punjab Gazette* (Amritsar) June 30, 1903, *Selections from the Native Newspapers Published in Punjab* (henceforth *SNNP*), 167, in IOR/L/R/5/187.
69. Anshu Malhotra, "The Body as Metaphor for the Nation," in *Rhetoric and Reality: Gender and the Colonial Experience in South Asia*, ed. Avril Powell and Siobhan Lambert-Hurley (Delhi: Oxford University Press, 2006), 121–53.
70. "Pañjāb Dayānand Dalitoddhār Maṇḍal kā Kārya," *Ārya*, June 1926, 16–17. On gender and Arya Dalit conversion, see Charu Gupta, "Intimate Desires: Dalit Women and Religious Conversions in Colonial India," *Modern Asian Studies* 73, no. 3 (2014): 661–87.
71. Amardeep Singh, "Swami Acchutanand and the Rise of Dalit Consciousness," *E-Journal of Dalit Literary Studies* 2, no. 3 (2013): 56–69, at 61.
72. NMML/DAV College Collection/Proceedings/Register F. No. 111, "Report of the Dayanand Anglo-Vedic College Society for 1927–28," pp. 103–4.
73. *Bharat Pratap* (Jhajjar), May 1903, *SNNP*, 182, IOR/L/R/5/187.
74. *Al Fazl* (Qadian), October 30, 1923, *SNNP*, 597, IOR/L/R/5/204.
75. Nicholas Goodrick-Clarke, *Hitler's Priestess: Savitri Devi, the Hindu-Aryan Myth, and Neo-Nazism* (New York: NYU Press, 2000).

76. Arjun Appadurai, *Fear of Small Numbers* (Durham, NC: Duke University Press, 2006).
77. Swami Shraddhananda, *Hindu Sangathan: Saviour of the Dying Race* (Delhi: Arjun Press, 1926).
78. "The Arya Samaj," in *Papers for the Thoughtful, No. 2*, ed. Lala Jivan Das (Lahore: Punjab Printing Works, 1902), 2.
79. Scott, *Spiritual Despots*, 166–73.
80. Lalla Ralla Ram, ed., *The Rules and the Scheme of Studies of the Gurukula, Sanctioned by the Arya Pratinidhi Sabha, Punjab* (Lahore: Punjab Printing Works, 1902), 11–12.
81. Chamupati, *The Ten Commandments of Dayananda* (Lahore: Rajpal, Arya Pustakalaya, ca. 1927), 119. For parallel rhetoric, see Chamupati, *Aryan Ideal*, 1.
82. Ṭhākurdās Mūlrāj Osvāl, *Dayānand Sarasvatī Mukh Capeṭikā* (Mumbai: Jagdīśvar Yantrālaya, 1882); Sītārām, *Tīrthanindak Mukhcapeṭikā* (Kapur: Ramik Yantrālaya, 1891). For the other titles, see Gerald Barrier Collection, Center for Research Libraries (Chicago).
83. See, for instance, Appaya Dīkṣita's *Madhvatantramukhmardana* and Vijaya Rāmācārya's *Pākhaṇḍacapeṭikā*, as discussed in Jonathan R. Peterson, "Polemics and Power in Early Modern South Asia, 1550–1700" (PhD diss., University of Toronto, 2021).
84. *Arya Gazette* (Lahore), August 3, 1905, ostensibly quoting *Al Bashir* (Etawah), SNNP, 222, in IOR/L/R/5/188.
85. On desecration and ritual pollution, see for instance Kajri Jain, "Taking and Making Offence: Hussain and the Politics of Desecration," in *Barefoot across the Nation: Maqbool Fida Husain and the Idea of India*, ed. Sumathi Ramaswamy (London: Routledge, 2011), 208.
86. NAI/Home/Political/September 1915/B/pp.205–7; IOR/L/PJ/6/1401.
87. Terry Eagleton, *The Ideology of the Aesthetic* (Oxford: Blackwell, 1990), 13.
88. Gupta, *Sexuality, Obscenity*.
89. See Lee, *Deceptive Majority*. For the caste-based distribution of the sensible, see Kajri Jain, *Gods in the Time of Democracy* (Durham, NC: Duke University Press, 2021).
90. Usha Sanyal, *Devotional Islam and Politics in British India: Ahmad Riza Khan Barelwi and His Movement, 1870–1920* (New York: Oxford University Press, 1996), 96. See, for instance, Bawa Arjan Singh, *Mela Chandapur* (Lahore: Arya Printing, Publishing, and General Trading, n.d.).
91. Frank Conlon, "The Polemic Process in Nineteenth Century Maharashtra: Vishnubawa Brahmachari and Hindu Revival," in *Religious Controversy in British India*, ed. Kenneth Jones (Albany: SUNY Press, 1992), 5–26, at 15–19.
92. Gupta, *Sexuality, Obscenity*, 97.
93. Kenneth Jones, "Sources for Arya Samaj History," in *Sources on Punjab History*, ed. W. Eric Gustafson and Kenneth Jones (Delhi: Manohar, 1975), 130–218, at 144.
94. *Arya Patrika*, July 11, 1885, 7, and July 18, 4.
95. Scott, *Spiritual Despots*, 150–76.
96. "Vigyāpan: Thiyosophisṭoṃ kī Golmāl Polpāl," in *Ṛṣi Dayānand Sarasvatī kā Patra-Vyavahār aur Vigyāpan*, ed. Bhagavad Datt, Māmarāj Ārya, and Yuddhiṣṭhara Mīmāmsaka (Sonipat: Ramlal Kapur Trust, 1996), 2:675–81.
97. Dayānand, *Satyārth Prakāś*, 413–15.

98. Dayānand, *Satyārth Prakāś*, 442, 461.
99. For a list of anti-pope Arya tracts from the 1880s and '90s, see Jones, *Arya Dharm*, 110, no. 51, and Jones, "Sources for Arya Samaj History," at 144–45. Sanatanists countered by referencing the term in their defenses of texts like the Tulsidas *Ramayan*, as in Chavirām Dhenusevak, *Alaulikakmālāmardan* (Etawah: Brahm Press, 1911), 41.
100. Jagganāth Dās, *Ārya-Praśnottarī* (Shahjahanpur: Ārya Darpaṇ Press, 1882), 16; *Arya Gazette* (Lahore), June 28, 1906, *SNNP*, 180, in IOR/L/R/5/188.
101. Girvar Sinha, *Pop-Pradīp* (Agra: Macchu Khan, 1889); Bābūrām Śarmā, *Īsāī Līlā* (Lakhīmpur Khīrī, Avadh: Hindī Prabhā Press, 1895), 3.
102. Śraddhānand, *Kalyān Mārg*, 75.
103. Dayānand, *Satyārth Prakāś*, 474–75.
104. Śraddhānand, *Kalyāṇ Mārg*, 132.
105. *Sanatan Dharm Gazette* (Lahore), April 3, 1904, *SNNP*, 82, in IOR/L/R/5/187.
106. Chamupati, *Glimpses*, 117.
107. NAI/Foreign and Political/Internal/1926/Nos. 557 (41)-I.
108. NAI/Political/Central India Agency/ F.92-A/1938.
109. Pandit Manasārāmjī, *Mere Pacchīs Miṇaṭ* (Bhiwani: Ambika Printing Works, ca. 1936), 14.
110. Elizabeth Kolsky, *Colonial Justice in British India: White Violence and the Rule of Law* (Cambridge, UK: Cambridge University Press, 2009).
111. *Tribune* (Lahore), November 2, 1911, in NAI/Home/Political/December 1911/Part B/ Nos. 19–20.
112. NAI/Home/Political/April 1912/Deposit/No. 4/Appendix/p.6.

CHAPTER 8

1. Quoted in C. S. Adcock, "Violence, Passion, and the Law: A Brief History of Section 295A and Its Antecedents," *Journal of the American Academy of Religion* 84, no. 2 (2016): 343–44.
2. For law's religion, see Benjamin Berger, *Law's Religion: Religious Difference and the Claims of Constitutionalism* (Toronto: University of Toronto Press, 2015); Winnifred Fallers Sullivan, *The Impossibility of Religious Freedom* (Princeton, NJ: Princeton University Press, 2018). For religion's law, see for instance Isaac Weiner, "The Corporately Produced Conscience: Emergency Contraception and the Politics of Workplace Accommodations," *Journal of the American Academy of Religion* 85, no. 1 (2017): 31–63.
3. *Sat Dharm Pracharak* (Jullunder), December 2, 1904, *Selections from the Native Newspapers Published in Punjab* (henceforth *SNNP*), 290, India Office Records (IOR)/ L/R/5/187. On the longer history of sex, class, and *nagar-kirtan* as eruptively "public" worship, see Varuni Bhatia, *Unforgetting Chaitanya: Vaishnavism and Cultures of Devotion in Colonial Bengal* (New York: Oxford University Press, 2017), 78–84.
4. C. S. Adcock, *The Limits of Tolerance: Indian Secularism and the Politics of Religious Freedom* (New York: Oxford University Press, 2014).

5. Akhil Gupta, *Red Tape: Bureaucracy, Structural Violence, and Poverty in India* (Durham, NC: Duke University Press, 2012), 208.
6. Bhavani Raman, *Document Raj: Writing and Scribes in Early Colonial South India* (Chicago: University of Chicago Press, 2012); Tania Sengupta, "Papered Spaces: Clerical Practices, Materialities, and Spatial Cultures of Provincial Governance in Bengal," *Journal of Architecture* 25, no. 2 (2020): 111–37.
7. Gauri Viswanathan, "The Ordinary Business of Occultism," *Critical Inquiry* 27, no. 1 (2000): 1–20.
8. *Indar* (Lahore), January 1909, SNNP, 137–39, IOR/L/R/5/190.
9. On the disarticulation of the Crown from colonialism, see Mithi Mukherjee, *India in the Shadows of Empire* (New York: Oxford University Press, 2011).
10. Compare Matthew Hull, *Government of Paper: The Materiality of Bureaucracy in Urban Pakistan* (Berkeley: University of California Press, 2012).
11. See J. Barton Scott, "Aryas Unbound: Print Hinduism and the Cultural Regulation of Religious Offense," *Comparative Studies of South Asia, Africa, and the Middle East* 35, no. 2 (2015): 294–309.
12. Mahārṣi Dayānand Sarasvatī, *Satyārth Prakāś* (Dehli: Arya Parivar Yojna, 2007), 8, 226, 434.
13. Smith and Frere, Solicitors High Court, to Pandit Dyanund Surswatee swamee [*sic*], June 13, 1882, in *Dayānand Sarasvatī Mukh Capeṭikā*, by Ṭhākurdās Mūlrāj Osvāl (Mumbai: Jagdishvar Press, 1882), 41–43; and Yudhiṣṭhir Mīmāṃsakaḥ, ed., *Ṛṣi Dayānand Sarasvatī ke Patra aur Vigyāpan*, 4th ed. (Sonipat: Ramlal Kapur Trust, 1996), 2:704–5.
14. Ṭhākurdās, *Dayānand*, 44–46.
15. Dayananda Sarasvati to Munśī Samarthdān, August 29, 1882, in Mīmāṃsakaḥ, *Patra aur Vigyāpan*, 738–39.
16. Chiranjiva Bharadwaja, *Light of Truth*, 3rd ed. (Lahore: Satya Vrata Bharadwaja, 1927 [1906]), iii; Durga Prasad, *An English Translation of the Satyarth Prakash* (Lahore: Virajanand, 1908), 66.
17. Dayānand, *Satyārth Prakāś*, 301–6; J. T. F. Jordens, "Dayananda and Karsondas Mulji," in *Dayananda Sarasvati: Essays on His Life and Ideas* (New Delhi: Manohar, 1998), 140–62.
18. See J. T. F. Jordens, *Dayānanda Sarasvati: His Life and Ideas* (Delhi: Oxford University Press, 1978), 190–93; John Cort, "History and Indology as Authoritative Knowledge," in *Trans-Colonial Modernities in South Asia*, ed. Brian Hatcher and Michael Dodson (London: Routledge, 2012), 137–61; and John Cort, "Jain Identity and the Public Sphere in Nineteenth-Century India," in *Religious Interactions in Modern India*, ed. Vasudha Dalmia and Martin Fuchs (New Delhi: Oxford University Press, 2019), 99–137.
19. Ṭhākurdās, *Dayānand*, 3–7.
20. Ṭhākurdās, *Dayānand*, 8–10.
21. Ṭhākurdās, *Dayānand*, 14–16.
22. Ṭhākurdās, *Dayānand*, 30.
23. Michael Warner, *Publics and Counterpublics* (Cambridge, MA: Zone, 2002).
24. Compare Hussein Ali Agrama, *Questioning Secularism: Islam, Sovereignty, and the Rule of Law in Modern Egypt* (Chicago: University of Chicago Press, 2012).

25. J. Barton Scott, *Spiritual Despots: Modern Hinduism and the Genealogies of Self-Rule* (Chicago: University of Chicago Press, 2016), 150–76.
26. *Muslim Outlook* (Lahore), July 19, 1927, 7.
27. Shiv Narayan Agnihotri, *Pandit Dayanand Unveiled: Part I* (Lahore: Tribune Press, 1891). For more on the trope of imposture, see J. Barton Scott, "Miracle Publics: Theosophy, Christianity, and the Coulomb Affair," *History of Religions* 49, no. 2 (2009): 172–96.
28. *Arya Patrika* (Lahore), July 1, 1890, 1.
29. On the relation between these newspapers, see *Muslim Outlook*, July 30, 1927, 6.
30. *Judgment in P. Gopi Nath Complainant against (1) Lala Munshi Ram, (2) Lala Wazir Chand, and (3) Lala Basti Ram Accused* (Haridwar: Sat Dharma Pracharak Press, ca. 1901). For the articles, see Mahāsáy Munśīrām Jigyāsu, *Satyadharmpracārak par Pahilā Mānhāni kā Abhiyog Jismeṃ Pandit Gopīnāth ke Pablik Jīvan kā Gupt Bhed Svayam hī Khul Gayā* (Ajmere: Vedic Press, 1901), 134–41.
31. *Judgment in P. Gopi Nath*, 8, 23.
32. *Judgment in P. Gopi Nath*, 6–7.
33. Munśīrām, *Satyadharmpracārak*; Mahāshe Munshī Rām Jigyāsu, *Satya Dharm Pracārak par Pahelā Lāībal Kes Jismeṃ Paṇḍit Gopīnāth kī Mukamal Pablik Lāīf kā Rāz Khūdbakhūd Khul Gayā* (Jullunder: Satya Dharm Pracharak, 1901).
34. Munśīrām, *Satyadharmpracārak*, 2, 30.
35. Munśīrām, *Satyadharmpracārak*, 24.
36. National Archives of India (NAI)/Home/Political/B/May 1911/p.64.
37. *Complete Judice File of Shriman Amar Singh, Complainant of Dev Samaj, versus Mahashay Dharmpal, Accused of Arya Samaj* (Lahore, ca. 1909).
38. Kenneth Jones, *Socio-Religious Reform Movements in British India* (Cambridge, UK: Cambridge University Press, 1990), 103–6.
39. *Complete Judice File*, 35, 43.
40. For Dharmpal's biography, see Ali Usman Qasmi, *Questioning the Authority of the Past: The Ahl al-Qur'an Movements in the Punjab* (Karachi: Oxford University Press, 2011), 122–25; Adcock, *Limits of Tolerance*, 132–38.
41. Mahāsay Dharmpāl, *Tark Islām* (Calcutta: Vedic Press, 1935), 3–8, 43–45, 74–75.
42. *Complete Judice File*, 6.
43. *Complete Judice File*, 38–40.
44. Dominic Janes, "The Confessional Unmasked: Religious Merchandise and Obscenity in Victorian England," *Victorian Literature and Culture* 41, no. 4 (2013): 677–90. On the Hicklin test in India, see Deana Heath, *Purifying Empire: Obscenity and the Politics of Moral Regulation in Britain, India, and Australia* (Cambridge, UK: Cambridge University Press, 2010), 105, 171.
45. For the trial, see "The Obscene Literature Case," *Arya Patrika*, July 1, 1890, 2–3 (reprinted from *Civil and Military Gazette*), and *Kitāb Dayānandioṇ kī Muśkilāt* (Lahore, 1890).
46. Jvālāsahāya, *Āj Kal ke Sādhuoṃ kī Kartūt*, transliterated by Durga Prasad (Lahore: Virajanand Press, 1888).
47. This detail comes from Denzil Ibbetson's recollection during a 1905 Arya obscenity scandal about a similar case fifteen years earlier. As Ibbetson was in Punjab at that

time, it seems probable that the earlier case was *Empress v. Arya Samaj*. See NAI/Home/Public/May 1905/A/23–4. I have relied on Professor Deana Heath's notes for this file, as it was deemed too brittle for consultation at the time of my research; I thank her for her collegial generosity. For the 1905 case, see also NAI/Home/Public/August 1905/A/185.
48. "The Obscene Literature Case," 3.
49. *Judgment, Showing How an Updeshak of the Sanatan Hindu Dharm Sabha Who Wanted to Poison the Ears of the Authorities against the Arya Samaj Was Punished* (Haridwar: Satya Dharm Pracharak Press, 1902), 3.
50. IOR/L/PJ/6/1401.
51. Munshi Ram and Rama Deva, *The Arya Samaj and Its Detractors* (Dayanandabad, 1910), i.
52. Munshi Ram and Rama Deva, *Arya Samaj and Its Detractors*.
53. Lord Minto to John Morley, March 5, 1907, IOR/MssEur/D573/p.11.
54. IOR/L/PJ/6/949/F.2457.
55. IOR/L/PJ/6/1261/F.3015.
56. [Edmund Candler], *Siri Ram, Revolutionist: A Transcript from Life, 1907–1910* (London: Constable, 1912).
57. Candler, *Siri Ram*, 487.
58. NAI/Foreign and Political/Internal/March 1919/Deposit/Progs. No. 52. For context, see Ian Copland, "The Maharaja of Kolhapur and the Non-Brahmin Movement, 1902–10," *Modern Asian Studies* 7, no. 2 (1973): 209–25; Christoph Jaffrelot, *Dr. Ambedkar and Untouchability* (New York: Columbia University Press, 2005), 28–29.
59. NAI/Foreign/Internal/July 1907/B/Nos. 447–49.
60. Munshi Rama and Rama Deva, *Arya Samaj and Its Detractors*.
61. NAI/Foreign and Political/Internal/July 1919/B/Progs/Nos. 561–82.
62. NAI/Foreign and Political/External/1926/F. No. 157; NAI/Foreign and Political/External/1933/F. No. 216.
63. Faiz Ahmad, *Afghanistan Rising: Islamic Law and Statecraft between the Ottoman and British Empires* (Cambridge, MA: Harvard University Press, 2017).
64. IOR/R/1/1/223/Foreign/Secret-I/Progs/June 1899/Nos. 13–7.
65. IOR/R/1/1/223/Foreign/Secret-I/Progs/June 1899/Nos. 13–7.
66. Spencer Lavan, *The Ahmadiyah Movement* (Delhi: Manohar, 1974); Yohanan Friedmann, *Prophecy Continuous: Aspects of Aḥmadī Religious Thought and Its Medieval Background* (Berkeley: University of California Press, 1989).
67. Mirza Ghulam Ahmad, *Barāhīn-e-Aḥmadiyya: Parts I and II* (Islamabad: Islam International Publications, 2012), 109.
68. Mirza Ghulam Ahmad, *Barāhīn-e-Aḥmadiyya*, 85.
69. NAI/Foreign/Secret/1891/F/Progs./Nos. 70–1.
70. Munśirām, *Ārya Pathik Lekhrām* (Haridwar: Gurukul Press, 1914), 193–96.
71. NAI/Foreign/Secret/1891/F/Progs./Nos. 70–1.
72. NAI/Foreign/Secret/1891/F/Progs./Nos. 70–71/September/pp.1–3.

CHAPTER 9

1. Śrīyut Devendranāth Mukhopādhyāy, *Dayānandcarit*, trans. Śrī Bābū Ghāsīrām (Meerut: Bhasker Press, 1912), 334; J. T. F. Jordens, *Dayānanda Sarasvati: His Life and Ideas* (Delhi: Oxford University Press, 1978), 236–37. For an expanded discussion of select material in this chapter, see J. Barton Scott, "Unsaintly Virtue: Swami Dayananda Saraswati and Modern Hindu Hagiography," *Journal of Hindu Studies* 7, no. 3 (2014): 371–91.
2. Lajpat Rai, *Collected Works of Lala Lajpat Rai*, ed. B. R. Nanda (New Delhi: Manohar, 2003), 1:270–71.
3. "Autobiography of Dayanand Saraswati, Swami," *The Theosophist* 1, no. 1 (October 1879): 9–13; *The Theosophist* 1, no. 3 (December 1879): 66–68; *The Theosophist* 2, no. 2 (November 1880): 24–25.
4. Jordens, *Dayānanda*, 20.
5. Satyaketu Vidyālaṅkār, and Haridatt Vedālaṅkār, *Āryasamāj kā Itihās* (New Delhi: Ārya Svadhyāya Kendra, 1982), 1:187–90; Jordens, *Dayānanda*, xiii–vii.
6. Śrī Śītalprasādjī Vaidya, ed., *Śrīmaddayānanad Citrāvalī* (Calcutta: Vaidik Pustakālaya, 1925), ii; cf. Kenneth W. Jones, "Arya Samaj in British India, 1875–1947," in *Religion in Modern India*, ed. Robert Baird, 2nd ed. (New Delhi: Manohar, 1989), 27–54.
7. Robin Rinehart, *One Lifetime, Many Lives: The Experience of Modern Hindu Hagiography* (Atlanta: Scholars Press, 1999); Timothy Dobe, *Hindu Christian Faqir: Modern Monks, Global Christianity, and Indian Sainthood* (New York: Oxford University Press, 2015), 182–257.
8. Mukhopādhyāy, *Dayānandcarit*, 5.
9. Akhilānanda Śarmmā, *Dayānanddigvijayam: Mahākāvyam* (Allahabad: Indian Press, 1910), 10–12; Candrakavi Varman, *Dayānand Caritra: Janm Prakaraṇ, arthāt Śrī 108 Mahārṣi Svāmīdayānandjī Sarasvatī Mahārāj kā Jīvancaritra Varttamān Dohā Lāvnī Ghazalādi Cāl meṃ* (Meerut: Globe Printing Works, 1916); Kṛṣṇa, *Śrīsvāmī Dayānand Sarasvatījī kā Jīvan Caritra*, 2 vols. (Delhi: Śrīmatī Vidyāvatī, 1924–25).
10. Sudarśan, *Dayānand-Nāṭak, arthāt Mahārṣi Svāmī Dayānandjī Mahārāj kā Pavitra Jīvan* (Lahore: Punjab Printing Works, 1917), 5–7.
11. Gosvāmī Yadukulbhūṣaṇ Śāstrī, *Dayānand aur Śivrātri kā Cūhā* (Lahore: Bombay Machine Press, 1929), 7.
12. Kajri Jain, *Gods in the Bazaar: The Economies of Indian Calendar Art* (Durham, NC: Duke University Press, 2007); Sumathi Ramaswamy, *The Goddess and the Nation: Mapping Mother India* (Durham, NC: Duke University Press, 2009).
13. My thanks to Kajri Jain for several of the ideas in this paragraph.
14. Durga Prasad, *A Triumph of Truth: Being an English Translation of Satya Dharm Vichar* (Lahore: Virajanand Press, 1889), 48, 41.
15. I thank Kajri Jain for the idea of "two-way traffic."
16. Paṇḍyā Mohanlāl Viṣṇulāl, *Svāmījī Śrī 108 Śrī Dayānandjī Sarasvatī kā Gurūtva vā Ācāryatva* (Meerut: Svāmiyantrālaya, 1901).
17. Hariścandra Vidyālaṅkār, *Ārya Samāj kā Itihās* (Delhi: 1949), 54.

18. Sivanandan Prasad Kulyar, *Swami Dayanand Saraswati: His Life and Teachings* (Madras: Ganesh, ca. 1914), 147.
19. Lājpat Rāy, *Maharṣi Svāmī Dayānand Sarasvatī aur Unkā Kām*, trans. Gopāldās Devguṇ Śarmmā (Lahore: Punjab Economical Yantrālay, 1898); Bawa Chhajju Singh, *Life and Teachings of Swami Dayanand Saraswati*, 2nd ed. (New Delhi: Jan Gyān Prakāshan, 1971 [1903]).
20. Varman, *Dayānand Caritra*, 4–5. Compare Santrām, *Dayānand* (Prayāg: Indian Press, 1930), 6.
21. Sudarśan, *Dayānand-Nāṭak*, 16–23.
22. Śāstrī, *Dayānand aur Śivrātri kā Cūhā*, 7.
23. *Prospectus of the Gurukul Mahavidyalaya* (Haridwar: Saddharma Pracharak Press, 1911), 48; J. T. F. Jordens, *Swāmi Shraddhānanda: His Life and Causes* (Delhi: Oxford University Press, 1981), 158–59.
24. *Ārya: Ārya Pratinidhi Sabhā Pañjāb kā Māsik Patra* (Lahore), May 1924, 45.
25. National Archives of India (NAI)/Foreign and Political/1925/30. For Brahmo Samajis being excused from work to celebrate their society's annual festival, see NAI/Home/Public/1883/May/81–82, and Home/Public/1883/ September/188&189.
26. Nehru Memorial Museum and Library (NMML)/Manuscripts/DAV College Collection/Register F.110/p.150; *Vedic Magazine* (Haridwar) March 1925, 56–59; *Leader* (Allahabad), February 16–26, 1925, and April 2, 1925, as quoted in Jordens, *Swāmi Shraddhānanda*, 158–59.
27. Pandit Nardev Vedalankar and Manohar Somera, *Arya Samaj and Indians Abroad* (New Delhi: Sarvadeshik Arya Pratinidhi Sabha, 1975), 106, 68.
28. NMML/Manuscripts/DAV College Collection/Register F.110/pp.121, 150, 167–70.
29. *Ārya*, November 1924, 38–39. See also *Ārya*, November 1924, 11–13; *Jyoti* (Delhi), February 1924, 555–56.
30. Dharmdev Siddhāntālaṅkār, "Vaidik Sabhyatā ke Punarūddhārak Ṛṣi Dayānand," *Vaidik Dharm*, February 1925, 61–63.
31. NMML/Manuscripts/DAV College Collection/Register F.111/p.63, and F.110/p.150.
32. For this polemic context, see G. R. Thursby, *Hindu-Muslim Relations in British India* (Leiden: Brill, 1975), 40–44.
33. *Vedic Magazine*, October 1923, 956–63; Chamupati, *Glimpses of Dayananda*, 2nd ed. (Delhi: Sharada Mandir, 1937 [1925]).
34. Svatantrānand, *Āryya Samāj ke Mahādhan* (Delhi: Sārvadeśik Ārya Pratinidhi Sabhā, 1948), 165.
35. Indra Vidyāvācaspati, *Āryasamaj kā Itihās*, vol. 2 (Delhi: Sarvadeshik Arya Pratinidhi Sabha, 1957), 167, as cited in Richa Raj, "A Pamphlet and Its (Dis)contents: A Case Study of *Rangila Rasul*," *History and Sociology of South Asia* 9, no. 2 (2015): 146–62.
36. Rājendra, "Sampādakīya," *Ārya*, January 1926, 46.
37. [Camupati], *Rangīlā Rasūl: Mūl Pustak Urdu kā Hindī Rūpāntar*, ed. Baldev Śarma (Banaras: Baldev Sharma, ca. 1927).
38. The only one of these hagiographies that I have found a copy of is Satyānand, *Śrīmaddayānand-Prakāś* (Mumbai: Vaibhav Press, 1918).
39. Wilfred Cantwell Smith, *Modern Islam in India* (Lahore: Muhammad Ashraf, 1963

[1943]), 65. For Smith's biography, see Ellen Bradshaw Aitken and Arvind Sharma, eds., *The Legacy of Wilfred Cantwell Smith* (Albany: SUNY Press, 2017).
40. Smith, *Modern Islam*, 65, 334; Annemarie Schimmel, *And Muhammad Is His Messenger* (Chapel Hill: University of North Carolina Press, 1985), 233, 241; Annemarie Schimmel, "The Golden Chain of 'Sincere Muhammadans,'" in *The Rose and the Rock*, ed. Bruce Lawrence (Durham, NC: Duke University Program in Comparative Studies on Southern Asia, 1979), 104–34. For a recent study, see Adil Mawani, "Devotion in Colonial Islam: Representations of Muhammad in Urdu *Sira*, 1842–1914" (PhD diss., University of Toronto, 2021).
41. Tarif Khalidi, *Images of Muhammad* (New York: Doubleday, 2009), 17–18.
42. Kecia Ali, *The Lives of Muhammad* (Cambridge, MA: Harvard University Press, 2014), 2.
43. Prabhat Kumar, "Colonialism, Modernity, and Hindi Satire in the Late 19th Century," *Zeitschrift für Indologie und Südasienstudien* 28 (2011): 1–25.
44. Jagannāthdās, *Muhammad Jīvan Caritra* (Moradabad: Sudarshan Press, 1887).
45. William Muir, *The Life of Mahomet from Original Sources* (London: Smith, Elder, 1878), 526–35.
46. Fazlur Rahman, "Sirat al-Nabi of 'Allama Shibli Numani," *Journal of the Pakistan Historical Society* 8, no. 1 (1960): 2–18, at 3–4.
47. Christopher Shackle and Javed Majeed, introduction to *Hali's Musaddas: The Flow and Ebb of Islam* (Delhi: Oxford University Press, 1997), 1–87, at 76–79. On late colonial *akhlaq* literature, see Margrit Pernau, *Emotions and Modernity in Colonial India* (New Delhi: Oxford University Press, 2019).
48. Ali, *Lives of Muhammad*, 169–72.
49. NAI/Home/Judicial/1928/794.
50. Ishita Pande, "Loving Like a Man: The *Colourful Prophet*, Conjugal Masculinity, and the Politics of Hindu Sexology in Late Colonial India," *Gender & History* 29, no. 3 (2017): 675–92; Charu Gupta, *Sexuality, Obscenity, Community: Women, Muslims, and the Hindu Public in Colonial India* (New York: Palgrave, 2002).
51. Mrinalini Sinha, *Specters of Mother India: The Global Restructuring of an Empire* (Durham, NC: Duke University Press, 2006).
52. *Ārya*, October 1926, 39; *Rāmparīkṣā* (Ludhiana: Ludhiana Mission Press, 1867), 4; Gosevak Paṇḍit Jagat Nārāyaṇ, *Muhammad Parīkṣā* (Banaras: Śrīkāśyāmamarantrālaya, 1888).
53. Lata Mani, *Contentious Traditions: The Debate on Sati in Colonial India* (Berkeley: University of California Press, 1998).
54. In effect, my argument here rereads Lata Mani via Eve Kosofsky Sedgwick, *Between Men: English Literature and Male Homosocial Desire* (New York: Columbia University Press, 2015). For a different development of the same move, see J. Barton Scott, *Spiritual Despots: Modern Hinduism and the Genealogies of Self-Rule* (Chicago: University of Chicago Press, 2016), 136–44.
55. Lala Hansraj, *A Lecture on the Arya Samaj, Delivered on the Occasion of the Last Anniversary of the Lahore Arya Samaj* (Lahore: Arcrbans, 1893).
56. Mrinalini Sinha, *Colonial Masculinity: The "Manly Englishman" and the "Effeminate*

Bengali" in the Late Nineteenth Century (New York: Manchester University Press, 1995); Peter van der Veer, *Imperial Encounters: Religion and Modernity in India and Britain* (Princeton, NJ: Princeton University Press, 2001), 83–104.

57. Compare Srinivas Aravamudan, *Guru English: South Asian Religion in a Cosmopolitan Language* (Durham, NC: Duke University Press, 2005).

58. Chamupati, *Glimpses*, 71–72, 93.

59. Afzal Iqbal, ed., *My Life: A Fragment: An Autobiographical Sketch of Maulana Mohamed Ali* (Lahore: Shaikh Muhammad Ashraf, 1942), v–vi.

60. Maulana Muhammad Ali, *Muhammad the Prophet* (Columbus, OH: Ahmadiyya Anjuman Isha'at Islam, 1993 [1924]), 164, 178, 187.

61. Syed Ameer Ali, *The Spirit of Islam: A History of the Evolution and Ideals of Islam, with a Life of the Prophet* (London: Chatto & Windus, 1964 [1922]), 1.

62. Ameer Ali, *Spirit*, 1, 223.

63. Ameer Ali, *Spirit*, 240.

64. For the ethical turn, see Shruti Kapila, "Self, Spencer, and Swaraj: Nationalist Thought and Critiques of Liberalism, 1890–1920," *Modern Intellectual History* 4, no. 1 (2007): 109–27. For life writing, see David Arnold and Stuart Blackburn, eds., *Telling Lives in India* (Delhi: Permanent Black, 2004); Javed Majeed, *Autobiography, Travel, and Postnational Identity* (New York: Palgrave, 2007); Vinayak Chaturvedi, "A Revolutionary's Biography: The Case of V. D. Savarkar," *Postcolonial Studies* 16, no. 2 (2013): 124–39; and Shinjini Das, "Biography and Homeopathy in Bengal," *Modern Asian Studies* 49, no. 6 (2015): 1732–71.

65. Śivnārāyaṇ Dvivedī, *Rājā Rāmmohan Rāy: Brahmsamāj ke Pravarttak Mahāpuruṣ kā Jīvan Carit* (Calcutta: Haridas, 1917); Śivnārāyaṇ Dvivedī, *Kolambas: Amerikā ke Āviṣkartā kā Jīvancarit* (Bombay: Hindi Granthratnākar Karyālaya, 1917); Sampūrṇānand, *Mahārāj Chhatrasāl* (Banaras: Shrilakshminarayan Press, ca. 1917); Śītalācaraṇ Vājpeyī, *Deśbhakt Lālā Lajpatrāy kā Jīvan Carit* (Prayag: Oṃkār Press, 1918); Sūryarām Someśvar Devāśrayī, *Mahādev Govind Rānaḍe*, trans. Jīvanśaṅkar Yāgyik and Kedārnāth Bhatt (from Gujarati) (Prayag: Indian Press, 1918); Dan Breen, *Merī Ātmākathā*, trans. Bhagat Singh (N.p.: n.p., 1931).

66. Dayācandra Goyalīya, *Sītācarit* (Lucknow: Jain Press, 1914); Adhyāpak Zahūrbakś, *Ārya Mahilā-Ratna: Terah Vīr-Viduṣi Ārya-Mahilāoṃ ke Sacitra Jīvan-Caritra* (Kolkata: Varman Press, ca. 1925). The introduction mentions a companion volume, *Muslim-Mahilā-Ratna*.

67. Ṭhākur Prasād Śāh, *Saṃkṣipt Jīvan Vṛtānt, arthāt Dharmvīr Svargvāsī Paṇḍitvar Lekhrām jī Śarmā Ārya Pathik ka Jīvan, Maraṇ, aur Śok* (Danapur: Thakur Prasad Shah, 1898 [Arya year 1,972,948,999]); Munśirām, *Āryapathik Lekhrām* (Haridwar: Gurukul Press, 1914); Ātmārām Amṛtsarī, *Mahātmā Śrī Svāmī Nityānand Sarasvatījī kā Jīvancarit* (Mumbai: Vaibhav Press, 1918); Svāmī Śraddhānand [Munshiram], *Kalyān Mārg kā Pathik, in Svāmī Śraddhānand Granthāvalī*, ed. Bhavānīlāl Bhāratīya, vol. 1 (Delhi: Govindaram Hasanand, 1987 [1924]).

68. Gaṅgāprasād Upādhyāy, *Ārya-samāj*, no. 9, Pratham Dayānand Janam Śatābdi Granthmālā (Mathura: Nārāyaṇ Svāmī, 1925), 3.

69. Vaidya, *Śrīmaddayānanad Citrāvalī*, ii.

70. Śrīyut Lakṣmīsahāya Māthur, trans., *Benjāmin Phreṅklin kā Jīvan Caritra* (Indore: Śrī Madhya-Bhārat Hindī Sāhitya Samiti, 1928), 6–7. The book had been translated into Gujarati in the 1890s and was adopted for library acquisition and book awards in both Bombay and Baroda; this Hindi edition is translated from the Gujarati edition.
71. Dvivedī, *Kolambas*, 3; Paṇḍit Śītalācaraṇ Vājpeyī, *Deśbhakt Lālā Lājpatrāy kā Jīvan Caritra* (Prayag: Oṅkār Press, 1918), 2.
72. Goyalīya, *Sītācarit*, 2.
73. Lakṣmodhar Vājpeyī, *Ebrāham Liṅkan*, trans. Vināyak Koṇḍadev Ok (Prayāg: Dīkṣit & Dvivedī, 1917), 2–3.
74. Vājpeyī, *Deśbhakt Lālā Lajpatrāy*, 2.
75. Rahman, "Sirat al-Nabi of 'Allaman Shibli," 3.
76. For more on "books and bodies," see Brannon Ingram, *Revival from Below: The Deoband Movement and Global Islam* (Berkeley: University of California Press, 2018).
77. Brian Hatcher, "Great Men Waking: Paradigms in the Historiography of the Bengal Renaissance," in *Bengal: Rethinking History: Essays in Historiography*, ed. Sekhar Bandyopadhyay (New Delhi: Manohar, 2001), 135–63, at 140.
78. Thomas Carlyle, *On Heroes, Hero-Worship and the Heroic in History*, ed. Michael K. Goldberg, Joel Brattin, and Mark Engel (Berkeley: University of California Press, 1993 [1840]), 3, 11–12.
79. See, for example, Syed Ahmed Khan, *Essay on the Question of Whether Islam Has Been Beneficial to Human Society in General and to the Mosaic and Christian Dispensations* (London: Trübner, 1870), 7. For context, see Philip Almond, *Heretic and Hero: Muhammad and the Victorians* (Wiesbaden: Otto Harrassowitz, 1989).
80. Nanda-Kiśora Śāstrī, *Kāṅgres ke Mahāpuruṣ* (Delhi, 1929).
81. The earliest instance is likely Prasad, *A Triumph of Truth*, v–vi.
82. Lala Munshi Ram, *The Future of the Arya Samaj: A Forecast* (Lahore: Virajanand Press, 1893), 9–10.
83. This text circulated in at least two forms: H. W. Dulcken, ed., *Worthies of the World: A Series of Critical and Historical Sketches of the Lives, Actions, and Characters of Great and Eminent Men of All Countries and Times* (London: Ward, Lock, ca. 1881), 209–24; *Ward & Lock's Library of National Information and Popular Knowledge: With Numerous Illustrations* (London: Ward, Locke, ca. 1888), 3:193–224.
84. *The Athenaeum*, October 2, 1880, 423.
85. I mean this in the sociologically precise sense developed in studies like Joan Shelley Rubin, *The Making of Middlebrow Culture* (Chapel Hill: University of North Carolina Press, 1992).
86. Priya Joshi, *Another Country: Colonialism, Culture, and the English Novel in India* (New York: Columbia University Press, 2002).
87. J. Barton Scott, "Translated Liberties: Karsandas Mulji's *Travels in England* and the Anthropology of the Victorian Self," *Modern Intellectual History* 16, no. 3 (2019): 803–33; Margrit Pernau et al., *Civilizing Emotions: Concepts in Nineteenth-Century Asia and Europe* (Oxford: Oxford University Press, 2015).
88. Michel Foucault, "What Is an Author," in *The Foucault Reader*, ed. Paul Rabinow (New York: Pantheon, 1984), 101–20.

89. Lājpat Rāy, *Maharṣi Svāmī Dayānand Sarasvatī aur Unkā Kām*, trans. Gopāldās Devguṇ Śarmmā (Lahore: Punjab Economical Yantrālay, 1898), 88–92.
90. Ayesha Irani, *The Muhammadan Avatara: Salvation History, Translation, and the Making of Bengali Islam* (New York: Oxford University Press, 2020).
91. Arjan Singh, *Dayananda Saraswati: Founder of Arya Samaj* (New Delhi: Ess Ess Publications, 1979), 47.
92. Paṇḍit Rāj Narāin, *Rishi Maṇḍal, Jis meṃ Ādī Srishṭī se Lekar Āj Tak Rishiomke Hālāt Darj Haiṃ* (Lahore: Hitkari Steam Press, 1902).
93. "Mahāpurūṣ Lenin," *Jyoti*, February 1924, 549–50.
94. Satyaketu Vidyālaṅkār, "Ṛṣi Dayānand kā Itihās meṃ Sthān," *Ārya*, February 1926, 24–31.
95. Vaidya, *Śrīmaddayānanad Citrāvalī*, i.
96. Har Bilas Sarda, ed., *Swami Dayanand Saraswati* (Ajmer, 1933), 1–2.
97. Extract from the Legislative Assembly Debates, Vol. IV," in NAI/Home/Political/1927/F.132/I. (Henceforth *LAD*.) I follow the printed pagination, which is organized by date. M. M. Malaviya (Allahabad and Jhansi), *LAD*, September 5, 17.
98. K. C. Roy (Bengal), *LAD*, September 5.
99. Tomoko Masuzawa, *The Invention of World Religions* (Chicago: University of Chicago Press, 2005), 132–33.
100. Dobe, *Hindu Christian Faqir*, 212–21. Compare C. S. Adcock, *The Limits of Tolerance: Indian Secularism and the Politics of Religious Freedom* (New York: Oxford University Press, 2014).
101. Brian Hatcher, *Eclecticism and Modern Hindu Discourse* (New York: Oxford University Press, 1999).
102. John Stevens, *Keshub: Bengal's Forgotten Prophet* (New York: Oxford University Press, 2018), 180.
103. Varuni Bhatia, *Unforgetting Chaitanya: Vaishnavism and Cultures of Devotion in Colonial Bengal* (New York: Oxford University Press, 2017), 46.
104. Keshub Chunder Sen, *Great Men* (Calcutta: Calcutta Central, 1868), 21.
105. Pandit Harishankar Vidyalankar, "Sansār ke Dhārmik Itihās meṃ Dayānand kā Sthān," *Jyoti*, February 1924, 507–12.
106. [Sardar Pritam Singh], "The Prophets of the World," *Gurukul Magazine* 2, nos. 10–12 (1908): 211–26.
107. Kajri Jain, *Gods in the Time of Democracy* (Durham, NC: Duke University Press, 2021), 102.
108. For context, see Smriti Srinivas, *A Place for Utopia: Urban Designs from South Asia* (Seattle: University of Washington Press, 2016), 50–86.
109. J. Barton Scott, "The Adyar Pantheon of World Religions," *Adyar Newsletter* (August 2008): 1–4.
110. Daniel Sheffield, "In the Path of the Prophet: Medieval and Early Modern Narratives of the Life of Zarathustra in Islamic Iran and Western India" (PhD diss., Harvard University, 2012), 194–204.
111. For context, see Jairam Ramesh, *The Light of Asia: The Poem that Defined the Buddha* (Gurugram, Haryana: Penguin-Viking, 2021). Hunt's 1860 painting was so widely

pirated that he not only sued for copyright infringement but also had to keep painting new and ever-larger versions of his famous theme to keep ahead of the reproductions; the last and largest went on world tour in 1905. See Jeremy Maas, *Holman Hunt and the Light of the World* (London: Scholar Press, 1984); Elena Cooper, *Art and Modern Copyright* (Cambridge, UK: Cambridge University Press, 2018), 219–36.

112. Jain, *Gods in the Time of Democracy*.

113. See, for instance, Brian Pennington, *Was Hinduism Invented?: Britons, Indians, and the Colonial Construction of Religion* (New York: Oxford University Press, 2005).

114. Swami Vivekananda, "The Work Before Us," in *Lectures: From Colombo to Almora*, rev. ed. (Almora: Prabuddha Bharata Press, 1908), 92–100.

115. Vivekananda, "Sages of India," in *Lectures*, 81–91.

116. Durga Prasad, *Maharṣi Dayānand Sarasvatī jī kā Jīvan Caritra* (Lahore: 1913), 2.

117. Śrī Paṇḍit Camūpati, "Ṛṣi kā Camatkār," *Prakāś* (Lahore): *Janm Śatābdī Ṛṣyaṅk*, October 26, 1924, 55–64.

118. M. G. Ranade, *Rise of the Maratha Power* (Bombay: Bombay University Press, 1961 [1900]), 80–81.

119. Schimmel, *And Muhammad*, 8, 23, 135, 231.

120. *Arya Patrika* (Lahore), June 9, 1891, 3.

121. Rai, *Collected Works*, 1:434.

122. Mahārṣi Dayānand Sarasvatī, *Satyārth Prakāś* (Dehli: Arya Parivar Yojna, 2007), 289; Amiya Sen, ed., *Bankim's Hinduism* (Ranikhet, Permanent Black, 2011), 227–34; Andrew Sartori, *Bengal in Global Concept History: Culturalism in the Age of Capital* (Chicago: University of Chicago Press, 2009), 109–35.

123. My thanks to Kajri Jain for this point.

124. Meenakashi Mukherkee, *Realism and Reality: The Novel and Society in India* (Delhi: Oxford University Press, 1994).

125. Dipesh Chakrabarty, *The Calling of History: Sir Jadunath Sarkar and His Empire of Truth* (Chicago: University of Chicago Press, 2015), 39.

126. Rinehart, *One Lifetime*, 37–38.

127. Mukhopādhyāy, *Dayānandcarit*, 1–2.

128. Harald Fischer-Tiné, "'The Only Hope for Fallen India': The Gurukul Kangri as an Experiment in National Education (1902–1922)," in *Explorations in the History of South Asia*, ed. Georg Berkemer et al. (Delhi: Manohar, 2001), 277–99, at 287.

129. Lala Har Dayāl, "Mahārṣi Svāmī Dayānand Sarasvatī," *Prakash* (Lahore), October 26, 1924, 10–12. For context, see J. Daniel Elam, *World Literature for the Wretched of the Earth* (New York: Fordham University Press, 2020), 19–43.

130. [Camupati], ed., *Raṅgīlā Rasūl: Mūl Pustak Urdu kā Hindī Rūpāntar*, ed. Baldev Śarma (Banaras: Baldev Sharma, ca. 1927), 35–38.

131. Camupati, *Raṅgīlā Rasūl*, 2.

132. Camupati, *Raṅgīlā Rasūl*, 5.

133. Camupati, *Raṅgīlā Rasūl*, 9.

134. Camupati, *Raṅgīlā Rasūl*, 2.

135. Camupati, *Raṅgīlā Rasūl*, 39–40.

136. Camupati, *Raṅgīlā Rasūl*, 2.

137. NAI/Home/Political/1927/132/I/p.39.
138. *Muslim Outlook* (Lahore), July 7, 1927.
139. Khalidi, *Images of Muhammad*, 15.
140. Compare Giorgio Agamben, *The Highest Poverty*, trans. Adam Kotsko (Stanford, CA: Stanford University Press, 2013).
141. NMML/Manuscripts/DAV College Collection/Register F. No. 109/Annual Report, 1912–5/p.66.
142. Saba Mahmood, "Religious Reason and Secular Affect," *Critical Inquiry* 35, no. 4 (2009): 835–62.
143. Smith, *Modern Islam*, 68. For expansion of the latter point, see David Gilmartin, "Democracy, Nationalism, and the Public," *South Asia: The Journal of South Asian Studies* 14, no. 1 (1991): 123–40; Faisal Devji, *Muslim Zion: Pakistan as a Political Idea* (Cambridge, MA: Harvard University Press, 2013), 208.
144. Francis Robinson, "Strategies of Authority in Muslim South Asia," *Modern Asian Studies* 47, no. 1 (2013): 1–21.
145. Indrani Chatterjee, "Monastic Governmentality, Colonial Misogyny, and Postcolonial Amnesia in South Asia," *History of the Present* 3, no. 1 (2013): 57–98.
146. Usha Sanyal, *Devotional Islam and Politics in British India: Ahmad Riza Khan Barelwi and His Movement, 1870–1920* (New York: Oxford University Press, 1996), 38–39, 129, 255–64; Barbara Daly Metcalf, *Islamic Revival in British India: Deoband, 1860–1900* (Princeton, NJ: Princeton University Press, 1982), 300–2.

CHAPTER 10

1. Lord Byron, as quoted on title page of W. Blake Odgers, *A Digest of the Law of Libel and Slander*, 2nd ed. (London: Stevens and Sons, 1887).
2. "Extract from the Legislative Assembly Debates, Vol. IV," in National Archives of India (NAI)/Home/Political/1927/F.132/I. (Henceforth *LAD*.) I follow the printed pagination, which is organized by date. Citation for the above quote is thus M. A. Jinnah (Bombay City), *LAD*, September 5, 6–7; September 16, 16.
3. N. C. Kelkar (Bombay Central Division), *LAD*, September 16, 3–5.
4. Lala Lajpat Rai (Jullunder), *LAD*, September 5, 5.
5. Rai (Jullunder), *LAD*, September 16, 37.
6. K. C. Neogy (Dacca), *LAD*, September 19, 12–14.
7. *LAD*, September 5, 5.
8. *LAD*, September 19, 26.
9. "Extract from the Council of State Debates, Vol. II, Nos. 36 and 37," in NAI/Home/Political/1927/F.132/I.
10. M. K. Acharya (South Arcot), *LAD*, September 5, 9.
11. *Bengalee* (Calcutta), *Bombay Chronicle*, and *Indian Daily Telegraph* (Lucknow), quoted in *Muslim Outlook* (Lahore) (henceforth *MO*), September 15, 1–2, and September 24, 2. Henceforth all press dates 1927 unless otherwise noted.

12. *MO*, September 20, 3.
13. *The People* (Lahore), September 29, 23.
14. NAI/Home/Political/1927/F.132/I/pp.3–27.
15. IOR/L/PJ/6/1941-F.1513/p.1.
16. Amar Nath Dutt (Burdwan), *LAD*, September 16, 19.
17. K. C. Roy (Bengal), *LAD*, September 16, 6.
18. A. Rangaswami Iyengar (Tanjore cum Trichonopoly), *LAD*, September 16, 1.
19. Mian Mohammad Shah Newaz (West Central Punjab), *LAD*, September 5, 14.
20. M. K. Acharya (South Arcot cum Chingleput), *LAD*, September 16, 41–42.
21. "Report of the Select Committee," Serials Nos. 1–39, pp. 38–41, in NAI/Home/Political/1927/F.132/I; T. A. K. Shervani (Cities of United Provinces), *LAD*, September 16, 21. Cf. Hari Singh Gour (Central Provinces), *LAD*, September 19, 24.
22. Lala Lajpat Rai, "Protecting Religions," *The People*, September 15, 99.
23. William James, *Writings, 1902–1910* (New York: Library of America, 1987), 33.
24. Compare Hussein Ali Agrama, *Questioning Secularism: Islam, Sovereignty, and the Rule of Law in Modern Egypt* (Chicago: University of Chicago Press, 2012).
25. Talal Asad, *Genealogies of Religion* (Baltimore: Johns Hopkins University Press, 1993); Émile Benveniste, *Indo-European Language and Society*, trans. Elizabeth Palmaer (Coral Gables, FL: University of Miami Press, 1973).
26. Winnifred Fallers Sullivan, *The Impossibility of Religious Freedom* (Princeton, NJ: Princeton University Press, 2018); Giorgio Agamben, *The Highest Poverty*, trans. Adam Kotsko (Stanford, CA: Stanford University Press, 2013).
27. Indrani Chatterjee, "Monastic Governmentality, Colonial Misogyny, and Postcolonial Amnesia in South Asia," *History of the Present* 3, no. 1 (2013): 57–98; Jacob Copeman and Aya Ikegame, "The Multifarious Guru," in *The Guru in South Asia* (London: Routledge, 2012), 1–45.
28. S. Srinivasa Iyengar (Madras City), *LAD*, September 16, 23–25.
29. John Durham Peters, *Courting the Abyss: Free Speech and the Liberal Tradition* (Chicago: University of Chicago Press, 2005).
30. Elaine Hadley, *Living Liberalism: Practical Citizenship in Mid-Victorian Britain* (Chicago: University of Chicago Press, 2010).
31. Compare Judith Butler, *Excitable Speech: A Politics of the Performative* (New York: Routledge, 1997).
32. See, for instance, Paul Gilroy, "'My Britain Is Fuck All': Zombie Multiculturalism and the Race Politics of Citizenship," *Identities* 19, no. 4 (2012): 380–97.
33. Alexander Brown, "The Racial and Religious Hatred Act 2006: A Millian Response," *Critical Review of International Social and Political Philosophy* 11, no. 1 (2008), https://www.tandfonline.com/doi/full/10.1080/13698230701880471.
34. UN General Assembly, Resolution 2200A (XXI), International Covenant on Civil and Political Rights, Article 20 (December 16, 1966), https://www.ohchr.org/en/professionalinterest/pages/ccpr.aspx.
35. Manu Bhagwan, "A New Hope: India, the United Nations, and the Making of the Universal Declaration of Human Rights," *Modern Asian Studies* 44, no. 2 (2010): 311–47.
36. Partha Chatterjee, *I Am the People* (New York: Columbia University Press, 2019), 64–65.

37. Tim Wu, "Is the First Amendment Obsolete?," *Michigan Law Review* 117, no. 3 (2018): 547–81.
38. Cherian George, *Hate Spin: The Manufacture of Religious Offense* (Cambridge, MA: MIT Press, 2016).
39. Deepak Mehta, "Words that Wound," in *Beyond Crisis: Reevaluating Pakistan*, ed. Naveeda Khan (Delhi: Routledge, 2010), 315–43, at 326.
40. John D. Kelly, *A Politics of Virtue: Hinduism, Sexuality, and Countercolonial Discourse in Fiji* (Chicago: University of Chicago Press, 1991), 208, 217–28.
41. See Snehal Shingavi, ed., *Angarey* (Delhi: Penguin, 2014).
42. Paul Fuller, "The Idea of Blasphemy in the Pali Canon and Modern Myanmar," *Journal of Religion and Violence* 4, no. 2 (2016): 159–81.
43. Sadia Saeed, *Politics of Desecularization: Law and the Minority Question in Pakistan* (Cambridge, UK: Cambridge University Press, 2017). Compare Humeira Iqtidar, *Secularizing Islamists: Jama'at-e-Islami and Jama'at-ud-Da'wa in Urban Pakistan* (Chicago: University of Chicago Press, 2011).
44. Asad Ali Ahmed, "Adjudicating Muslims: Law, Religion, and the State in Colonial India and Postcolonial Pakistan" (PhD diss., University of Chicago, 2006); Osama Siddique and Zahra Hayat, "Unholy Speech and Holy Laws: Blasphemy Laws in Pakistan," *Minnesota Journal of International Law* 17, no. 2 (2008): 303–85; Farhat Haq, *Sharia and the State in Pakistan: Blasphemy Politics* (New York: Routledge, 2019).
45. See Asad Ali Ahmed, "Specters of Macaulay: Blasphemy, the Indian Penal Code, and Pakistan's Postcolonial Predicament," in *Censorship in South Asia*, ed. Raminder Kaur and William Mazzarella (Bloomington: Indiana University Press, 2009), 172–205.
46. See, for instance, Jeffrey Redding, *A Secular Need: Islamic Law and State Governance in Contemporary India* (Seattle: University of Washington Press, 2020).
47. Tisa Wenger, *Religious Freedom: The Contested History of an American Ideal* (Chapel Hill: University of North Carolina Press, 2017); Elizabeth Shakmun Hurd, *Beyond Religious Freedom: The New Global Politics of Religion* (Princeton, NJ: Princeton University Press, 2015).
48. Taraknath Das, "Review of *Mother India*," *The People* (Lahore), August 18, 1927, 124.
49. Quoted in Joy Dixon, *Divine Feminine: Theosophy and Feminism in England* (Baltimore: Johns Hopkins University Press, 2001), 217.
50. M. K. Acharya (Madras), *LAD*, September 16, 41–42. See also the brief reference to Mayo in Amar Nath Dutt (Burdwan), *LAD*, September 16, 20.
51. Mrinalini Sinha, *Specters of Mother India: The Global Restructuring of an Empire* (Durham, NC: Duke University Press, 2006).
52. See Laurie Patton, *Who Owns Religion?: Scholars and Their Publics in the Late Twentieth Century* (Chicago: University of Chicago Press, 2019).
53. For full discussion, see Brian Pennington, ed., "Roundtable on Outrage, Scholarship, and the Law in India," *Journal of the American Academy of Religion* 84, no. 2 (2016): 323–72.
54. Compare Michael Hardt and Antonio Negri, *Empire* (Cambridge, MA: Harvard University Press, 1999).
55. For broad context, see Deonnie Moodie, "Corporate Hinduism," *Religion Compass* 15,

no. 2 (2020): 1–9, and Manisha Basu, *The Rhetoric of Hindu India* (Cambridge: Cambridge University Press, 2016). For an analogous phenomenon, see Winnifred Sullivan, *A Ministry of Presence: Chaplaincy, Spiritual Care, and the Law* (Chicago: University of Chicago Press, 2014).

56. Ajoy Ashirwad Mahaprashasta, "Why the Hindu Right, Not Usually a Champion of Free Speech, Is Supporting Charlie Hebdo," *The Wire*, September 5, 2020, https://thewire.in/politics/hindu-right-charlie-hebdo-cartoons-free-speech.

57. For wounded attachments, see Wendy Brown, *States of Injury: Power and Freedom in Late Modernity* (Princeton, NJ: Princeton University Press, 1995).

58. "Tandav Row," *Hindustan Times*, January 27, 2021, https://www.hindustantimes.com/entertainment/web-series/tandav-row-as-supreme-court-refuses-to-grant-protection-here-are-all-the-controversies-surrounding-saif-ali-khan-s-amazon-show-101611755000552.html.

INDEX

abolitionism, 90, 107, 117–18. *See also* race; slavery
Acchutanand, Swami, 156
Acharya, M. K., 23, 59, 70, 227
Adcock, Cassie, 63, 138. *See also* tolerance/toleration
aesthetics, 23, 41, 58, 66, 71–75, 113, 157–60, 202–5. *See also* Jain, Kajri; Naidu, Sarojini
affect, 12, 47, 59–60, 81, 86–88, 96–98, 107, 138–39, 169, 176, 184, 186, 218, 229; religious, 20–28, 43–45, 52–53, 86–87, 103, 135–36, 163–64, 171, 220–21. *See also* body/bodies/flesh; emotion; sentiment; violence
affections, 21, 101, 110, 114, 118–19, 146. *See also* affect; disaffection
Agnihotri, Shiv Narayan, 161, 172, 174–76
Agrama, Hussein Ali, 6, 129
Ahmad, Mirza Ghulam, 161, 182, 227
Ahmed, Asad Ali, 89, 233
Ali, Maulana Muhammad, 46, 68–69
Ali, Syed Ameer, 194, 197
Ambedkar, B. R., 37, 181, 226
Amritsar, 39–40, 155
Anandilal, 170–71
Anglo-Hindu law, 82–86, 100, 103
Anglo-Muhammadan law, 82–85, 103
Arabic, 71, 74, 85, 200
Arnold, Edwin, 205, 207
Arya Musafir, 158, 178
Arya Patrika, 186, 208
Arya Samaj, 23–24, 27–28, 40–42, 48–49, 139–43, 172–73, 178, 181–82, 206, 208–9, 212, 222; Gurukul, 143, 146, 150, 157, 159, 162, 192; hagiography, 185, 187, 190, 192, 199, 202, 215; insult, 141–65; penal code, 166–84; *prachar*, 145, 150; Vedic publicity, 145–55, 159, 166. *See also* hagiography; polemic
asceticism, 39, 41, 48–49, 53, 65–66, 78, 96, 114–15, 142, 156–57, 159, 188, 197, 211–12, 224. *See also* body/bodies/flesh; celibacy; masculinity: manly self-rule
atheism, 7, 129, 153
Atma, Bhagwan Dev. *See* Agnihotri, Shiv Narayan
Auto-Icon, 98–99. *See also* Bentham, Jeremy
Avory, Horace, 135–36

Bagehot, Walter, 18–19
Baksh, Khuda, 48–49
Barelwi, Ahmad Riza Khan, 215
Batra, Dinanath, 228
Begum of Bhopal, 181–83
Bentham, Jeremy, 80, 83–84, 90, 96–104, 120–21, 124, 129, 133, 138, 220–21. *See also* Auto-Icon; utilitarianism
Bentinck, William, 82, 104
Besant, Annie, 11, 74, 227
Bhagavad Gita, 74, 192. *See also* Hinduism
Bhagavati, Mai, 148–49
Bhargava, Pandit Thakur Das, 56, 217
Bhargava, Rajeev, 4–5
Bible, 7, 10, 84, 90, 115–16, 118, 121, 168, 203. *See also* Christianity; Jesus
biography, 28, 39, 108, 185–87, 194–99, 207–9, 212–13

biopolitics, 10, 42–43, 52, 59, 85, 122, 129, 157, 204. *See also* Foucault, Michel; governmentality
birth control, 11–12, 135
Blackstone, William, 7, 83, 134
blasphemy, 1–15, 17, 67, 77–78, 80–81, 89–92, 94, 97, 100, 135–36, 225, 227; blasphemous libel, 10, 24–25, 123–26, 135; common law of blasphemy, 2, 6, 9, 224; Danish cartoon, 2, 214. See also *Charlie Hebdo*; defamation; Indian Penal Code: Section 298; libel; obscenity; polemic; sedition
Blasphemy Bill, 5, 54, 57. *See also* Religious Insults Bill
body/bodies/flesh, 10–11, 18–20, 22–24, 27–28, 36–44, 51–53, 55–59, 81–83, 92–94, 98–99, 119–20, 129–30, 136–37, 145–46, 150–51, 155–61, 163–65, 175–76, 212–13, 220–21. *See also* affect; asceticism; corpses; habitus; physicality; public/private distinction; purity; race; sexuality
Bombay, 5, 67–68, 72, 91, 142, 169, 205, 218, 226
Bonaparte, Napoleon, 194, 197–200
bourgeoisie, 22–23, 42, 59, 92–94, 106–7, 110, 135, 148, 150. *See also* caste; class; domesticity
Bradlaugh, Charles, 11, 26
Brahmo Samaj, 74, 203
Brougham, Henry, 25, 127
Buddha, 23, 197, 202–5, 210, 226
Buddhism, 7, 42, 73 144, 155, 197
Bulwer-Lytton, Robert, 15, 224
Burke, Edmund, 77, 83, 101–3, 220

Calcutta, 34, 65, 69, 79–82, 85, 89, 91, 97, 104–5, 111–14, 116, 131–32, 179
Cambridge, 90–91, 116, 127
Candler, Edmund, 179–80
Carlile, Richard, Jane, and Mary Ann, 89–90, 93, 116, 127
Carlyle, Thomas, 199–204, 208. *See also* great men; masculinity: heroes
caste, 35–36, 41–42, 55–56, 62, 142–46, 155–58, 162, 178, 193, 195–96, 226. *See also* body/bodies/flesh; bourgeoisie; class; Dalit; *savarna*
caste sensorium, 23–24, 222. *See also* affect; disgust
Catholicism, 10, 82, 90–92, 94–95, 97, 128, 177. *See also* Christianity
celibacy, 23, 106, 144–45, 150, 157, 196–97, 210–11. *See also* asceticism; sexuality
Chamupati, Pandit, 34, 42, 141, 144, 150, 154, 157, 185, 207, 210, 212; *Glimpses of Dayananda*, 194, 196
Charlie Hebdo, 4, 228. *See also* blasphemy
Chatterjee, Bankimchandra, 208, 219
Chatterjee, Partha, 16, 35–36, 58
Christianity, 6–11, 14–15, 73–74, 97–98, 115–20, 155–56. *See also* Bible; Catholicism; Jesus; missionaries, Christian; Protestantism
Clapham/Claphamites, 117–21
class: economic, 10, 89, 92–94, 114–15, 119–21, 135, 171; in Indian Penal Code, 59–62, 67–69, 86, 130–33, 219–21, 225. *See also* bourgeoisie; caste; enmity/hatred/contempt; violence
Cockburn, Alexander, 177
Code of Criminal Procedure, 85, 104
Coke, Edward, 134
Coleridge, John, 10–12, 25, 127, 135
commensuration. *See* Jain, Kajri
communalism, 18, 28, 34, 41–42, 45–46, 48, 55, 60, 62–63, 72–73, 132, 141–45, 159, 172, 184–85, 196, 220. *See also* riots; violence
comparative prophetology, 202–6, 210, 214–15
confession, 106, 110, 114, 121, 174–77. *See also* letters/letter writing
convent. *See* erotica
conversion, 9, 19, 41–42, 48, 63, 65, 75, 115–17, 155–56, 162, 174, 181, 217. *See also* proselytism
corpses, 51, 57, 98, 101, 135, 221. *See also* body/bodies/flesh
Crerar, James, 64, 217
crowd theory, 46–48

Dalit, 24, 41–42, 62–63, 112, 146, 155–56, 159, 163, 178, 193, 226. *See also* caste

INDEX

Darstellung, 41, 45, 58. *See also* Spivak, Gayatri; *Vertretung*
Daryabadi, Abdul Majid, 21
Das, Nilakantha, 60, 70
Dayananda Saraswati, Swami, 23, 51, 142–43, 152–54, 161–64, 168–72, 181–82, 185–89, 192–94, 197–200, 209–10, 212–13, 217, 226; *Satyarth Prakash*, 145–46, 152, 161–62, 168–69, 171, 194, 202. *See also* Arya Samaj
Dayanand Chitravali, 189–90, 202
defamation, 13, 123, 125, 129, 133, 135, 161, 225. *See also* blasphemy; libel; slander
desire, 96, 106–7, 110, 112, 122, 164, 176, 218. *See also* incest; passion; sexuality
Dev Samaj, 161, 174–76. *See also* Agnihotri, Shiv Narayan
Dewey, John, 35, 37
Dharmpal, 174–76
disaffection, 130–32. *See also* affection
disenchantment, 36, 190–92, 206–9
disgust, 23, 41, 43, 88, 93–94, 135, 158–59. *See also* caste sensorium
domesticity, 22, 85–86, 91–92, 106–7, 112, 118–19, 135. *See also* bourgeoisie; femininity; public/private distinction; sweet bondage
Doniger, Wendy, 1, 228
Durkheim, Emile, 44–45

East India Company, 15, 79, 81–83, 85, 91, 100, 104, 106, 111, 115, 118, 224
emotion, 21–22, 105, 108, 111–12, 116, 131, 134–35, 220–21, 229. *See also* affect; fanaticism; outrage; sentiment
empire, 3–4, 14–15, 81–82, 89–92, 95–96, 101–2, 106–9, 116–20, 227–29. *See also* intimacy; mission, civilizing; "West," the
Enlightenment, 9, 11, 82–84, 101, 119, 142, 220
enmity/hatred/contempt, 7–8, 12–14, 33, 39–41, 60–61, 77, 83, 130–33, 174–75, 178–79, 203, 211, 224–25. *See also* class; emotion
erotica, 128, 177. *See also* pornography
ethics, 8, 21, 78, 120–21, 137–39, 142, 154, 161, 195, 198, 206–9
ethnographic state, 16, 35–37, 41, 56, 58, 60
evangelicalism, 19, 27, 82, 90, 108, 115–16, 120–22. *See also* Christianity; missionaries, Christian; proselytism; Protestantism

family. *See* incest
fanaticism, 34, 45, 48, 66, 97, 164, 218–19. *See also* affect; emotion; religious feeling
feeling/feelings. *See* affect; emotion; religious feeling; sentiment
femininity, 22, 49, 72, 106, 150, 157, 197, 210. *See also* domesticity; masculinity
feminism, 38, 108, 150, 196
flesh. *See* body/bodies/flesh; habitus
Foucault, Michel, 28, 138–39, 154, 221. *See also* biopolitics; ethics; governmentality
free speech, 1, 28, 54, 70, 90, 132, 163, 219, 223–24. *See also* liberalism; speech
freethought, 3, 8, 10–11, 117, 135, 142. *See also* Ramsay, William, and George Foote
French revolution, 80, 83, 93, 101
friendship, 107–8, 112, 115. *See also* masculinity: homosocial/homoerotic/homosexual
frotteurism, 174, 176. *See also* Singh, Amar

Gandhi, M. K., 39, 42, 48, 56, 63, 65, 71–72, 139, 202, 224, 227
Garibaldi, Giuseppe, 202, 208–9
Gay News, 12, 26. *See also* newspaper
gender/sexuality. *See* body/bodies/flesh; desire; domesticity; femininity; incest; masculinity; public/private distinction; sexuality
Gentoo law. *See* Anglo-Hindu law
Ghafur, Abdul. *See* Dharmpal
Ghasiram, 187, 209, 212
Ghaznavi, Maulvi Muhammad Daud, 40–41, 134
Gladstone, William, 78, 133–34
Gopinath, 172–73
gossip, 109, 130, 161–62
Gott, John, 12, 135
Gour, Hari Singh, 5–6, 14–15, 26, 63–64, 66–67, 133, 137
governmentality, 16–17, 35–38, 65–66, 75, 108, 121, 138, 168, 186, 215, 226; spiritual, 154–57, 221–23. *See also* biopolitics; Foucault, Michel

Grant, Charles, 106, 118
graphomania, 112–14, 139. *See also* print culture
great men, 199–204, 209, 214–15. *See also* Carlyle, Thomas; masculinity: heroes
Gujarati, 148, 170, 187, 200, 218
Gurukul. *See* Arya Samaj

habitus, 12, 19, 23, 120, 122, 214–15. *See also* body/bodies/flesh
hagiography, 185, 187, 190, 192–94, 198–99, 202, 208–10, 215. *See also* Arya Samaj
Hale, Matthew, 9–10, 13, 20, 81, 124
Halhed, Nathaniel, 86, 100. *See also* Anglo-Hindu Law
Hall, Catherine, 108, 110, 112, 117, 121
Harishchandra, Bharatendu, 195
Hastings, Warren, 82–83, 102
hate speech, 12–13, 26, 28, 224–26, 131, 142, 224–26. *See also* blasphemy; enmity/hatred/contempt; Indian Penal Code: Section 153A; speech
hatred. *See* enmity/hatred/contempt
heroes. *See* Carlyle, Thomas; great men; masculinity: heroes
Hicklin test, 128, 277
Hinduism, 55, 73–74, 86, 142, 145, 185, 189, 196, 203, 205, 227–28; Hindu nationalism, 5, 140, 218, 228; Puranic, 145, 152, 159, 192, 208. See also *Bhagavad Gita*; Puranas
homoeroticism. *See* masculinity: homosocial/homoerotic/homosexual
House of Commons, 79, 92
Hunt, William Holman, 205, 207, 280n111
Hussain, M. F., 1

iconoclasm, 2, 49, 188, 190, 192, 196
incest, 27, 43, 78, 106, 108, 110–11, 122, 178. *See also* desire; domesticity; intimacy; Macaulay sisters; war on nature
Indian Penal Code, 24–26, 77–78, 84–89, 103, 105–6, 121–23, 129–31, 168–72, 218–19, 225–26; Section 124A, 130–32, 166, 179; Section 153A, 14, 39, 60–61, 77, 130, 132, 167, 174–75, 178–799, 218, 225–26; Section 295A, 1–2, 4–7, 12–14, 17–18, 21, 25, 27, 33,

55, 59–66, 68, 77, 130, 132–33, 135, 137–38, 166, 185–86, 216–18, 220–23, 225–28; Section 298, 18, 25, 93, 105, 169, 171, 182, 226; Section 377, 105, 121; Section 499, 131, 175. *See also* blasphemy; caste; enmity/hatred/contempt; Macaulay, Thomas Babington
injury, 1, 9, 28, 39, 57, 65, 87, 97, 131, 133, 141, 166, 168–69, 171, 175–77, 214, 219, 224. *See also* speech
insult. *See* blasphemy; intimacy
intimacy, 24, 27–28, 103, 105–10, 112–14, 117–18, 122, 123–24, 134, 137, 162, 168, 175–76. *See also* domesticity; empire; incest
Islam, 7, 13, 39, 41–44, 60, 62–63, 73–74, 84–85, 103, 133, 136, 145, 181–82, 210, 214–15, 225, 227. *See also* Islamophobia; Muhammad, Prophet; Qur'an
Islamophobia, 33, 42, 53, 63, 178, 204, 209, 215–16, 228
Iyengar, S. Srinivasa, 64–66

Jain, Kajri, 74, 204. *See also* aesthetics
Jainism, 73, 145, 155
James, William, 22, 219
Jayakar, M. R., 5–8, 13, 15, 63–64, 67, 70, 137, 227
Jesus, 2, 7, 9, 12, 23, 51, 71, 119, 125, 161, 196–97, 202–5, 210. *See also* Bible; Christianity
Jones, William, 83
Judaism, 10, 81, 90–92, 94–95, 97, 100–101, 103, 228

Kenny, Courtney, 25–26
Khadijah, 42, 195, 210–11
Kittler, Friedrich, 28, 112, 139
Krishna, 71, 143, 159, 164, 192, 196, 199, 202–5, 208, 210, 220, 226
Krishnavarma, Shyamji, 143
Kunwar, Ved, 149–51

Lahore, 13, 33–34, 39, 41, 46, 78, 174, 190, 194, 212
Lahore High Court, 43, 57, 61, 67, 133, 211, 225
Lawrence, D. H.: *Lady Chatterley's Lover*, 42

INDEX

Legislative Assembly, 5, 7, 14, 23, 37, 54–56, 58, 60, 63–64, 69, 133, 137, 203, 216, 218, 221–22
Lekhram, Pandit, 155, 158–60, 163, 172, 181–83, 187, 194
letters/letter writing, 112, 114, 121, 175–76. *See also* confession; paper
libel, 123–36, 173, 185. *See also* blasphemy; obscenity; polemic; sedition
liberalism, 18, 46, 57, 82, 106, 140, 151–52, 214, 219, 224. *See also* Bagehot, Walter; free speech; Mill, John Stuart
Lippmann, Walter, 35–37, 46, 225
Locke, John, 15, 19, 116
Lowe, Lisa, 107, 222
Luther, Martin, 84, 199, 200, 202

Macaulay, Selina Mills, 98, 110, 112, 117, 119
Macaulay, Thomas Babington, 17, 19, 24–25, 27–28, 35–36, 77–80, 82–85, 87–88, 90–98, 100–104, 105–22, 129–30, 221, 253n64; *History of England*, 104, 208; "Minute on Education," 89, 105, 114–16, 118. *See also* Indian Penal Code
Macaulay, Zachary, 90. 107, 109, 117, 119
Macaulay Code. *See* Indian Penal Code
Macaulay sisters (Hannah and Margaret), 106–7, 109, 111–16, 122. *See also* domesticity; incest
Madonna, 2, 229
Maharaj Libel Case, 130, 169
Mahmood, Saba, 15–16, 214–15, 219
Mahmud, Ghazi. *See* Dharmpal
Maine, Henry, 6
Malaviya, M. M., 61, 203, 205
Mani, Lata, 82, 196
Marathi, 187, 200, 226
Marsh, Joss, 2, 78, 123–24, 129–30, 166, 225
martyr, 3, 48–52, 120, 190
Marx, Karl, 90, 253n64
masculinity: heroes, 199–202, 210, 214; homosocial/homoerotic/homosexual, 12, 107, 112, 114–15, 121, 196; hypersexual, 24, 42, 209; independent man, 106–7, 109, 112, 114, 120; male body, 59, 148, 150, 196, 210, 215; manly self-rule, 106, 120. *See also* body/bodies/flesh; celibacy; femininity; frotteurism; phallic communion; sexuality
Mathura, 185, 192–93
Mayo, Katherine, 196, 227. *See also* Mother India
Mere Pacchis Minet, 163–64
merry prophet. *See* Rangila Rasul
Mill, James, 21, 79–80, 102, 104, 115, 127; *History of British India*, 83, 97
Mill, John Stuart, 12, 19–21, 79–80, 89–90, 101–3. *See also* liberalism
Milton, John, 17, 116
mission, civilizing, 10–11, 82, 89, 118, 120. *See also* empire
missionaries, Christian, 11, 82, 118, 130, 146, 152, 155, 162, 168, 228. *See also* Christianity; conversion; evangelicalism; Protestantism
monster meetings, 46–48. *See also* Rajpal affair
Moolraj, Lala Thakurdas, 168–72
moral force, 20, 48, 51, 65, 139
More, Hannah, 117, 119
Morvi, 192, 194
Moses, 10–11, 84, 202–4
Mother India, 73, 188–89, 192
Muhammad, Prophet, 1, 4, 7, 13, 23, 28, 34, 39, 41–44, 60, 67, 78, 133–34, 182, 185, 194–99, 202–4, 208–12, 214–15, 221, 225–26. *See also* Islam; Islamophobia; Rajpal affair
Muir, William, 194–95, 209
Mukhopadhyay, Devendranath, 187
Muller, Max, 146
Munshiram, 48–49, 153–54, 156–57, 162, 165, 172–73, 192, 200. *See also* Shraddhananda
Muslim Outlook, 43, 47, 67, 134–35, 217. *See also* newspaper

Naidu, Sarojini, 55, 68, 71–75, 203. *See also* aesthetics; Respect for All Prophets
necropolitics, 51–52
Nehru, Jawaharlal, 73
Nehru, Motilal, 45
newspaper, 4, 33, 37–38, 40, 43, 47, 53, 55, 68–69, 90, 133, 150, 172–73, 179, 200, 214. *See also* paper; print culture
Numani, Shibli, 194–95, 197–98

Obscene Publications Act of 1857, 128, 177
obscenity, 11, 23, 41–42, 78, 123–29, 135, 158, 166, 177–78, 182. *See also* libel
Odgers, W. Blake, 127–28
Olcott, Henry Steel, 204–5
Orientalism, 83, 85–87, 114, 146
outrage, 1, 5, 11–12, 14, 17–18, 30, 34, 54–55, 59–60, 75, 88, 95, 218, 225, 227–28. *See also* emotion

pain/pleasure, 77, 81, 94–102, 121, 129, 158, 224. *See also* utilitarianism
Paine, Thomas, 9, 89, 92–93
paper, 27, 40–41, 57, 78, 113–14, 139, 146–47, 159, 164, 167–68, 174–77, 182, 186, 192–93, 213. *See also* letters/letter writing; newspaper; physicality; print culture; tracts
Parliament, 79, 88, 91, 94, 100, 106, 110, 112–13, 126, 129
passion, 17–18, 21–22, 45, 59, 96–97, 101, 109. *See also* affect; desire; religious feeling; violence
personal law, 84–87, 103
persuasion, 19–20, 58, 94, 140, 151, 153
phallic communion, 125–26. *See also* masculinity
photography, 146, 189–90
photorealism. *See* photography
physicality, 47, 57, 146, 151, 157–58. *See also* body/bodies/flesh; paper; print culture
polemic, 23, 41, 137–40, 142, 145, 151–54, 158–59, 165–67, 185–86, 194–97, 209–11. *See also* libel; tracts
pornography, 125, 128, 196. *See also* erotica
prachar. *See* Arya Samaj
pracharaks, 148, 152–53
prejudice, 77, 89, 100–103, 220. *See also* Burke, Edmund
print culture, 46–48, 53, 92–94, 114–16, 125, 139–40, 144, 146, 157–60, 165, 176, 181, 193. *See also* empire; graphomania; paper; physicality; tracts
proselytism, 42, 63. *See also* conversion; evangelicalism; missionaries, Christian

Protection for Prophets law, 67–68, 70, 72, 74–75, 222
Protestantism, 82, 84, 90, 95, 97, 103, 114–16, 118–19, 146, 151–52, 177. *See also* Christianity
public/private distinction, 22–23, 27, 34–38, 53, 78, 84–86, 103, 105–6, 122–23, 221–22. *See also* domesticity
Puranas, 162, 164. *See also* Hinduism
purity, 23–24, 42, 130, 155, 157, 178. *See also* body/bodies/flesh

Qur'an, 211, 220, 226. *See also* Islam

race, 1, 10–11, 15, 28, 36, 72, 85, 91–92, 103, 115, 117–18, 120, 130, 145, 155–57, 224, 228. *See also* body/bodies/flesh
Rai, Lajpat, 37, 49, 69, 179, 186, 198–99, 201–2, 208–9, 217–18
Rajpal, Mahashe, 13, 33–34, 132, 141, 194, 217. *See also* Rajpal affair; *Rangila Rasul*
Rajpal affair, 27, 33–34, 38, 40, 43, 45–46, 48, 52–57, 63, 78, 133, 138, 216–17, 226–27. *See also* Rajpal, Mahashe; *Rangila Rasul*
Rajpal v. Emperor, 13, 60, 133–34
Rama, 71, 192, 196, 202, 208, 210, 228–29
Ramsay, William, and George Foote, 10, 12, 17, 25
Ranade, M. G., 198, 208
Rangila Rasul, 13, 23, 27–28, 33–34, 38–39, 42–43, 137–39, 185–86, 193–97, 209–12, 216–19, 226–27. *See also* Muhammad, Prophet; Rajpal affair
Regina v. Hicklin, 128, 177
Regina v. Ramsay and Foote, 10–11
religion, 3–8, 19–23, 59–60, 86–87, 103–4, 226–29. *See also* Christianity; Hinduism; Islam
religious feeling, 1, 5, 12, 17–18, 23–26, 33–34, 57–62, 68–70, 86–89, 103–4, 116–17, 135, 169, 182–83, 215. *See also* fanaticism; passion; violence
Religious Insults Bill, 5, 54. *See also* Blasphemy Bill

INDEX

Respect for All Prophets, 71–72, 137, 139, 203, 222. *See also* Naidu, Sarojini
Rex v. Taylor, 9, 13, 61
Rida, Rashid, 194
riots, 14, 46, 60, 132. *See also* communalism; violence
Risala-i-Vartman, 40–41, 172. *See also* newspaper
Risley, Herbert, 35–36
Roy, Rammohun, 80, 198, 217
Rushdie, Salman, 1–3, 12

Sanatan Hindu Dharm Sabha, 177–78
Sanatanism, 158, 163, 178
Sanskrit, 71, 74, 85, 144, 148–50, 152, 157, 170, 187
Sarda, Har Bilas, 202
Savarkar, V. D., 143
savarna, 23–24, 41, 59, 62, 159, 178. *See also* caste
Savigny, Friedrich Carl von, 84
scatology, 39, 41, 126, 158, 163
schesis. *See* habitus
Scott, Joan Wallach, 22, 222
secular/secularism, 1–3, 8–13, 15–16, 22–23, 54–56, 62–64, 66–67, 70–75, 105–6, 219, 224; colonial, 6, 13–17, 23, 27, 52, 56, 107–8, 129, 227, 229; Company, 14–15, 81–84; governmental, 16–17, 55–56, 62, 94, 138; Indian, 14–16, 34, 54, 62–63, 67, 70–71, 75, 138, 203, 222, 227; liberal-constitutional, 16, 35–37, 41, 54–56, 58, 62, 64, 88–89, 94, 96, 204, 219; penal, 17, 55, 62, 87, 219–20; Victorian, 10, 129, 208
sedition, 78, 123–25, 126, 128, 130–33, 135, 166, 178–79, 181, 197. *See also* blasphemy; libel
Sedley, Charles, 125–26
self, 107, 120, 138–39, 214. *See also* ethics
Sen, Keshub Chunder, 74, 161, 203
sentiment, 1, 16, 21–23, 43–44, 53, 72, 77, 82, 86, 95, 99–103, 105–7, 116, 165, 183, 225, 228. *See also* affect; emotion
sexuality, 41–43, 103, 105, 112, 120–22, 130, 142, 157, 175–77, 184, 195–97, 222, 227.

See also body/bodies/flesh; celibacy; desire; masculinity
sex work, 23, 41, 164
Shakespeare, William, 17, 115, 199
Shankaracharya, 155, 202
Shastri, Manasaram, 162–64
Shimla, 54–56, 58–59, 69–70, 137
Shiva, 70–71, 179, 186, 188, 190–92, 228–29
Shivaji, 70–71, 199, 202
Shraddhananda, Swami. *See* Munshiram
shuddhi, 24, 42, 155–58
Singh, Amar, 174–77. *See also* frotteurism
Singh, Kanwar Dalip, 13–14, 39, 46, 60, 134–35, 210–11. *See also* Rajpal affair
sira, 185, 194–95, 208–9, 212
Sita, 185, 198
slander, 39, 67, 69–70, 123–26, 129–31, 133–34, 160–62, 172, 186, 209, 212, 225, 227. *See also* defamation; libel
slavery, 56, 92, 107, 117–18. *See also* abolitionism; race
Smiles, Samuel, 200
Smith, Wilfred Cantwell, 194, 214
Socrates, 50, 203
speech, 93–94, 140, 146, 150–53. *See also* free speech; hate speech
Spiritualism, 26, 34
Spivak, Gayatri, 41, 58. See also *Darstellung*; *Vertretung*
Starkie, Thomas, 127–28
Stephen, James Fitzjames, 19–20, 24–25, 130, 134, 139
subjectivity, 10–11, 59, 93, 101, 107, 121, 139–40, 152, 161, 214
suffering, 48, 65, 92
Sullivan, Robert, 108, 115
sweet bondage, 107, 114, 120. *See also* domesticity
sympathy, 71–75

Tagore, Rabindranath, 199
Tarde, Gabriel, 47, 53
Taylor, John, 9, 14, 125
Tejani, Shabnum, 62–63

Theosophist, The, 186, 190
theosophy/Theosophical Society, 74, 161, 167, 204. *See also* Besant, Annie; Olcott, Henry Steel
Tiele, Cornelis, 21
Tilak, B. G., 23, 131
tolerance/toleration, 15, 19, 39, 55–56, 63–67, 71, 73, 75, 88, 90, 92, 102, 115, 118, 223–24. *See also* Adcock, Cassie
tracts, 10–13, 33–35, 38–40, 42–43, 92–93, 157–58, 162–67, 185–86, 194–97, 209–12, 157–58, 211. *See also* libel; paper; polemic; print culture
Trevelyan, Charles, 111–12

Unnisvi Sadi ka Maharshi, 38–39
Urdu, 21, 33, 148, 150, 173, 187, 194, 197, 200
utilitarianism, 82, 96–99, 101–3. *See also* pain/pleasure

Vedas, 7, 49, 142, 145–46, 157, 161, 168, 187, 204
Vedic modernity, 142–45, 181

Vedic publicity. *See* Arya Samaj
Vertretung, 41, 44, 58. *See also* Spivak, Gayatri
Victoria (Queen), 15, 63, 167–68
violence, 16–20, 55–57, 61, 64–65, 87–88, 94–95, 156, 163–65, 178, 219–20. *See also* affect; communalism; fanaticism; religious feeling; secular/secularism
Viswanathan, Gauri, 14, 91, 115

war on nature, 106, 111, 121, 122. *See also* incest
"West," the, 3–6. *See also* empire
Whig-liberal narrative of blasphemous modernity, 3–5, 9–10, 25, 228
whore-master. *See* Jesus
Wilberforce, William, 110, 117–19, 121
witchcraft, 9, 124
word crime. *See* blasphemy; Marsh, Joss
Wright, Peter, 133–35

Yogi-Raj, 188–89

Zoroaster/Zoroastrianism, 73, 204–5